Haida Gwaii

Pacific Rim Archaeology

This series is an initiative of UBC Laboratory of Archaeology and UBC Press. It provides a source of scholarly reporting on significant new archaeological research along the entire Pacific Rim, spanning the region from Southeast Asia to western North America and Pacific Latin America. The series will publish reports on archaeological fieldwork in longer monograph form as well as edited volumes of shorter works dealing with contemporary themes.

The general editors of the series are Michael Blake and David Pokotylo, both faculty members in the Department of Anthropology and Sociology at the University of British Columbia.

Other books in the series include *Hidden Dimensions: The Cultural Significance of Wetland Archaeology,* edited by Kathryn Bernick; *Since the Time of the Transformers: The Ancient Heritage of the Nuu-chah-nulth, Ditidaht, and Makah,* by Alan D. McMillan; and *Emerging from the Mist: Studies in Northwest Coast Culture History,* edited by R.G. Matson, Gary Coupland, and Quentin Mackie.

Edited by Daryl W. Fedje and Rolf W. Mathewes

Haida Gwaii: Human History and
Environment from the Time of
Loon to the Time of the Iron People

UBCPress · Vancouver · Toronto

15 14 13 12 11 10 09 08 07 06 05   5 4 3 2 1

Printed in Canada on ancient-forest-free paper (100% post-consumer recycled)
that is processed chlorine- and acid-free, with vegetable-based inks.

Library and Archives Canada Cataloguing in Publication

Haida Gwaii : human history and environment from the time of loon to the
time of the iron people / edited by Daryl W. Fedje and Rolf W. Mathewes.

(Pacific Rim archaeology, ISSN 1483-2283)
Includes bibliographical references and index.
ISBN-13: 978-0-7748-0921-4 (bound); 978-0-7748-0992-1 (pbk.)
ISBN-10: 0-7748-0921-3 (bound); 0-7748-0922-1 (pbk.)

1. Queen Charlotte Islands (B.C.) – Antiquities. 2. Paleoecology – British
Columbia – Queen Charlotte Islands. 3. Queen Charlotte Islands (B.C.) –
History. I. Fedje, Daryl W. II. Mathewes, Rolf W. III. Series.

FC3845.Q3H35 2005   971.1'2   C2005-903358-4

Canadä

UBC Press gratefully acknowledges the financial support for our publishing
program of the Government of Canada through the Book Publishing Industry
Development Program (BPIDP), and of the Canada Council for the Arts, and
the British Columbia Arts Council.

This book has been published with the help of a grant from the Canadian
Federation for the Humanities and Social Sciences, through the Aid to Scholarly
Publications Programme, using funds provided by the Social Sciences and
Humanities Research Council of Canada.

Printed and bound in Canada by Friesens
Set in Stone by Artegraphica Design Co. Ltd.
Copy editor: Francis Chow
Proofreader: Gail Copeland
Indexer: Noeline Bridge

UBC Press
The University of British Columbia
2029 West Mall
Vancouver, BC V6T 1Z2
604-822-5959 / Fax: 604-822-6083
www.ubcpress.ca

Contents

Illustrations

Tables

Foreword

Guujaaw

It Was Told

At the time before people, these islands were under water. The Supernaturals occupied the first rock to come above those waters. Our ancestors came later, from the sea.

Our people knew the time when it was like twilight and there was little difference between night and day. Our people told of *Kaalga Jaad* (Ice Woman) hovering in front of a glacier in what is now Skidegate Inlet. When the waters left Hecate Strait, our people hunted and lived there in the treeless landscape. Our relatives saw the first tree and recount floods and tidal waves in their time and before. In one instance, they were saved by the rings on *Qingi's* hat; in another, the ones who had dogs on their rafts were not upset by the bears; in another, they found salvation in the mountains of *Duu Guusd*.

We have a song of the grizzly bear that came down to kill people, even though grizzly bears don't exist here, and a story of a young hero who slays a mountain lion near Copper Bay.

This was all myth, of course, comparable to fairytales put together to make some sense of things – at least until a few years ago.

For years the scientific community has debated whether these islands had been entirely covered by ice during the last ice age or had contained an ice-free refuge. Scientists have now concluded that while there was an ice-free and inhabitable corridor where Hecate Strait now lies, and while we were clear of the continental ice field, there were indeed local glaciers. They know that our people were here before cedar; in fact, they know the precise sequence of the arrival of plants, as generations of our people would have witnessed. In our west coast mountains were found the grizzly bear bones that are now in the hands of science.

Science has come to see that the ice age came to an end much more abruptly than previously thought. We can now look beneath the waters at the sea floor and appreciate the effects of the great meltwaters and the havoc unleashed upon our people as the lands were swallowed by the sea. We all know now that in addition to floods, tsunamis had been, and will continue to be, a reality of coastal life.

It isn't science, however, but the Tibetans who also remember the time when they lived in twilight. As we have known *Sgulhgu Jaad* (Seafoam Woman), the Egyptians and people of Peru knew of a "god" called "Seafoam" in their own languages. The Hopi talk about their people coming out of the earth; we told them that it was *Nangkilstlas* who stomped his feet to call the different tribes from the earth.

Science is coming of age, and while there is a convergence and a reconciling of science with our histories, scientists may have to take our word on certain facts.

It was because Raven fooled around with his uncle's wife that *Gahllns Kun* (his uncle) spun his hat and caused the water to rise, accounting for one of the floods.

Scientists are still trying to figure out how the sun and the moon got up there, and while they have theories, give them time and they will come back to us. And we can tell them, because it was told ...

Foreword

Knut Fladmark

I would like to thank Daryl Fedje and Rolf Mathewes for asking me to contribute to this volume, albeit from the largely historical perspective of someone who has had no involvement with archaeological or paleoenvironmental research in Haida Gwaii since 1970. As I read this book, my first reaction was a sense of awe about how much more is now known about the natural and human history of those islands than when I began exploring those topics thirty-four years ago. Although archaeologists routinely deal with the effects of time on human knowledge, it still seems remarkable when such a profound increase in data occurs on one's own intellectual doorstep over such a relatively short period. I also cannot help wondering how my original research perspectives and efforts might have differed if only a fraction of the information contained in this volume had been available.

This represents a major advance in knowledge and sets a very high standard for future multidisciplinary archaeological-paleoecological projects. Only thirty to forty years ago, for the general public, Quaternary scientists, and archaeologists alike, the Queen Charlotte Islands (Haida Gwaii) were one of the least accessible and least understood parts of the province of British Columbia. Before regular ferry connections with Port Hardy and Prince Rupert began in the early 1970s, very few mainlanders of any professional orientation had ever visited them. Indeed, their human story was so poorly known that I remember being told as a student in the mid-1960s that they had probably been uninhabited before about 2,500 years ago, because the boat-building capabilities needed for people to reach them would not have existed before then.

In the early to mid-1960s, a fairly recent age for initial human occupation of Haida Gwaii also seemed to be supported (or at least not denied) by all existing archaeological information from those islands. That consisted, however, of only four to five individual publications, none particularly informative. They included the results of Harlan I. Smith's pioneering excavations at the Yakan Point village site in 1919, now in a heavily forested part of

Naikoon Park at the northeastern end of Graham Island. He thought that the village must have been abandoned at least "several centuries ago" on the basis of the size of its trees, but other information about the site was very limited (Smith 1929:42, 46). Smith also commented on a series of peculiar low-lying rectangular earthworks that he saw in 1919 in a pioneer homestead north of Yakan Point, among the sand dunes of Rose Spit. He thought that they were anthropogenic features, possibly representing Haida garden-plots, also implying a recent age (Smith 1927:111). The first modern archaeological excavations in Haida Gwaii were small-scale efforts conducted in the historical Haida village site of Ninstints at the southern end of the archipelago in 1956 and 1957 (Duff and Kew 1958:50-54). While they demonstrated some depth of midden deposits, artifacts were infrequent and dominated by European trade goods, all still compatible with a relatively recent overall age of human occupation of the islands.

Reflecting the marked increase in archaeological research throughout the entire province since the mid-1960s, the level of published archaeological data from Haida Gwaii is now vastly larger. We now can be certain that those islands were first occupied by people at least as early as any other part of the British Columbia coast, as demonstrated by the archaeological chapters in this volume. Also, a count of all the different references cited by the contributors to this volume, plus my own bibliographic files, indicates that currently there are at least forty-seven journal articles, professional monographs, and graduate theses bearing directly on the archaeology of these islands. There also are a great many unpublished reports filed in the Provincial Archaeologist's Office, which simply did not exist in the 1950s and 1960s.

My first contact with Haida Gwaii was in the summer of 1967, when as a student fieldworker with George MacDonald's North Coast Archaeological Project, based in Prince Rupert, I participated in a ten-day trip to those islands. We spent most of our time excavating a large test unit in the deep Honna River shell midden near Queen Charlotte City. While the resulting artifact assemblage was small, two associated radiocarbon dates (the first from any archaeological site in Haida Gwaii) demonstrated that people had definitely lived on those islands for at least 3,000-3,300 years (MacDonald 1969:249). We also explored the road-accessible portions of northern Haida Gwaii, finding the Skoglund's Landing site near Masset. It displayed a simple unifacial lithic industry in an apparent non-shell midden context, unlike any other site then known on the northern British Columbia coast and suggestive of a substantial age. Involvement in that discovery made me aware of the possibility of a very early human record in Haida Gwaii and fuelled a personal interest in conducting further archaeological investigations on those islands.

As a result, after entering graduate studies at the University of Calgary, I directed excavations at Skoglund's Landing and three other island sites in the summers of 1969 and 1970, supported by a total of budget of $5,000. My field crews of about four to five people each year (largely unpaid volunteers, with little or no previous field experience) had to survive very primitive living conditions and unvarying canned-food diets. Minimal resources also were reflected in the kinds of research that we were able to accomplish, emphasizing very basic cultural-historical and cultural-ecological goals. Also, because we could afford no air charter or practical water transport, our areal coverage was restricted entirely to the road-accessible portions of eastern Graham and northeastern Moresby Islands. This was unfortunate because, as clearly demonstrated in this book, the greater physiographical and environmental diversity of the South Moresby–Gwaii Haanas region seems to have retained a longer, richer, and more complete paleoecological and archaeological record.

The amount of published information about past (and present) environments of Haida Gwaii available to me in 1969 and 1970 was also very small, being limited only to Dawson (1880), Heusser (1955, 1960), Sutherland-Brown and Nasmith (1962), Foster (1965), Sutherland-Brown (1968), and Calder and Taylor (1968). Those pioneering works provided only preliminary suggestions about the chronology and effects of past glaciations, sea level changes, and other natural factors that could have affected past human occupations. Nevertheless, they still offered hints of a unique biological and environmental history for those islands, including a role as a late Wisconsin biotic refugium. As a result, by 1969 increasing awareness that a chain of similar refugia along the outer Pacific coast could have been used by early human migrants moving south from Beringia alerted me to the possibility that Pleistocene-aged archaeological sites might be found on those islands. As represented by this volume, today there is a vastly greater stock of paleoenvironmental and archaeological information about Haida Gwaii than in 1969 and 1970. Counting the contributions in this volume and the different sources that they cite, plus other references that I am aware of, there are now at least 118 articles and monographs bearing on this topic. One of their most significant conclusions is that indeed there are now strong indications that a late Wisconsin biotic refugium existed somewhere around these islands, most likely on the emergent continental shelf.

A unique and much debated aspect of the natural history of Haida Gwaii has been its potential role as a late Pleistocene biotic refugium. Some biologists have argued in favour of that concept because of the unique array of disjunct and endemic species or subspecies of plants and animals found today on those islands. Their degree of divergence from mainland counterparts has been thought to indicate the survival of distinct populations of ancestral plants and animals on those islands during all or part of the last glaciation (e.g., Heusser 1955:446, 1960:201-203; Calder and Taylor 1968:112). As stated in Chapter 5 of this book, "genetic data of a mid-Pleistocene split of vertebrate taxa and geographic distribution of the mitochondrial lineages of stickleback, black bear, marten, and short-tailed weasel cumulatively suggest that a refugium existed on the continental shelf off the central coast of British Columbia. Genetic data are consistent with geological and stratigraphic data demonstrating that the continental shelf separating Haida Gwaii from the mainland contained a large ice-free area during the glacial maximum."

I think that one of the most important suggestions made in this volume is that older ice-free areas probably existed on the now submerged continental shelf adjacent to the islands, particularly in the "Hecatian" area. Plans apparently are under way to seriously investigate this possibility, and I suspect that if anyone has the resources and expertise needed to locate and effectively study such deeply submerged terrestrial surfaces (and hopefully any associated archaeological sites), it is Daryl Fedje and his research team.

At the risk of breaking scientific conventions, I would like to make one final comment. This involves a subjective impression that I think arises in virtually anyone who spends much time in Haida Gwaii, particularly in wilderness areas in close interaction with the natural environment. I suspect that it also underlies the personal interests and research perspectives of at least some of the contributors to this volume, although it would not be considered appropriate to mention in scientific discussions. It is the sense of being in a truly special place – an awareness that one is in a very insular realm that has always followed its own unique directions distinctly removed from those of the adjacent continent. As far as I know, the Queen Charlotte archipelago is the most disjunct large landmass associated with the continent of North America. Newfoundland, the Kodiak group, and the Caribbean Islands are all separated from the adjacent mainland by shorter minimal water distances, often involving steps across intervening smaller islands.

Haida Gwaii, particularly the Gwaii Haanas area, is also a remarkably beautiful place, with wisps of clouds weaving through dense dark forests. It cannot help but evoke a sense of spiritual power, however one wishes to define that concept, even to the most agnostic of observers. When this feeling happens to coincide with the arrival of a large raven, loudly asserting his command of the landscape, modern scientific perspectives merge with older views stretching back to the arrival of the first people on these islands, sometime before 10,000 years ago. If the coastal migration route hypothesis is correct, then Haida Gwaii may well have been the first part of modern Canada to hear human voices.

Knut Fladmark
Simon Fraser University

Preface and Acknowledgments

Daryl W. Fedje and Rolf W. Mathewes

The human history of Haida Gwaii (the Queen Charlotte Islands), and the environmental context within which this history has unfolded, is a story of dramatic long-term change. People have lived in this archipelago for at least 10,500 radiocarbon years. During the time of human occupation, they saw glaciers retreat, climate change over millennia, and sea levels rise high over their grandparents' villages and then fall back so that new villages could be built on their ancestors' fishing grounds. They saw forests develop and then change their composition. They saw the first cedar tree and the last Dawson caribou, the first European and the last sea otter. Over time they have seen brown bears replaced by black bears in response to environmental change, and the black bears, in turn, change their diet from land to ocean and change in stature. Over this time, people developed new tools, such as microblades, slotted antler harpoons, and ground stone adzes, and they came to live in big houses, carve monumental art, and paddle their seagoing canoes the length of the coast. The Haida people have seen and been part of a long-term process of environmental transformation and cultural change. In oral histories they remember the history of the islands.

Haida Gwaii is an archipelago with a combined land mass of approximately 10,000 square kilometres. The archipelago includes two large islands (Graham Island to the north and Moresby Island to the south), and more than 100 smaller islands. Adjacent waters are the open Pacific Ocean to the west, Hecate Strait to the east, and Dixon Entrance to the north. Haida Gwaii is separated from continental North America by at least 70 kilometres in any direction, making it the most isolated archipelago on the west coast of the Americas. Over the long term, Haida Gwaii has been both slightly smaller and considerably larger due to sea level change. The archipelago includes three major physiographic regions: the Queen Charlotte Ranges, the Skidegate Plateau, and the Queen Charlotte Lowland (Sutherland-Brown and Yorath 1989). Haida Gwaii is dominated by temperate rain forest in which spruce, western hemlock, and western red cedar are dominant. Endemic large mammals are limited to black bear and a now-extinct caribou, while the surrounding waters are rich in fish, shellfish, marine mammals, and sea birds. Haida Gwaii is the home of the Haida people, whose history is known through both oral tradition and archaeology.

This volume builds on the publication *The Outer Shores* (Scudder and Gessler 1989), which provided synthetic summaries of environmental and human histories as then understood. In the years since *The Outer Shores* was published, much new and exciting research has taken place in Haida Gwaii and Hecate Strait. Now a grand story is emerging of the long-term human and environmental history of Haida Gwaii, a story this book attempts to tell in a precise, approachable, and sensitive manner.

This book is a compendium of paleoenvironmental, traditional, and archaeological records for Haida Gwaii and adjacent areas of Hecate Strait. The forewords are by Guujaaw and Knut Fladmark. Guujaaw, currently president of the Haida Nation, is a strong environmental advocate with considerable expertise in Haida history. Knut Fladmark conducted extensive fieldwork and analysis of the archaeology of Haida Gwaii in the 1960s and 1970s and developed a theory of a coastal migration route from Asia to southern North America. The chapters of this book represent the latest research results and interpretations of current research into the long-term human and natural history of these islands. The chapters are presented grouped in three parts, each introduced by a short introductory chapter. Paleoenvironmental histories are presented in Part 1, traditional histories in Part 2, and archaeological histories in Part 3.

The editors wish to express their thanks to all those who helped bring this volume to publication. We appreciate the support of the editors of the Pacific Rim Archaeology Series, Michael Blake and R.G. Matson, who reviewed an early draft and encouraged us to submit the manuscript for inclusion in the series. Knut Fladmark and two anonymous reviewers are thanked for providing comment on the volume. We are also grateful to Quentin Mackie and Marty Magne, who, in addition to contributing to chapters in this volume, provided comments on several archaeological chapters and on the more general integration of the cultural and environmental histories presented. We wish to thank the staff at UBC Press, in particular Jean Wilson, who guided the manuscript through the review process, and Darcy Cullen, who oversaw the editing and production of the book. Frank Chow's role as copy editor was invaluable, as he managed to ensure consistency of style throughout the collection. We also wish to acknowledge the funding provided for the index by the University Publications Committee at Simon Fraser University.

We are grateful to Guujaaw, president of the Council of the Haida Nation, for maintaining a strong interest in the archaeology and paleoecology of Haida Gwaii and Hecate Strait, for giving insightful comments on select chapters, and for preparing a foreword that brings a Haida perspective to the volume. We thank Knut Fladmark for his foreword, which represents a Western perspective, and note that his contribution to Pacific Rim archaeology is profound and ongoing: while much new information about Haida Gwaii has come to light over the past few decades, it is remarkable how well it all fits into the archaeological and environmental framework Knut devised over thirty years ago. Working with better tools and a multidisciplinary team has allowed us to expand and enhance this story but most key tenets are unchanged. Captain Gold of Skidegate has played a vital role in the archaeology and history of Haida Gwaii since the early 1970s. We thank him for his participation in, and encouragement of, the archaelogy program and his willingness to share his perspectives on the connections between archaeology, environmental reconstructions, and traditional history. Parks Canada managers Ernie Gladstone, Marty Magne, and Ron Hamilton were key supporters of the Gwaii Haanas Archaeology and Paleoecology Project and without their support much of the research presented here would not have taken place. And, of course, a big thanks to the efforts of all the contributors who shared with us their knowledge so that this fascinating history could be told.

To Donna, Kimberley, and Brooke – thanks for all the times I was in the field and you had to look after the chores at home. – *Rolf*

To Joanne, Edana, Freia, and Erika – for all your time with me in Gwaii Haanas and for keeping the home fires burning when I was up there without you. – *Daryl*

And in fond memory of Tucker Brown (K̲'oyas), Captain of the Parks Canada vessels *Shearwater* and *Gwaii Haanas*. Tucker will be remembered by those who were fortunate enough to cross his path for his knowledge, humour, and endless stories, and for always getting the "Archy's" to where they needed to go. Howa.

A Note on Radiocarbon Dating

In this book dates are presented in radiocarbon years before present (BP) unless otherwise indicated. For technical reasons, radiocarbon years are not the same as calendar (solar) years, and the relationship between these two scales varies across the centuries. Corrections – or calibrations – are now available for late glacial and Holocene time (Stuiver et al. 1998), which convert one scale into another. The following table is derived from CALIB 4.1 derived using the CALIB 4.1 program (Stuiver et al. 1998). The calibrated age is the median age derived from the program, and the Christian era age is obtained by subtracting the present, which is fixed at AD 1950. From this, the term *years ago* would be the calibrated age plus the number of years before AD 1950. For example, a radiocarbon age estimate of 3000 BP is calibrated at 3,180 calendar years ago (3,180 cal yrs ago), or a calendar date of 1230 BC.

Radiocarbon Calibration Table

Radiocarbon years	Calibrated age	Calendar date
1000 BP	930 cal yrs ago	1020 AD
2000 BP	1,940 cal yrs ago	10 AD
3000 BP	3,180 cal yrs ago	1230 BC
4000 BP	4,490 cal yrs ago	2540 BC
5000 BP	5,730 cal yrs ago	3780 BC
6000 BP	6,820 cal yrs ago	4870 BC
7000 BP	7,810 cal yrs ago	5860 BC
8000 BP	8,870 cal yrs ago	6920 BC
9000 BP	10,190 cal yrs ago	8240 BC
10,000 BP	11,400 cal yrs ago	9450 BC
11,000 BP	13,000 cal yrs ago	11,050 BC
12,000 BP	14,060 cal yrs ago	12,110 BC

13,000 BP	15,630 cal yrs ago	13,680 BC
14,000 BP	16,790 cal yrs ago	14,840 BC
15,000 BP	17,940 cal yrs ago	15,990 BC
16,000 BP	19,090 cal yrs ago	17,140 BC
17,000 BP	20,240 cal yrs ago	18,290 BC
18,000 BP	21,390 cal yrs ago	19,440 BC
19,000 BP	22,540 cal yrs ago	20,590 BC
20,000 BP	23,690 cal yrs ago	21,750 BC

Part 1
Paleoenvironmental History

The great mystery of the peopling of the Americas, once thought to be solved by the "Clovis-first" scenario, is once again reopened as a focal point of argument, speculation, and a host of new scientific data. Of special interest to us on the Pacific coast is the growing evidence for early native populations with strong maritime adaptations, which almost certainly included boat building as well as marine foraging strategies. How early such peoples were present on the coast is a key question that has yet to be answered, but it is highly probable that they predate the beginning of the Holocene. The current search for evidence of these early coastal colonists is well described by Dixon (1999) and most recently in *Lost World, Rewriting Prehistory: How New Science Is Tracing America's Ice Age Mariners* by Tom Koppel (2003). In order to theorize rationally about the possible timing of early coastal migrations, we need to first understand the physical and biological environments along the Pacific coast during the late glacial and early Holocene time periods. Much of the evidence that Koppel discusses was gleaned from discussions with and publications of contributors to this book.

Since publication of *The Outer Shores* in 1989, significant advances have been made regarding the glacial history, sea level history, archaeology, and paleoecology of the Pacific Northwest Coast. In order to improve the current state of knowledge about past environments along the coastal strip of British Columbia, data from pollen analysis and plant macrofossils need to be expanded, synthesized, and integrated with other lines of evidence. Several studies not reviewed in *The Outer Shores* have since been published, and they provide intriguing, although preliminary, insights into the now submerged "Lost World" that has played an important role in the biological recolonization of British Columbia since the last glacial maximum. The "Lost World" terminology (Mathewes 2000a, 2000b) is used, with apologies to Sir Arthur Conan Doyle, since it is now clear that large portions of the continental shelf of the Pacific Northwest Coast were emergent during the Fraser Glaciation, and that these landscapes were subsequently "drowned" due to rising postglacial sea levels. A key element of current interest in this submerged landscape is the evidence that the earliest migration of humans to the Americas could have occurred along the coastal corridor during deglaciation, if not earlier. Hence, the nature of the plant cover and terrestrial environment of the Lost World becomes important not only as a clue to paleoclimates and wildlife habitats but as a potential source of food, fibres, and medicines for early human occupants.

Intimately linked to the emerging interest in the coast as a biotic migration corridor is the long-standing controversy regarding the possibility that plants and animals may have survived along the coast during the last glacial maximum in ice-free refugia. This controversy is not yet settled, but new lines of evidence regarding molecular data of genetic divergence have recently become available for plants, insects, and terrestrial vertebrates. Although the search for continuously unglaciated refugia on the coast has gone on for over forty years, the critical evidence for such a site has not yet been presented. Along the Vancouver Island coast, radiocarbon-dated evidence of non-glacial environments is restricted to the intervals before about 16,000 BP (radiocarbon years) and after about 14,000 BP (Ward et al. 2003; see also Lian et al. 2001 – Port Moody Interstade). On Haida Gwaii, deglaciation was under way by 15,000 BP, following conditions that peaked sometime between 21,000 and 16,000 BP. In southeastern Alaska, fossil ringed seal and arctic fox bones dating through the glacial maximum hint at a productive marine environment, and possible refugia in the Alexander Archipelago.

Recent research suggests that the best possibility of a continuous refugium is around Haida Gwaii on the now-submerged continental shelf in Hecate Strait, east of north Moresby Island and Graham Island ("Hecatia" in Fladmark 1975). Studies are ongoing to examine the terrestrial vegetation and paleoenvironment of Hecate Strait and Queen Charlotte Strait to the south. Long cores of lake sediments on northern Vancouver Island and in the Gwaii Haanas National Park Reserve have been dated and studied (Lacourse 2004), and the pollen profiles will be compared with the late glacial portions of cores taken from submerged lakes on the continental shelf. These studies will emphasize the interval between 15,000 and 10,000 BP, which includes the probable time of human migration from the north. Evidence so far points to expanses of treeless shrub-tundra vegetation between 15,000 and 12,500 BP. Forests of pine and spruce expanded rapidly over the landscape after 12,500 years ago (12,500 BP) but were flooded on the lowlands when sea levels rose quickly after 12,000 BP (Lacourse et al. 2003). The optimum interval for human migration was likely between 13,500 and 12,000 BP, when the landscape was open and climatic conditions supported a diverse and relatively productive plant cover (Mathewes 2000a).

History of Investigation

In the late 1800s, Dawson (1880) explored the archipelago and reported extensively upon the geological and environmental history of Haida Gwaii. His reports provide a plethora of information and include descriptions of evidence for glacial history and sea level as well as sedimentary history, biology, and anthropology. After a long hiatus, interest in the late Pleistocene environments of the Pacific coast was rekindled by the publication of a seminal report by Calvin Heusser (1960). Based on cores collected in numerous peat bogs from the Aleutian Islands to California, Heusser provided pioneering information on postglacial vegetation succession and climate for the Pacific Northwest. Subsequent refinements in pollen analytical techniques and radiocarbon dating have greatly expanded our ability to reconstruct environmental histories, but we owe a great deal to these early investigations.

The next comprehensive synthesis of the geology and environmental history of Haida Gwaii was prepared by Sutherland-Brown (1968), who conducted extensive fieldwork in the archipelago. He provided substantial interpretation of structural geology and glaciation, including discussions of glacial deposits, ice movement, paleontology, sea levels, and refugia. His interpretation of glacial history left little opportunity for organisms to have survived on Haida Gwaii during the last glaciation, contrary to the interpretations of many biologists who argued from the presence of endemic plants and animals that glacial refugia must have been present (Heusser 1960, 1989; Calder and Taylor, 1968). A breakthrough paper published in the journal *Science* (Warner et al. 1982) provided the first radiocarbon-dated evidence for early deglaciation on Haida Gwaii, suggesting that ice-free areas existed near Cape Ball on Graham Island by 15,000 BP, with accompanying evidence of a tundra-like terrestrial vegetation cover by that time (Mathewes 1989a).

With respect to both human and glacial history, a seminal report was published by Knut Fladmark in 1975. Based on his doctoral dissertation, Fladmark's "Paleoecological Model for Northwest Coast Prehistory" set the scene for many subsequent investigations into the paleogeography, oceanography, sea level history, and archaeology of Haida Gwaii. His sea level curves for the North Coast (Fladmark 1975, figure 6) were the first to document that relative sea levels during the late glacial on Haida Gwaii were lower than they are today, setting the scene for the problem of recovering archaeological evidence from a much larger but now drowned landscape, a theme that appears in several of the chapters in this book. Similarly, he concurred with Heusser's earlier findings (1960) that during the last glacial period lower sea levels and incomplete glaciation provided a possible chain of refugia that might have been used by early human travellers between coastal Alaska and the south. Updates on many of these issues are summarized in the various chapters of *The Outer Shores* by Scudder and Gessler (1989) and in the following chapters of this book. Nevertheless, new information relating to paleoenvironments and the potential for early human migration along the coast appears regularly (e.g., Ward et al. 2003; Hetherington and Reid 2003), and interested individuals need to monitor the primary scientific literature to keep up with new developments.

The six chapters that follow build on data already available in *The Outer Shores* to provide an overview of physical and biological conditions that humans may have encountered in their settlement of the Haida Gwaii region. In Chapter 1, Vaughn Barrie and colleagues document the late Quaternary geology of Haida Gwaii and the surrounding marine areas, with an emphasis on processes and timing of sedimentation, glaciation, and deglaciation. In Chapter 2, Daryl Fedje and colleagues outline the long-term history of sea level change, showing how at different periods sea level has been both much lower and somewhat higher than it is today. This chapter lays a baseline for the book as a whole. By knowing the size and shape of Haida Gwaii at any given time, we can better reconstruct environment and potential for human occupation. This theme is elaborated in Chapter 3, in which Terri Lacourse and Rolf Mathewes outline the terrestrial paleoecology of Haida Gwaii and the adjacent continental shelf, paying special attention to the problems and prospects of the late Pleistocene environment for human subsistence and as a potential migration corridor into the Americas. This is followed by a more focused study by Richard Hebda and colleagues, who examine in detail data from Anthony Island (*SGang gwaay*) to focus attention on long-term vegetation history, climate change, and their relationship to human settlement. Since the ancient village of Ninstints is a UNESCO World Heritage Site, this study of Anthony Island provides an important environmental link to understanding the human history of this special place. Haida Gwaii has long been known for its unique biota, and the final two chapters outline the evolution of endemic species and paleontological evidence of the vertebrate faunal history.

1

Late Quaternary Geology of Haida Gwaii and Surrounding Marine Areas

J. Vaughn Barrie, Kim W. Conway, Heiner Josenhans,
John J. Clague, Rolf W. Mathewes, and Daryl W. Fedje

The present morphology of Haida Gwaii (Queen Charlotte Islands) (Figure 1.1) and surrounding seabed has developed under the influence of glaciation, tectonism (changes in the earth's surface due to earthquakes), sea level change, and dynamic oceanography over the late Quaternary geological period (approximately the last 30,000 years). Change brought on by these processes, acting independently and in combination, is complex. Coastal change is continuous today and is strongly influenced by global climatic events such as El Niño and earthquake activity along the Queen Charlotte Fault (Figure 1.2), which separates the North America and Pacific plates along the west coast of Haida Gwaii. The interaction of these processes throughout the late Quaternary are briefly described here to lay a physical environmental framework for human colonization of these spectacular islands.

Haida Gwaii encompasses two physiographic regions (Holland 1964): (1) the Queen Charlotte Ranges, part of the Insular Mountain Belt, and (2) the Coastal Trough, which includes the Hecate Depression. The Queen Charlotte Ranges form the backbone of the islands and are extremely rugged, dropping steeply into the Pacific Ocean off the west coast of Moresby Island. The Hecate Depression is a broad area of low relief, with shorelines of basaltic lavas west of Masset Inlet and thick beach sand and gravel east and southeast of Masset Sound (Figures 1.1 and 1.5A).

Late Quaternary Geological Processes

Tectonism

Tectonism gave rise to the existence and location of Haida Gwaii. The Pacific plate slides northward and slightly into North America at an average rate of 50 to 60 millimetres per year along the Queen Charlotte Fault (Riddihough 1988; Rohr et al. 2000). At the junction of the two plates (Figure 1.1), this motion has been accompanied by frequent earthquakes that vary in intensity along the fault (Figure 1.2), although the overall pattern has been stable since records have been kept (Bird 1997). Along with numerous small events, four large earthquakes have occurred in the past century, with the largest (magnitude 8.1) occurring adjacent to the northwestern edge of the continental shelf of Graham Island in 1949 (Figure 1.1), and the most recent on 17 February 2001 (magnitude 6.1). During the 1949 earthquake, approximately 7 metres of movement occurred over 490 kilometres during the rupture (Bostwick 1984).

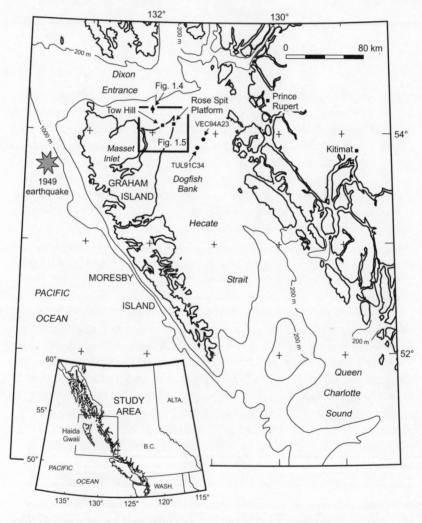

Figure 1.1   Haida Gwaii and surrounding marine areas. Location of figures, sediment cores discussed in the text, and the epicentre of the 1949 earthquake are shown.

This active plate boundary defines the shape and physiography of the Pacific margin of Haida Gwaii. The western continental shelf is extremely narrow, extending offshore less than 5 kilometres in the south and up to 30 kilometres at latitude 54°N to the shelf edge, at roughly 200 metres water depth (Figure 1.1). Earthquakes along the fault have resulted in rupturing of the ground surface and seabed and produced local "tidal waves," more properly called tsunamis (Barrie and Conway 1996b). For example, a tsunami was observed in Tasu Sound at the time of the 1949 earthquake, the result of a large submarine failure that occurred along the southern arm of the inlet near the entrance.

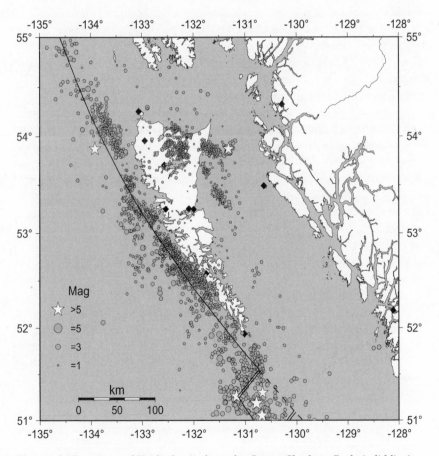

Figure 1.2 Seismicity of Haida Gwaii along the Queen Charlotte Fault (solid line), in northern Graham Island and Hecate Strait from data collected at eleven recording stations (diamonds) between 1984 and 1996, after Bird 1997.

Late Wisconsin Glaciation

Glaciation has occurred many times on Haida Gwaii, although extensive evidence has been found for only the youngest glacial episode over much of the islands and offshore (Clague et al. 1982b). The Fraser Glaciation, as the last main phase of continental glaciation is known in British Columbia, began approximately 25,000 to 30,000 years ago (Clague 1977, 1981). However, the relatively low Queen Charlotte Mountains may have resulted in glaciers developing more slowly and much later than in southern British Columbia. On Haida Gwaii, ice formed small ice caps flowing from the mountains up to 500 metres thick, independent of the Cordilleran Ice Sheet that covered mainland British Columbia (Clague et al. 1982b; Clague 1983). There may have been ice-free areas on the islands and on the coastal lowlands of Graham Island, where glaciation was weak and of short duration (Clague et al. 1982b; Clague 1989). The limited size and extent of the Queen Charlotte Mountains source areas and the proximity of the deep water of the open Pacific Ocean, Dixon Entrance, and Queen Charlotte Sound limited the expansion of Queen Charlotte ice (Clague 1981, 1989; Warner et al. 1982; Barrie et al. 1993; Barrie and Conway 1999).

Ice from the massive Cordilleran sheet extended westward across northern Hecate Strait and through Dixon Entrance and coalesced with ice from Haida Gwaii, deflecting it westward along Dixon Entrance (Sutherland-Brown 1968; Hicock and Fuller 1995; Barrie and Conway 1999). This coalescence was probably short-lived (Clague 1989). Ice also moved south down the central trough in Hecate Strait (Barrie and Bornhold 1989), coalescing with ice coming through the troughs of Queen Charlotte Sound to the edge of the shelf (Luternauer and Murray 1983; Luternauer et al. 1989a; Josenhans et al. 1995) (Figure 1.3).

Glaciation reached its maximum extent sometime after 21,000 BP (Blaise et al. 1990). The late Fraser Glaciation terminated with rapid climatic amelioration, resulting in rapid retreat and melting of the ice. Glaciers had retreated from the lowland areas of the Queen Charlotte Islands beginning around 15,000 BP (Warner et al. 1982), but mountain valleys and cirques supported remnant ice masses until much later (Clague et al. 1982b; Clague 1989). Offshore glacial retreat began sometime after 15,000 BP and ice had largely left the lowlands and offshore of the region by 13,500 to 13,000 BP (Barrie and Conway 1999).

Icebergs were calved from the retreating glacial ice front. These icebergs impacted the seafloor and left characteristic plough features or iceberg furrows that are ubiquitous in the troughs of the basin between depths of 110 and 350 metres (Luternauer and Murray 1983; Barrie and Bornhold 1989; Barrie and Conway 1999). The curvilinear furrows have incision depths of up to 7 metres but are mostly less than 3 metres deep. They typically display a preferred orientation in the direction of the trough.

Distribution of glacial extent on the continental shelf surrounding Haida Gwaii (Figure 1.3) is inferred from glacial deposits that suggest ice-contact sediments extending to the shelf edge through the large troughs that empty into Queen Charlotte Sound (Josenhans et al. 1995) and also Dixon Entrance (Barrie and Conway 1999). A minimum ice thickness of 400 metres is suggested for the shelf areas, allowing the ice to infill the 300-metre-deep troughs and maintain a 100-metre ice thickness before spilling onto the bank tops (Josenhans et al. 1995; Barrie and Conway 1999). This same geophysical evidence (lack of ice-contact deposits) also suggests that glacial ice was not present on the bank tops in Queen Charlotte Sound (Josenhans et al. 1995) and on southern Dogfish Bank (Figure 1.1) in Hecate Strait (Barrie and Bornhold 1989). Sutherland-Brown (1968) suggests that ice also moved out onto the shelf, off western Haida Gwaii, and formed a small ice shelf

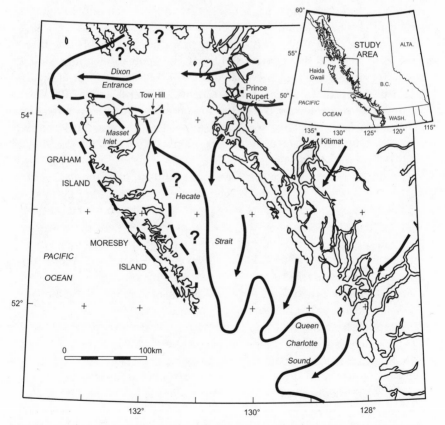

Figure 1.3 Late Wisconsin glacial maximum for Haida Gwaii and surrounding marine areas. Dashed lines indicate the approximate limit of the Queen Charlotte ice cap and solid lines show the approximate westward limit of the Cordilleran glacier. Question marks indicate potentially unglaciated areas.

from evidence of low-level cirques and glacial grooves and scratches. However, Clague (1989) implies that the ice extent was limited and that some areas of the shelf could have been free of ice during the last glaciation (Figure 1.3). Offshore work so far suggests that there is no evidence for glacial till or any other identifiable glacial or deglaciation features, such as iceberg scours or boulders, usually common in such glaciated areas (Barrie and Conway 1996b).

Sea Level History

A regional lowering of sea level along the northern Pacific margin of Canada began soon after the late Fraser glacial maximum and continued during deglaciation. The oldest known record of open marine conditions occurs at 14,380 BP (Core VEC94A23 in Figure 1.1) at the present-day water depth of 37 metres in northern Hecate Strait (Barrie and Conway 1999). At this time, relative sea level was above 30 metres but not higher than present-day sea level, as there is no record of submergence of the eastern coast of Haida Gwaii (Clague et al. 1982a). Just 9 kilometres southwest of this site, three cores were collected that contain terrestrial sediments formed in a tundra environment (Barrie et al. 1993) dated to 13,790 BP (TUL91C34 in Figure 1.1). This means that sea level dropped significantly in as little as 590 years (using a 600-year reservoir correction to compare marine with terrestrial radiocarbon dates). Relative sea level had reached a maximum lowering after 13,000 BP and remained low until approximately 12,400 BP (Josenhans et al. 1997; Barrie and Conway 1999).

At peak glaciation, the ice mass over the mainland had compressed the earth's crust. As ice retreated from the marine areas, the load of the mainland glacier caused the outer coast to be lifted (similar to a teeter-totter), while the mainland was depressed. The rise of the earth's crust after the ice load had been removed from the marine areas would account for most of the relative drop in sea level during this period of regression. Global sea level rose approximately 10 metres in the same period due to melting ice (Fairbanks 1989). When the ice melted over the mainland, the mainland also rebounded upward, but the outer coast dropped in elevation (the reverse motion of the teeter-totter), causing relative sea level to rise (Clague 1983). Sea levels reached the present shoreline on Haida Gwaii by about 9400 BP and reached a maximum of 13 to 16 metres above current levels by 8900 BP, returning to the present level by 2000 BP (Clague et al. 1982a; Clague 1983; Josenhans et al. 1995, 1997; Fedje and Josenhans 2000).

The Haida Gwaii archipelago is located at the western margin of the North American lithospheric plate (Figure 1.2), where high heat flow and a relatively thin crust imply rapid crustal response to changes in surface load and a short wavelength (James et al. 2000). The amount of change varies dramatically from east to west in response to loading and rebound from the

Cordilleran ice advance (Clague 1983; Barrie and Conway 1999; Chapter 2). As the eastern ice load retreated, the crust responded, with the maximum flexure occurring nearest the area of maximum change in the ice load.

Late Glacial Stratigraphy

Late glacial stratigraphy of coastal Haida Gwaii can be broadly divided into three dominant units that overlie the glacial deposits (till) offshore (Luternauer et al. 1989a; Barrie et al. 1991; Barrie and Conway 1999) and onshore (Alley and Thomson 1978). Glaciomarine mud (Unit A) containing approximately equal but varying proportions of sand, silt, and clay occurs in depths generally greater than 200 metres. Initial deposition of the glaciomarine sediments began during deglaciation between 15,000 and 13,000 BP. The unit is interpreted to have been deposited by rafting of sediment by icebergs and floating sea ice, similar to present-day conditions on the Labrador margin of eastern Canada (Gilbert and Barrie 1985). The depositional environment changed somewhere between 13,600 and 12,900 BP (Luternauer et al. 1989b) with the complete retreat of the ice from the continental shelf, ending the ice rafting.

Onshore sediments carried by meltwater are found in the lowlands of Haida Gwaii and in some valleys, and attain thicknesses of several tens of metres. A similar thick deposit of well-sorted sand and gravel (outwash) underlies northeastern Graham Island (Clague et al. 1982b). This deposit accumulated between a local glacier and the Cordilleran Ice Sheet during the last glaciation. This outwash extends into Dixon Entrance to the 150-metre isobath (Barrie and Conway 1999) and likely existed across northern Hecate Strait. Late glacial lake sediments have also been identified at several sites on the islands, similar in character to the offshore glaciomarine sediments (Alley and Thomson 1978).

Overlying the glaciomarine mud in the offshore troughs is a sedimentary sequence, designated Unit B, up to 20 metres thick. The sequence was subdivided by Luternauer and colleagues (1989b) into three subunits that reflect the radiocarbon age and texture of the sediments. B1, lowermost in the package, has been dated to between 13,000 and 12,000 BP. This mud unit is thought to have developed as sea levels were falling on the shelf and, unlike the glaciomarine muds, contains no material of ice-rafted origin.

Unit B2 overlies B1 or, where B1 sediments are not found, overlies the glaciomarine mud. This sandy mud unit, 0.01 to 4.0 metres thick, is found within the shelf troughs and represents a lag formed between 12,900 BP and approximately 10,500 to 10,200 BP. In shallower water depths of 160 and 100 metres, at the edge of the shelf banks, Unit B2 thickens into a wedge of nearshore laminated sands (Barrie 1991). In Dixon Entrance, Unit B2 is consistently thicker in section, varying between 0.5 and greater than 3.0 metres in thickness with consistently greater than 50 percent sand, with the remainder consisting of equal amounts of gravel, silt, and clay. This unit is thought to have been deposited over a period of several hundred years when sea level was lower than at present (Luternauer et al. 1989b; Barrie et al. 1991; Barrie and Conway 1999). In Dixon Entrance, however, the extensive distribution of the unit to water depths of greater that 450 metres suggests that wave and current energy at the seabed was much higher than at similar water depths in Hecate Strait and Queen Charlotte Sound during the period of deposition. The upper contact of Unit B2 is sharp, implying that the conditions that caused the formation of the lag in the deeper waters and the rapid deposition in shallower waters were abruptly terminated. The rapid sea level transgression that began shortly after 12,400 BP brought about this dramatic change. At a few locations in the troughs, Unit B3 overlies Unit B2; Unit B3 is a mud unit of limited aerial distribution that was deposited between about 10,500 and 9700 BP.

Onshore, alluvium deposits formed during the late glacial period, primarily in the river valleys of Haida Gwaii (Clague 1989). They commonly overlie deltaic deposits where streams enter lakes or the sea, and active delta foreslopes are present off the mouths of many streams. The alluvium is texturally highly variable, ranging from sand and silt in some valleys near the coast to gravel in the mountain valleys (Clague 1989).

Offshore sedimentation during the Holocene has resulted in up to 40 metres of olive, clay-rich mud (Unit C) in the troughs and a thin (usually less than 10 metres) sand and gravel unit on the bank tops deposited as the coast migrated during sea level rise. Marine sediments also occur up to 15 metres elevation in coastal areas of Haida Gwaii (Clague et al. 1982b; Clague 1989). They include both shallow marine sands rich in shell, estuarine muds, and beach sands and gravels. Present-day sedimentation in the region is minimal.

Onshore Holocene deposits also include windblown (aeolian) sands (Harper 1980a; Clague and Bornhold 1980) and extensive organic deposits from near sea level to the subalpine zone (Alley and Thomson 1978; Warner 1984). Where strong onshore winds occur and there is a supply of sand, aeolian dunes form. In particular, along the northeastern coast of Graham Island the aeolian sands have formed an extensive belt adjacent to the present shoreline (Harper 1980a). Decomposition of plant material to form peat results in the ubiquitous organic deposits on the islands. These can be greater than 10 metres thick in level areas (Clague 1989).

Processes of Deposition and Erosion

Outside the coastal areas, the landscape of Haida Gwaii has changed little (Clague 1989). Sediment supply and wave and tidal current energy were the primary factors that controlled coastal response to the late Quaternary relative sea level changes. Coincident with deglacial regression of the shelf, a significant volume of sediment was delivered by the retreat of the Cordilleran Ice Sheet to the continental margin. This resulted in extensive glacial outwash and glaciomarine deposition except where wave and current energies were high, such as outer Dixon Entrance and the western coast of Haida Gwaii. During the early Holocene transgression of the shelf, sediment supply was primarily restricted to the erosion of the previously deposited late glacial deposits and landforms, resulting in the rapid formation of drowned wave-cut terraces and spit platforms (Figure 1.4) as sea level rose in steps. The rapid transgression also overstepped lakes and estuarine environments (Josenhans et al. 1995). Wave energy removed sediment on the western shelf and coastal zone of Haida Gwaii, except in very protected basins and fjords (Barrie and Conway 1996a). In one of the protected basins east and north of Anthony Island, a fine-grained carbonate deposit has formed. The extensive exposure of a rough bedrock surface and the vertical mixing that occurs off southwestern Moresby Island (Crawford et al. 1995) provides both the substrate and nutrient-rich water required for carbonate production. Similar high-latitude carbonate deposits occur over about 4,000 square kilometres off southeastern Haida Gwaii, overlying bedrock and gravel lag deposits (Carey et al. 1995).

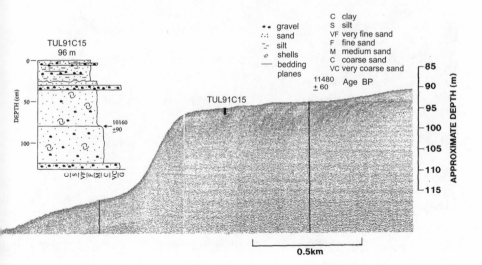

Figure 1.4 Lithology and coincident Huntec DTS sub-bottom profile of a sea level lowstand spit platform (terrace) in Dixon Entrance. Accretion is suggested in the dipping reflectors in the subsurface of the terrace.

Plate tectonics, on the other hand, played a secondary role in coastal evolution. The recurrence of earthquakes (see Figure 1.2) has resulted in disturbance of the limited Quaternary deposits and bedrock faulting and folding at the seabed (Barrie and Conway 1996b). However, the active Queen Charlotte Fault does not control the large-scale adjustment in relative sea

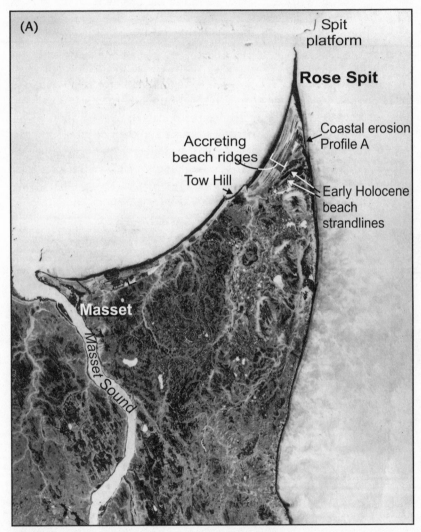

Figure 1.5   SPOT satellite image (A) of northeastern Graham Island taken on 19 May 1992, showing the accreted beach ridges, the Holocene highstand beach strandline, and the Rose Spit platform. An oblique aerial photograph (B) looking landward off the northeastern corner of Haida Gwaii shows the extensive spit platform at spring low tide in June 1998.

level that has been recorded in the late Quaternary. Riddihough (1982) suggests that isostatic adjustment along Haida Gwaii is dominant over stepwise tectonic movements, which would be small. Vertical tectonic movements are at least an order of magnitude lower than maximum rates of isostatic movements during and soon after deglaciation, based on tidal records and precise levelling (Clague et al. 1982b; Clague 1983).

Present Conditions
During the early Holocene highstand of 13 to 15 metres above present sea level, wave energies were greater due to the increased fetch. In addition,

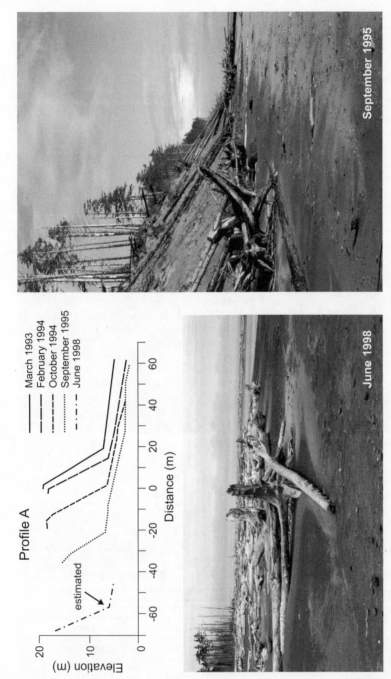

Figure 1.6 Successive cliff erosion at Profile A (Figure 1.5A) along the northeastern coast of Haida Gwaii between March 1993 and June 1998. The photographs, taken at approximately the same location looking north, demonstrate the drastic coastal retreat that occurred at Profile A as a result of the 1998 El Niño, when sea levels were as much as 40 centimetres above normal levels.

little new sediment was available, as the rapid transgression had reworked and mobilized most sediment offshore. Consequently, most of Haida Gwaii has a rocky coastline up to the present day, except for the Hecate Lowland of northeastern Graham Island. Here continuous sand and gravel beaches are found, nourished through erosion of sea cliffs composed of unconsolidated sands and gravel and glacial sediments. Accretive landforms, mainly spits and shore-attached bars, were and still are common along the 120-kilometre stretch of beach. Erosion of these areas may have slowed during the slow fall in sea level between approximately 9000 to 2000 BP, while the present mean rate of coastline retreat is 1 to 3 metres per year (Barrie and Conway 1996a). Most of the sediment released by this erosion is transported to a Holocene spit platform (Rose Spit) that extends 10 kilometres off the northeastern corner of Haida Gwaii (Figure 1.5A and 1.5B), similar to those that developed during the Holocene as sea level rose (Figure 1.4).

Periodic sea level anomalies occur during El Niño events in this region that significantly affect the shoreline of Haida Gwaii. In 1982-83 and 1997-98, sea levels recorded at Prince Rupert (see Figure 1.1) were over 40 centimetres above normal at the height of El Niño. An average of 12 metres of coastal retreat occurred during the most recent event just south of Rose Spit (Figure 1.6), measured at two coastal profiles. This is the result of only four months of sustained sea levels 10 centimetres or greater above present sea levels during the stormy season. The apparent pattern of coastal change is similar to what it was during the early Holocene transgression. Sediment eroded from the upper beach (shoreface) is transferred to longshore bars that extend for several kilometres northward. Longshore transport driven by the dominant southeasterly storms provided the sediment needed for the development of the Rose Spit platform (Amos et al. 1995; Barrie and Conway 1996a).

Coastal Processes and Human Habitation
The discovery of prolific stone tools on former shoreline deposits (Chapter 10) demonstrates that the early inhabitants of Haida Gwaii lived within close proximity to former coasts. We have demonstrated that sea levels have changed rapidly and that the coastlines have moved accordingly, depending on sediment supply, oceanography, topography, and local geology. The location of stable past shorelines can thus be predicted (see Chapter 2).

Conclusions
The morphology of Haida Gwaii and adjacent marine areas is a product of seismic uplift, the action of glaciers through the Pleistocene, and river and marine erosion and deposition. Ice from the mainland extended across northern Hecate Strait and through Dixon Entrance to briefly coalesce with ice

from Haida Gwaii, deflecting the ice sheet in Dixon Entrance westward. Glaciation reached its maximum extent sometime after 21,000 BP. Deglacial retreat began sometime after 15,000 BP and ice had completely left the region by 13,500 to 13,000 BP, except for local remnant ice masses that still existed in the mountain valleys and cirques.

Coastal evolution through the late Quaternary has shaped Haida Gwaii primarily by dramatic sea level change, sediment supply, wave energy, and tidal currents. During deglacial regression, sediment supply was abundant. This resulted in extensive glacial outwash and glaciomarine deposition except where wave and current energies were high, such as Dixon Entrance and the western coast of Haida Gwaii. During the early Holocene transgression of the continental shelf, sediment supply was primarily restricted to the erosion of the previously deposited deglacial deposits, resulting in the formation of drowned wave-cut terraces and spit platforms as the sea level rose in steps. Sediment supply was reduced as sea levels increased, except for the northeastern coastline of Haida Gwaii. Here, Holocene sea level changes still impact the coastal zone and transfer sediment offshore.

Acknowledgments
We would like to thank the captains and crews of *CCGS John P. Tully* and *CCGS Vector* for their support in the collection of the field data over the past twelve years. Technical support for all field operations was provided by B. Hill, I. Frydecky, and B. Macdonald. The manuscript for this chapter was improved and enhanced by discussion with J. Dowdeswell and C.O. Cofaigh and the critical revision of M. Blake and R.G. Matson.

2
Hecate Strait Paleoshorelines
Daryl W. Fedje, Heiner Josenhans, John J. Clague,
J. Vaughn Barrie, David J. Archer, and John R. Southon

Archaeological research from southeastern Alaska, Haida Gwaii, and Queen
Charlotte Sound has revealed a record of maritime occupation extending
back to about 10,000 BP (Ackerman 1996b; Carlson 1996; Fedje and
Christensen 1999; Dixon 1999). It has been proposed that a much longer
human (Fladmark 1975, 1979a; Dixon 1999, 2002) and vegetation (Mathewes
1989a, 1989b; Chapter 4) record may be associated with paleoshorelines
both drowned and stranded as a result of sea level change.

This chapter describes results and implications of paleoshoreline research
in the environs of Hecate Strait (Figure 2.1). It builds on the pioneering
work of researchers such as Fladmark (1975) and Clague (1983). Paleoshoreline histories are key to the development of investigative approaches
in the study of environmental change and early human occupation in late
glacial and early Holocene time. Three regional sea level histories are presented to demonstrate the magnitude of regional differences (Figures 2.1
and 2.2). The data derive from archaeological and geological investigations
conducted between 1970 and 2002.

Geological Processes
The paleoshoreline record is primarily a function of glacio-eustatic, glacio-
isostatic, and tectonic change. Glacio-eustatic change entails global shifts
in sea levels due to variations in the amount of water stored on land as
glacier ice. Globally, sea level was about 120 metres lower than at present
during the Wisconsin glacial maximum (ca. 17,000 BP) (Fairbanks 1989).
Subsequent eustatic rise, during deglaciation, was about 1 centimetre per
year until the mid-Holocene (Figure 2.2). Eustatic rise is the rise in sea level
resulting from worldwide melting of glacial ice. By about 5000 BP, eustatic
rise had slowed to less than 0.2 centimetres per year.

Glacio-isostatic change reflects the uplift or depression of land in response
to loading and unloading by glacier ice. Direct effects include compression
of the earth's crust by the weight of glacier ice and rebound following

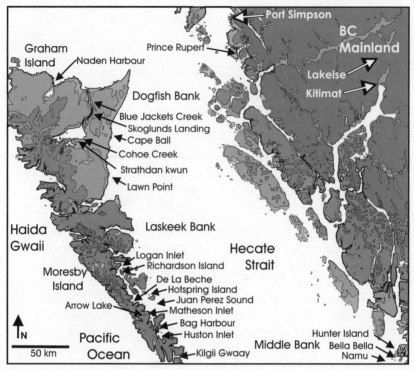

Figure 2.1   Study area

deglaciation. Indirect effects include the effect of glacio-isostatic depression on adjacent unglaciated or less glaciated terrain. Terrain immediately adjacent to the ice load will be depressed. A forebulge develops beyond the isostatically depressed area as subcrustal material is displaced outward (Clague 1983). A forebulge is an area where the earth's crust is bowed upward by the lateral displacement of subcrustal material. On the Pacific coast, this forebulge migrates seaward in response to continental ice load and back to its source upon deglaciation (Figure 2.3).

In the Hecate Strait area, tectonic change is the result of interaction between the North American and Pacific plates. The tectonic component of relative sea level change has been determined through analysis of historical data (Riddihough 1982). Currently, land is rising about 2 millimetres per year in western Hecate Strait (southern Moresby Island), subsiding approximately 1 millimetre per year on the outer mainland coast (Prince Rupert) and subsiding about 2 millimetres per year on the inner mainland coast (Kitimat). Our observations suggest that the scale of tectonic movement during the early Holocene is minor compared with isostatic and eustatic sea level changes. Projection of these rates to earlier Holocene time is consistent with mid to late Holocene data from Haida Gwaii (see below) and from elsewhere on the north Pacific coast (Friele and Hutchinson 1993).

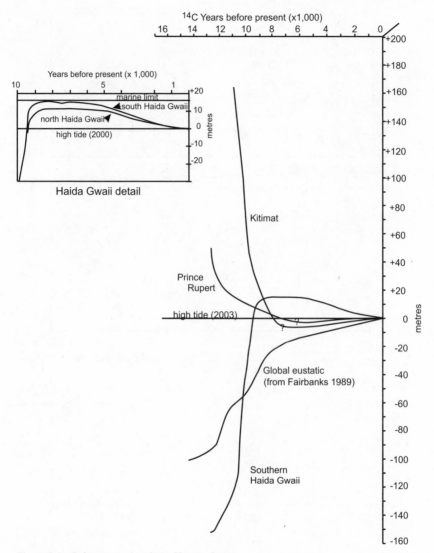

Figure 2.2 Relative sea levels in Hecate Strait.

Sea Levels: Regional Histories from the Environs of Hecate Strait

Regional sea level histories have been developed by dating transgressive (flooding during a rise of sea level) and regressive (lowering of sea level) events and by establishing tidal limits. This work involves analysis of ancient landforms, isolation basins (sediment basins flooded by or isolated from ocean waters as a result of sea level change), and archaeological sites (Fladmark 1975; Clague 1983; Pienitz et al. 1990; Fedje 1993). In this chapter, sea level is measured relative to high tide for ease of application in a

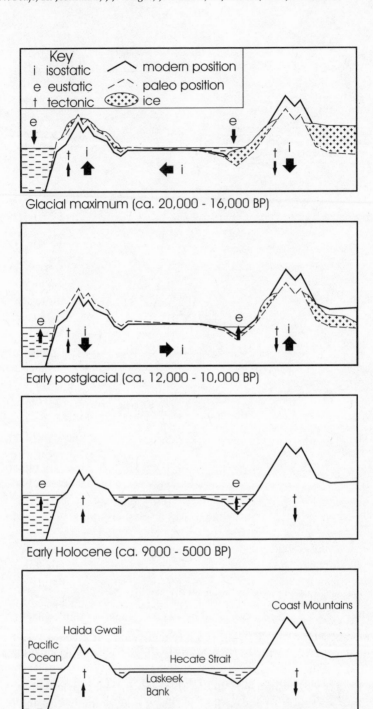

Figure 2.3 Schematic of isostatic, eustatic, and tectonic effects.

terrestrial context. Radiocarbon ages presented in the text are in years before present (AD 1950) and include a reservoir correction of –600 years for marine samples (Southon et al. 1990; Southon and Fedje 2003). Oceanic carbon dioxide, in the northeast Pacific, is approximately 600 years older than atmospheric carbon dioxide, thus marine organisms (fish, shellfish, sea mammals) have radiocarbon ages 600 years older than terrestrial plants and animals of the same age (Table 2.1).

Western Hecate Strait

The post-12,000 BP sea level history of western Hecate Strait has been reconstructed in detail through marine geological and archaeological work (Table 2.1; Figure 2.2; Fladmark 1975; Clague et al. 1982a; Josenhans et al. 1997; Fedje and Josenhans 2000).

Data from southern Haida Gwaii show that sea level was at least 150 metres lower than it is at present at 12,200 BP and rose rapidly over the next three millennia. Relative sea level rose above the present-day shoreline approximately 9400 BP. The maximum transgression of 15 to 16 metres elevation occurred at about 8900 BP and relative sea level remained within 1 metre of this elevation until about 5000 BP. After this time, sea level dropped slowly. The –150-metre relative sea level position resulted primarily from a combination of global eustatic lowering and isostatic uplift. The uplift is interpreted as a forebulge of westerly displaced subcrustal matter caused by isostatic depression of the mainland coast by up to 2,500 metres of glacier ice (Clague 1983). The subsequent rapid rise of relative sea level from about 12,000 to 9000 BP was largely the result of forebulge collapse and sinking of land following disintegration of the late Wisconsin ice sheet, coupled with eustatic rise. The tectonic component of relative sea level change was small, likely less than 10 percent of the total, but may have moderated the rate of rise by about 2 millimetres per year (Riddihough 1982). Isostatic collapse appears to have been complete by about 9000 BP. The 4,000-year period of high sea levels (9000 to 5000 BP) is interpreted as a period of equilibrium between slow late Holocene eustatic rise and tectonic uplift. Possibly, some residual isostatic change may also be represented. Subsequent and continuing lowering of relative sea level is largely from tectonic uplift. The 10-to-15-metre fall in sea level from 5000 BP implies a rate of uplift of about 2 to 3 millimetres per year (Riddihough 1982).

The paleoshoreline record for northern Haida Gwaii is not known in detail for the period before about 9200 BP but is assumed to be similar to that for southern Haida Gwaii. The record from 9200 BP to present exhibits similar trends, but with a slightly lower sea level highstand, to that in the south (Figure 2.2). These data derive from investigations conducted in the 1970s and from recent work by Parks Canada and consulting archaeologists (Fedje et al. 1995; Stafford and Christensen 2000; Chapter 13).

Table 2.1

Radiocarbon ages constraining Hecate Strait and Kitimat-Lakelse sea level positions

Elevation (m aht[a]) and location	Context	Material	Lab no.	[14]C age BP	Source
South Haida Gwaii					
−145 Juan Perez	Brackish	Wood	CAMS-26271	12,460 ± 60	Fedje and Josenhans 2000
−153 Juan Perez	Fluvial + marine	Wood	CAMS-26276	12,380 ± 70	Fedje and Josenhans 2000
−147 Juan Perez	Supratidal	Wood	CAMS-59768	12,240 ± 50	Fedje and Josenhans 2000
−147 Juan Perez	Supratidal	Wood	CAMS-59769	12,190 ± 50	Fedje and Josenhans 2000
−147 Juan Perez	Fluvial	Wood	CAMS-26273	11,830 ± 60	Fedje and Josenhans 2000
−147 Juan Perez	Fluvial	Wood	CAMS-27940	11,810 ± 70	Fedje and Josenhans 2000
−133 Juan Perez	Intertidal	Shell	CAMS-54600	10,850 ± 50	Southon and Fedje 2003
−128 Juan Perez	Intertidal	Shell	CAMS-47675	11,080 ± 50	Fedje and Josenhans 2000
−128 Juan Perez	Intertidal	Shell	CAMS-47674	10,940 ± 50	Fedje and Josenhans 2000
−125 Juan Perez	Intertidal	Shell	CAMS-54601	10,950 ± 50	Fedje and Josenhans 2000
−123 Juan Perez	Intertidal	Shell	CAMS-48155	10,690 ± 50	Fedje and Josenhans 2000
−122 Juan Perez	Intertidal	Shell	CAMS-49631	11,120 ± 50	Fedje and Josenhans 2000
−113 Juan Perez	Estuarine	Shell	CAMS-18997	10,720 ± 60	Southon and Fedje 2003
−113 Juan Perez	Estuarine	Wood	CAMS-18601	10,670 ± 60	Southon and Fedje 2003
−113 Juan Perez	Estuarine	Shell	CAMS-18996	10,550 ± 60	Southon and Fedje 2003
−113 Juan Perez	Estuarine	Wood	CAMS-18995	10,490 ± 60	Southon and Fedje 2003
−110 Juan Perez	Intertidal	Shell	CAMS-49630	10,180 ± 50	Fedje and Southon n.d.
−108 Laskeek	Lacustrine	Wood	TO-3495	10,360 ± 80	Southon and Fedje 2003
−108 Laskeek	Marine	Shell	TO-3735	10,180 ± 70	Southon and Fedje 2003
−83 Logan	Lacustrine	Wood	CAMS-18752	10,560 ± 70	Fedje and Southon n.d.
−83 Logan	Marine	Shell	CAMS-19007	10,550 ± 60	Southon and Fedje 2003
−83 Logan	Marine	Shell	CAMS-18751	10,440 ± 50	Southon and Fedje 2003
−59 Juan Perez	Intertidal	Shell	CAMS-49628	9930 ± 40	Fedje and Josenhans 2000
−57 Juan Perez	Intertidal	Shell	CAMS-49629	9980 ± 40	Fedje and Josenhans 2000

Sample	Environment	Material	Lab no.	Age	Reference
-53 Juan Perez	Supratidal	Wood	CAMS-50947	10,500 ± 40	Fedje and Josenhans 2000
-48 Huston	Lacustrine	Wood	CAMS-19005	10,790 ± 80	Southon and Fedje 2003
-48 Huston	Lacustrine + marine	Wood	CAMS-18602	10,630 ± 110	Southon and Fedje 2003
-48 Huston	Marine	Wood	CAMS-19001	9940 ± 70	Southon and Fedje 2003
-30 Matheson	Intertidal	Shell	CAMS-9992	9890 ± 80	Fedje et al. 1996
-30 Matheson	Intertidal	Shell	CAMS-10837	9600 ± 60	Fedje et al. 1996
-30 Matheson	Intertidal	Wood	CAMS-10817	9530 ± 60	Fedje et al. 1996
-30 Matheson	Intertidal	Wood	CAMS-9991	9530 ± 60	Fedje et al. 1996
-28 Matheson	Fluvial	Wood	CAMS-9989	9780 ± 60	Fedje et al. 1996
-28 Matheson	Fluvial	Wood	CAMS-9990	9670 ± 60	Fedje et al. 1996
-28 Matheson	Fluvial	Wood	CAMS-10601	9630 ± 70	Fedje et al. 1996
-28 Matheson	Fluvial	Wood	CAMS-9988	9540 ± 80	Fedje et al. 1996
-3 Matheson	Intertidal	Shell	CAMS-10848	9430 ± 100	Fedje et al. 1996
-3 Matheson	Intertidal	Wood	CAMS-10847	9430 ± 100	Fedje et al. 1996
-3 Matheson	Intertidal	Shell	CAMS-9969	9370 ± 70	Fedje et al. 1996
-3 Matheson	Intertidal	Wood	CAMS-9968	9990 ± 90	Fedje et al. 1996
-2 Matheson	Intertidal	Shell	CAMS-10853	9420 ± 60	Fedje et al. 1996
-2 Matheson	Intertidal	Wood	CAMS-10846	9320 ± 100	Fedje et al. 1996
+1 Logan	Intertidal	Wood	CAMS-54596	9490 ± 70	Fedje et al. 1996
+1 Logan	Intertidal	Shell	CAMS-54595	9370 ± 50	Fedje et al. 1996
+1 Matheson	Intertidal	Shell	CAMS-9983	9220 ± 80	Fedje et al. 1996
+1 Matheson	Intertidal	Wood	CAMS-9982	9390 ± 60	Fedje et al. 1996
+4 Matheson	Intertidal	Wood	CAMS-8378	9290 ± 60	Fedje et al. 1996
+4 Matheson	Intertidal	Shell	CAMS-8374	9060 ± 60	Fedje et al. 1996
+4 Matheson	Intertidal	Wood	CAMS-8384	9150 ± 80	Fedje et al. 1996
+12 De La Beche	Fresh	Wood	CAMS-6249	9010 ± 70	Fedje 1993
+12 De La Beche	Marine	Wood	CAMS-19015	8750 ± 60	Fedje 1993
+12 De La Beche	Marine	Shell	CAMS-19016	9590 ± 60	Fedje 1993
+12 De La Beche	Brackish	Wood	CAMS-3969	6250 ± 90	Fedje 1993

▲

▼ *Table 2.1*

Elevation (m aht[a]) and location	Context	Material	Lab no.	[14]C age BP	Source
+13 Richardson*	Supratidal	Wood	CAMS-39876	9290 ± 50	Fedje and Christensen 1999
+15 Richardson*	Supratidal	Wood	CAMS-16202	9010 ± 60	Fedje and Christensen 1999
+17 Richardson*	Supratidal	Wood	CAMS-26262	8470 ± 60	Fedje and Christensen 1999
+16 Arrow 1*	Fluvial	Wood	CAMS-33909	8880 ± 50	Fedje et al. 1996
+16 Arrow 1*	Supratidal	Wood	CAMS-33906	7410 ± 60	Fedje et al. 1996
+15 Arrow 1*	Supratidal	Wood	CAMS-4111	5650 ± 70	Fedje et al. 1996
+15 Arrow lk.	Brackish	Wood	CAMS-18998	6100 ± 60	Fedje and Southon n.d.
+15 Arrow lk.	Brackish	Wood	CAMS-18999	8850 ± 70	Fedje and Southon n.d.
+6 Bag Harbour	Brackish	Wood	CAMS-2325	4140 ± 150	Fedje 1993
+6 Bag Harbour	Brackish	Wood	CAMS-2324	3720 ± 110	Fedje 1993
+3 Hotspring Is.*	Supratidal	Wood	CAMS-10843	1850 ± 60	Southon and Fedje 2003
+3 Hotspring Is.*	Supratidal	Wood	CAMS-10873	1820 ± 60	Southon and Fedje 2003
0 Gadadjans*	Supratidal	Wood	CAMS-15356	300 ± 90	Fedje and Southon n.d.
North Haida Gwaii					
+3 Naden	Intertidal	Wood	CAMS-14432	9200 ± 60	Fedje et al. 1995
+3 Naden	Intertidal	Shell	CAMS-15371	9090 ± 60	Fedje et al. 1995
+4 Cape Ball	Supratidal	Wood	GSC-3129	9160 ± 90	Clague et al. 1982b
+5 Cape Ball	Intertidal	Wood	GSC-3120	8750 ± 80	Clague et al. 1982b
+12 Cohoe*	Supratidal	Wood	CAMS-54599	6980 ± 50	Chapter 13
+11 Cohoe*	Supratidal	Wood	CAMS-50956	5590 ± 50	Chapter 13
+11 Naden	Supratidal	Wood	BTS-2217	4900 ± 55	Stafford and Christensen 2000
+12 Lawn Point*	Supratidal	Wood	S-679	7400 ± 140	Fladmark 1971a
+12 Lawn Point*	Supratidal	Wood	GaK-3272	7050 ± 110	Fladmark 1971a
+12 Strathdan*	Supratidal	Wood	CAMS-19023	5740 ± 60	Fedje et al. 1995
+10 Strathdan*	Supratidal	Wood	CAMS-16203	4520 ± 60	Fladmark 1971a

Site	Environment	Material	Lab No.	Age	Reference
+9 Blue Jackets Creek*	Supratidal	Wood	GSC-1554	4290 ± 130	Fladmark 1971a
+9 Skoglund's Landing	Supratidal	Wood	GX-1695	4165 ± 80	Fladmark 1971a
+6 Naden 1*	Supratidal	Wood	CAMS-14436	3070 ± 60	Fedje et al. 1995
+6 Naden 2*	Supratidal	Wood	CAMS-14435	3250 ± 60	Fedje et al. 1995
Prince Rupert					
+50 Port Simpson	Intertidal	Shell	Beta-14465	12,440 ± 70	Archer 1998
+50 Port Simpson	Intertidal	Shell	Beta-14464	12,370 ± 50	Archer 1998
+10 Kaien Is.	Marine	Shell	GSC-2290	12,100 ± 200	Clague 1984
+5 Ridley Is.	Marine	Shell	CAMS-33900	8880 ± 70	Archer 1998
+2 McNeil R.	Estuarine	Wood	GSC-2248	8460 ± 90	Archer 1998
0 Venn Pass	Supratidal	Wood	S-924	4965 ± 95	MacDonald and Inglis 1981
1 Tugwell Is.	Supratidal	Wood	CAMS-49623	2040 ± 50	Southon and Fedje 2003
Kitimat-Lakelse					
+98 Lakelse	Delta	Shell	GSC-2492	9500 ± 160	Clague 1984
+90 Lakelse	Marine	Shell	CAMS-40363	10,210 ± 60	Fedje and Southon n.d.
+90 Lakelse	Marine	Shell	CAMS-40363	10,150 ± 50	Fedje and Southon n.d.
+90 Lakelse	Marine	Shell	GSC-523	10,190 ± 180	Clague 1984
+90 Lakelse	Marine	Shell	GSC-535	9820 ± 160	Clague 1984
+38 Kitimat	Marine	Shell	GSC-522	9280 ± 160	Clague 1984
+35 Kitimat	Marine	Wood	CAMS-40371	9320 ± 140	Southon and Fedje 2003
+35 Kitimat	Marine	Shell	CAMS-40372	9340 ± 60	Southon and Fedje 2003
+35 Kitimat	Marine	Wood	CAMS-40366	8920 ± 80	Southon and Fedje 2003
+35 Kitimat	Marine	Shell	CAMS-40365	9230 ± 60	Southon and Fedje 2003
+30 Kitimat	Marine	Wood	GSC-2425	9300 ± 90	Clague 1984

a aht = above high tide

Notes: Only basal dates are given for archaeological sites (*) unless there is evidence for sea level change within the site stratigraphy; see Southon and Fedje 2003 for full listing. Shell dates have been corrected for the local marine carbon reservoir effect (Southon et al. 1990; Southon and Fedje 2003). The ages have been reduced by 600 years from the raw radiocarbon ages.

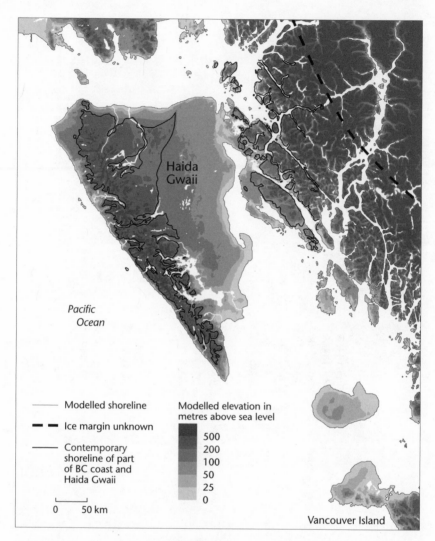

Figure 2.4   Northern BC coast ca. 12,000 BP.

Outer Mainland Coast

The post-12,000 BP sea level history of the outer mainland coast is based on a small number of geological and archaeological data points (Clague et al. 1982a; Archer 1998; Barrie and Conway 1999). This history was developed through the analysis of isolation basins, ancient beaches, and archaeological sites (Table 2.1; Figure 2.4).

The data show that sea level was 50 metres higher than at present at 12,500 BP at Prince Rupert and fell rapidly over the following millennium. Subsequently, relative sea level fell gradually and approached the elevation of the present-day shoreline by early Holocene time. Investigation of mid-

Holocene subtidal shell middens (to –1 metre) and an absence of any archaeological sites older than about 5000 BP have been suggested as possible evidence for lowering to below modern levels during the early Holocene (Clague et al. 1982a; Ames and Maschner 1999).

The approximately 12,500 BP paleoshoreline at 50 metres elevation is the net result of global eustatic lowering (ca. 100 metres) and isostatic depression in the order of 150 metres. The subsequent rapid fall from about 12,500 to 12,000 BP was largely the result of isostatic rebound due to decay of late Wisconsin ice. Relative sea level fall was moderated by eustatic rise. The tectonic component of relative sea level change was small in proportion to the isostatic and eustatic components but may have increased the rate of fall by approximately 1 millimetre per year. Gradual relative sea level rise from the mid-Holocene to recent time is likely a function of tectonic depression (Riddihough 1982).

Inner Coast

The post-12,000 BP sea level history for the inner mainland coast at Kitimat is based on a small number of geological data points (Clague et al. 1982a; Clague 1984; Southon and Fedje 2003). This history was developed through the analysis of ancient beaches and marine sediments (Table 2.1; Figure 2.2). The data show that relative sea level was about 200 metres higher than at present in late glacial times and fell rapidly over the subsequent millennia. Relative sea level reached 30 metres above the present level by the early Holocene. There are no data for mid-Holocene sea level positions.

The late glacial transgression of 200 metres is the net result of global eustatic lowering (ca. 100 metres) and isostatic depression on the order of 300 metres. The subsequent rapid fall after 11,000 BP on was largely the result of isostatic rebound during disappearance of late Wisconsin ice. Sea level fall was moderated by eustatic rise. Tectonic depression would have increased the rate of fall about 2 millimetres per year. While isostatic rebound appears to have slowed considerably by about 9500 BP, this is at least partly an artifact of the moderating effect of global eustatic rise. The area was still rebounding more rapidly than the sea was rising.

Imaging Early Postglacial Landscapes and Corroboration of the Sea Level History

Integrating the sea level histories of western and eastern Hecate Strait and the inner mainland coast into a coherent model will require considerably more data than are currently available. There are sufficient data, however, for a general reconstruction at specific times. In Figures 2.4 and 2.5, the northern BC coast is modelled at about 12,000 and about 10,000 BP. In these images, an elevation model produced from hydrographic and terrestrial data sets is draped over a generalized sea level correction model. The

Table 2.2

North Coast sea level data points for 12,000 and 10,000 BP

Location	Elevation (m)	Context	Age	Source
12,000 BP				
Lakelse	+200	Early postglacial shores	ca. 12,000 BP	Clague et al. 1982a
Kitimat	+200	Early postglacial shores	ca. 12,000 BP	Clague et al. 1982a
Port Hardy	+50	Dated shoreline	ca. 12,500 BP	Howes 1983
Port Simpson	+50	Dated shoreline	12,400 BP	Archer 1998
Bella Bella	+15	Dated shoreline	11,800 BP	Clague et al. 1982a
Dogfish Bank	-100	Dated shoreline	12,500 BP	Barrie and Conway 1999
Middle Bank	-100	Early postglacial shores	ca. 12,000 BP	Josenhans et al. 1993
Rennel Sound	-150	Dated shoreline	12,300 BP	Barrie and Conway 1996a
Juan Perez Sound	-150	Dated shoreline	12,400 BP	Fedje and Josenhans 2000
West Moresby	-200	Early postglacial shore	ca. 12,000 BP	Barrie and Conway 1996a
10,000 BP				
Lakelse, Kitimat	+100	Dated shoreline	10,200 BP	Clague et al. 1982a; Southon and Fedje 2003
Prince Rupert	+6	Dated shoreline	9700 BP	Archer 1998
Namu	+5	Dated shoreline	10,000 BP	Cannon 2000
Juan Perez Sound	-60	Dated shoreline	10,000 BP	Fedje and Josenhans 2000
Cook Bank	-90	Dated shoreline	10,000 BP	Luternauer et al. 1989a

sea level model is based on sea level positions determined from radiocarbon and geological interpretation of sedimentary records across the study area (Tables 2.1 and 2.2), and on 1:20,000 topographic and 1:50,000 hydrographic data. The images provide a preliminary visualization of paleoshorelines at relatively coarse (ca. 200 metres horizontal and ca. 10 metres vertical) resolution. Ongoing research continues to provide greater detail and more extensive modelling of the Haida Gwaii–Hecate Strait area (Hetherington and Reid 2003; Clague et al. 2004).

The application of seismic, side-scan, and newly developed marine mapping technologies produced significantly higher resolution imagery of

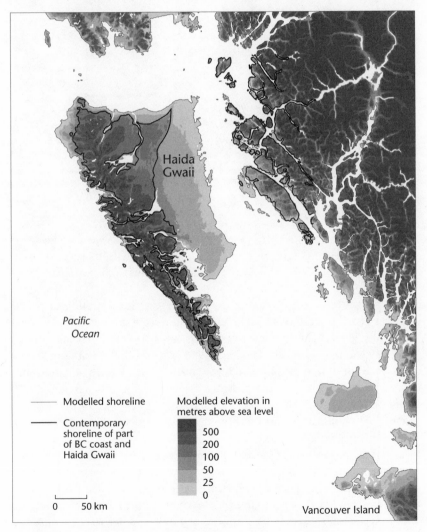

Figure 2.5 Northern BC coast ca. 10,000 BP.

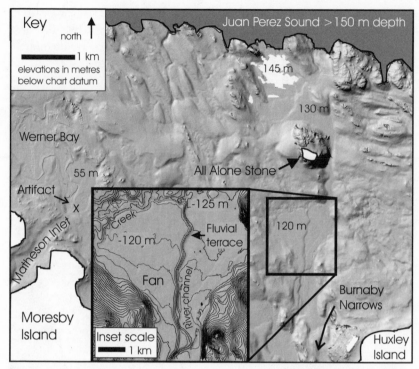

Figure 2.6   Juan Perez Sound bathymetric elevation model with an inset showing detail of ancient river channel south of All Alone Stone.

drowned paleoshorelines and adjacent landscapes than was possible with pre-1990s hydrography (Fedje and Josenhans 2000). This imagery was used to ground truth sea level and paleoecological histories from the Hecate Strait area.

Seismic and side-scan imaging provided targets for sampling drowned sediment basins and fluvial systems. These sites were subsequently sampled to detail vegetation and sea level change (Luternauer et al. 1989a; Josenhans et al. 1995, 1997; Barrie and Conway 1999). Portions of the seafloor of western Hecate Strait were also imaged using swath bathymetry to obtain a more detailed interpretation of the drowned landscapes (Figures 2.6 and 10.7). These images provided target sites for recovery of evidence of past human use of these landscapes and for more detailed paleoenvironmental records (Fedje and Josenhans 2000).

In terrestrial settings, sea level histories have been established from geological mapping and study of sediment exposures. Imaging of past landscapes associated with raised paleoshorelines has been carried out at a few locations in southern Haida Gwaii through the use of elevation models created from aerial photography (Fedje and Christensen 1999; Chapter 10). A number of early to mid-Holocene archaeological sites were found using this approach.

Projections of Archaeological Visibility Based on Sea Level History

The nature of sea level change across Hecate Strait has considerable implications for the study of early human occupation in the region. By looking at the rates and times of marine transgression and regression within a context of environmental productivity, we can gain a sense of the potential for discovery of early postglacial and Holocene archaeological sites.

The sea level history of western Hecate Strait implies that any evidence for coastal occupation is drowned for the period from before 12,500 BP to 9500 BP, intertidal at about 9500 to 9400 BP, and above sea level after about 9400 BP. Most paleoshorelines associated with the marine transgression between about 12,000 BP and 9000 BP would be ephemeral because of the rapid rate of sea level rise. Associated archaeological sites would have low visibility because of the short time available for cultural deposition at any one elevation and because of subsequent buildup of marine sediments on drowned shorelines, and deep forest soils or alluvial deposits on raised shorelines. Additionally, shoreline erosion and bioturbation by mollusks are likely to have destroyed or degraded most archaeological sites during the transgression. However, intertidal survey results (Chapter 16) show that sites can be located readily in lag contexts and, as has been seen from excavations at Kilgii Gwaay (Chapter 11), archaeological sites can survive intact despite being subjected to rapid transgression and subsequent marine processes. Paleoshorelines dating from about 9000 to about 5000 BP can be expected to have a fairly rich archaeological record, as this period of relative stability would allow more substantive buildup of archaeological material and thus heightened visibility. After 5000 BP sea level fell slowly. Archaeological visibility should be moderately good for this period.

The sea level history of the outer mainland coast implies that any archaeological evidence for coastal occupation is stranded above the modern shoreline for the period from 12,500 BP until at least 8000 BP, is possibly subtidal from about 8000 to 5000 BP, and is associated with a near-modern shore position thereafter. Paleoshorelines associated with the marine regression from about 12,000 BP to 9000 BP are located back from the modern shore. The paucity of data points does not permit identification of any changes in the rate of regression (i.e., stillstands) through this period. Paleoshorelines dating from about 9000 to 4000 BP may be drowned and thus destroyed or degraded (Clague 1984).

The sea level history of the inner mainland coast near Kitimat implies that any evidence for coastal occupation is stranded above the modern shoreline for the period from 11,000 BP to at least 9000 BP, and is likely subtidal from about 8000 to 1000 BP. Although data points are few, the very rapid regression from 10,000 BP to 9300 BP implies that any archaeological record would be sparse along receding shorelines. The absence of archaeological sites older than the late Holocene is consistent with the interpretation that 8000 to

1000 BP shorelines are below present sea level. This transgression is ongoing and is caused by tectonic depression and eustatic sea level rise.

Results of Applying Sea Level History to Archaeological Investigation
The archaeological record from Haida Gwaii is closely linked to sea level history (see Chapter 10). A large number of archaeological sites ($N > 100$), many of which are associated with 9500 BP to 9400 BP transgressive shorelines, have been found in the modern intertidal zone (see Chapter 16). Their association with rapidly rising sea level suggests intensive use of the early Holocene landscape. Heightened visibility because of the very large amount of lithic detritus produced by early Holocene stone tool technology may inflate apparent occupation density.

The abundance of early Holocene stone artifacts observed at the Haida Gwaii intertidal sites suggests that similarly abundant evidence for early human presence may be found on the mainland coast. This may be especially true on the outer mainland coast (e.g., Prince Rupert) where the rate of sea level change after about 12,500 BP was less than a third of that determined for Haida Gwaii.

Refugia and Early Postglacial Human History: Impetus for Applied Sea Level Research in Eastern Hecate Strait
The debate over full glacial refugia and early postglacial pioneering and occupation of the Hecate Strait area by plants and animals, including humans, remains contentious. It is only recently that the history of human occupation of the Northwest Coast has been extended beyond 10,000 BP (Dixon 1999; Fedje et al. 2004b). It is clear that the evidence for human presence at this time and the potential for earlier records is strongly limited by visibility, which in turn has been largely determined by shoreline position.

The use of sea level histories in archaeological surveys has substantially expanded the early Holocene archaeological record (Fedje and Christensen 1999; Chapter 10). This approach has been very successful in Haida Gwaii, where radiocarbon-dated history of human occupation has been pushed from about 7500 BP to 10,500 BP in the last few years. Sea level research has also opened a number of avenues for detailing late glacial environmental history by identifying paleoenvironmental targets in western Hecate Strait, including drowned lakes and ponds in areas suggested as possible refugia (Mathewes 1989a, 1989b).

While the drowned landscapes of western Hecate Strait offer considerable promise in the search for biological refugia and early human occupation, logistical challenges and the cost of investigation have limited field investigations to a few weeks over several years. Eastern Hecate Strait and the mainland coast may hold considerable promise for at least the later part of the early postglacial period and pose fewer logistical and resource constraints.

Recently developed tools, such as laser ranging (LIDAR) terrain imaging, provide detailed morphological resolution through the tree canopy, which could help to locate early habitation sites now raised above the former shoreline and obscured by forest cover. Paleoenvironmental data suggests that by 13,000 BP the coastal margins along Hecate Strait were ice-free (Chapters 1 and 3). Discovery of a 12,500 BP beach at 50 metres above sea level near Prince Rupert that is rich in intertidal shellfish (Archer 1998) suggests potential for associated terrestrial resources and an environment suitable for animals and people in early postglacial time. The shellfish include several edible species utilized by First Nations people during Holocene and modern times.

Further detailing of the regional sea level record should enhance the potential for locating both additional paleoenvironmental and archaeological sites in this narrow zone of the outer mainland coast where sea level range and coastal erosion may be relatively limited.

Conclusions

Sea level research in the Hecate Strait area demonstrates a dynamic history with considerable variation in paleoshoreline positions on a regional scale. This is especially true as one moves from areas proximal to Wisconsin ice loading westward to the less loaded and earlier deglaciated continental margin. Even on the relatively local scale of Haida Gwaii, however, there are differences in transgressive limits. These differences are of sufficient magnitude to be critical to locating paleoshorelines and associated environmental and cultural records.

Investigations integrating sea level research with recently developed technologies have been successful in modelling and sampling drowned early postglacial landscapes in western Hecate Strait. This area holds a great potential for a very early paleoenvironmental record, but logistical costs of the work are high. Sea level research on the BC mainland currently lacks sufficient detail for early postglacial shoreline survey, although preliminary research has identified isolated raised paleoshorelines dating as early as 12,500 BP. The logistical costs of research on these raised beaches should be substantially less than for the drowned lands of western Hecate Strait.

Acknowledgments
The 1991-99 paleoshoreline research was supported by Parks Canada's Western Service Centre, Parks Canada, and the Council of Haida Nations through the Gwaii Haanas Archipelago Management Board and by the Geological Survey of Canada. This work built upon previous research published by John Clague and Knut Fladmark. The 1990s field crews included David Archer, Vaughn Barrie, Kim Conway, Daryl Fedje, Martin Geertsema, Guujaaw, Captain Gold, René Hetherington, Heiner Josenhans, Quentin Mackie, Joanne McSporran, Rod Pickard, and Bert Wilson. GIS models were prepared by Greg MacMillan of Parks Canada, using hydrographic data from the Canadian Hydrographic Service. Dating was conducted by the CAMS group at Lawrence Livermore National Laboratory, California.

3

Terrestrial Paleoecology of Haida Gwaii and the Continental Shelf: Vegetation, Climate, and Plant Resources of the Coastal Migration Route

Terri Lacourse and Rolf W. Mathewes

Since the publication of *The Outer Shores* (Scudder and Gessler 1989), significant advances have been made regarding the glacial history, sea level history, archaeology, and paleoecology of the western margin of Canada. In order to improve the current state of knowledge about paleoenvironments along the coast of British Columbia, results from pollen and plant macrofossil analyses need to be expanded, synthesized, and integrated with other lines of evidence. Several new paleoecological studies have been published, and they provide intriguing insights into a drowned landscape that played an important role in the biological recolonization of British Columbia since the last glacial maximum.

As explained in Chapter 1, large portions of the continental shelf were exposed during the last glaciation, and were subsequently flooded due to rising relative sea levels. A key element of increasing interest in this drowned landscape is the hypothesis that the earliest migration of humans to the Americas occurred along a coastal corridor during deglaciation, if not earlier (Bryan 1941; Heusser 1960; Fladmark 1979a). By 14,000 BP, the Northwest Coast was a viable route for human movement into the New World with sufficient time depth to allow for pre-Clovis human history such as the 12,500 BP occupations at Monte Verde in Chile (Dixon 1999; Fedje and Josenhans 2000; Mandryk et al. 2001). Paleoecological studies that reconstruct the nature and extent of the vegetation during this critical time are important pieces of the puzzle. In addition to determining local and regional vegetation dynamics, these studies describe potential sources of food, medicines, or fibres for early human migrants, and also provide proxy records of past climates.

Intimately linked to the emerging interest in the coast as a biotic migration corridor is the long-standing controversy over whether plants and animals survived during the last glacial maximum in ice-free refugia along the coast (Heusser 1989). This controversy is not yet settled, but new lines of evidence, such as molecular data on genetic divergence, have recently become available for some of the region's plants, insects, birds, and terrestrial vertebrates (i.e., O'Reilly et al. 1993; Zink and Dittmann 1993; Heaton et al. 1996; Byun et al. 1997; Hamann et al. 1998). Although the search for continuously ice-free refugia on the coast has gone on for over forty years, the critical evidence for such a site has not yet been found. Along the central British Columbia coast, radiocarbon-dated evidence of non-glacial environments is restricted to the intervals before 21,000 BP and after 16,000 BP. In southeastern Alaska, a fossil ringed seal bone dated to 17,565 ± 160 BP (AA-18450) hints at a productive marine environment and possible refugia in the Alexander Archipelago (Heaton et al. 1996; Dixon et al. 1997). Recent research suggests that the best possibility of a continuous refugium around Haida Gwaii (Queen Charlotte Islands) is on the now submerged continental shelf in Hecate Strait (Byun et al. 1997; Chapter 5).

Paleoecological evidence thus far points to expanses of treeless herb and dwarf shrub tundra from the Olympic Peninsula in Washington to southeastern Alaska between at least 15,000 and 13,000 BP (Figure 3.1), marked by the presence of willow (*Salix*), crowberry (*Empetrum*), grasses (Poaceae), sedges (Cyperaceae), and a variety of other herbaceous plants (Warner et al. 1982; Heusser 1985; Mathewes 1989a; Barrie et al. 1993; Lacourse 2004). On Haida Gwaii, this tundra-like plant cover gave way to coniferous forests around 12,500 BP with the rapid expansion of lodgepole pine (*Pinus contorta*), followed by spruce (*Picea*) at about 11,200 BP and then western hemlock (*Tsuga heterophylla*) at about 10,000 BP. Portions of the continental shelf were ice-free, vegetated, and available to humans between ca. 14,000 and 10,000 BP; moderate climatic conditions supported diverse and productive vegetation while adjacent mainland areas remained glaciated.

Review of New Late Glacial Paleoecological Evidence

Mathewes (1989a) summarized the history of vegetation on Haida Gwaii from the middle Jurassic period to the present. Since then, significant progress has been made in expanding our understanding of the late glacial paleoecology of Haida Gwaii and the surrounding areas. This new evidence is presented first, as an update to Mathewes (1989a). Botanical nomenclature follows Douglas and colleagues (1989).

Marine sediment cores from the continental shelf have been particularly useful for investigating the local vegetation of landscapes that were exposed during the regional late Wisconsin deglaciation. Paleoecological analyses of sediments from Dogfish Bank in Hecate Strait (Figure 3.2) demonstrate that at 13,200 BP the landscape was treeless and locally characterized by wet sedge tundra (Barrie et al. 1993). The fossil pollen assemblage includes high frequencies of sedge pollen and horsetail (*Equisetum*) spores, and relatively high values of crowberry pollen. Total tree pollen frequency is only 4 percent, a very low value, which suggests a treeless local environment.

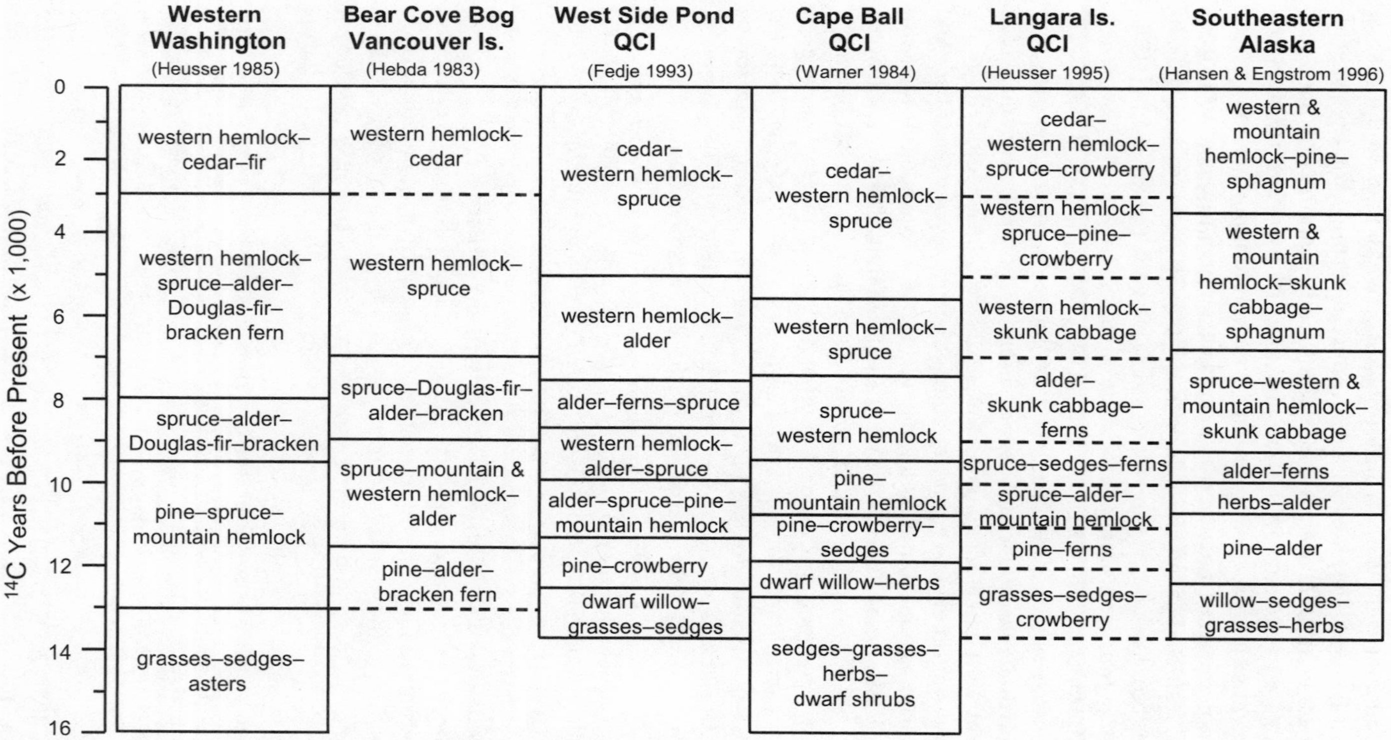

Figure 3.1 Summary of vegetation histories reconstructed from paleoecological analyses for selected sites along the Pacific coast. Vegetation assemblages are indicated by major species, and are reported as published. Dashed horizontal lines indicate inferred radiocarbon ages. QCI = Queen Charlotte Islands (Haida Gwaii).

The few arboreal pollen types found likely arrived by long-distance transport or were reworked from melting ice or glacial drift. Total pollen and spore concentrations are relatively low, about 5,600 grains per cubic centimetre of sediment. This may indicate small vegetation populations and/or rapid sediment accumulation rates. Pollen and plant macrofossil studies west of Dogfish Bank at Cape Ball, Graham Island (Figure 3.2), document the presence of willow shrub tundra with abundant sedges, grasses, and mosses in lowland areas on Haida Gwaii between 14,000 and 13,000 BP (Barrie et al. 1993). Abundant willow macrofossils are from a dwarf species, likely net-veined willow (*Salix reticulata*) or stoloniferous willow (*S. stolonifera*), but the specific identifications are uncertain. Pollen from other herbs and dwarf shrubs such as sage (*Artemisia*), Jacob's-ladder (*Polemonium*), and Sitka valerian (*Valeriana sitchensis*) was also found at Cape Ball.

The most dramatic and incontrovertible evidence for well-developed forests that once occupied the continental shelf comes from a drowned paleosol in Juan Perez Sound (Figure 3.2) (Fedje and Josenhans 2000). A pine stump

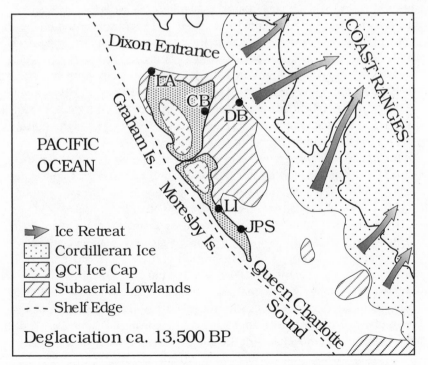

Figure 3.2 Schematic reconstruction of ice retreat around the Queen Charlotte Islands (Haida Gwaii) approximately 13,500 BP. As Cordilleran ice retreated eastward, large expanses of lowlands were exposed in Hecate Strait and elsewhere. Major paleoecological sites are LA = Langara Island, CB = Cape Ball, DB = Dogfish Bank, LI = Logan Inlet, and JPS = Juan Perez Sound.

(ca. 20 centimetres in diameter), still rooted in a peaty soil, was recovered from a drowned fluvial terrace at a present water depth of 145 metres and yielded an accelerator mass spectrometric (AMS) radiocarbon age of 12,240 ± 50 BP (CAMS-59768). This drowned forest site appears to have occupied a relatively large area but was transgressed by marine waters prior to 11,500 BP. The recovered sediments also contained abundant lodgepole pine cones and needles, and twigs of deciduous wood, one of which dates to 12,190 ± 50 BP (CAMS-59769). Fedje and Josenhans (2000) also note that spruce tree roots dating to 10,500 ± 40 BP (CAMS-50947) were collected from a fluvial terrace at 51 metres water depth and that wood was abundant at several other locations on the shelf.

Further south, on Cook Bank off northern Vancouver Island, Luternauer and colleagues (1989a) report pollen and plant macrofossil evidence of well-developed soils and colonization by trees, herbs, ferns, and mosses about 10,500 BP, when relative sea level at Cook Bank was 95 metres lower. Studies of now submerged terrestrial sediments with in situ roots show that lodgepole pine is the dominant pollen type but spruce, alder (*Alnus*), and both western hemlock and mountain hemlock (*Tsuga heterophylla* and *T. mertensiana*) were also present. Total pollen and spore concentrations in a silt bed at this site reach 760,000 grains per cubic centimetre, suggesting high productivity from a well-established plant cover, possibly combined with slow sedimentation rates in a shallow freshwater environment. Local wetland conditions are represented by the pollen of sedges, marsh marigold (*Caltha*) and members of the parsley family (Apiaceae), and spores of various ferns and *Sphagnum* moss. Algal cysts such as those of *Spirogyra* indicate the presence of standing pools of freshwater.

To improve our understanding of the vegetation on the continental shelf during the latest period of subaerial exposure, Lacourse and colleagues (2003) conducted further paleoecological analyses on the radiocarbon-dated terrestrial deposits of Fedje and Josenhans (2000) and Luternauer and colleagues (1989a). At both sites on the continental shelf, conifers in growth position are preserved, confirming that terrestrial vegetation was well established. Microscopic identification of fossil wood and analyses of pollen and plant macrofossils (Figure 3.3) from the associated paleosols and overlying shallow pond sediments indicate that productive lodgepole pine–dominated communities with green alder (*Alnus crispa*), willow, and ferns grew on the shelf adjacent to and on Haida Gwaii around 12,200 BP. The presence of other shade-intolerant species such as crowberry, Canada burnet (*Sanguisorba canadensis*), and hanging moss (*Antitrichia curtipendula*) suggests open gaps in the woodland vegetation. The riparian nature of the landscape is supported by the presence of plants such as cow parsnip (*Heracleum lanatum*), common mare's tail (*Hippuris vulgaris*), northern maidenhair fern (*Adiantum aleuticum*), quillwort (*Isoëtes*), horsetail, and sedges.

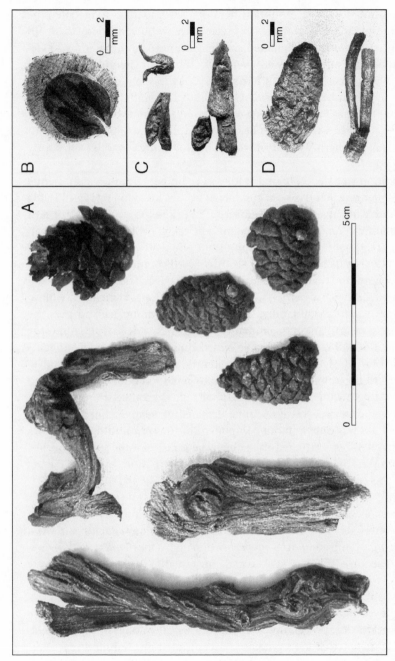

Figure 3.3 Selected plant macrofossils from Juan Perez Sound. (A) Willow twigs (left) and female cones of lodgepole pine (right); (B) Cow parsnip fruit; (C) Willow buds and capsules; (D) Male cone and paired needle base of lodgepole pine (from Lacourse et al. 2003, © Elsevier Science, reprinted with permission).

Scattered individuals of mountain hemlock accompanied lodgepole pine on more upland sites, along with green alder, willow, and crowberry in open areas. At Cook Bank, mixed coniferous forests dominated by lodge-pole pine with spruce, western hemlock, mountain hemlock, red alder (*Alnus rubra*), green alder, and ferns occupied the shelf at 10,500 BP. Pol-len of yellow sand-verbena (*Abronia latifolia*), a creeping perennial typical of coastal beaches but infrequent on Vancouver Island today (Douglas et al. 1989), indicates that sandy beach vegetation grew along the ancient shoreline of northern Vancouver Island and that shoreline soils were poorly developed.

In addition to paleoecological studies of sediments from the continental shelf, similar research has been conducted using lake sediments from Haida Gwaii and Vancouver Island. Heusser (1995) presents an account of past vegetation from analyses of a sediment core taken on Langara Island that, based on regional chronostratigraphy from other sites, spans an estimated 13,500 ^{14}C years (Figures 3.1 and 3.2). The record commences with a coastal tundra community that is dominated by grasses, sedges, and heath (Ericaceae) shrubs, including crowberry. This herbaceous tundra also included willow, members of the parsley family, sage, Jacob's-ladder, and Iceland purslane (*Koenigia islandica*), an arctic annual typical of wet sites (Porsild and Cody 1980). By 12,000 BP, open lodgepole pine communities with alder and ferns were established. Heusser (1995) attributes the widespread success of lodge-pole pine to the absence of competition, its rapid reproductive ability, and its ability to grow on coarse, nutrient-poor soils. As competition with alder and spruce increased, lodgepole pine declined in relative abundance, and by 10,000 BP was only a minor component of the surrounding vegetation.

Fedje (1993) reconstructed the late glacial and Holocene vegetation his-tory from West Side Pond, a small basin on southern Moresby Island (Figure 3.1). In this case, basal sediments that date to 13,500 ± 480 BP (CAMS-2523) are dominated by herbaceous pollen, including sedges and grasses and other herbs such as sage and cow parsnip. Reinvestigation of this site has shown that a variety of other herbs were also present: lupine (*Lupinus*), fireweed (*Epilobium*), swamp gentian (*Gentiana douglasiana*), dock (*Rumex*), and Jacob's-ladder (Lacourse 2004). These taxa all suggest that local conditions were moist to wet. Willow and crowberry shrubs soon became more common and probably occupied drier upland sites while ferns and clubmosses (*Lyco-podium*) were likely restricted to moist sites. By 12,500 BP, lodgepole pine dominated the local vegetation as it did at other sites along the Pacific coast. The local presence of lodgepole pine is confirmed by abundant macrofos-sils, including a lodgepole pine needle that dates to 12,190 ± 140 BP (CAMS-2525). A sharp decline in the percentage of lodgepole pine pollen concomitant with marked increases in alder and spruce pollen occurred between 11,500 and 10,000 BP. Spruce needles and alder leaf fragments and seeds demonstrate the local presence of these trees. Mountain hemlock also arrived about 11,000 BP. It was a minor yet significant component of the vegetation since its presence indicates cool temperatures and deep snow-packs (Pojar and MacKinnon 1994).

Paleoecological studies have also been conducted on Brooks Peninsula, a reputed glacial refugium on the west coast of Vancouver Island. Hebda and Haggarty (1997) present reconstructed vegetation histories for six sites on Brooks Peninsula. At both high- and low-elevation sites, the landscape was characterized by lodgepole pine forest between 13,000 and 12,000 BP that included scattered mountain hemlock. Mountain hemlock, spruce, and Pacific silver fir (*Abies amabilis*) populations expanded, at the expense of lodgepole pine, between 12,000 and 10,000 BP, forming mixed coniferous forests. Western hemlock was abundant on lower slopes. Basal radiocarbon ages from these sites are based on bulk sediments, which typically yield significantly older radiocarbon ages than AMS radiocarbon dating on plant macrofossils at the same depth. The radiocarbon dates should therefore be viewed as maximum ages.

Current Studies at Logan Inlet

To gain further knowledge about the terrestrial vegetation and paleo-environment of Hecate Strait, the late glacial portions of sediment cores retrieved from submerged lakes on the continental shelf are currently being studied. These studies emphasize the late glacial interval before 10,000 BP, which includes the probable time of human migration from the north. Here we present the results of pollen analysis from submerged lake sediments in Logan Inlet (52°47'N, 131°41'W), which is located immediately north of Richardson Island, one of the 150 islands that compose the Haida Gwaii archipelago (Figure 3.2). Logan Inlet is a formerly subaerial basin with a sill depth of –80 metres (Josenhans et al. 1997). At the end of the Pleistocene, lowered relative sea levels isolated basins such as Logan Inlet, creating sediment-trapping lakes. At that time, as little as 5 kilometres of water may have separated the enlarged archipelago from the mainland (Josenhans et al. 1995). Diatom analysis indicated that marine incursion of the basin occurred about 10,400 BP (Josenhans et al. 1997).

Methods

A 12-metre piston core (VEC94A-018) was retrieved from Logan Inlet by the Geological Survey of Canada (Josenhans et al. 1997). The core penetrated marine and paleolake sediments, revealing a sharp contact between stratified lake sediment and overlying slumped marine deposits at 4.4 metres. Plant macrofossils were removed from the lake sediments, identified, and then submitted to Lawrence Livermore National Laboratory for AMS radiocarbon dating (Josenhans et al. 1997). The paleolake sediments date between

12,000 and 10,400 BP (Table 3.1). Sediment ages were estimated for all depths using linear interpolation between radiocarbon ages.

Sediment subsamples were prepared for pollen analysis following standard methods (Fægri and Iversen 1989; Cwynar et al. 1979). Known quantities of *Eucalyptus* pollen were added to each sample prior to chemical treatment in order to determine pollen and spore accumulation rates (grains per square centimetre per year) (Benninghoff 1962). A minimum sum of 600 pollen and spores, excluding pollen from aquatic plants, was counted for each sample. Pollen and spore identifications were made with the help of reference material at Simon Fraser University and published dichotomous keys. Percentages are based on the sum of all tree, shrub, and herb pollen and fern spores.

Vegetation Reconstruction

At Logan Inlet there is no evidence of the tundra-like herb assemblage that predates 12,500 BP (Lacourse 2004). The pollen spectra begin during the period of lodgepole pine dominance, about 12,000 BP, and record the transition from pine to spruce-dominated forests (Figure 3.4). Evidence for lodgepole pine abundance is strong here: pine pollen concentrations are high (up to 135,000 grains per cubic centimetre), as are relative frequencies, which account for 85 percent of all terrestrial pollen and spores at the base of the sequence (Figures 3.4 and 3.5A). Lodgepole pine needles, one of which dates to 12,020 ± 70 BP, were recovered from the lake sediments at this location and confirm its local presence (Table 3.1). Pine stomata are present in the pollen preparations (Figure 3.5B) and also suggest its nearby presence. Pine is a prolific producer of pollen that have low susceptibility to corrosion and oxidation relative to other pollen types such as willow (Havinga 1984). It is likely, then, that pine did not cover the landscape to the extent that the pollen spectra suggest, but rather that its pollen is overrepresented in the Logan Inlet sediments. This may explain why taxa such as willow appear to be only minor components of the vegetation at a time when there is abundant plant macrofossil evidence from nearby sites for its presence (Lacourse et al. 2003). Similarly, there is limited pollen evidence of crowberry; however, an AMS radiocarbon age of 11,990 ± 50 BP on crowberry seeds (CAMS-61255) from a small pond on Richardson Island confirms its local presence.

Although lodgepole pine dominates the Logan Inlet record between 12,000 and about 11,200 BP, fern spores are also consistently abundant (Figure 3.4), including polypody fern (*Polypodium*, Figure 3.5B), northern maidenhair fern (Figure 3.5D), and lady fern (*Athyrium filix-femina*) as well as numerous undifferentiated fern spores (Polypodiaceae), which may be lady fern and spiny wood fern (*Dryopteris expansa*) spores that have lost their diagnostic outer perines. Northern maidenhair fern and lady fern are strong indicators

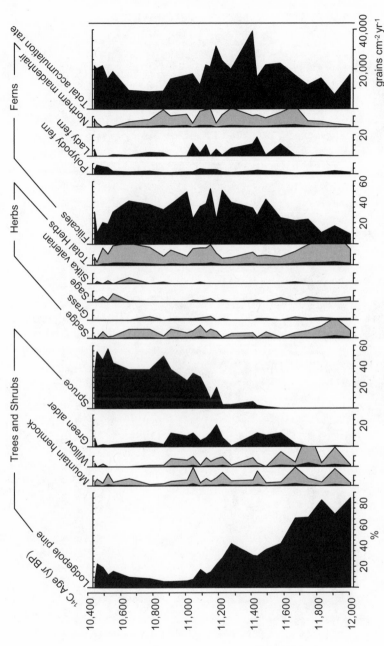

Figure 3.4 Pollen and spore percentage diagram for late glacial sediments (VEC94A-018) from a freshwater lake now submerged in Logan Inlet, Haida Gwaii. Only the most abundant pollen and spore types, plus a few selected indicator taxa, are shown. Grey curves represent 10× exaggeration. Total accumulation rates include pollen and spores from all taxa with the exception of aquatics.

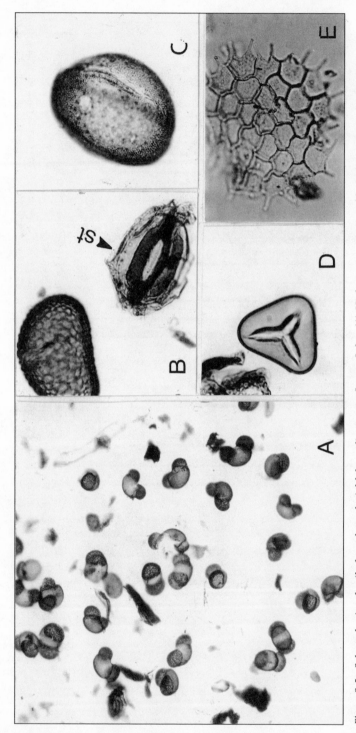

Figure 3.5 Selected microfossils from late glacial lake sediments at Logan Inlet. (A) High concentration of lodgepole pine pollen (100×); (B) characteristic stomata (st) from pine needles, and part of a polypody fern spore (500×); (C) Sitka valerian pollen (500×); (D) trilete spore of northern maidenhair fern, showing the prominent margins of the apertures (500×); (E) colony of freshwater green algae, *Pediastrum* (500×).

Table 3.1

AMS radiocarbon dates for the Logan Inlet paleolake sediments (VEC94A-018)

Depth (cm)	Material	Lab no.	^{14}C age (yrs BP ± 1σ)
444	Spruce needle	CAMS-18751[a]	10,440 ± 50
481	Spruce branchlet	CAMS-18752[a]	10,560 ± 70
510	Unknown twig	CAMS-18735[a]	10,870 ± 60
639	Pine needle	CAMS-19510	12,020 ± 70

a Previously published in Josenhans et al. 1997.

of moist to wet, nitrogen-rich soils (Klinka et al. 1989); ferns probably dominated the understorey vegetation. It appears that the only other upland tree that accompanied lodgepole pine before 11,000 BP was mountain hemlock; although its frequencies are low, they are sufficient to imply its local presence (e.g., Hebda 1983).

The major palynological change in the Logan Inlet core occurs about 11,200 BP, when lodgepole pine pollen decreased to less than 20 percent and spruce pollen increased to more than 30 percent. This increase in spruce pollen has also been recorded near Cape Ball (Figure 3.2) on Graham Island (Mathewes et al. 1993). It has been attributed to the expansion of Sitka spruce (*Picea sitchensis*), although this is uncertain in light of the analysis by Warner and Chmielewski (1987) at Cape Ball, which indicates that late glacial spruce cones probably represent hybrids of Sitka spruce and white spruce (*P. glauca*). Total pollen and spore accumulation rates are highest during the transition from pine to spruce forests. Green alder and ferns, vegetation typical of moist soils such as riparian fringes or floodplains, increased in relative abundance during this transitional period. Meadow vegetation is represented by grasses, sage and other composites (Asteraceae), fireweed, and cow parsnip pollen. Pollen from Sitka valerian (Figure 3.5C), which is common in open, coniferous forests at montane to subalpine elevations (Klinka et al. 1989), suggests moist, nitrogen-rich soil. In general, however, there is little change in the relative frequencies of pollen from herbaceous plants (Figure 3.4). The presence of *Pediastrum* algae (Figure 3.5E) and pollen from the aquatic perennial water-milfoil (*Myriophyllum spicatum* type) confirm that Logan Inlet was a freshwater lake between 12,000 and 10,400 BP.

Discussion

Paleovegetation between 15,000 and 10,000 BP
Sea cliff exposures at Cape Ball on Graham Island (Figures 3.1 and 3.2) provide the earliest radiocarbon-dated record of plants from the late Wisconsin glaciation on the British Columbia coast. AMS radiocarbon dating of a twig from basal ponded sediments indicate an age of 14,700 ± 700 BP (RIDDL-3)

(Mathewes et al. 1985); as expected, conventional radiocarbon dating on mixed plant macrofossils indicates older ages of 15,400 ± 190 (GSC-3319) and 16,000 ± 570 BP (GSC-3370) (Warner et al. 1982). These ^{14}C ages, combined with pollen and plant macrofossil analyses, suggest that terrestrial vegetation was established by 15,000 BP at Cape Ball, beginning with early-successional herbaceous plants such as rushes (*Juncus*), docks, chickweeds (Caryophyllaceae), and Jacob's-ladder as well as grasses, sedges, and mosses. Grass, alpine bistort (*Polygonum viviparum*), and sage pollen suggest the presence of drier meadows, while Alaska plantain (*Plantago macrocarpa*) and sedge pollen indicate locally wet conditions. Mineral-rich sediments with low pollen concentrations suggest that areas of open, poorly vegetated soil were common and available for erosion. The shallow ponds and drainage systems that formed during deglaciation were inhabited by aquatic plants such as buttercups (*Ranunculus*) and pondweed (*Potamogeton*), as well as green algae. Hence, a mosaic of different habitats and plant communities characterized the area, and the richness of the flora at this time, when adjacent areas were glaciated, suggests the presence of nearby refugia. It is unclear, however, how widespread such early communities were, since no other localities are available for comparison prior to 13,500 BP.

By 13,500 BP, paleoecological evidence from other sites becomes available for comparison with Cape Ball. The pollen record from Pleasant Island in the Panhandle of southeastern Alaska (Figure 3.1) is instructive, since it begins around 13,500 BP with a herb and dwarf shrub tundra that includes grasses, sedges, willow, heath shrubs, and a variety of herbs (Hansen and Engstrom 1996). This is similar to Cape Ball after 13,000 BP, where the vegetation can also be described as tundra-like, with pollen and leaf remains of dwarf willow, crowberry, and an abundance of grasses, sedges, and other herbs. A similar pollen assemblage is found on Kodiak Island in southwestern Alaska in sediment that dates to 13,420 ± 20 BP (Beta-26607) (Peteet and Mann 1994). There, grasses, sedges, and crowberry shrubs dominate a landscape that is also characterized by a diverse array of herbaceous plants. A non-arboreal community is also recorded in a core from Dogfish Bank around 13,200 BP (Figure 3.2), where a wet tundra community dominated by sedges, horsetail, and crowberry was described by Barrie and colleagues (1993) from terrestrial sediment deposited when the bank was exposed due to low relative sea level. Low crowberry shrubs probably grew on drier, exposed hummocks within the sedge tundra that likely would have been subject to strong winds. Crowberry and other heath shrubs are a prominent element of many late glacial sites along the Pacific coast. On Langara Island (Figures 3.1 and 3.2), Heusser (1995) also identified an early plant community from about 13,000 BP where crowberry, along with grasses, sedges, and members of the parsley family, defined the tundra communities. A relatively cool climate and moist but poorly developed soils are indicated by pollen of the arctic-alpine annual Iceland purslane. On the west coast of southern Moresby Island, this tundra assemblage was present as early as 13,500 BP (Fedje 1993; Lacourse 2004). Willow, heath shrubs, grasses, and especially sedges dominated the lowland environment. There is ample evidence to conclude that herb-dominated plant communities with dwarf willow and crowberry shrubs were widespread along the Pacific coast before 12,500 BP.

At most of these early sites, some tree pollen, mostly that of lodgepole pine, is typically recorded: pine commonly accounts for up to 5 percent of the pollen sum. The abundance of tree pollen is sufficiently low, however, that treeless tundra is still the most appropriate interpretation for the vegetation cover. Occasional tree pollen is most likely a product of long-distance transport, and/or reworking from melting glacier ice or other surficial deposits. Wood or other tree macrofossils are absent from the largely inorganic sediments deposited during this time. Based on the high pollen frequencies of grasses, sedges, willow, heath shrubs, and members of the parsley family, the closest match between these herb- and shrub-dominated fossil pollen spectra and modern vegetation communities appears to be with sites in the Gulf of Alaska region, from Kodiak Island to the Aleutian Islands (Heusser 1985, 1990). This similarity and the presence of indicator taxa such as Iceland purslane and alpine bistort suggest a cold, arctic-like aspect to the vegetation and landscape in general, which accords well with the interpretation of tundra. In general, the vegetation is indicative of cool, wet, and probably windy conditions that were locally controlled by topography, soils, and disturbance.

Reconstructed climate records and paleoclimate simulations from the region also corroborate a cold late glacial climate (e.g., Heusser et al. 1985; Bartlein et al. 1998). Climate in the late glacial period was likely characterized by an anticyclonal high-pressure system centred on the continental ice sheet, which generated subcontinental katabatic easterly winds and increased seasonality (COHMAP 1988; Bartlein et al. 1998). Paleoclimate simulations suggest that before 12,000 BP, the ice sheet shifted the jet stream south, causing cooling in mid-latitudes, intensifying cold, dry easterly winds, and reducing available winter moisture (Bartlein et al. 1998).

A rapid expansion of coniferous forest began about 12,500 BP. Lodgepole pine was the first tree species to colonize the coast following deglaciation. Abrupt increases in lodgepole pine pollen percentages and accumulation rates, and the rooted pine stump (Fedje and Josenhans 2000) with associated forest litter, document its rapid colonization and the formation of open pine communities. Its local presence is also demonstrated by needles and their stomata, cones, and other lodgepole pine macrofossils (Figure 3.3) (Lacourse et al. 2003). It appears that by 12,000 BP, mountain hemlock was also present, probably as scattered upland trees. Green alder and ferns were important components of the understorey and edge communities of these early forests. Much of the landscape would have been characterized by fluvial features such as extensive fan and delta complexes (Fedje and Josenhans 2000). Free of competing tall vegetation, lodgepole pine would have colonized the moist but well-drained sands and gravels quickly, due to its efficient seed dispersal, rapid growth and maturation, and wide edaphic tolerance.

Around 11,200 BP, spruce joined the pine forests on the Queen Charlotte Islands and soon dominated forests along much of the coast. Green alder and ferns expanded during the transition from pine- to spruce-dominated forests. Due to greater shade tolerance, spruce forests were denser than earlier forests, and soils were moist with increasing humus accumulation. Global climate model simulations suggest that the climate was likely characterized by the northward shift of the jet stream that resulted from the decreasing size of the continental ice sheet and increased seasonality due to changes in the seasonal cycle of insolation (Berger 1978; Whitlock and Bartlein 1997; COHMAP 1988; Bartlein et al. 1998). Summer conditions were progressively warmer and drier, and winters were cooler than at present. As the continental ice sheet receded, moist westerly winds may have become more important in the region (COHMAP 1988). After rapid initial expansion, spruce declined in abundance at Cape Ball (Figures 3.1 and 3.2) (Mathewes et al. 1993), and herbaceous plants expanded their cover. The pine and spruce forests appear to have opened up into conifer parkland around 10,700 BP, with meadows of sedges, grasses, members of the parsley family, and other herbs. Western hemlock expansion was delayed until after 10,500 BP. Rising sea levels began to flood the lower elevations of the continental shelf around the same time (Josenhans et al. 1997; Fedje and Josenhans 2000), submerging the late glacial landscapes and their vegetation (Lacourse et al. 2003). The vegetation history after this time is recorded in lakes, fens, and bogs above the limit of marine inundation.

The Coastal Migration Route

The dramatic sea level changes at the end of the last glaciation, which resulted in the exposure of large banks in Hecate Strait, caused a near twofold increase in land area for Haida Gwaii compared with today (Fedje and Christensen 1999). These broad, low-relief plains were therefore available to plants, animals, and humans during deglaciation. It has been proposed that the entry of humans into North America was by a marine-adapted people travelling down the coast in the late glacial period both on land and by simple watercraft (Bryan 1941; Heusser 1960; Fladmark 1979a). If early human populations were moving south from Beringia along the Pacific coast, then these emergent landmasses would have been important surfaces along that route.

The Northwest Coast was deglaciated and available for human migration and habitation by at least 13,500 BP (Barrie et al. 1993; Mann and Hamilton 1995; Josenhans et al. 1997; Mandryk et al. 2001), while the hypothesized ice-free corridor would not have been passable until after 11,000 BP (Arnold 2002). It is likely that a coastal route was available well before 13,500 BP as coastal glaciers were retreating and could have been easily bypassed. The initial Paleoindian migration from Beringia probably occurred about 13,500 BP, when temperatures rose in the northern hemisphere (Hoffecker et al. 1993; Goebel 1999; Mandryk et al. 2001). Intertidal fauna were an abundant source of food available to marine-adapted peoples by 13,200 BP (Hetherington and Reid 2003; Fedje and Christensen 1999). However, archaeological evidence to support the coastal migration hypothesis is inconclusive because known archaeological sites along the Northwest Coast do not predate 10,500 BP (Dixon et al. 1997; Josenhans et al. 1997; Dixon 1999; Cannon 2005; Fedje 2005). Fedje and Josenhans (2000) recovered a stone tool, almost 10 centimetres in length, from a drowned fluvial terrace 53 metres below sea level in Juan Perez Sound (Figure 3.2). The stone tool was recovered from lag sediments and is encrusted with modern subtidal barnacles; however, on the basis of reconstructed sea level history, an age of about 10,000 BP is suggested for the site (Fedje and Josenhans 2000). With a well-defined striking platform and a shallow bulb of percussion, both diagnostic features of humanly fractured stones (Andrefsky 1998), it is clearly the product of human workmanship. By 10,500 BP, however, humans could have taken an inland route and then travelled north up the coast. Older archaeological sites would have been rapidly transgressed by rising sea levels (Fedje and Josenhans 2000). Such sites may be preserved on drowned landscapes but will be difficult to locate and may have been exposed to significant erosion and/or subsequent sedimentation. Additional underwater archaeology is desperately needed to further evaluate the possibility of pre-Holocene human occupation of the outer shelf region (Easton 1992).

Paleoecological records provide considerable information as to the food plants that would have been available to humans migrating southward along the coast in late glacial times (Table 3.2). Animal products probably dominated the total food intake of early migrants. Rick and colleagues (2001) provide evidence that early New World peoples in coastal California fished intensively, and suggest that fish and shellfish provided 50 percent and 30 percent, respectively, of their edible meat. Plant products, however, would have provided nutritional diversity and dietary support when yields from fishing and hunting were low. Food plants would have been predictable seasonal resources, requiring minimal searching and little effort and technology to gather. For example, cow parsnip and fireweed pollen and plant macrofossils have been identified in late glacial sediments at several locations in coastal British Columbia, and many Aboriginal groups in British

Columbia have used the leaves of these plants as green vegetables (Compton 1993; Turner 1995). The Haida have been known to eat the young leaves and red-coloured stems of dock, which was growing on the shelf around 13,000 BP. The roots of cinquefoil (*Potentilla*) may also have been harvested; when steam-cooked, they apparently taste like sweet potato (Turner 1995). Early migrants could also have eaten cambium cakes, a mixture of berries such as crowberries or bunchberries (*Cornus canadensis*) and the nutrient-rich cambium of pine, spruce, or alder (Turner 1995). The leaves and rhizomes of alpine bistort are still eaten by the Inuit of Alaska and Siberia (MacKinnon et al. 1992), and could have been used as a food plant by humans on the coast in the late glacial period. The presence of northern rice-root (*Fritillaria camschatcensis*) pollen at Cape Ball suggests that the starch-rich bulb of this plant, which was widely eaten by coastal peoples in British Columbia, was already available in the late glacial period. Finally, fern spores are abundant at all late glacial sites; the young shoots and rhizomes of various ferns could have been steamed and eaten, as done for centuries by coastal peoples in British Columbia (Turner 1995).

Plants would also have provided materials for fuel, manufacture, dyes, and medicinal purposes. Fern fronds, bark, stems, leaves, and root fibres could have been used to make twine, nets, baskets, mats, and clothing (Turner

Table 3.2

Selected food plants available on the Pacific coast during the late glacial period, based on fossil evidence

Common name	Latin name	Known Aboriginal foods[a]
Bistort	*Polygonum viviparum*	Leaves and rhizomes
Bunchberry	*Cornus canadensis*	Fruit
Burnet	*Sanguisorba canadensis*	Leaves (for tea)
Cinquefoil	*Potentilla*	Roots
Cow parsnip	*Heracleum lanatum*	Young stems and leaf stems
Crowberry	*Empetrum nigrum*	Fruit
Dock	*Rumex*	Young stems and leaves
Ferns (various)	Polypodiaceae	Young stems and rhizomes
Fireweed	*Epilobium angustifolium*	Young stems and leaves
Horsetail	*Equisetum*	Young stems
Lodgepole pine	*Pinus contorta*	Cambium and phloem
Lupine	*Lupinus*	Rhizomes
Northern rice-root	*Fritillaria camschatcensis*	Bulbs
Pacific hemlock-parsley	*Conioselinum pacificum*	Taproots
Red alder	*Alnus rubra*	Cambium and phloem
Sitka spruce	*Picea sitchensis*	Cambium and phloem
Soapberry	*Shepherdia canadensis*	Fruit
Yellow pond lily	*Nuphar luteum*	Seeds and rootstocks

a Sources: Turner 1995; MacKinnon et al. 1992; Compton 1993.

1979). The large leaves of plants such as cow parsnip are ideal surfaces for drying berries and as liners for baskets or other containers (Turner 1979). Other examples of useful plant materials include silica-rich horsetail, which has been used as sandpaper, and fireweed and willow seed fluff and *Sphagnum* mosses, which, due to their absorbent properties, could have been used for a variety of purposes.

Evidence for Younger Dryas–like Cooling
Several paleoecological studies from coastal British Columbia and Alaska record a reversion to a cooler climate between 11,000 and 10,000 BP, similar in timing and extent to the Younger Dryas cooling documented first in Europe and then in eastern North America (Mangerud et al. 1974; Watts 1980; Mott et al. 1986; Peteet et al. 1990). Based on peaks in cold-water benthic foraminiferans in marine sediment cores, Mathewes et al. (1993) document the cooling of ocean waters on the British Columbia coast between 11,000 and 10,200 BP. Similarly, many temperate-water bivalves seem to have disappeared from waters around Haida Gwaii between 11,000 and 10,000 BP and been replaced by only a few cold-tolerant species (Hetherington and Reid 2003). Using pollen-climate transfer functions, Mathewes et al. (1993) estimate a drop of 2°C to 3°C in summer temperature as well as increasing precipitation during this interval. In particular, late glacial peaks in mountain hemlock pollen suggest a cooling event on the Pacific coast between 10,700 and 10,000 BP (Mathewes 1993). Mountain hemlock is a good indicator of cool and moist conditions; it requires cool temperatures and substantial snow for insulation during winter months (Pojar and MacKinnon 1994). Mountain hemlock pollen is severely underrepresented in modern pollen assemblages, even in areas where it accounts for 40 percent of the tree cover. In the subalpine zone of Brooks Peninsula on Vancouver Island, where it is a co-dominant in the forest, mountain hemlock accounts for only 9 percent of the pollen sum (Hebda 1983; Hebda and Haggarty 1997). Therefore, even minor increases in mountain hemlock pollen are good indicators of climatic cooling and increased moisture. Mountain hemlock pollen is abundant in sediments from Cook Bank off northern Vancouver Island that date to this critical time period (Luternauer et al. 1989a; Lacourse et al. 2003). Similar peaks in mountain hemlock pollen occur in sediments from Haida Gwaii (Warner 1984; Fedje 1993; Heusser 1995), including preliminary evidence from Hippa Island on the west coast of the archipelago (R.W. Mathewes, unpublished data), and elsewhere along the Pacific coast (Mathewes 1993; Heusser 1960, 1985; Lacourse 2004).

At Cape Ball (Figure 3.2), a cooler climate during the Younger Dryas chronozone is suggested not by increases in mountain hemlock pollen but by a reversion from forest to open, herb-rich parkland vegetation (Mathewes

et al. 1993). In southeastern Alaska, pollen analysis revealed a similar reversion (Figure 3.1): open lodgepole pine forest, which had become established
sometime after 12,500 BP, was replaced by shrub and herb-dominated tundra between 10,800 and 9800 BP (Engstrom et al. 1990; Hansen and Engstrom
1996). Late glacial cooling also appears to have caused dramatic vegetation
changes on nearby Kodiak Island (Peteet and Mann 1994). A shift from
forest to herb-rich vegetation is also a common feature of Younger Dryas
landscapes around the North Atlantic (e.g., Mott et al. 1986; Williams et al.
2002).

Trends in Holocene Vegetation and Climate

Several paleoecological records from Haida Gwaii and southeastern Alaska
demonstrate significant changes in vegetation and climate after 10,000 BP
(Figure 3.1). In general, the early Holocene climate along the Northwest
Coast was marked by relatively high summer temperatures, low winter temperatures, and low mean annual precipitation (Heusser et al. 1985; Bartlein
et al. 1998). The mid-Holocene was characterized by a gradual trend towards cooler and wetter conditions, resulting in relatively low temperatures
and high annual precipitation in the late Holocene. The typically cool and
moist modern climate was established between 4000 and 3000 BP (Heusser
1985; Pellatt and Mathewes 1997).

Two sites on eastern Graham Island, Serendipity Bog and Boulton Lake,
have detailed and well-dated records of vegetation change with basal sediments that are early Holocene in age (Warner 1984). Mixed coniferous forests of lodgepole pine, spruce, and mountain hemlock with abundant alder
and ferns characterized this area and much of the region at the beginning
of the Holocene. After 9400 BP, spruce populations expanded at the expense of lodgepole pine and formed forests with western hemlock. Spruce
and western hemlock forests dominated the area until 5500 BP, when decreasing temperature and increasing precipitation promoted the development of forest-bog complexes throughout Haida Gwaii, but particularly in
poorly drained lowlands (Quickfall 1987). As a result, cedar (Cupressaceae),
lodgepole pine, and heath shrubs became more common. The modern western hemlock and cedar forest was established by 3000 BP, although the relative contributions of western red cedar (*Thuja plicata*) and yellow-cedar
(*Chamaecyparis nootkatensis*) are unknown due to indistinguishable pollen
morphologies.

At the northwestern tip of Haida Gwaii, on Langara Island, Heusser (1995)
found a similar record of Holocene vegetation change (Figures 3.1 and 3.2).
There, lodgepole pine was a minor component of the vegetation by 10,000
BP, due to the expansion of alder, spruce, and, later, western hemlock. The
high proportion of fern spores in early Holocene sediments suggests, however, that local forests remained partially open, providing good habitat for

light-demanding ferns. Between 9000 and 5000 BP, the pollen record on Langara Island records the local development of an open alder and skunk cabbage (*Lysichiton americanum*) community. The abrupt increase in skunk cabbage pollen suggests that local paludification, a process in which sites become waterlogged, had commenced about 9000 BP. About 5000 BP, heath shrubs and sedges replaced skunk cabbage. The climate cooled in the mid-Holocene but humidity increased, allowing western hemlock, spruce, and pine populations to expand once again. Cedar pollen increased after 3000 BP, suggesting establishment of present-day coastal forest with western red cedar, western hemlock, and spruce.

Several other sites further to the south on Haida Gwaii have been studied. Fedje (1993) conducted pollen analysis on lake sediments from two lowland sites, Skittagetan Pond and West Side Pond (Figure 3.1). There, western hemlock, spruce, and alder dominated the early Holocene landscape. Ferns were the dominant understorey vegetation and horsetail was locally abundant. Spruce, alder, and skunk cabbage expanded around 8700 BP as western hemlock declined in importance. Western hemlock re-expanded after 7500 BP, reflecting an increase in precipitation. Vegetation assemblages similar to modern communities were established around 5000 BP, with the addition of cedar. It is interesting to note that the expansion of western red cedar in coastal forests between 5000 and 2500 BP is strongly correlated with the development of massive woodworking technology (Hebda and Mathewes 1984). A similar vegetation history was reconstructed from sediments on Anthony Island, a small island located at the southern tip of the archipelago (see Chapter 4). Human activities in the last few thousand years have promoted increases in lodgepole pine populations and, more recently, the expansion of western hemlock. Forest clearing, fire, and harvesting of western red cedar for building purposes exposed the soil, allowing other conifers such as lodgepole pine to increase in abundance.

Pollen and plant macrofossil records from three subalpine ponds on Moresby Island provide a unique alpine perspective on Holocene vegetation change (Pellatt and Mathewes 1994, 1997). Mountain hemlock, along with spruce, alder, and western hemlock, characterized the late glacial upland vegetation. The relatively warm climate of the early Holocene allowed western hemlock to expand and resulted in a tree line higher in elevation than present-day tree line. About 7000 BP, temperatures began to decrease, forest productivity declined, and tree line decreased in elevation. By 6000 BP, lower temperatures allowed mountain hemlock to dominate subalpine forests, and higher precipitation allowed yellow-cedar to expand soon after. Open mountain hemlock and yellow-cedar forests were established by 3500 BP. Reconstructed vegetation histories from subalpine ponds (Pellatt and Mathewes 1994, 1997) and lowland sites (Fedje 1993) on the Queen Charlotte Islands suggest that a relatively short-lived cooling occurred about 3500

BP. This corresponds with glacial advances in the Coast Mountains of British Columbia and in the Rocky Mountains, and with climatic cooling documented along the Pacific coast (Pellatt and Mathewes 1997).

Given their proximity, paleoecological records from southern Alaska (Heusser 1960, 1985; Cwynar 1990; Hansen and Engstrom 1996) are both relevant and interesting (Figure 3.1). Trees consistently arrived later at more northwesterly sites, suggesting that the migration of the major trees was primarily northward and that local refugia did not support trees during the last glacial maximum (Cwynar 1990). Lodgepole pine may be an exception to this because its dominance at late glacial coastal sites must be explained by either refugia in Alaska or British Columbia or exceptionally high migration rates (Peteet 1991). Sitka spruce arrived in the Glacier Bay region by 9500 BP (Hansen and Engstrom 1996), forming productive forests with green alder and various ferns about 1,500 ^{14}C years after similar vegetation had developed on Haida Gwaii. Alder was an important component of the vegetation from 12,000 BP but, like the Logan Inlet record, it reached its peak abundance during the transition from pine- to spruce-dominated forests. Spruce forests were subsequently replaced when increased summer temperatures and annual precipitation allowed western hemlock and mountain hemlock to form closed forests between 8500 and 8000 BP. Lodgepole pine re-expanded about 7000 BP due to widespread paludification. Local edaphic conditions at this time were also favourable for *Sphagnum* moss, skunk cabbage, and heath shrubs. Due to a late Holocene increase in precipitation, western hemlock, lodgepole pine, and other bog vegetation became more abundant about 3400 BP.

Acknowledgments
We are grateful to V. Barrie and K. Conway for providing access to the Logan Inlet core (VEC94A-018), D.W. Fedje for supplying a previously unpublished radiocarbon date (CAMS-19510), and R.W. Stein, D.M. Peteet, J.J. Clague, E. Elle, and two anonymous reviewers for critical reviews of a draft of this chapter. Financial support was provided by the Natural Sciences and Engineering Research Council of Canada through a Postgraduate Scholarship to T. Lacourse and Research Grants to R.W. Mathewes, and by a Geological Society of America Research Grant to T. Lacourse.

4
Vegetation History of Anthony Island, Haida Gwaii, and Its Relationship to Climate Change and Human Settlement

Richard J. Hebda, Marlow G. Pellatt, Rolf W. Mathewes, Daryl W. Fedje, and Steven Acheson

Interest in Haida Gwaii stems in considerable part from its isolation from mainland North America. Its unique flora, ecosystems, and culture are a consequence of that isolation. The scientific investigation of islands such as Haida Gwaii often allows a better understanding of fundamental ecological processes because the reduced complexity makes it easier to isolate the key factors influencing those processes. For example, MacArthur and Wilson's classic study and theories of island biogeography (1967) provided insights into evolution that we now apply to mountains, lakes, and other discrete populations on continental landscapes.

As Haida Gwaii is to mainland North America, so are the small islands and islets in the archipelago to the large islands. Of these, Anthony Island (*SGang gwaay*) off the south end of Moresby Island is an excellent example of an island apart, exposed to the most extreme climatic phenomena characteristic of Haida Gwaii as a whole, and distant from the influence of the continental mainland.

Anthony Island's small size (approximately 2 square kilometres) and limited flora offer an opportunity to examine ecological changes and their relationship to climate change through an investigation of postglacial vegetation history. The island is fully exposed to the open Pacific Ocean, providing an opportunity to understand vegetation-climate interactions under a highly oceanic climatic regime (Figure 4.1). Also, Anthony Island was once home to a large Haida settlement (Abbott and Keen 1993; Acheson 1985) and provides an opportunity to examine the ecological effects of First Nations on a discrete and limited landmass.

This chapter examines the vegetation and climate history of Anthony Island using pollen analysis. Three sediment sequences at three different time intervals (> 10,000 years, < 2,000 years, and 100 to 200 years ago) serve to outline the dynamic ecosystem history of the island. The results are discussed with respect to regional ecosystem and climate history, biogeography, and the effect of human activities on the island's vegetation.

Figure 4.1   Aerial photograph of Anthony Island showing its location in Haida Gwaii (Queen Charlotte Islands) and location of study sites and geographical features. A = *SGang gwaay* Crevasse Flats site; B = Location of *SGang gwaay* Pond, with basal age of 1750 ± 120 BP; c = South *SGang gwaay* Meadow (SSM) site. The solid white line points to Ninstints village and the location of Site S84-52B.

Setting

Anthony Island is situated at the extreme south end of Haida Gwaii and is a low outlier (maximum elevation of slightly over 60 metres above sea level) of the Queen Charlotte Mountains. The island is located about 5 kilometres west of Kunghit Island and only 1.5 kilometres south of Moresby Island, near the mouths of Louscoone, Moresby, and Rose inlets (Figure 4.1).

The relatively mild climate is strongly influenced by the Pacific Ocean. The mean daily temperature (based on the Cape St. James climatic station) is 8.7°C, with a January mean of 4.6°C and July mean of 13.0°C (Atmospheric Environment Service 1993). The mean annual precipitation is 1,542 millimetres, almost all of which falls as rain. October to January is the rainy season, but rain falls even in July. Wind is a major climatic factor, with the average annual wind speed probably slightly less than the 32 kilometres per hour recorded at Cape St. James. Although winds are strongest in the winter, they blow on average in the 25 to 27 kilometres per hour range even in the summer (Atmospheric Environment Service 1993).

Anthony Island lies within the Very Wet Hypermaritime subzone of the Coastal Western Hemlock biogeoclimatic zone (CWHvh) (Banner et al. 1993). This lowland subzone is typical up to 25 kilometres inland along the north coast of BC. It consists of a mosaic of productive forests and poor forest and bog ecosystems, which are well represented on the islands adjacent to Anthony Island. The relatively productive forests largely occur on moderate to steep slopes and floodplains and form a fringe along the shoreline.

Common tree species in CWHvh include western red cedar (*Thuja plicata*), yellow-cedar (*Chamaecyparis nootkatensis*), western hemlock (*Tsuga heterophylla*), shore/lodgepole pine (*Pinus contorta*), Sitka spruce (*Picea sitchensis*), and red alder (*Alnus rubra*). Under the highly oceanic conditions and low elevation of Anthony Island, Sitka spruce (especially near the shore) and western hemlock predominate. Western red cedar occurs relatively frequently but shore pine is rare. Sitka alder (*Alnus crispa*) is present in openings along with salal (*Gaultheria shallon*), but most other shrubs are uncommon today because of heavy deer browsing. Deer were introduced to Haida Gwaii in the twentieth century (Banfield 1974). Grasses, especially Pacific reedgrass (*Calamagrostis nutkaensis*), occur in windblown settings. Pacific crabapple (*Malus fusca*) is present on headlands and in scattered moist areas.

Cultural History

Arguably, human settlement of Anthony Island, beginning 1,600 years ago, had a perceptible impact on the island's vegetation through time. A number of archaeological sites occur on Anthony Island, or "Red Cod Island," including *SGang gwaay*, the last and largest of the villages once occupied by the Kunghit Haida. The Kunghit Haida, or "island end people," were the original inhabitants of the region and constituted one of three historically recognized Haida dialectic-territorial divisions on Haida Gwaii. The archaeology of *SGang gwaay* village (also known as Ninstints), located on the eastern shore of Anthony Island, has revealed four depositional phases or events spanning the established 1,600-year history of the site. These events include initial settlement, two periods of expansion, and abandonment, all of which may be traceable in the island's vegetation history.

Initial settlement of *SGang gwaay* around AD 360 (Acheson 1985) coincided with falling sea levels and a newly emerging coastline within the last 2,000 years (Hebda and Mathewes 1986). Radiocarbon dating of basal-pond sediments (Figure 4.1B) at 1750 ± 120 BP places an age limit on occupation of the Ninstints locality. Archaeological evidence for the rapid colonization of

Anthony Island is followed by major depositional changes indicative of heightened cultural activity and expansion at *SGang gwaay*, and also at a number of neighbouring sites on Moresby Island between AD 1200 and 1400. During this time the houses at the southern end of *SGang gwaay* village were established. At the neighbouring village of *Taaji*, there is similar evidence of a series of living floors at the western edge of the site dating from around AD 1400. The nearby village of *xuud jihldaa* ("to go for cedar") was also established at about the same time (Acheson 1998), suggesting that this is a regional phenomenon rather than a localized trend in settlement growth.

The third major depositional phase at *SGang gwaay* coincides with the onset of the maritime fur trade and introduction of a suite of devastating diseases during the late 1700s and mid-1800s. With smallpox rampant on the coast by the late 1700s, many settlements simply dissolved as surviving remnant populations moved and regrouped at villages such as *SGang gwaay* (Acheson 1998:61-62). This event led to a brief period of rapid growth for *SGang gwaay* at the expense of neighbouring settlements. As Newcombe (n.d.b) observed at the turn of the nineteenth century:

> [*SGang gwaay*] ... was inhabited by the dwindling population of the numerous villages near[by]. Within a radius of fourteen miles from this village there were no less than thirty-five permanent villages of which the names are still preserved; in addition, there were eight or nine isolated forts sometimes occupied for months together, and as many camping places, in good fishing harbours or streams.

A declining population, heightened conflict, and access to a massive short-lived influx of new wealth from the maritime fur trade encouraged the creation of the large, strategically located settlement of *SGang gwaay*. Both Swanton (n.d., 1905a:94) and Newcombe (n.d.a) reported on the resettlement of Chief Ninstints's lineage from Gowgaia Bay to *SGang gwaay*, during which time the Ninstints name became synonymous with the village. According to Newcombe (n.d.a), "the south end of the village belonged to Ninstints people who originally lived at gao-gia [Gowgaia Bay]" and had moved at the outbreak of the first smallpox epidemic. Robert Haswell's remark (n.d.; see also Howay 1941:327) on visiting Gowgaia Bay in 1792 that the area was now "visited [only] casually by strangers from Coyah's [Xoya] tribe," in reference to the then senior most ranking Kunghit chief at *SGang gwaay*, suggests that the resettlement of the Ninstints Sa'ki lineage at *SGang gwaay* had already taken place. One of the last groups to settle at *SGang gwaay* was from *Qayjuu* ("songs-of-victory") village at Benjamin Point. This group settled at the north end of *SGang gwaay* village on the eve of the last smallpox epidemic to strike the Haida in 1862-63 (Acheson 1998:93; Newcombe n.d.a). The accounts of the in-migration of these groups agree with the depositional history of *SGang gwaay,* with the last cluster of houses appearing at the north end of the village before 1860 (Abbott and Keen 1993; Acheson 1998; Duff and Kew 1958:54).

In addition to an expanding village, a feature of *SGang gwaay* relevant to the island's vegetation history was the potato garden, located in the meadow area behind the houses at the south end of the village. The growing and trading of potatoes, introduced on the coast as early as 1825, had become a major Haida enterprise within a few short years. Potatoes were sought after by traders to supplement their monotonous, heavily salted provisions. For John Work (1945:45), factor at Fort Simpson in the 1830s, potatoes were "a great acquisition, as they serve to enable the people to be fed with salt fish." J. Dunn (1844:294), who was also at Fort Simpson intermittently through the 1830s, estimated that upwards of "500 to 800 bushels" were being traded by the Haida in a season. The growing importance of this trade to both Haida and fur trader alike is illustrated by the fact that within just ten days in 1840 the fort had acquired 1,119 bushels of potatoes from the "Queen Charlotte Islanders," arriving in "no less than 48 Canoes" (Hudson's Bay Company n.d.a). Although the Skidegate people appear to have cornered much of this trade, most villages, including *SGang gwaay,* had potato gardens (Newcombe n.d.a; Hudson's Bay Company n.d.a, n.d.b, n.d.c; Work 1945:76, 78).

Despite the influx of people to *SGang gwaay* from surrounding villages throughout the historical period, the growing isolation, the crippling small-pox epidemic of 1862-63, and internecine conflicts all took their toll on the Kunghit Haida. The Hudson's Bay Company census of 1836-41 tallied 308 people at *SGang gwaay,* living among twenty houses (Douglas n.d.). By 1885 their number had dropped to less than 30 individuals (Acheson 1998:93-94). The final act for the Kunghit came in the winter of 1887-88, when the few surviving residents abandoned *SGang gwaay* for the settlements of New Clue and Skidegate (United Church of Canada 1888).

Methods

This study approaches vegetation history from two directions. A long post-glacial record (*SGang gwaay* Crevasse Flats) representing regional vegetation was obtained from a small depression near the height of land on the island; and two short sediment sequences were sampled from the main archaeo-logical site (*SGang gwaay* or Ninstints) to investigate the relationship be-tween vegetation and human settlement. Standard pollen analysis (Fægri and Iversen 1989) and radiocarbon dating were used to analyze the sedi-ment profiles.

Results

SGang gwaay Crevasse Flats (SCF)

The SCF site is located in a small forest hollow at 29 metres above sea level, about 200 metres inland from the south end of the main settlement (Figure 4.1). The samples were taken from thick organic deposits filling a depression within the mixed inland forest. The depression is located in a saddle between the east and west sides of the island.

The forest is dominated by young western hemlock with scattered western red cedar and Sitka spruce. There is no significant shrub or herb understorey due to deer browsing, but a nearly continuous feather moss layer consisting primarily of *Kindbergia oregana* carpets the forest floor.

The SCF profile is 1.65 metres deep and rests upon a stony brown diamicton. Matted sedge peat with organic detritus and macrofossils such as yellow waterlily (*Nuphar polysepalum*) seeds occurs from 1.15 to 1.65 metres. Wood from the base of this layer was dated at 12,300 ± 300 BP (WAT 1204), whereas the peat adjacent to the wood was dated at 10,570 ± 180 BP (WAT 1195). The older date is taken as the start of organic sedimentation. Crumbly dark peat occurs between 1.15 and 0.95 metres. A sample from 1.05 to 1.10 metres was dated at 9870 ± 140 BP (WAT 1198). Dark woody peat spans 0.95 to about 0.80 metres, where it is replaced by brown peat with sedge lenses and twigs. Dark slimy peat begins at about 0.35 metres and grades up into brown fibrous peaty litter at the surface. Wood at the base of the dark slimy peat was determined to be 2,580 ± 90 radiocarbon years old. The detailed stratigraphy and dates are summarized in Hebda and Mathewes (1986).

Pollen Zones and Interpretation

For the different pollen zones, see Figure 4.2.

Zone SCF-1: Pinus (165 to 145 cm, > 12,300 to 11,700 BP)
Dominated by 70 to 80 percent *Pinus* pollen, this zone is typical of late glacial pollen assemblages from the northwest Pacific coast (Hebda and Whitlock 1997) and on Haida Gwaii (Mathewes 1989a; Fedje 1993). The earliest part of this interval is interpreted as forest with shrubby patches dominated by heath plants (Ericaceae and possibly *Empetrum*). There is no clear record of the treeless vegetation observed at slightly older sites on Haida Gwaii (Mathewes 1989a; Fedje 1993). A 10 percent value for *Picea* pollen in the zone suggests that spruce likely grew on Anthony Island during this late glacial interval.

The occurrence of *Ligusticum calderi* pollen (see Hebda 1985) at the base of the record is notable. It confirms that this Pacific coast endemic grew on the late glacial landscape of Haida Gwaii at the same time as populations on the Brooks Peninsula of southern Vancouver Island (Hebda 1997). This species does not inhabit Anthony Island today, although it grows on adjacent Moresby Island. This record strongly suggests that this plant and possibly

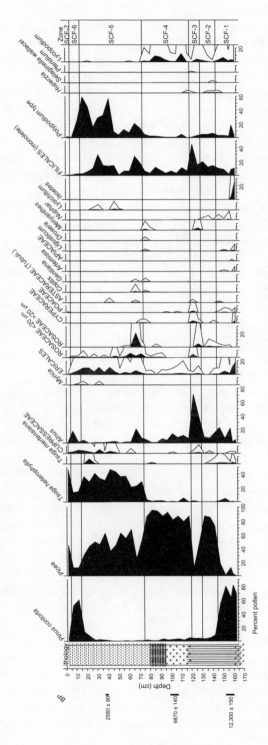

Figure 4.2 Percentage pollen diagram for *SGang gwaay* Crevasse Flats (SCF) site, Anthony Island (R. Hebda, analyst). Hollow curves represent 10× exaggeration. Radiocarbon dates are listed to the left of the diagram.

others of the endemic group (Ogilvie 1994) are members of a once wide-spread coastal flora that is now restricted to non-forest sites. The occurrence of *L. calderi,* a perennial of open habitats (Ogilvie 1997), confirms that pine stands of this time must have been open or interspersed with meadowlike patches.

Zone SCF-2: Picea (145 to 130 cm; ca. 11,700 to 11,000 BP)

Picea pollen rapidly replaced pine at about 11,700 BP, reducing pine to a minor forest element. Alder occupied openings among the spruces on the island, perhaps becoming more widespread at the end of the zone. There may have been a few mountain hemlock trees, but their pollen is sparse. The understorey probably still contained ericaceous shrubs. Fedje (1993) also noted the expansion of spruce during this time on the west side of Moresby Island to the north, and Mathewes and colleagues (1993) also saw an expansion of spruce on northeast Graham Island, beginning around 11,200 BP.

The replacement of pine by spruce takes place within 5 centimetres, or less than 200 years. This change in vegetation is more or less contemporaneous with changes at other sites along the coast (Hebda and Whitlock 1997) and in Haida Gwaii (Mathewes 1989a), but nowhere else does spruce become so abundant in the interval.

Zone SCF-3: Alnus-Picea (130 to 120 cm; ca. 11,000 to 10,600 BP)

The spruce-dominated stage is interrupted by a brief but prominent alder peak during which alder reaches 70 percent of pollen and spores. Small peaks of other non-arboreal types such as Rosaceae and Poaceae occur at the same time. Spruce values are sharply reduced, dropping to less than 20 percent in one of the samples.

The abrupt change, timing, and disturbance of the ground implied by the high alder percentage strongly suggest that this brief interval may represent a Younger Dryas–type cooling event on Anthony Island. Apparently alder, assumed to be Sitka alder (*Alnus sinuata*), briefly replaced spruce as the dominant vegetative cover. Among the alder there appear to have been openings that harboured other shrubs and herbs. Unlike other sites in Haida Gwaii, there is little in the way of an increase in mountain hemlock (Mathewes 1993) at this time, perhaps because it did not grow on the island.

Zone SCF-4: Picea (120 to 75 cm; 10,600 to 6900 BP)

Picea predominates in pollen spectra of this mostly early Holocene assemblage. Alder pollen and fern spores are the only other significant types. Western hemlock pollen is uncommon, and considering modern spectra (Hebda and Allen 1993; Pellatt et al. 1997; Allen et al. 1999), did not grow on the island. The vegetation likely consisted of continuous dense Sitka spruce forest, perhaps with a fern understorey and patches of alder in unstable sites. The occurrence of buckbean (*Menyanthes*) pollen near the end of the zone suggests that the site was still open and wet.

This spruce-alder forest was characteristic not only of Anthony Island but also of many sites along the north coast (Hebda 1995). Unlike sites in the main part of Haida Gwaii (Mathewes 1989a; Pellatt and Mathewes 1994, 1997), however, Anthony Island spruce forests contained little western hemlock.

Zone SCF-5: Picea-Tsuga (75 to 15 cm; 6900 to 1100 BP)
This mid to late Holocene zone begins with a sharp rise in western hemlock values at the expense of spruce, and presumably reflects the arrival and spread of western hemlock on Anthony Island. Whether this was simply a chance migration to an isolated island or a response to climate change is not clear. In the early Holocene, sea levels were about 15 metres higher and the island was much smaller than today (Hebda and Mathewes 1986).

This zone has two parts. Between 6900 and 4300 BP (75 to 50 centimetres), cedar-type pollen was essentially absent and Rosaceae pollen was more abundant than Ericales. From 4300 to 1400 BP, cedar-type pollen increased, although it never became abundant. Ericales values reached 10 percent in several samples, and monolete fern spores are very abundant. The change in understorey pollen and spore types coincides with approximately the end of the mesothermic interval (Hebda 1995), but is earlier than changes noted at high-elevation sites on nearby Moresby Island (Pellatt and Mathewes 1994, 1997).

In terms of vegetation, the earlier portion of the zone suggests a more open landscape with salmonberries (*Rubus spectabilis*) or other Rosaceae growing in moist openings. With cooling and increased moisture at about 4,300 years ago, western red cedar became a prominent forest component, the canopy closed completely, and ericaceous shrubs formed an understorey layer. Peat bogs were expanding actively around this time on both Moresby and Graham Islands, blanketing many areas with wet peat of variable thickness (Quickfall 1987).

Zone SCF-6: Pinus (15 to 5 cm; 1100 to 500 BP)
Pine pollen values rise to nearly 60 percent in this late Holocene zone at the expense of both spruce and western hemlock. The pine pollen values indicate the re-expansion of *Pinus contorta* on the island and around the site. *Alnus* values also increase in the latter part of the zone. Such an assemblage is not known in other late Holocene records of the British Columbia coast or in Haida Gwaii (Hebda 1995; Mathewes 1989a; Pellatt and Mathewes 1994, 1997). No climatic change is demonstrated at this time, certainly none of a magnitude sufficient to explain the change in forest composition at the beginning of this zone.

The most likely explanation would be a local disturbance event, such as a fire, or perhaps progressive clearing on the island associated with colonization by people. The absence of a charcoal layer near the surface favours the clearing hypothesis. The first confirmed occupation of the island occurred about 1400 BP (Acheson 1985), around the same time as the development of the pine zone. When people first arrived, they presumably began to use the nearby timber for firewood and other uses, thereby opening up the previously dense and closed forest. Progressive clearing and other disturbances likely provided opportunities for disturbance-adapted pines to expand their populations.

Zone SCF-7: Tsuga-Picea (5 to 0 cm; 500 to 0 BP)

The most recent zone, represented by a single sample, exhibits a resurgence of western hemlock and spruce pollen values, mostly at the expense of pine but also associated with a decline in alder. The most straightforward explanation for the zone could be successional recovery of climax forest after the disturbances responsible for SCF-6 as well as historical events. The characteristics of this most recent interval are resolved in detail in the following section from the South *SGang gwaay* Meadow locality.

South *SGang gwaay* Meadow (SSM)

This record (see Figure 4.3) originates from an 81-centimetre-long sequence of sediment from a wet grassy meadow at the south end of the main settlement (Acheson 1985). A layer of 15 to 20 centimetres of slimy black peat rests upon cobbles and pebbles in a coarse sand matrix. The upper contact of the slimy peat is well marked and has an undulating boundary with fibrous brown peat above. The lower portion of the fibrous peat is dense and dark and contains roots and wood, whereas the upper 15-centimetre segment is lighter in colour and comes in contact with the darker underlying peat at about 15 centimetres. A piece of wood from 65 centimetres below the surface at the contact with slimy black peat was dated at 1020 ± 70 BP.

The current vegetation is an open stand of Sitka spruce with an understorey of Pacific reedgrass (*Calamagrostis nutkaensis*). Adjacent to the site, Sitka spruce, western hemlock, western red cedar, and a single Sitka alder shrub grow on the rocky cliff.

Three pollen zones are identified (Figure 4.3).

Zone SSM-1: Picea–Monolete Ferns (81 to 45 cm; >1020 to 750 BP)

High arboreal pollen (AP) and spruce values (mostly about 80 percent) characterize this zone, along with abundant monolete fern spores. Western hemlock pollen is relatively uncommon, and alder values are less than 5 percent. Aside from the fern spores, Ericaceae pollen is the most abundant

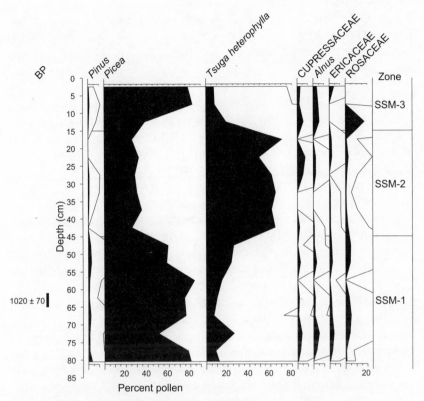

Figure 4.3 Percentage pollen diagram for South *SGang gwaay* Meadow (SSM) site, Anthony Island (R. Hebda and D. Fedje, analysts). Hollow curves represent 10× exaggeration. Radiocarbon dates are listed to the left of the diagram.

non-tree type, although Rosaceae and rare Caprifoliaceae (twinberry type) pollen are also present.

This assemblage represents a wet shoreline habitat. Sitka spruce trees grew at the site, with openings occupied by shrubs such as salal, salmonberry, and black twinberry (*Lonicera involucrata*). Masses of ferns likely grew in moist pockets. Open meadow and herb vegetation likely occurred along the shoreline only a few metres away.

Zone SSM-2: Tsuga-Picea (45 to 15 cm; 750 to 200 BP)
High tree pollen values continue from the preceding zone but are dominated by western hemlock rather than spruce. Fern spores are much less abundant than before. Non-tree types are also rarer than in SSM-1. The sharp decline in spruce can be ascribed to the local decline of spruce trees at the site. The only sites where western hemlock pollen predominates to such

an extent on Anthony Island are within western hemlock stands inland from the shore. The zone may reflect deliberate removal of spruce trees during expansion of the village site, and the transport of pollen from nearby western hemlock forest.

Zone SSM-3: Picea (15 to 0 cm; 200 to 0 BP)
Spruce pollen again replaces western hemlock in this zone. The early part records a diversity (> 5 percent) of shrubs such as Rosaceae and Caprifoliaceae as well as Cyperaceae. The recent age and the return of spruce suggest that SSM-3 represents post-abandonment vegetation succession at the site. Shrubs such as black twinberry and possibly salmonberry colonized the surrounding landscape and the core site as human activity declined and ceased. Sedges (Cyperaceae) probably expanded in the wettest portion of the meadow.

None of the samples from the near-surface part of this record contain potato pollen despite the documented use of the area for potato cultivation (Acheson 1985). Perhaps the sampling site remained too wet for potato culture, or the plants rarely flowered, or the pollen was not preserved. Even if the plants bloomed, potato pollen is not wind-dispersed and would not be expected to occur outside the potato patch.

Fedje (1991) carried out enhanced counts for SSM samples and noted in the basal 21 centimetres the occurrence of Apiaceae, Asteraceae, and Chenopodiaceae. This group, particularly Chenopodiaceae, are good indicators of an upper-intertidal and beach environment, and their occurrence might be expected in association with the inferred pebble and sand beach deposits. The proportion of these pollen types is very low compared with examples of intertidal sediments (Hebda 1977), and probably testifies to the limited extent of the vegetation and the overwhelming representation of the adjacent non-strand community.

Fedje (1991) also noted a marked increase in Rosaceae and Caprifoliaceae (rose and honeysuckle families) pollen values in the 25-to-10-centimetre interval, as well as a diversity of herbaceous types such as Asteraceae and Apiaceae. These observations are consistent with clearing, expansion of the village site, and possibly local cultivation of fields.

Site S84-52B
A 13-centimetre-long sequence of litter and shell midden debris from within the main portion of the settlement was sampled and analyzed to identify what the vegetation may have been like during occupation, and how it changed with abandonment. The sample site was located near the middle of the village (B in Figure 4.1).

This sequence of six samples exhibits major changes in pollen and spores from the time of occupation and changes associated with abandonment (see Figure 4.4). The deepest sample (10 to 13 centimetres) from shell midden

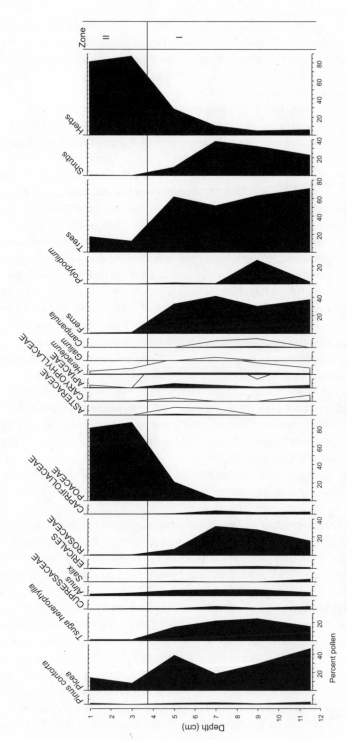

Figure 4.4 Percentage pollen diagram for Site S84-52B, Anthony Island. Hollow curves represent 10× exaggeration (R. Hebda, analyst).

debris is dominated by spruce, western hemlock, and Rosaceae pollen. Willow (*Salix*) pollen occurs at about 3 percent. Monolete fern spores are exceptionally abundant. Notable non-arboreal types include Caprifoliaceae (presumably *Lonicera involucrata*) and Apiaceae (including both *Heracleum lanatum* and *Angelica lucida* pollen).

The sample from the 8-to-10-centimetre level is similar to the basal sample in most respects, except that western hemlock pollen is almost as abundant as spruce pollen and Rosaceae pollen is more abundant. Similar non-arboreal pollen types occur.

In the sample from the 8-to-10-centimetre level, arboreal pollen values are lower than in the preceding two samples, and western hemlock pollen is more abundant than that of spruce. Rosaceae pollen is exceptionally abundant. Other shrubs, especially Caprifoliaceae, occur at relatively high values, as does Apiaceae pollen. Monolete fern spores remain abundant.

From 6 centimetres to the surface, the sample consists mostly of herbaceous roots in organic debris. Poaceae pollen increases until it overwhelmingly dominates the pollen spectrum at 70 to 80 percent. The relatively uncommon tree pollen is composed mainly of spruce, and by the uppermost sample (0 to 2 centimetres) western hemlock nearly disappears from the record. Other major changes include the near-disappearance of Rosaceae pollen and the previously predominant fern spores. Apiaceae pollen is notably abundant at the 4 to 6 centimetre level.

The S84-52B sequence appears to match the upper 50 centimetres of the SSM sequence, in which western hemlock rises to dominance and then is replaced by Sitka spruce. The spruce-hemlock-spruce dominance pattern suggests that the western hemlock peak at SSM reflects a more general change in vegetation, and supports the suggestion that people may have cleared locally growing spruce trees. Historical photographs reveal that late in the 1800s, places where spruce trees have now become re-established were once open.

The site also reveals the nature of the vegetation cover that occupied the village site. Plants of the rose family apparently grew between the structures. Likely candidates include Pacific crabapple (*Malus fusca*) and salmonberry (*Rubus spectabilis*). Black twinberry likely grew mixed in the thickets on the site. Cow parsnip and angelica occurred abundantly, a conclusion supported by historical photographs. Pollen of *Campanula* occurs in one sample (8 to 10 centimetres), suggesting that *Campanula rotundifolia* (Scotch harebell) occupied very open spots. In addition to the flowering plants, ferns were widespread within the settlement.

Grass pollen becomes abundant late in the sequence, apparently coincident with the abandonment of the settlement. Several exotic grasses, such as velvet grass (*Holcus lanatus*) occur in open portions of the site today. Had native grasses been a major element of village settlement before European contact, much higher percentages of grass pollen would have been expected. The record suggests that weedy communities before the advent of Europeans were very different from today.

Discussion and Conclusions

Pollen and spore analyses of organic deposits reveal that Anthony Island has experienced a dynamic environmental history. In the late Pleistocene, open lodgepole pine forest covered the island. The openings supported at least one Pacific coast endemic herb, *Ligusticum calderi*, suggesting that the island was one of several sites where such species may have survived the last glacial advance.

Spruce rapidly replaced lodgepole pine about 11,700 years ago, presumably in response to climatic change. It is assumed that Sitka spruce or a hybrid (Warner and Chmielewski 1987) was involved, although macrofossil analysis is required to verify this interpretation. Macrofossils of spruce confirm its occurrence on the coast of Graham Island (Mathewes 1989a) and confirm Sitka spruce on northern Vancouver Island (Hebda 1997) at the same time. This spruce expansion occurs slightly earlier than on northeast Graham Island (Mathewes et al. 1993), a difference perhaps related to differences in radiocarbon dating. At West Side Pond, located at the midpoint of the west side of Moresby Island, the increase in spruce abundance occurs at about the same time as on Anthony Island (Fedje 1993). Alder pollen predominates in the interval rather than spruce, however, possibly because of the more exposed setting and shallower soils at that site.

The late Pleistocene spruce increase on Anthony Island corresponds in general to the spread of the regional mixed coniferous forests (Hebda and Whitlock 1997) ascribed to various factors such as increased moisture compared with the preceding pine zone (Hebda 1995) or perhaps Younger Dryas–type cooling and disturbance (Mathewes 1993).

The occurrence of spruce forest between 11,700 and 11,000 BP, rather than mixed coniferous forest, might be ascribed to the absence of the other tree species. True fir appears to have been absent from Haida Gwaii since deglaciation (Mathewes 1989a). Western hemlock was an important element of mixed coniferous forests on the coast under similar past climatic conditions (Hebda 1997), but not in Haida Gwaii. Hence its absence is most easily explained by a migrational delay or lag on its way to Anthony Island. The difference in vegetation is likely the result of small size and isolation of the island compared with larger landmasses nearby.

The occurrence of a brief but prominent alder zone at the SCF site in the thousand years preceding the beginning of the Holocene is notable. Alder is a recognized indicator of disturbance. Landscape instability resulting from climatic deterioration such as the Younger Dryas (see Mathewes 1993) is a possible explanation.

A contemporaneous brief alder peak occurs in diagrams from several other sites with similar climatic regimes (Hebda 1997, 1983; Mathewes 1989a). This concurrence of the alder peak suggests a regional rather than local phenomenon, favouring a climatic cause such as Younger Dryas cooling.

The return of spruce at approximately 10,600 BP, and predominance of Sitka spruce until 6900 BP, signals the development of relatively stable climate. Spruce forests were widespread along the North Pacific coast at this time (Hebda 1995; Hebda and Whitlock 1997). Curiously, though, alder and western hemlock, not spruce, predominated at West Side Pond (Fedje 1993). Pellatt and Mathewes (1997) identified the early Holocene as an interval of warmer-than-present climate and higher-than-present tree lines in Haida Gwaii. On Anthony Island, it appears that western hemlock was absent. Late migration to the island is a likely explanation, and even if western hemlock had arrived, it may have found conditions inhospitable because of the high sea levels with strong influence of sea spray. Sitka spruce thrives under these conditions but western hemlock does not. The small size and isolation of Anthony Island again contributed to a unique vegetation history.

The end of the spruce zone coincides with the end of the "xerothermic" interval throughout British Columbia about 7000 BP (Mathewes 1985; Hebda 1995). This observation emphasizes the importance of this horizon as a time of significant regional climatic change. Even highly oceanic Anthony Island was sensitive to the increasing moisture and possible cooling at this time.

The spruce zone is followed by a long interval of combined spruce and western hemlock dominance, the second half of which includes western red cedar as a notable element. This spruce-hemlock combination with increasing red cedar is a typical pattern for maritime sites in the mid to late Holocene (Hebda and Mathewes 1984; Hebda 1995). The forest took on its modern form and composition typical of the Coastal Western Hemlock biogeoclimatic zone (Meidinger and Pojar 1991) as climate moistened and cooled. The increase in red cedar appears to occur slightly earlier than vegetation changes at higher elevations nearby where mountain hemlock expands (Pellatt and Mathewes 1997). Nevertheless, the sequence indicates changes in climate more or less consistent with the regional pattern (Hebda 1995), resulting in cool and moist modern conditions becoming established about 4000 BP. It is notable that on Anthony Island, as on the Brooks Peninsula, the mid to late Holocene climate and vegetation appear to be relatively stable, unlike drier and less exposed sites inland (Hebda 1997).

A unique feature in the vegetation history of Anthony Island compared with other sites in the region is the establishment of pine stands around 1500 BP. Today a few pine trees grow south of the main archaeological site but contribute little to the modern pollen rain on the island. There are no major regional climatic changes at this time of a scale that can account for this marked change in vegetation (Hebda 1995; Pellatt and Mathewes 1994, 1997), hence it is probably a consequence of human activities on Anthony Island that are documented archaeologically. Clearing of the forest, perhaps combined with fire of limited extent, is the most likely cause of pine expansion. Both activities would have exposed the thick organic forest soil developed under the spruce-hemlock forests and created high light conditions needed for pine establishment. Pine expansion would have been favoured particularly under a regime of regular clearing, perhaps for firewood. The persistence of pine also raises the question of whether pines were encouraged or favoured for human use (see Turner 1998). It is important to emphasize that the pine zone begins just after the time of permanent settlement of *SGang gwaay* village (Acheson 1985).

The occurrence of the unique pine zone on Anthony Island raises questions about the impact of First Nations settlements on nearby landscapes. Although people of coastal settlements lived off the sea (Hebda and Frederick 1990), they certainly used resources such as wood from the adjacent forest. As population grew, timber of various sizes must have been cut for fuel and for building, and harvesting must have moved progressively further and further from the original settlement. The pollen records of the SSM and S84-52B sections also support the conclusion that people altered the nearby landscape by cutting spruces as the village grew. As the spruce cover near the site was reduced, the signal from hemlocks on the surrounding uplands became relatively more important, recorded as the hemlock-dominated pollen zone in both these records. It is notable that the SSF section near the crest of the upland also exhibits a western hemlock rise in the past few centuries consistent with the two shorter sections. Neither of the shorter sections appears to include the pine zone, although they overlap somewhat in time. In any case, it is very likely that the advent of human settlement had major consequences for the island's vegetation cover.

This observation raises the question of why such ecological effects have not been observed clearly on the northwest coast before. The main reason is that few archaeological sites and their nearby environs have been studied in similar detail. Regional vegetation and climate summaries have been developed (Mathewes 1985; Hebda 1995) but the archaeological sites themselves have received little or no attention. Our analysis of shell midden deposits at *SGang gwaay* demonstrates that even these alkaline and oxidized sediments may contain sufficient pollen to merit study. They hold the potential for detailed reconstructions of the local environment. As we demonstrate, shrubs of the rose and honeysuckle families and cow parsnip and angelica grew on site between the houses.

Our study further demonstrates that the advent of Europeans and their weeds led to a change in local ecology, particularly in early-successional vegetation. Instead of salmonberry, twinberry, and cow parsnip plants, grasses took over and predominated. The pre-contact settlement likely looked very different from times recently past, when it was covered in shrub thickets rather than a grassy sward. It is important to note that many of the original successional shrubs and forbs were important food species (Turner 1995), whereas the grasses had no such value.

Our study of Anthony Island demonstrates the value of examining small, isolated areas to understand climate-vegetation interactions and impact of humans on coastal forests. The response of the vegetation differed from that in the adjacent regions because of phytogeographic phenomena such as differences in immigration times and colonization, and the unique ecological circumstances (influence of ocean spray) of small islands. The study further demonstrates that First Nations peoples had direct ecological effects on the local environment. Furthermore, the advent of Europeans and their introduced plant species affected the way the human-influenced ecosystems responded to disturbance. Finally, our study clearly demonstrates the potential value of looking at human-landscape relationships at other sites in Haida Gwaii and the Pacific Northwest Coast to better understand the role that humans may have played in shaping coastal ecosystems.

Acknowledgments
Petro-Canada Resources and the British Columbia Heritage Trust generously funded the archaeological investigations in Gwaii Hanaas with the cooperation of the Skidegate Band Council. Members of the field crew included Roberta Aiken, Alan and Morgan Brooks, Herman Collinson, Vicky Mills, Roberta Olson, Carmen Pollard, Bert Wilson, and Jordan Yeltatzie, all from Skidegate, and Doug Edgars of Masset. Sandra Zacharias directed the initial fieldwork with the assistance of Geordie Howe and Barbara Stucki. Captain Gold of Skidegate provided valuable practical field assistance and guidance, and Alexander Mackie and Laurie Williamson helpful advice and encouragement. Parks Canada assisted with the dating of a number of radiocarbon samples and the Archaeology Branch of the Government of British Columbia and the Royal British Columbia Museum provided field equipment and laboratory facilities.

We thank Bob Powell for assistance in the field and for preparing pollen samples. We thank Dave Gillan for additional sample preparation. Resources from the Royal British Columbia Museum in part supported the study, and Rolf Mathewes thanks the Natural Sciences and Engineering Research Council of Canada for research support.

5
The Evolution of Endemic Species in Haida Gwaii

Tom Reimchen and Ashley Byun

Highly distinctive and geographically restricted plants and animals characterize the biota of islands. Such endemism results from a complex interplay of geographical, ecological, and evolutionary processes. One of the central tenets of island biogeography is that number of species is reduced compared with equivalent areas on the adjacent mainland, and that the extent of the deficiency is directly proportional to the distance from the mainland and inversely proportional to island size (MacArthur and Wilson 1967). Significant ecological consequences result from this deficiency because species experience reduced competition, which allows for ecological expansion into unoccupied niches. Consequently, island species often exhibit striking morphological and genetic differences from ancestral populations. Galapagos finches and Hawaiian honeycreepers are classic examples of such divergence. Because evolutionary rates can be rapid in such conditions of ecological release (Gingerich 1993), the morphological distinctness may represent geologically recent adaptations to novel habitats rather than long periods of isolation and gradual divergence.

One of the largest and most isolated archipelagos in western North America is Haida Gwaii, and similar to other islands, it exhibits a rich diversity of biologically unique plant and animal taxa. The prevalence of such endemics relative to adjacent continental regions led to an emerging view that areas on or near Haida Gwaii escaped glaciation and allowed survival of these relict forms when other coastal and continental regions were subject to glacial advances during the Pleistocene (Scudder 1989). However reasonable such a view, available geological evidence indicates that Haida Gwaii was subject to major ice cover with few prospects of ice-free areas other than mountaintops, which would not have supported diverse ecological communities (Sutherland-Brown and Nasmith 1962; Clague 1989). If true, this would suggest that the endemism in Haida Gwaii was derived during postglacial times (Holocene) rather than through extended periods of isolation. In this chapter, we consider the conflicting evidence for relictual versus Holocene origin of endemic animals in Haida Gwaii and summarize recent studies using genetic markers in mitochondrial DNA, which allow times of divergence or antiquity of populations to be estimated.

The endemism of biota in Haida Gwaii is taxonomically and ecologically diverse (Figure 5.1). It occurs in mosses (Schofield 1989), flowering plants (Calder and Taylor 1968), beetles (Kavanaugh 1992), fish (Moodie and Reimchen 1973), birds, and mammals (Foster 1965; Cowan 1989). In virtually all cases, endemics are differentiated from mainland forms to the level of subspecies or, rarely, full species. In this review, we will focus on seven endemic animals: the three-spined stickleback (*Gasterosteus aculeatus*), Dawson caribou (*Rangifer tarandus dawsoni*), black bear (*Ursus americanus carlottae*), marten (*Martes americana nesophila*), Haida short-tailed weasel (*Mustela erminea haidarum*), saw-whet owl (*Aegolius acadicus brooksi*), and ground beetles (*Nebria* spp.). We provide brief descriptions of the life history, distinguishing attributes from mainland source populations, evidence for adaptation, and results for molecular phylogenies for some of the endemics.

Endemic Taxa of Haida Gwaii

Three-spined Stickleback
This small fish is widespread in marine and freshwater habitats of northern latitudes and is extensively studied in ecological, behavioural, and evolutionary disciplines (Bell and Foster 1994). Marine stickleback are anadromous, entering freshwater streams each year for reproduction, and this has led to multiple invasions of freshwater lakes during the recession of ice and establishment of populations restricted to fresh water. Collections of the fish by multiple researchers from throughout Europe, Asia, and North America show evidence for high levels of morphological variability among freshwater populations, much of which is due to genetic differences (see Wootton 1984 for summary). It has become apparent that the sticklebacks from Haida Gwaii exhibit greater morphological variability among lakes than that found throughout the rest of the distribution of the species (Moodie and Reimchen 1973, 1976a; Reimchen 1994a). This extensive variability over such a small geographical area provides a model for evaluating the origin of endemic taxa in Haida Gwaii.

Surveys of 95 percent of all watersheds in Haida Gwaii (Reimchen 1992b, 1994b) have identified stickleback in 110 lakes, most of which occur on northeastern Graham Island, with the remainder in low-elevation lakes on both Graham and Moresby Islands. Collections of stickleback yielded geographically isolated populations with gigantism in body size (Moodie 1972), complete loss of bony armour (Reimchen 1980, 1984), diversity in body pigmentation, and breeding colour ranging from blue iridescence and crim-

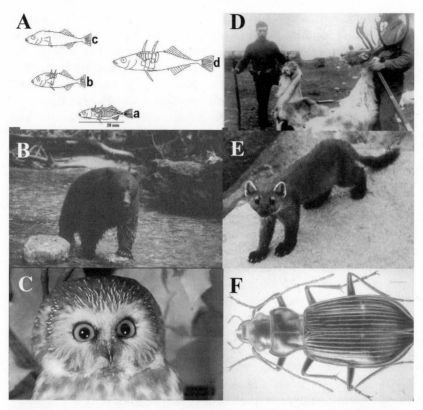

Figure 5.1 Representatives of endemic animals from Haida Gwaii: (A) Three-spined stickleback; (a) ancestral marine form, (b) typical stream and small lake form, (c) unarmoured forms of northeastern Graham Island, (d) giant stickleback from Drizzle Lake, Mayer Lake, Skidegate Lake, and Coates Lake. (B) Coastal black bear. (C) Saw-whet owl (courtesy Bristol Foster). (D) Last Dawson caribou (1908) seen from northern Graham Island (BC Archives F-00235). (E) Marten (courtesy Bristol Foster). (F) *Nebria*.

son displays to black forms (Moodie 1972; Reimchen 1989). Such large differences also occur over short distances within watersheds where genetic interchange among populations is possible (Reimchen et al. 1985).

The majority of highly divergent stickleback are found in the tea-coloured and low-productivity lakes of the Argonaut Plain. This high level of divergent body forms in Haida Gwaii stickleback was consistent with trends found in other endemic species and initially appeared to represent relict populations that diverged during long periods of isolation in ice-free conditions. There is, however, a striking congruence between morphological characteristics of the fish in each lake and ecological attributes of the habitat (Moodie and Reimchen 1976b). These and subsequent studies show strong support for the primary role of natural selection in shaping the characteristics of the divergent stickleback. Gigantism in body size, independently derived in six different populations, represents a defensive adaptation against gape-limited piscivores such as trout and diving birds (Moodie 1972; Reimchen 1988, 1991). Lateral bony plates on the fish vary extensively in number among populations and are tightly correlated with the presence or absence of predatory trout (Moodie and Reimchen 1976b). Variability in the defensive apparatus ranging from robust development of spines and bony armour to complete loss of spines and armour represents a functional adaptation to the relative proportions of puncturing, compression, and grappling predators in a given lake (Reimchen 1983, 1992a, 1994a). These predator groups correspond to trout, bird, and macroinvertebrate piscivores that forage, capture, and manipulate their prey in a distinctive manner, leading to different defences of the stickleback to each predator. The speed of evolutionary adaptation among these populations may be very high, as there is evidence for yearly and seasonal shifts in morphological traits that respond to yearly and seasonal shifts in predation regime (Reimchen 1995; Reimchen and Nosil 2004). This suggests that the morphological endemism in the Haida Gwaii populations could have developed postglacially without extended periods of isolation.

One of the most distinctive populations of stickleback in Haida Gwaii occurs at Rouge Pond on the Argonaut Plain. These fish are unarmoured and represent the most morphologically derived condition relative to the marine ancestral form (Reimchen 1984). The fish are also unusual in that most have a mucous layer on their body containing thousands of nonpathogenic dinoflagellates of unknown taxonomic affinity (Reimchen and Buckland-Nicks 1990). Recent studies demonstrate that the dinoflagellate has a particularly complex life cycle (Buckland-Nicks and Reimchen 1995) and represents a new species that is apparently restricted globally to a small region of the Argonaut Plain (Buckland-Nicks et al. 1997). The restricted distribution of this atypical dinoflagellate and its association with a highly divergent and unarmoured stickleback is suggestive of extended historical persistence and perhaps a relictual status of this stickleback population.

Molecular studies using mitochondrial DNA have been employed to investigate phylogenetic affinities or relatedness among populations and species (Avise 1994). Ideally, the extent of genetic divergence in the DNA can be used to determine whether endemic species from islands are ancient relictual lineages that survived in ice-free regions or whether they are closely related to mainland forms and therefore of postglacial origin. Two hypotheses for the evolution of Haida Gwaii stickleback are reasonable: (1) that freshwater populations such as the unarmoured stickleback at Rouge Pond and the giant stickleback at Mayer Lake and Drizzle Lake are relictual, from which one would predict major genetic differences among these endemic freshwater populations as well as a major separation between each of these

THREE-SPINED STICKLEBACK

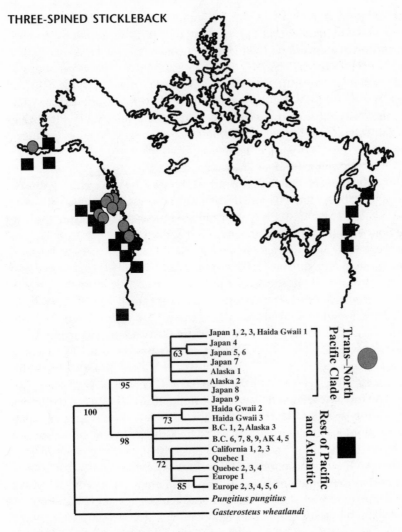

Figure 5.2 Molecular phylogeny of three-spined stickleback and North American geographical distribution of lineages.

populations and the ancestral marine populations; and (2) that freshwater populations are postglacially derived, from which one would predict a single major genetic lineage among all freshwater and marine populations.

Results from genetic studies (Gach and Reimchen 1989; O'Reilly et al. 1993; Orti et al. 1994; Deagle et al. 1996) demonstrate a complex and unanticipated history consistent with both of these hypotheses. Two highly divergent mitochondrial DNA lineages have been identified globally for marine and freshwater stickleback, and these lineages separated from a common ancestor near the beginning of the Pleistocene (Figure 5.2). The Euro–North

American lineage is common and widespread and is found in marine and freshwater habitats around Europe, eastern North America, and western North America, including California, Vancouver Island, Alaska, and most lakes in Haida Gwaii. The latter includes marine ancestral populations as well as highly derived freshwater populations such as the spine-deficient form at Boulton Lake and the giant forms at Mayer Lake and Drizzle Lake. This is consistent with the second hypothesis, that these endemic stickleback in Haida Gwaii are not relicts but rather originated from marine ancestors in postglacial (Holocene) periods.

The second mitochondrial lineage identified from the global survey, referred to as the Japanese lineage on the trans–North Pacific clade (Johnson and Taylor 2004), is much more restricted but predominates in Japan and in several localities in Alaska. It is also found in Haida Gwaii lakes, primarily in the northeastern corner of Graham Island and usually in the same lakes as the widely distributed lineage (Figure 5.3). Frequencies of this more restricted lineage are highly variable in Haida Gwaii lakes, with the higher frequencies in localities where stickleback are most dissimilar morphologically to marine ancestral forms. The highest frequency of the Japanese lineage (100 percent) is found in Rouge Pond, where the stickleback are the most divergent from marine ancestors and show the strange association with dinoflagellates. While there is potential for recent transoceanic dispersal of stickleback from Japan (Deagle et al. 1996), the apparent absence of the Japanese lineage in marine waters surrounding Haida Gwaii, combined with the prevalence of this lineage in the most morphologically divergent stickleback populations, suggests that these comprise older and possibly relictual populations, results consistent with the first hypothesis. Recent investigations also show the Japanese lineage on Vancouver Island, but these populations do not exhibit any morphological divergence (Johnson and Taylor 2004).

However, the ponds and lakes containing the most divergent stickleback populations are underlain by glacial outwash gravels (Sutherland-Brown 1968) and are clearly postglacial in origin (Warner 1984). Consequently, the current prevalence of the Japanese lineage in ponds and lakes on the northeastern corner of the Argonaut Plain would suggest early postglacial colonization from adjacent freshwater habitats that persisted during late Pleistocene. These habitats, including large freshwater lakes, occurred on the now submerged continental shelf separating Haida Gwaii from the mainland (Josenhans et al. 1993; Chapter 1) and could have allowed early postglacial colonization by a relictual lineage of the Argonaut Plain.

Dawson Caribou

One of the most interesting endemics known to Haida Gwaii is the now extinct Dawson caribou. The last caribou ever seen on the islands (a herd consisting of two bulls and a cow near Naden Harbour) were shot in 1908

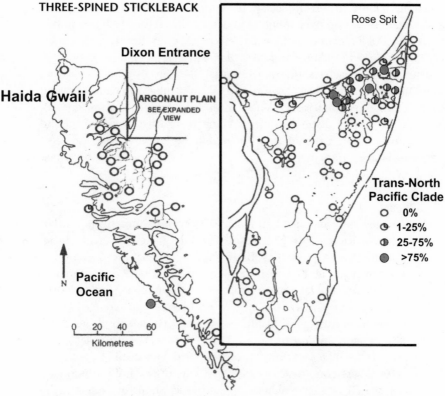

Figure 5.3 Haida Gwaii distribution of two divergent molecular lineages in stickleback.

and the species is believed to have become extinct shortly thereafter (Cowan and Guiget 1978; Banfield 1961). The 1908 specimens of Dawson caribou were small in stature. The antlers on the males were poorly developed and remarkably irregular, while the females lacked antlers altogether, a condition atypical for caribou (Cowan and Guiget 1978). Fossil evidence indicates that Haida Gwaii was inhabited by caribou at least 5500 years BP (Chapters 6 and 13), and there is recent evidence for interglacial presence based on an antler dated at > 40,000 BP (R.W. Mathewes, personal communication). The large diameter and length of these fossil caribou bones indicate close affinity to large-bodied woodland or mountain caribou on the mainland, suggesting that the small stature of the Dawson caribou is of recent origin and not relictual.

Many of the Dawson caribou's divergent characteristics, such as small stature and reduced antlers, are typical of insular ungulates (Foster 1965). This is clearly illustrated by the decrease in body size and reduction in antler size of black-tailed deer introduced to Haida Gwaii in the late 1800s. These morphological changes have been attributed to a variety of factors, including poor nutrition and lack of predators (Foster 1965) and is possibly an adaptation for improved mobility in dense forest (Lister 1993). Both Foster (1965) and Banfield (1961) considered the Dawson caribou to be a postglacial colonist of Haida Gwaii rather than a glacial relict.

Byun (1998) extracted short mitochondrial DNA (mtDNA) fragments from four museum specimens of Dawson caribou for comparison with mainland caribou. Based on the base sequences from these fragments, Dawson caribou did not have a distinctive mtDNA lineage relative to woodland and mountain caribou on the adjacent mainland. Such results based on short fragment lengths are tentative, but these suggest that the Dawson caribou was a postglacial colonist of Haida Gwaii (Byun et al. 2002).

Black Bear

It has been generally assumed that black bears persisted in refugia south of the Cordilleran Ice Sheet in North America during the Wisconsin glacial advance (Kurtén and Anderson 1980). From these refugia, they recolonized the Pacific Northwest and its offshore islands by 12,000 BP and ultimately differentiated into the various subspecies in this region. Across North America, sixteen subspecies of black bear have been recognized (Hall 1981), seven of which occur in the Pacific Northwest. These subspecies differ principally in skull and tooth morphology. The Haida Gwaii black bear (*U. americanus carlottae*) was originally described as a distinct species by Osgood (1901) based on its robust skull, heavy dentition, and exceptionally large body size. It was later reduced to subspecies status but remains the most morphologically distinct of all coastal bears and the largest black bear in North America.

Cowan and Guiget (1978) and Foster (1965) suggested that the Haida Gwaii bear was a glacial relict, having developed heavy molars and a massive skull in response to foraging on marine resources over long periods of isolation from mainland bears. Given the rapid evolutionary rates observed in many Quaternary mammals (Gingerich 1993), however, the adaptations observed in the Haida Gwaii black bear may have been derived following early postglacial colonization of the islands.

To determine whether Haida Gwaii bears are glacial relicts or recently separated from mainland bears, we undertook an examination of mitochondrial DNA from black bears of western North America. Earlier genetic studies of interior continental black bears (Cronin et al. 1991) suggested that these bears were represented by a single and widespread genetic lineage. If Haida Gwaii black bears are glacial relicts that diverged from other black bears prior to the Fraser Glaciation, then they should be genetically distinct.

Our results are only partially consistent with this hypothesis. Phylogenetic analyses of 719 base pairs of the mtDNA clearly identified two major lineages in black bear, which we distinguish as continental and coastal (Byun et al. 1997). The continental lineage includes black bears from locations as diverse as Alaska, Alberta, Montana, and Pennsylvania, while the coastal lineage comprises all of the coastal subspecies, including the Haida Gwaii bear, the Kermode bear of the mainland coast, and the Vancouver Island black bear (Figure 5.4). The average sequence divergence within these coastal

BLACK BEAR

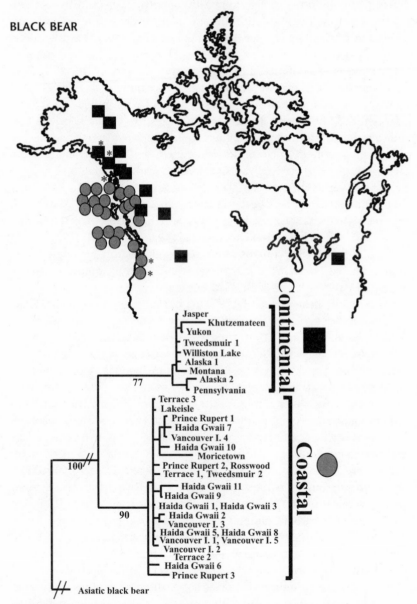

Figure 5.4 Molecular phylogeny of black bear and geographical distribution of lineages.

lineages is low (0.1 percent), suggesting that diversification of the various subspecies in each lineage occurred during the Holocene. In contrast, the average sequence divergence between coastal and continental lineages was high (3.6 percent). Using the standard rate of change for vertebrate mtDNA of 2 percent per million years (Brown 1985), these two lineages apparently diverged 1.8 million years ago. Application of other rate estimates, including those for silent base substitutions and a rate calibrated from *Ursus* subfossils, both yielded divergence times in the range of 360,000 to 1.8 million years ago.

The close genetic affinity of the Haida Gwaii black bear with those from the mainland and Vancouver Island suggests that these bears shared a common ancestor in the early Holocene. Consequently the unique and highly divergent morphology of Haida Gwaii bears relative to the Kermode bear and to the Vancouver Island bear must be postglacially derived and not the product of long-term isolation. Recently discovered skeletal remains from three bears on northwestern Vancouver Island (carbon-dated to 10,000 BP) suggest that early Holocene colonists to Vancouver Island were significantly larger than modern black bears on both Vancouver Island and adjacent continental regions (Nagorsen et al. 1995). If true, then large body size, currently observed in the Haida Gwaii black bear, may be ancestral among the coastal subspecies, perhaps as a foraging adaptation for intertidal resources that currently predominate and would have predominated in the periglacial habitats of the late Pleistocene.

It is generally believed that black bears in the Pacific Northwest are derived from southern Washington (Kurtén and Anderson 1980). Northern dispersal from Washington probably occurred during the late glacial and early Holocene on newly deglaciated landscapes, although somewhat impeded by changing sea levels on the coast and instability of ecosystems at the edge of retreating glaciers. Occurrence of the two highly divergent mtDNA lineages differentiating coastal bears from continental bears contradicts the supposition that black bears in the Pacific Northwest are derived from a single southern refugial population. The divergent lineage restricted to Haida Gwaii, Vancouver Island, and coastal regions of mainland British Columbia suggests that these areas were colonized by the same source population, but one different from the bears that recolonized deglaciated areas on the continent. The current distribution of mtDNA lineages in coastal British Columbia can be most readily interpreted if one assumes that the source population of coastal bears had equal access to Haida Gwaii, the coastal mainland, and Vancouver Island prior to the rise in sea levels.

Two major glacial refugia in the Pacific Northwest are currently recognized, one south of the ice front in Washington and a second in unglaciated parts of Alaska and the Yukon (Pielou 1992). Various lines of evidence suggest that a third mid-coastal glacial refugium persisted on the now submerged continental shelf separating Haida Gwaii from the mainland. Cores taken midway between Haida Gwaii and the mainland indicate that large portions of Hecate Strait were terrestrial and ice-free during the Fraser Glaciation (see Josenhans et al. 1993; Barrie et al. 1993; Josenhans et al. 1995). The coastal plain would have connected Haida Gwaii to the mainland and may have extended far enough south along the mainland to allow access along the coast to Vancouver Island. The distribution of the coastal mtDNA lineage can be explained if the black bear persisted in the Hecate refugium and, during the early stages of deglaciation, recolonized Haida Gwaii, the coastal mainland, and Vancouver Island. Recent molecular studies (Stone and Cook 2000) have also identified the coastal lineage in southeastern Alaska, immediately north of Haida Gwaii, consistent with our suggestions. The coastal lineage is rare further inland, probably since movement into the interior of British Columbia would have been impeded by Cordilleran ice. The rapid rise in sea level in early postglacial times would have further isolated the mainland from Vancouver Island and Haida Gwaii, resulting in the present lineage distribution. The continental lineage, which likely resided south of the Cordilleran Ice Sheet, repopulated the interior regions more effectively due to greater accessibility to the mid-continental corridor, which became more habitable by the Holocene (Pielou 1992). Some black bear populations in interior British Columbia contain both lineages and may represent recent easterly dispersal of the coastal lineage and a westerly or northerly dispersal of the continental lineage (see Stone and Cook 2000).

The early to mid-Pleistocene split between the two black bear mtDNA lineages indicates that they have persisted through multiple glacial and interglacial periods. This is surprising given the numerous population bottlenecks and opportunities for lineage sorting that would occur in a large mammal with low population size (see Avise 1994). These two lineages could have been maintained if they had been reproductively isolated, but there is no evidence to suggest any reproductive barriers. These lineages could also have persisted if they had been geographically isolated for the past 360,000 years. It is not clear how this could have occurred. Given the cyclic pattern of glaciations, the coastal lineage could have been isolated from the continental lineage by surviving in coastal refugia during glacial advances and in Haida Gwaii during interglacials. If true, this would make the Haida Gwaii black bear the ancestral form for the recolonization of the coastal Pacific Northwest (Byun et al. 1997).

Marten

Based on fossil evidence, marten likely crossed to North America from Eurasia via the Bering land bridge during the mid to late Pleistocene (Anderson 1994). These early colonists spread eastward and were subsequently isolated in eastern North America by the Laurentide Ice Sheet. Following retreat of the glaciers, eastern marten expanded westward but were largely excluded from the Pacific Northwest by a second group of marten, which had independently colonized this region from Eurasia (Anderson 1994; see, however, Stone and Cook 2002). These two colonizing groups are currently recognized as morphotypes *caurina* and *americana*. They are differentiated on the basis of skull characteristics, including shape of the auditory bullae and relative size of the upper molar teeth (Grinnell and Dixon 1926; Hagmeier 1961). *Caurina* occurs in western North America and has greater morphological affinity to a Eurasian ancestor than does the eastern *americana*. Hagmeier (1955) suggested that both morphotypes persisted during the late Pleistocene, with *caurina* isolated from *americana* in west coast refugia.

There are seven subspecies currently recognized within each of the two morphotypes. These subspecies, differentiated by variations in pelage colour, body size, and skull shape, are believed to have originated postglacially (Hagmeier 1955; Foster 1965). Of all the subspecies in North America, the Haida Gwaii marten (*Martes americana nesophila*) is the most distinct. It is the largest marten in North America and is characterized by thick nasal bones, robust molar teeth, orange breast patch, and marked sexual dimorphism (Foster 1965; Giannico and Nagorsen 1989). Both Hagmeier (1955) and Foster (1965) suggest that these characteristics are too distinct to have evolved in postglacial times, suggesting that these morphological features evolved during extended isolation in a refugium in Haida Gwaii.

Phylogenetic analyses of a 311-base-pair fragment of the cytochrome b gene indicate the presence of two distinct marten mtDNA lineages in the Pacific Northwest (Figure 5.5). The coastal lineage was found exclusively in Haida Gwaii and on Vancouver Island while the continental lineage was found on mainland British Columbia and Newfoundland. An average sequence divergence within the coastal lineage of 0.8 percent suggests that the morphological features characterizing both the Haida Gwaii and Vancouver Island marten may have evolved during postglacial times. Similarly, marten of mainland British Columbia exhibit relatively low sequence divergence (0.6 percent) for this molecular marker, again implying that the morphological differences distinguishing each of these continental subspecies evolved within the last 12,000 years.

The average sequence divergence of 1.8 percent between these mtDNA lineages suggests that the continental martens of British Columbia and Newfoundland diverged from marten in Haida Gwaii and on Vancouver Island prior to the Wisconsin glaciation. These results suggest that the biogeographical history of marten in the Pacific Northwest is more complex than previously thought. More recent molecular data on marten from a broader region of the Pacific Northwest (Small et al. 2003) confirm our results of two distinctive lineages. The coastal lineage that we identified in

MARTEN

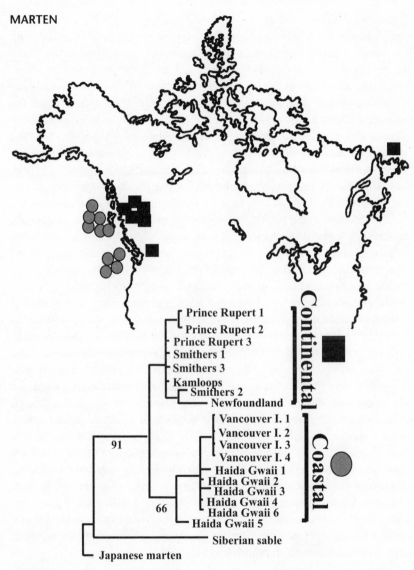

Figure 5.5 Molecular phylogeny of marten and geographical distribution of lineages.

Haida Gwaii and Vancouver Island was also found on Admiralty Island and Kuiu Island in southeastern Alaska. While this lineage was not found on the Alaskan mainland, it was detected in Oregon and southern Montana. Given the broadly similar phylogeographic pattern observed in black bear, the distribution of coastal and continental marten lineages is largely consistent with postglacial recolonization of the Pacific Northwest from both continental and coastal refugia.

Haida Short-tailed Weasel

The short-tailed weasel first appeared in North America from Eurasia during the mid-Pleistocene and spread over Canada and northern United States (Kurtén and Anderson 1980). During the last glacial advance, the short-tailed weasel appears to have persisted both north and south of the Cordilleran Ice Sheet (Kurtén and Anderson 1980). From these refugia, they are believed to have recolonized the Pacific Northwest, undergoing extensive morphological diversification to produce the twenty subspecies identified in North America (Hall 1981). The Haida short-tailed weasel is the most morphologically distinct of all short-tailed weasels, with large body size and proportional difference in the breadth and depth of the rostrum (Cowan and Guiget 1978; Foster 1965; Eger 1990). Like the black bear and marten, the Haida short-tailed weasel is believed to be from a coastal glacial refugium that was distinct from the continental refugia that occurred north and south of the ice sheet (Foster 1965). Alternatively, the Haida short-tailed weasel may not be relictual but part of the Holocene dispersal and differentiation that occurred among many subspecies on the continent.

Mitochondrial DNA was extracted from museum skins of short-tailed weasels collected throughout their North American distribution (Byun 1998). Two predictions are considered. If Haida short-tailed weasels are relictual, then three major lineages would be expected to exist in northwestern North America, representing each of the isolated refugial populations. Alternatively, if Haida short-tailed weasels are recent and derived only from the two major refugia, then only two molecular lineages should occur. Although the data are limited by the short fragment length of DNA and small number of specimens, results from the mtDNA are more consistent with the first hypothesis, as they reveal a Beringian and southern lineage as expected but also a unique lineage for Haida short-tailed weasels, indicating that the attributes of the Haida short-tailed weasel are relictual (Figure 5.6). In fact, phylogenetic reconstructions demonstrate that the Haida weasels may constitute the source populations for postglacial recolonization of British Columbia (Byun 1998), rather than weasels from south of the ice front as previously assumed (Kurtén and Anderson 1980).

Saw-whet Owl

Because of the lack of fossil evidence, little is known about the distribution of various owl species during Wisconsin glaciation (Fedduccia 1996). There is no direct information regarding the postglacial source for the saw-whet owl. Given their high dependence on trees for nesting sites, however, they are considered unlikely to have persisted in the tundra regions north of the Cordilleran Ice Sheet and are most likely to have recolonized northern North America from southern refugia. There are two subspecies of saw-whet owl in North America. One subspecies is found on the continent while the other

SHORT-TAILED WEASEL

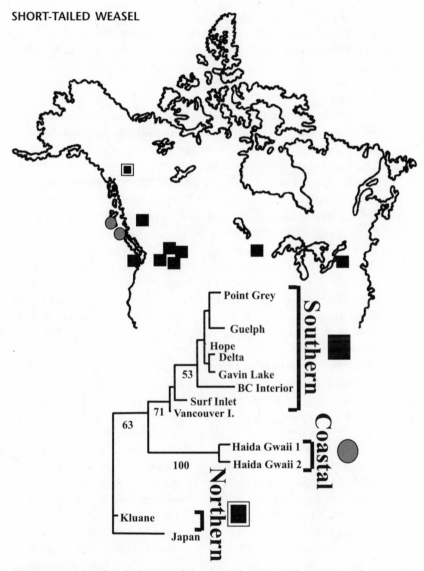

Figure 5.6 Molecular phylogeny of short-tailed weasel and geographical distribution of lineages.

is found in Haida Gwaii. The Haida Gwaii saw-whet owl (*Aegolius acadicus brooksi*) was first described by Fleming in 1916 as a dark, slightly larger race, although Brooks and Swarth (1925) regarded the Haida Gwaii owl to be a distinct insular species. The darker feathers and larger body that characterize the Haida Gwaii owl are typical for insular avifauna (Murphy 1938; Foster 1965) and are considered to have evolved in situ in response to local selective regimes.

Phylogenetic analyses of a 241-base-pair fragment of cytochrome b amplified from DNA isolated from preserved skins indicated little genetic differentiation between the Haida Gwaii saw-whet owl and owls from across Canada.

Ground Beetles

Ground beetles of the *Nebria gregaria* group are distributed in the Pacific Northwest from Haida Gwaii to the Aleutians. Haida Gwaii is inhabited by three species of *Nebria,* one that is restricted to cobble beaches on Graham Island, a second found in similar habitats on Moresby Island, and a third found only in alpine locations on Graham and Moresby Islands and on a mountaintop north of Prince Rupert, BC. These beetles are thought to have survived in ice-free habitats in Haida Gwaii during the Pleistocene, during which their morphological differences developed (Kavanaugh 1992). Their closest relatives occupy beaches on the Alaskan coastline.

There are two lines of evidence that suggest relictual status of these beetles in Haida Gwaii. First, the beetles are flightless and have limited dispersal ability; second, *Nebria* occur across North America and are highly conserved morphologically, suggesting that the differences among Haida Gwaii beetles are unlikely to be of recent origin (Kavanaugh 1992). There are, however, alternate interpretations for the distribution and differentiation of Haida Gwaii *Nebria,* including postglacial colonization and subsequent diversification. The beetles are common on high intertidal and supratidal habitats, including drift logs. Given the abundance of large woody debris in coastal waters and the prevalence of such drift logs in virtually all shorelines in Haida Gwaii (personal observation), it seems plausible that these beetles could have colonized these habitats in this manner. Furthermore, the morphological traits that differentiate the three *Nebria* species in Haida Gwaii are subtle shape differences in the body (Kavanaugh 1992), raising the potential that these represent recent ecological adaptations to the distinctive habitats that the beetles encountered upon colonizing the archipelago.

To differentiate between relictual and recent status, analyses were undertaken (Clarke 1998) of the mtDNA sequence of *Nebria* from Haida Gwaii and from related species on the mainland. One predicts the occurrence of three distinct lineages if the three species are relictual but only a single lineage if the beetles colonized and differentiated postglacially. Results show high genetic similarity among the Haida Gwaii species and suggest that *Nebria* probably colonized the islands and differentiated there during postglacial times (Clarke et al. 2001).

Discussion and Conclusions

Morphological and molecular examination of the major endemic species yields two major results:

1 The morphological features characterizing the endemic forms of highly divergent stickleback, dwarf Dawson caribou, large black bear and marten, dark saw-whet owls, and *Nebria* ground beetles appear to have been derived postglacially. Where more detailed investigations were made on endemics such as the Haida Gwaii stickleback, it is evident that morphological differentiation is not the result of isolation per se but rather due to natural selection and adaptation to the distinct ecological habitats found in the archipelago.

2 Genetic data of a mid-Pleistocene split of vertebrate taxa and geographic distribution of the mitochondrial lineages of stickleback, black bear, marten, and short-tailed weasel cumulatively suggest that a refugium existed on the continental shelf off the central coast of British Columbia. Genetic data are consistent with geological and stratigraphic data demonstrating that the continental shelf separating Haida Gwaii from the mainland contained a large ice-free area during the glacial maximum (Josenhans et al. 1993, 1995; Chapter 1). The assemblage of taxa that might have persisted here during the last glaciation, including top-level carnivores such as bear and marten, suggests that this refugium was ecologically productive and likely an important source area for the postglacial recolonization of northwestern North America. Recent cave discoveries in southern Haida Gwaii show both black bear and brown bear fossil material, with preliminary dates as old as 11,500 BP and 14,000 BP, respectively (Chapter 6). This unambiguous evidence of two bear species in Haida Gwaii during the early Holocene is concordant with our interpretation based on molecular data.

If the coastal refugium was a major source area that influenced the phylogeographic distributions of these endemics, then other species in the Pacific Northwest should have been affected similarly. There are additional data to suggest that this is the case. Molecular studies of brown bear (*Ursus arctos*) show two divergent lineages, one found throughout Europe, Asia, and North America and a second lineage largely restricted to Admiralty, Baranof, and Chicagof Islands in Alaska immediately north of Haida Gwaii (Talbot and Shields 1996). Protein analyses of sockeye salmon have also suggested that three genetic lineages exist in northwestern North America that may correspond to northern, southern, and coastal refugia (Wood et al. 1994).

In addition to these molecular studies, data from other disciplines point to similar conclusions. There are currently eighteen disjunct liverworts, twelve disjunct mosses, and nine vascular plants found only in the Pacific Northwest. In addition, seven disjunct bryophytes in North America are found only in Haida Gwaii. The strong affinity of many of these disjunct bryophytes with bryophytes found in western Europe or southeastern Asia suggests that they are relicts of formerly more widespread species, possibly dating back to the Tertiary Period (over 2.5 million years old). The persistence of these suspected relicts and disjuncts in Haida Gwaii is considered evidence for continuity during multiple Pleistocene glacial advances (Calder and Taylor 1968; Ogilvie and Roemer 1984; Schofield 1989). Perhaps even more compelling is evidence of early deglaciation on the east coast of Graham Island near 16,000 BP, followed by rapid recolonization of a plant community. Because of the absence of any known source areas in the region at this time of glacial maximum, it was suggested by Warner et al. (1982) that these plants dispersed from well-established plant communities in a nearby coastal refugium.

There are alternate interpretations of our molecular data. It is possible that the rare mitochondrial lineage detected in the unarmoured stickleback is not relictual but rather a second postglacial colonizing event. This is possible because the rare lineage was detected in samples of stickleback from the mid-Pacific, raising the possibility of recent colonization (Deagle et al. 1996). However, the combination of this lineage in headwater lakes on the northeastern corner of the Argonaut Plain and the highly derived morphology of the fish is suggestive of extended isolation. The presence of divergent mtDNA lineages in Haida Gwaii in black bear, marten, and short-tailed weasel might be solely due to northward dispersal from southern populations (Demboski et al. 1999). If this had occurred, the dispersal would have to have occurred during the early stages of deglaciation, prior to sea level rises. Massive glacial lakes (Lake Missoula and Lake Columbia) (Pielou 1992), high sea levels, and large rivers would have severely impeded northward movement, particularly for small-bodied and uncommon apex predators such as marten and weasel. On the coast, eustatic and isostatic changes resulted in flooding of the Puget Lowland about 11,500 to 13,500 BP (Easterbrook 1992). From about 13,000 BP to 9000 BP, sea levels rose along the eastern shores of Haida Gwaii, isolating Haida Gwaii from the mainland (Josenhans et al. 1995; Chapter 2). These changes were exacerbated by tilting of tectonic plates that effectively increased sea levels along the coastal mainland while decreasing sea levels further west (Chapter 1). Furthermore, the divergent lineages of black bear, marten, and short-tailed weasel in Haida Gwaii suggest that these lineages dispersed from nearby source populations and not from southern refugia over 600 kilometres away (see Byun et al. 1999 for a review of arguments).

The current most plausible interpretation for the high similarity of molecular lineages in Haida Gwaii, Vancouver Island, and coastal British Columbia and major differences from interior continental lineages is persistence of a complex ecosystem on the continental shelf that provided the source populations for the postglacial recolonization of the Pacific

Northwest during the Holocene. Subsequent morphological differentiation among colonists to Haida Gwaii, the coastal mainland, and Vancouver Island probably comprises ecological adaptation to the distinctive selective regimes of each region in the Pacific Northwest.

6
History of the Vertebrate Fauna in Haida Gwaii
Rebecca J. Wigen

This chapter summarizes the current information available on the history of the vertebrates of Haida Gwaii and adjacent southeastern Alaska. There has been a long debate about the possible existence of a glacial refugium in Haida Gwaii and/or the adjacent British Columbia and Alaska coasts (Heusser 1989). Recent evidence about the sea level history of the Haida Gwaii region (Chapter 2), the presence of extensive paleontological deposits in southeastern Alaska, genetic work done on modern Haida Gwaii vertebrates (Chapter 5), pollen deposits at Cape Ball, and an early date on a fossil bear from K1 Cave have added new support to the idea of a refugium in the area (Heusser 1989; Fladmark 1989; Ramsey et al. 2004).

Fossil data on the history of the vertebrate fauna of Haida Gwaii and adjacent areas come from two sources, paleontological and archaeological sites. There are a few scattered vertebrate paleontological finds from Haida Gwaii and two cave sites providing vertebrate material from the early postglacial period (Ramsey et al. 2004; Wigen 2003a, 2003c). Some very important sites in caves are now being investigated in southeastern Alaska (Dixon et al. 1997; Heaton 1995a, 1995b; Heaton et al. 1996). These caves span the preglacial, glacial, and early postglacial time periods. Extensive vertebrate fauna have been recovered, with more than 100 radiocarbon dates (Heaton and Grady 2003). They are close enough to Haida Gwaii to be of significance, especially regarding the possibility of glacial refuges.

The bulk of the vertebrate faunal record from Haida Gwaii comes from postglacial archaeological sites, with a modest amount from paleontological sources. The paleontological deposits in caves from Haida Gwaii and southeastern Alaska are likely mostly the result of accidental deaths (i.e., falling into the caves), deaths while using the caves as den sites (particularly in the case of the bears, arctic foxes, and otters), or food remains deposited by the den residents (mainly fish and bird remains from the foxes and otters). The vertebrate remains in the archaeological sites are mainly the result of collection by humans occupying the sites. These data are the best sources of direct information on the past vertebrates in Haida Gwaii, despite the small sample sizes and human and environmental filtering.

I have divided the last 40,000 years into several periods. These periods are fairly broad, based on a combination of glacial and climatological events. All ages are given in radiocarbon years before present (BP). A summary of the material is shown in Table 6.1.

Preglacial, Up to 24,000 BP

Only a single definite sample of preglacial vertebrate remains has been recovered from Haida Gwaii. A fragment of robust caribou antler from White Creek on northern Graham Island has been radiocarbon-dated at > 40,000 BP (R.W. Mathewes, personal communication), indicating a pre–Fraser Glaciation presence in Haida Gwaii for this ungulate. In addition, there is one partially documented find of either mammoth or mastodon remains (Dalzell 1968:244-245). These bones were reported found at Sandspit in 1907 and were put on display in Vancouver, but their current whereabouts are unknown. Tusks recovered were described as being 18 feet long and nearly straight. This suggests that the bones were American mastodon (*Mammut americanum*), but this cannot be considered conclusive. If these tusks are mastodon, they would represent one of few occurrences on the British Columbia coast (Harington 1975:907, table 1a). No age is available, but a preglacial origin is possible.

There are several paleontological sites from this period in the region, predominantly from the Alexander Archipelago of southeastern Alaska, where Heaton (Dixon et al. 1997; Heaton and Grady 2003) has excavated a series of karst caves with extensive bone deposits. Dated remains from On Your Knees Cave (49-PET-408) on Prince of Wales Island include brown bear (4 dates), black bear (15 dates), caribou (3 dates), hoary marmot (5 dates), harbour seal (2 dates), arctic fox (4 dates), large puffin (2 dates), oldsquaw (1 date), and a bovid, possibly saiga (2 dates) (Heaton and Grady 2003). In addition, one ringed seal element is dated at 24,150 ± 490 BP, right on the boundary of this time period. Also recovered from this cave and likely of similar age are red fox, heather vole, and brown lemming. A single marmot element, possibly hoary marmot, was recovered from Devil's Canopy Cave (49-PET-221), also on Prince of Wales Island, which is beyond the limit of radiocarbon dating, indicating that it is older than 44,500 BP (Heaton and Grady 2003). Isotopic analysis of black bear bone collagen from On Your Knees Cave indicates a terrestrial diet, while the brown bear from this time appears to have had a particularly large marine component in its diet (Heaton 1995b:96). It is not known whether many of the southeastern Alaskan species were present in Haida Gwaii during this period, but they do give an idea of possible habitats in the broader area.

Table 6.1

Summary of taxa with confirmed dates recovered from paleontological and archaeological sites in southeastern Alaska and Haida Gwaii, by time periods

	Preglacial to 24,000 BP		Glacial 24,000 to 13,500 BP		Early postglacial 13,500 to 9000 BP		Postglacial 9000 to 4000 BP		Recent 4000 to present	
	SE Alaska	Haida Gwaii	SE Alaska	Haida Gwaii	SE Alaska	Haida Gwaii	SE Alaska	Haida Gwaii	SE Alaska	Haida Gwaii
Mammals										
Beaver (*Castor canadensis*)							A (< 8200)			C
Porcupine (*Erethizon dorsatum*)							P (1 date)			
Heather vole (*Phenacomys intermedius*)	P									
Brown lemming (*Lemmus sibiricus*)	P									
Hoary marmot (*Marmota caligata*)	P (6 dates)		P (1 date)						C	
River otter (*Lontra canadensis*)					P (1 date)	A (9440)	P	A (6150-4990)	C	A, C
Sea otter (*Enhydra lutris*)						A (9440)		A (5000-3000)	C	A, C
Wolverine (*Gulo gulo*)					P				C	
Marten (*Martes americana*)									C	A, C
Harbour seal (*Phoca vitulina*)	P (3 dates)					A (9440)		A (6150-4990)	C	A, C

Taxon								
Ringed seal (*Phoca hispida*)	P (28 dates)							
Northern sea lion (*Eumetopias jubatus*)	P (1 date)			A (9440)	A (< 8200)		C	A, C
Dolphin (Delphinidae)	P (2 dates)					A (6150-4990)	C	A, C
Pacific white-sided dolphin (*Lagenorhynchus obliquidens*)							C	A, C
Whale (Cetacea)					P	A (5000-3000)	C	A, C
Domestic dog (*Canis familiaris*)						A (6150-4990)	C	P, A, C
Red fox (*Vulpes vulpes*)	P		P (1 date)					
Arctic fox (*Alopex lagopus*)	P (4 dates)		P (2 dates)					
Brown bear (*Ursus arctos*)	P (4 dates)	P (14,500)	P (9 dates)	P (3 dates), A (7205)			C	
Black bear (*Ursus americanus*)	P (15 dates)		P (15 dates)	P (16 dates), A (9440)	P (5 dates), A (6415)	A (6150-4990)	C	A, C
Mastodon (*Mammut americanus*)?	P?			P?				
Bovid – *Saiga*? (Bovidae – cf. *Saiga tatarica*?)	P (2 dates)							
Cervid (Cervidae)	P (2 dates)			P (11,005)	A (< 8200)		C	
Caribou (*Rangifer tarandus*)	P (2 dates)	P (3 dates) P (> 40,000)			P (2 dates)	A (6150-4990)		A, C
Mule deer (*Odocoileus hemionus*)				P (6 dates), A (8108)		A (6150-4990)	C	
Large land mammal						A (9010-8500)		

Table 6.1

	Preglacial to 24,000 BP		Glacial 24,000 to 13,500 BP		Early postglacial 13,500 to 9000 BP		Postglacial 9000 to 4000 BP		Recent 4000 to present	
	SE Alaska	Haida Gwaii	SE Alaska	Haida Gwaii	SE Alaska	Haida Gwaii	SE Alaska	Haida Gwaii	SE Alaska	Haida Gwaii
Birds										
Albatross cf. short-tailed (*Phoebastria* cf. *albatrus*)						A (9440)				A
Geese (Anatidae)									C	A, C
Ducks (Anatidae)								A (6150–4990)	C	A, C
Canada goose (*Branta canadensis*)								A (6150–4990)	C	A, C
Snow goose (*Chen caerulescens*)						A (9440)			C	C
Oldsquaw (*Clangula hyemalis*)	P (1 date)								C	C
White-winged scoter (*Melanitta fusca*)			P				P (1 date)		C	A, C
Loons (*Gavia* sp.)							A (<8200)		C	A, C
Common loon (*Gavia immer*)								A (6150–4990)	C	A, C
Grebe (Podicipedidae)							A (<8200)		C	A, C

Species					
Red-necked grebe (*Podiceps grisegena*)		A (9440)		C	A, C
Cormorant (Phalacrocoracidae)		A (< 8200)		C	A, C
Double-crested cormorant (*Phalacrocorax auritus*)		A (9440)		C	A, C
Pelagic cormorant (*Phalacrocorax pelagicus*)			A (6150-4990)	C	A, C
Peregrine falcon (*Falco peregrinus*)				C	A, C
Ptarmigans (*Lagopus* sp.)				C	
Gulls (Laridae)				C	A, C
Alcids (Alcidae)		A (9440)	A (9010-8500)	C	A, C
Large puffin (*Fratercula*)	P (2 dates)				
Cassin's auklet (*Ptychoramphus aleuticus*)				C	A, C
Common murre (*Uria aalge*)	P (2 dates)	A (9440)		C	A, C
Tufted puffin (*Fratercula cirrhata*)				C	A, C
Pigeon guillemot (*Cepphus columba*)		A (9440)		C	A, C
Rhinoceros auklet (*Cerorhinca monocerata*)		A (9440)		C	A, C
Raven (*Corvus corax*)		A (9440)	A (5000-3000)	C	A, C
Songbirds (Passeriformes)		A (9440)		C	A, C

▼ *Table 6.1*

	Preglacial to 24,000 BP		Glacial 24,000 to 13,500 BP		Early postglacial 13,500 to 9000 BP		Postglacial 9000 to 4000 BP		Recent 4000 to present	
	SE Alaska	Haida Gwaii	SE Alaska	Haida Gwaii	SE Alaska	Haida Gwaii	SE Alaska	Haida Gwaii	SE Alaska	Haida Gwaii
Fish										
Fishes (Pisces)							P (2 dates)		C	A, C
Dogfish (*Squalus acanthias*)						A (9440)		A (9010-8500)	C	A, C
Skate (Rajidae)						A (9440)		A (6150-4990)	C	A, C
Herring (*Clupea harengus*)						A (9440)		A (9010-8500)	C	A, C
Salmon (*Oncorhynchus* sp.)						P (2 dates), A (9440)		A (9010-8500)	C	A, C
Rockfish (*Sebastes* sp.)						A (9440)	A (< 8200)	A (9010-8500)	C	A, C
Tomcod (*Microgadus proximus*)								A (9010-8500)	C	A, C
Pacific cod (*Gadus macrocephalus*)							A (< 8200)	A (6150-4990)	C	A, C
Greenling (*Hexagrammos* sp.)						A (9440)	A (< 8200)	A (9010-8500)	C	A, C
Lingcod (*Ophiodon elongatus*)						A (9440)		A? (9010-8500)	C	A, C
Jack mackerel (*Trachurus symmetricus*)									C?	A, C?
Striped seaperch (*Embiotoca lateralis*)						A (9440)		A (6150-4990)	C	A, C

Prickleback (Stichaeidae)				A (9010-8500)		
Sculpin (Cottidae)				A (9010-8500)		
Irish lord (*Hemilepidotus* sp.)	A (9440)	A (<8200)			C	A, C
Great sculpin (*Myoxocephalus polyacanthocephalus*)			A (6150-4990)		C	A, C
Staghorn sculpin (*Leptocottus armatus*)					C	A, C
Cabezon (*Scorpaenichthys marmoratus*)	A (9440)				C	A, C
Starry flounder (*Platichthys stellatus*)					C	A, C
Halibut (*Hippoglossus stenolepis*)	A (9440)		A (6150-4990)		C	A, C

Note: In cases where taxa are present in more than one archaeological site, the earliest date is given.
P = paleontological fossils; A = archaeological fossils; C = current occupant. Number in parentheses = date before present.

The caribou and mastodon give some idea of habitats in Haida Gwaii during this period. Caribou inhabit tundra and taiga, extending into the northern boreal forest and up into mountains above the tree line in alpine meadows and subalpine forests (Miller 1982:928). Miller states that "the climate of caribou ranges is characterized by long, cold winters; short, cool summers; and low precipitation" (1982:929). Mastodons are considered browsers typically found in open spruce woodlands or spruce forests (Harington and Clulow 1973:705).

Lemmings are typically found in tundra or into subalpine parklands (Banfield 1974:187; Cowan and Guiget 1978:200). The hoary marmot resides in talus slopes and alpine meadows (Banfield 1974:112). The marmot elements suggest the necessity for open rocky areas, probably alpine or subalpine. Evidence is sparse, but there is an impression of a colder, and possibly drier, climate, with less forest cover than today in southeastern Alaska, and probably also in Haida Gwaii. Examination of floral data from Haida Gwaii gives a similar climatic picture (Clague 1989:72).

Finally, it should be pointed out that the preglacial fauna might not have been like any that followed. Today, red fox and lemmings are not found on any of the coastal islands of British Columbia or southeastern Alaska and the brown bear is not found on outer coastal islands south of Frederick Sound. Mastodons and mammoths have not been found in this area since the end of the Pleistocene (about 10,000 years ago).

Glacial, Approximately 24,000 to 13,500 BP

The earliest remains from this period are known from On Your Knees Cave in Alaska. There is a large sequence of twenty-eight dates from ringed seal, starting at 24,150 ± 490 BP and ending at 13,690 ± 240 BP (Heaton and Grady 2003). The bulk of these dates fall between 24,000 and 17,000 BP, with no dates between 17,000 and 14,500 BP. Two ringed seal specimens have been dated at the very end of this period. These dates suggest that the peak of the glacial period was between 17,000 and 14,500 BP. Other species identified and dated from the early part of the glacial period are hoary marmot, red fox, northern sea lion, arctic fox, and white-winged scoter. All of these species appear before 19,000 BP. These data appear to illustrate the increasing cooling of the area of Prince of Wales Island to a peak at about 17,000 to 16,000 BP and then enough amelioration to permit the return of the ice-loving ringed seals at the very end of the glacial period.

Ringed seals and arctic foxes inhabit the Arctic today. Ringed seals are associated with land-fast or pack ice and occasionally ice floes on open water (Banfield 1974). They eat krill; small fish such as cod, herring, and whiting; and crabs and prawns. Arctic foxes inhabit "the arctic and alpine tundra zones and the boreal forest border during the winter months" (297). Arctic foxes eat lemmings in particular, and also birds, ringed seal pups, mollusks, crabs, and fish (296-297). The presence of ringed seal means that a significant amount of ice was present to the north of Haida Gwaii during this period and suggests the potential for substantial ice in the immediate Haida Gwaii area. An ice-free marine ecosystem is also indicated by the presence of harbour seal, northern sea lion, and white-winged scoter. All of these species require open water.

On Your Knees Cave also has a large collection of bird bones, which appear to have been accumulated by the arctic foxes (Heaton and Grady 2003). The only specimens dated from this time period are the white-winged scoter mentioned above and two puffin elements. The arctic foxes are dated from preglacial times to 11,275 ± 90 BP, except for the period 17,000 to 14,500 BP, so the birds are probably of similar time span. The birds include at least forty-four taxa. The most commonly recovered taxa based on the number of elements identified are parakeet auklet, common murre, oldsquaw, tufted puffin, pelagic cormorant, common eider, songbirds, brant, surf scoter, white-winged scoter, double-crested cormorant, and pigeon guillemot, in that order (T.H. Heaton, personal communication). The bulk of the birds recovered are marine species, but Heaton also reports two species of ptarmigan, an owl, and a variety of songbirds, indicating that terrestrial habitats were available.

The only known fossil from this time period in Haida Gwaii is a partial bear femur dated at 14,540 ± 70 BP found in K1 Cave on the northwest coast of Moresby Island (Table 6.2). This element is from a juvenile individual, which makes it difficult to determine whether its size best matches black or brown bear. Isotopic analysis of the collagen from this bear indicates a mixed terrestrial and marine diet. Heaton and Grady's data (2003:32) show a range of collagen values of –19.5 to –15.9 for brown bears and a range of –23.6 to –18.4 for black bears. If the Haida Gwaii bears follow the same pattern as the Prince of Wales Island bears, the $D^{13}C$ value of –18.2 supports the identification as a brown bear rather than a black bear. Black bears tend to eat more plant food than brown bears and inhabit more forested areas (Banfield 1974:306). An exception to this is seen in Labrador, where black bears live beyond the tree line. Black bears colonized this area in Labrador fairly recently, after the extirpation of the resident brown bear population (Veitch and Harrington 1996:245). This Haida Gwaii fossil bear could be a brown bear as suggested by the mixed terrestrial and marine diet, living in a probably treeless habitat (Chapter 3). Alternatively, it could be a black bear living in an unusual habitat, possibly because there were no brown bears as competition.

Whichever species it is, the presence of this bear fossil proves the existence of a habitat to support it. Black and brown bears are omnivores, eating many animals from insects to mammals, combined with a wide variety of plants. Modern coastal black bears add fish and marine invertebrates to this

Table 6.2

Dates from K1 vertebrate elements

Sample	Material	D¹³C	D¹⁵N	¹⁴C age (BP)
K1S7H	Brown bear	−18.2		14,540 ± 70
K1L11BB8	Brown bear	−16.7	10.9	12,090 ± 35
K1L11Ab12	Brown bear	−16.8	7.5	12,070 ± 40
K1S11X3 54	Brown bear	−17.7		12,065 ± 40
K1S7B12 12	Black bear	−20.5		11,280 ± 40
K1 S11B	Black bear	−20.2		11,250 ± 70
K1S7X1-6 0	Black bear	−20.5		11,180 ± 40
K1S7A	Black bear	−20.0		11,150 ± 50
K1L11Cb3a	Black bear	−20.7	1.2	10,960 ± 35
K1S11A20	Black bear	−21.1		10,950 ± 40
K1L11Ab6a	Ungulate	−21.6	2.5	10,905 ± 35
K1S11B20	Black bear	−20.5		10,660 ± 40
K1S11A30	Black bear	−20.4		10,640 ± 60
K1S11B10	Black bear	−20.9		10,525 ± 50
K1L11CB2a	Black bear	−19.9	1.0	10,510 ± 35
K1S7ANW 0-10	Black bear	−21.3		10,480 ± 45
K1S11F	Black bear	−21.1		10,450 ± 60
K1S8	Black bear	−21.7		9370 ± 50
K1S6B	Domestic dog	−11.8		2350 ± 40

list, although, as mentioned above, this may not apply to the fossil bears (Cowan and Guiget 1978:290).

Early Postglacial, 13,500 to 9000 BP

The retreat of ice from Dixon Entrance marks the beginning of this period (Chapter 1).

Vertebrate remains have been recovered from K1 Cave, found in the karst area of Graham Island's west coast (Ramsey et al. 2004). The species definitely dating from this time period are brown bear, black bear, and ungulate (Wigen 2001, 2003a). Seventeen bear elements have radiocarbon dates from this time period (Table 6.2). Three bear bones are identified as brown bear with dates of ca. 12,000 BP. Note that their collagen signatures match brown bear as well. The remaining dated bear bones are tentatively identified as black bear since most of them are similar in size to those of modern black bears. Stable isotope analysis of these bears indicates a terrestrial diet, similar to the fossil and modern black bears of Prince of Wales Island (Heaton and Grady 2003), which further supports their identification as black bears.

K1 Cave has also produced mouse elements and a few artiodactyl bones, one of which dates to 10,900 BP (Wigen 2001, 2003a). Only two artiodactyls are known to have existed in Haida Gwaii, the now extinct Dawson

Table 6.3

Dates from Gaadu Din				
Sample	Material	$D^{13}C$	$D^{15}N$	^{14}C age (BP)[a]
GD1SOB1	Black bear	−20.6	0.8	10,515 ± 35
GD2T2L4	Black bear	−20.3	−1.1	10,485 ± 35
GD2T2L7	Black bear	−21.3	2.7	10,575 ± 35
GD2T5L2	Black bear	−21.7	2.3	10,585 ± 45
GD2T5L2	Black bear	−21.5	2.4	10,550 ± 35
GD2T2L15	Brown bear?	−16.3	12.1	12,205 ± 40
GD2T5L7	Brown bear?	−17.0	9.3	11,985 ± 50
GD2T4L6	Ungulate (deer?)	−20.7	2.2	11,005 ± 45
GD2T2L4	Salmon	−14.8	15.0	10,955 ± 35
GD2T2L7	Salmon	−15.4	15.6	10,935 ± 35

a Marine reservoir corrections (Southon and Fedje 2003) will reduce the brown bear and salmon ages by 400-600 years.

caribou (*Rangifer tarandus dawsoni*) and the recently introduced Sitka black-tailed deer (*Odocoileus hemionus sitkensis*). One element, a metapodial fragment, is not caribou and is similar in size to modern black-tailed deer (*Odocoileus hemionus columbianus*). The remaining elements are too fragmentary to identify beyond the artiodactyl order.

Gaadu Din, a cave on the east coast of Moresby Island, has also produced a moderate vertebrate sample (Fedje and Sumpter 2004). Bones were recovered from surface and excavated deposits during 2003 and 2004. In addition to screening in the field, sediment samples were collected and sieved in the lab, producing an assemblage of bone from small animals. The samples collected in 2003 have been analyzed (Wigen 2004), and analysis of the 2004 material is in progress. Ten dates from this site all fall within this time period (Table 6.3).

Mammalian taxa definitely identified include shrew, bat, mouse, and black bear. In addition, river otter, canid, brown bear, and mule deer were tentatively identified. As discussed above, it is often difficult to definitively separate black and brown bears skeletally. However, the size of these elements fits brown bear better than black bear, as do the isotope values. Note that in both K1 and Gaadu Din the tentative brown bear bones are consistently older than the black bears. Gaadu Din also contains ungulate bones that fit mule deer characteristics more closely than caribou. The dated specimen from Gaadu Din is a mandible fragment with M1-3 present. These teeth are smaller than caribou teeth and fit comfortably within the mule deer size range (T.H. Heaton, personal communication). If this mandible is mule deer, it represents the oldest postglacial mule deer on the coast. The other mammals are undated. The small rodent remains are most common in the upper levels and surface, but some elements are scattered throughout the deposits, suggesting that some may be as old as 10,000 BP or older. A single canine is tentatively identified as small canid, such as fox or domestic dog. It was recovered stratigraphically below the dated ungulate mandible, suggesting an age of greater than 11,000 BP.

A wide variety of fish have been identified from Gaadu Din, including smelt (Osmeridae), possible Dolly Varden (*Salvelinus malma*), salmon, rockfish, greenling, buffalo sculpin (*Enophrys bison*), Irish lord, herring, tidepool sculpin (*Oligocottus* sp.), longfin sculpin (*Jordania zonope*), black prickleback (*Xiphister atropurpureus*), gunnels (Pholididae), and flatfish (Pleuronectiformes). The majority of the fish bone is concentrated in the upper levels. Only salmon is found throughout the deposit. The small size and shallow water habitat of most of the fish strongly suggest collection and deposition by river otters (Wigen 2004). Two samples of salmon vertebrae from 45 centimetres and 55 centimetres below the surface were dated to about 10,500 years ago (Table 6.3 and reservoir correction), making these the oldest dated salmon elements on Haida Gwaii. However, salmon elements were found throughout the deposits in even lower levels with bear bones dated to almost 12,000 years ago. All the dates in the cave appear to be in correct stratigraphic order, so there is every reason to believe that some salmon are as much as 12,000 years old. It is difficult to determine the age of the remaining fish taxa, which were probably collected by the otters or other small predators. They are concentrated in the upper levels of the units, implying that they could be of relatively recent origin. In some units, however, they are in the same levels as bear bones dated to about 10,000 BP, suggesting that they may be equally old. The presence of strictly marine fish, as opposed to anadromous fish such as salmon and Dolly Varden, implies that marine waters had to be within reach of whatever predator deposited the remains. At 10,000 BP the ocean shoreline would have been about a kilometre from Gaadu Din. This adds further weight to the interpretation that the small marine fish remains are relatively recent.

A few bird taxa are present in Gaadu Din, including ancient murrelet, small duck, and two sizes of songbird. The ancient murrelet (*Synthliboramphus antiquus*) remains are on the surface and could be quite recent. The small duck is deep in the deposits, suggesting an age of over 10,000 BP. The songbird remains are scattered throughout the deposits, indicating that some are probably 10,000 years or older.

Excavations at Kilgii Gwaay (1325T) on Ellen Island recovered a large sample (3,129 elements) of faunal material dating to about 9450 BP (Fedje et al. 2001; Chapter 11). Ellen Island is in Houston Stewart Channel between Moresby and Kunghit Islands. The site is located in the intertidal zone. Rockfish, dogfish, lingcod, and cabezon are the most common fish present. Salmon, greenling, skate, herring, Irish lord, striped seaperch, and halibut are present in small numbers. The two most common mammal species present are harbour seal and black bear, with small amounts of river otter, sea otter, and sea lion. The most common birds recovered are albatross, probably the short-tailed albatross, and Cassin's auklet. Other birds include red-necked grebe, snow goose, cackling Canada goose, scoter, ducks, double-crested cormorant, common murre, pigeon guillemot, rhinoceros auklet, and common raven.

Again there is an extensive record of animals from Prince of Wales Island in southeastern Alaska. Heaton and Grady (2003) record the presence of brown and black bears, with dates ranging from 12,295 ± 120 to 9670 ± 75 BP, caribou dated at 11,560 ± 100 BP, and red fox dated at 10,050 ± 100 BP from El Capitan Cave. Other fauna recovered from this cave that may date to this period are wolverine, river otter, and a wide variety of fish (presumed to be prey of the otters). In Bumper Cave, three brown bear elements and a caribou metacarpal were recovered (Heaton and Grady 2003). Blowing in the Wind Cave has a single dated brown bear element. Arctic fox is still present in On Your Knees Cave deposits, dated at 12,700 ± 140 BP and 11,275 ± 90 BP, during the early part of this period. None of more recent date have been recovered (Heaton and Grady 2003).

Caves on Vancouver Island are another source of vertebrate material from this time period. Although the caves are considerably further from Haida Gwaii than Prince of Wales Island, it is still interesting to consider these specimens. Several black bear bones have been recovered dating from 9760 ± 140 BP (Nagorsen et al. 1995:14). In another cave on Vancouver Island, mountain goat (*Oreamnos americanus*) elements were recovered and dated at slightly over 12,000 BP (Nagorsen and Keddie 2000:669). Mountain goats are not present on Vancouver Island today.

It is clear that southeastern Alaska was still quite cold during early deglaciation. Arctic foxes are found in colder, ice-laden areas. Today arctic foxes occupy the "arctic and alpine tundra zones and the boreal forest border" (Banfield 1974:297) and will venture far out onto frozen sea ice. As noted earlier, caribou inhabit tundra and taiga, in areas of long, cold winters and short, cool summers. The wide variety of birds and the presence of bears show that early in the postglacial period, the climate had ameliorated sufficiently to encourage an expanding vertebrate assemblage, which appeared very rapidly. For example, bears appear at most only 2,000 years after the ringed seal. This strongly implies a refugium somewhere close to these Alaskan islands.

By the middle of this period, about 11,000 to 10,000 BP, Haida Gwaii clearly had a wide variety of vertebrate fauna resident. Four taxa are directly dated: brown bear, black bear, salmon, and an ungulate most closely resembling mule deer. Other probable residents include mice, ducks, and some type of canid. The presence of these disparate animals requires a wide variety of habitats.

The Ellen Island material indicates that by the end of this period the fauna of Haida Gwaii was similar to current fauna. The variety of fish species and the presence of harbour seal, sea lion, and otters indicate a fully functioning marine habitat, and that people were present to utilize it by 9500 BP. Note that many of the fish species identified are predators and therefore require typical prey species to be present in good numbers as well.

Postglacial, between 9000 and 4000 BP

Paleontological sites in southeastern Alaska include specimens from this time period as well as older material. Heaton et al. (1996:189) report mule deer dated 8180 ± 70 BP from Nautilus Cave, Heceta Island, as well as black bear dated 6415 ± 130 BP. In addition, there are fish bones dated 5770 ± 130 BP and 6810 ± 65 BP from El Capitan Cave and brown bear dated 7205 ± 65 BP from Bumper Cave, both on Prince of Wales Island.

A small amount of vertebrate material from the Richardson Island site dates from 9010 to 8500 BP (Chapter 12). Only small fragments of burned bones were recovered and identifications were very difficult. Taxa identified include large land mammal (such as bear or caribou), large alcid (such as puffins or murres), and rockfish. Subsequent excavations have expanded that list to include dogfish, herring, salmon, prickleback, sculpin, greenling, and tentatively lingcod, hake, and halibut (Wigen 2003b).

Excavations at Lyell Bay (site number 1355T6) have uncovered a small amount of fauna (333 elements), predominately herring with one rockfish element, from a hearth feature. This site has a single date of 8210 ± 50 BP (CAMS 42480) based on charcoal (Chapter 12).

Somewhat more recent than Richardson Island or Lyell Bay is the Chuck Lake site on Heceta Island in southeastern Alaska (Ackerman 1988). This archaeological site has a basal age of 8200 BP, with all vertebrate fauna coming from the oldest levels. Mammals recovered include beaver, a cervid, and northern sea lion. Cormorants, grebes, and loons were also present, as well as salmon, Pacific cod, greenling, Irish lord, and rockfish.

Still more recent, and with considerably more vertebrate material present (about 8,000 elements), is the site of Cohoe Creek on Masset Inlet, Graham Island. This site was excavated by Ham (1988, 1990) in 1988 and Christensen in 1998 (Chapter 13). Ham reports dates of 6150 ± 70 BP to 4990 ± 100 BP (Ham 1990:206-207). A large series of dates were taken from the 1998 material, ranging from 5700 to 4400 BP (Wigen and Christensen 2001:16). Ham recovered a small amount of faunal material, including black bear, caribou, harbour seal, dolphin, a large bird (possibly goose or swan), and an unidentified fish, thought to be a type of Carangidae. The analysis of the vertebrate fauna from Christensen's excavation is still ongoing, but at this time the following taxa have been added: river otter, domestic dog, Canada goose, large, medium, and small-sized ducks, pelagic cormorant, common loon, dogfish, skate, salmon, great sculpin, Pacific cod, and flatfish.

Christensen also found large numbers of the same type of carangid bones recovered by Ham. Christensen and I have examined them carefully and concluded that these are jack mackerel (*Trachurus symmetricus*). Ham (1990:211) suggests that their presence in the area indicates warmer marine temperatures than today. However, Eschmeyer and Herald (1983:211) give the jack mackerel range as southeastern Alaska to Baja and state that "larger individuals often move inshore and north in the summer." Neave and Hanavan (1960:229), using survey data collected in 1956 and 1957, show jack mackerel moving north into the Gulf of Alaska during the summer, possibly reaching the latitude of Haida Gwaii by July, definitely by August and September. It is therefore not necessary to have warmer marine temperatures for the jack mackerel to be present. They do seem to be a strong seasonal indicator, probably having been caught in late summer. It is interesting that there is no record of them in Masset Inlet in historical times.

Another site that includes this time period is Blue Jackets Creek, excavated by Severs in 1972, 1973, and 1974. The oldest date from this site is reported to be 4290 ± 130 BP (Severs 1974a:169), although Fladmark (1989:214) reports that human skeletons from this site are dated at 4500 to 5000 BP. The site was occupied for at least 2,000 years. A preliminary analysis of the fauna shows that the following species are present: sea otter, black bear, caribou, dog, seal, whale, common loon, raven, salmon, and halibut (Severs 1974a:198). Fladmark (1989:216) also notes the presence of a beaver incisor artifact, adding that species to the list. Severs states that "large sea mammal bones were found to occur more often in upper levels of the site" (1974a:169), but there is no other information on the age of the different taxa.

The caribou bones from these two sites are of particular interest, because caribou is now extinct in Haida Gwaii. Shackleton suggests that the last Dawson caribou died "shortly after 1910, or in the early 1920's" (1999:180). This subspecies of woodland caribou is described as a small animal, close to the size of a coast deer with poorly developed antlers (Cowan and Guiget 1978:386), but the description is based on very few specimens. It is variably classified as *Rangifer tarandus dawsoni* (see Shackleton 1999) or *Rangifer dawsoni* (see Cowan and Guiget 1978). The caribou bones recovered from both Cohoe Creek and Blue Jackets Creek are not from small individuals. Severs reports that "the four worked metapodials appear to be comparable in size to equivalent specimens of barren ground caribou" (1974a:198). The specimens recovered from Cohoe Creek are very similar in size to the modern female woodland caribou specimen used in the identifications. It is quite clear that there is no indication of dwarfing of the caribou at either of these sites. This also suggests that calling these archaeological specimens Dawson caribou is inappropriate, as they do not match the description of the type specimen.

Post-4000 BP

Unfortunately, there are relatively few archaeological sites with faunal data from Haida Gwaii in this time period. Blue Jackets Creek was occupied until about 3000 BP, but it is unknown which taxa are present in the more recent deposits.

Three dog bones were collected from an apparently complete skeleton in K1 Cave. One element has been dated to 2350 ± 40 BP (Wigen 2001).

A very small excavation took place on Department of National Defence property in Masset in late 1999 (Christensen and Stafford 2000). A single corrected date of 1310 ± 50 BP was obtained. I identified the few bones recovered, including caribou, large goose, dogfish, greenling, lingcod, and sculpin. The caribou showed no signs of dwarfing. This is the most recent archaeological caribou known, consisting of several teeth and a cranial fragment. Once again, these elements appear to be from a normal-sized caribou, although teeth are less indicative of the individual's size than other skeletal elements.

A slightly larger test excavation was carried out at Second Beach (FhTx19) on Graham Island (Christensen et al. 1999). No date is available, although historical items were found in the upper levels. The mammals recovered included dog, black bear, Pacific white-sided dolphin, sea otter, and harbour seal, with the latter two being the most common. The fish remains include dogfish, skate, herring, salmon, Pacific cod, tomcod, rockfish, lingcod, staghorn sculpin, red Irish lord, great sculpin, halibut, and starry flounder. The bird remains include common loon, red-necked grebe, albatross, pelagic cormorant, great blue heron, Canada goose, white-winged scoter, large alcid, large gull, and raven.

The most extensive data are from nineteen sites excavated on Kunghit Island and the southern end of Moresby Island (Acheson 1998; Wigen 1990). These sites span the period from about 2000 BP to historical times (Acheson 1998:39). A total of 105 vertebrate taxa, including 32 fish, 8 terrestrial and 6 marine mammals, and 58 birds were identified from the more than 300,000 elements recovered (Acheson 1998:47-48; Wigen 1990:1). The most common are sea otter, harbour seal, and whale among the mammals; rockfish and salmon among the fish assemblage; and Cassin's auklets among the birds. It is also worth mentioning that the first evidence of fossil marten appears at this time in these sites. The vertebrates found in these sites are essentially a selection of the modern vertebrate fauna, showing its long presence. None of these sites shows any sign of caribou, which supports the interpretation that they were restricted to Graham Island.

The vertebrate fauna of Haida Gwaii today consists of restricted mammal and freshwater fish faunas, a moderately restricted bird fauna, and an extensive marine fish fauna. A total of 13 indigenous land mammals are known to reside on the islands, with an additional 8 mammal species that have been introduced in the last 100 years (Cowan 1989:179). The indigenous mammals include black bear, caribou, river otter, marten, weasel, 4 species of bat, and 2 each of mouse and shrew. There are at least 49 breeding terrestrial bird species and 22 breeding marine or shorebird bird species (Cowan 1989:185). Many more species of birds visit the islands. At the Delkatla Wildlife Sanctuary, at least 132 bird species have been recorded over the last 100 years (Hamel 1989:190). Cowan also points out that it "seems apparent that the islands are still gaining avifauna and have not yet reached an equilibrium state" (1989:177). The freshwater fish fauna consists of only 14 species, and 8 of these are anadromous salmonids (Northcote et al. 1989:147). The marine fish fauna is the least well known of the vertebrate faunas, with Northcote and colleagues (1989) suggesting that 315 species may be present.

The faunal lists from these sites indicate that the vertebrates were essentially identical to those of the present, although some species, such as the short-tailed weasel, have not yet been identified from archaeological sites.

Discussion and Conclusions

The preglacial vertebrates of Haida Gwaii are poorly known. Caribou is the only species known definitely from this time period. The mastodon from Sandspit might be from this time period, but could be more recent as well. In southeastern Alaska, deposits have shown a rich vertebrate fauna, including several species, such as red fox and lemmings, that are not present today. The vertebrate fauna from southeastern Alaska suggests a colder environment than today and seems to fit the vegetation data from Haida Gwaii. I think it quite probable that a rich bird and marine vertebrate assemblage was present in Haida Gwaii, and likely a variety of land mammals also.

One question to be considered when discussing the vertebrate fauna of Haida Gwaii is whether or not a glacial refugium existed on the islands during the last glacial maximum. At this time the data suggest that the answer is "not on the existing islands," at least for large vertebrates. The very good paleontological record of southeastern Alaska provides evidence of a modest number of vertebrates during the early glacial period. At the beginning of the period in southeastern Alaska, there are red fox and marmot. By the middle of the period, about 20,000 BP, only marine animals and arctic foxes are present in southeastern Alaska. And despite the extensive list of dates from the Prince of Wales Island caves, none are found between 17,000 and 14,500 BP, suggesting abandonment of the caves at that time. Throughout the glacial period in Haida Gwaii, floral and insect data suggest that nunataks were present in both places (for example, see

Ogilvie 1989 and Kavanaugh 1989). These could have provided habitat for small mammals, such as lemmings or mice, for example, and possibly a variety of small birds, but probably not for such animals as caribou or bears. Late in the period, at 14,500 BP, there is evidence of bears, probably brown bears, in Haida Gwaii, indicating the presence of a terrestrial ecosystem with a variety of plants and presumably other animals. Bears are not known to be present in southeastern Alaska at this time, suggesting that it may still have been too cold in that area to support big terrestrial mammals. Large vertebrates certainly moved into the area very rapidly after the glacial maximum, implying their presence close by. Byun and colleagues (1997:1651) examined the genetic relationships of the Haida Gwaii black bear, and on the basis of its distinctiveness suggest that a refugium existed somewhere in the immediate area, most plausibly on the Argonaut Plain, between Haida Gwaii and the mainland. This is further supported by the genetic relationships of the Haida Gwaii subspecies of marten and short-tailed weasel (Byun 1998). In Chapter 5 of this volume, Reimchen and Byun also argue for the possibility of a refugium in Hecate Strait.

The early postglacial period shows the end of the arctic fauna in southeastern Alaska. The last ringed seal date is just on the boundary, at 13,690 ± 240 BP (Heaton and Grady 2003). Arctic foxes lasted several thousand years longer, dating to 11,275 ± 90 BP. Bears appeared in southeastern Alaska early in this period. The oldest postglacial brown bear from El Capitan Cave on Prince of Wales Island is dated at 12,295 ± 120 BP. Black bears are dated at slightly over 11,000 BP in southeastern Alaska. The presence of black bears, salmon, and ungulates in K1 and Gaadu Din caves by 11,500 to 11,000 BP indicates the rapid colonization of Haida Gwaii by these, and probably other, taxa. By 9400 BP the list of mammals, birds, and fish from Ellen Island already looked very similar to the vertebrates found on the islands today.

The possible presence of deer in Haida Gwaii in the early postglacial period is both exciting and perplexing. Deer require both forested and open habitats such as alpine or subalpine areas or early-stage successional forest. In addition, they need protection from deep winter snow, usually dense forested areas (Shackleton 1999:139). In order for them to be present, some combination of these habitats must have been present on Haida Gwaii (Chapter 3). Then there is the question of what became of the deer. Certainly, none were present on the islands at the time of European contact, and none have been recovered from archaeological sites. If they were on the islands at 11,000 BP, they appear to have become extinct in a fairly short time. Further speculation will have to wait on the recovery of some unequivocal deer specimens.

The next oldest material from Haida Gwaii comes from the Cohoe Creek site and is several thousand years younger. Dating from about 6000 to 4500

BP, this site shows the presence of the basic Haida Gwaii fauna that is known today. Both large land mammals, caribou and black bear, are present, as well as a variety of fish and birds.

The caribou of Haida Gwaii deserve special consideration. At European contact, a rare dwarf form of caribou called Dawson caribou was present, but it became extinct about AD 1920. Only a few specimens were ever collected. The oldest archaeological caribou specimens in Haida Gwaii appear at about 6000 BP, and the most recent archaeological specimens are dated at about 1500 BP. None of these specimens is dwarf. This implies that dwarfing of the Haida Gwaii caribou took place after 1500 BP, a very short time for such a change to occur. Possibly only some individuals in the population were dwarf. As the archaeological record improves, it will be very interesting to watch the caribou elements for evidence of the first dwarf specimens.

The postglacial history of the vertebrates of Haida Gwaii is becoming clearer with recent discoveries. The establishment of a marine fish fauna similar to that of today occurred very early, perhaps before 10,000 BP. As far as mammals are concerned, it now appears that brown bear, possibly mule deer, and perhaps a small canid of some type were found early but did not survive into modern times (unless the canid was a dog). Brown bears appear not to have survived past about 10,000 BP. Many questions still remain. For example, the timing of the disappearance of the other taxa (assuming that their presence is confirmed) is unknown at this point. There is also the question of when the dwarfing of the Dawson caribou occurred. And there is little or no fossil evidence of the presence of other endemic species such as the marten and short-tailed weasel (*Mustela erminea*). Considering the evidence available at this point, I suggest that postglacially Haida Gwaii was colonized by a wide variety of mammalian species, some of which did not survive the subsequent climatic changes. I expect future work on Haida Gwaii to solve some of these puzzles and raise others.

Part 2
Haida Traditional History

The survival of many elements of First Nations' traditional heritage despite the effects of Western expansion and policies, such as disease, forced resettlement, mission schooling, and outlawing of traditional practices, underscores the strengths of these cultures and their continuity from past to present. For many First Nations, oral records are an integral element of their culture and are often seen as a key to their identity as a people. These traditions provide a link to the past that is important in affirmation of the community in a Western-dominated world. In oral traditions is seen a potential for both valid interpretation of the past and social relevance and support for the living.

Many anthropologists have looked at oral histories not as mere myth but as tools to unlock high-level cultural constructs or as illustrations of theories (e.g., Lévi-Strauss 1963). In many parts of the world, oral history can be shown to be both an account of the past that a culture tells itself and an account of the past that contains accurate information about past events or the past environment. Examples of correspondence between oral histories and scientifically documented events include work by Hutchinson and McMillan (1997), who demonstrate a connection between oral histories and prehistoric tsunamis on Vancouver Island; Moodie and colleagues' connection (1992) of an Athapaskan oral tradition to the White River volcanic eruption of about AD 720 (and some of its demographic consequences); Harris's association (1997) of oral histories with millennia-long archaeological and environmental histories; and MacDonald's investigation (1983b) into the Kaigani Haida expansion into what is now southeastern Alaska about AD 1700. On the northern Pacific Northwest Coast there are many recorded oral accounts of what appear to be Pleistocene environmental conditions. Swanton (1905a, 1905b, 1908), for example, documents oral histories with possibly great time depth, such as those describing a time when Haida Gwaii was joined to the mainland, a time when the climate was much warmer, a time when it was cold, and a time before the first trees.

Haida traditional history includes the oral records of people and events dating from very early to recent times. This history is less complete than it was a few hundred years ago as a result of the major disruptions to Haida society that occurred when European-introduced diseases and epidemics drastically reduced the population of Haida Gwaii (Boyd 1990, 1999; Gibson 1992). At the time of European contact, the population of Haida Gwaii was about 10,000 to 15,000. By the time the first comprehensive ethnographic records were being compiled, this population had been reduced to about 500. The portion of this history that has been carried forward includes the living memory of Haida elders as well as histories and stories recorded by ethnographers over the last 200 years. These stories also include details of founding villages and the history of budding of named lineages (Swanton 1905a).

Substantial compilations of Haida oral history were transcribed by ethnographers and others beginning a century ago and continuing to the present. Among the more important collections of these transcribed histories are Swanton 1905b, 1908; Deans 1895, 1899; Barbeau 1953; and Enrico 1995, n.d.

In Chapter 7 Barbara Wilson and Heather Harris provide an overview of Haida oral history, and in Chapter 8 James Young presents an oral history of Taadl (the loon) from the beginning of Haida time.

7
Tllsda X̲aaydas K̲'aaygang.nga: Long, Long Ago Haida Ancient Stories
K̲ii7iljuus (Barbara J. Wilson) and Heather Harris

The subject of this chapter is X̲aayda (Haida) knowledge of *tllsda gaagwii* (long, long time ago). It is the same past discussed in the chapters in this book that have been written by western scientists, but from a X̲aayda perspective as preserved in oral histories, called k̲'aaygang.nga (long, long ago ancient stories).

The knowledge of the X̲aayda and other indigenous peoples has long been dismissed as myths and legends by colonial authorities. In recent years, however, some western scientists have begun to recognize the correlations between the oral histories and the archaeological and geological evidence. For example, McMillan and Hutchinson (2002) have shown clear correspondence between a number of geological events such as earthquakes and tsunamis along the British Columbia coast, while Moodie and colleagues (1992) document connections between Athapaskan oral histories and the White River volcanic eruption. Archaeologists working in X̲aayda Gwaayaay (Haida Gwaii, also known as the Queen Charlotte Islands) in the last couple of decades have made extensive use of our stories in locating and interpreting historic and prehistoric sites across the archipelago (Mackie and Wilson 1994, 1995; Fedje et al. 2002; Josenhans et al. 1997; Mandryk et al. 2001).

In light of the efforts of missionaries and governments to destroy our culture through residential schools and the banning of the potlatch, compounded with changes in the economic system away from the large nuclear family and through the devastating ravages of smallpox and other diseases, we can only be thankful for the remaining body of knowledge that has come to us. While the written words of 100 years ago are a treasure, our elders continue to tell the stories they heard, even as we lament the great losses of people and knowledge.

The spoken word is being written as X̲aayda families gather and preserve their oral histories through the Skidegate Haida Language Program (SHIP) and the Haida Gwaii Museum at Qay'llnagaay. Clan members concerned that their stories will be overlooked, forgotten, or misinterpreted can place these stories with SHIP or the Haida Gwaii Museum, using video and audio recordings. Today, we can utilize the _k'aaygang.nga_ to understand the ancient past while employing information from scientific sources, and appreciate the value of both sources of knowledge. We believe that the conjunction of data provided by the _k'aaygang.nga_ and archaeological/geological evidence can produce synergies in which the two kinds of knowledge combine to create something greater than the two separately. While the scientific sources can provide dates of occupations, confirmation of _k'aaygang.nga,_ and considerable information about material culture, settlement patterns, diet, and trading patterns, the _k'aaygang.nga_ can provide lessons in life and an insight to the ancient world.

The stories captured through electronic or written records of our ancient past are valuable as a record of our occupation of _Xaayda Gwaayaay._ They are filled with information about the beliefs and practices of the _Tllsda Gaagwii Xaadagaay_ (all the ancient Haida). The stories describe the origin of the lands, resource ownership, crests, songs, names, how medicinal plants are used, facial paintings, and the names and locations of places. These stories tell of places where people lived and travelled, marriage patterns and relations between groups, motivations for actions and events, spiritual beliefs and practices, values, and many other kinds of information unobtainable from other sources. The various alliances and other important relationships can be derived from these stories, since only members of the clans involved should tell the stories.

The _k'aaygang.nga_ describe the types of major human and geological events that are included in this book. For western scholars interested in the ancient past, the _k'aaygang.nga_ can provide information that cannot be easily obtained, or that can be completely missed by the methods of archaeology and geology.

Besides the _k'aaygang.nga_ retained in memory are those written down by early scholars, especially during the late nineteenth and early twentieth centuries. A significant number of these stories were recorded and published by Swanton (1905a, 1905b, 1908), Boas (1895), Deans (1895, 1899), Curtis (1916), and Newcombe (n.d.a). Many of the works that followed (MacDonald 1983b, 1989; Enrico 1995) have relied upon the earlier works, especially Swanton. While some contemporary scholars (such as Enrico), have worked closely with _Xaayda_ elders to assess earlier works, others have not. Some of the stories gathered show the variety of natural and creation stories being told before the distractions of foreign values.

Discussions with _Nang Kiing.aay7uuans_ (James Young) indicate that stories gathered and written by some of the visitors may have been interpreted incorrectly. James Young is presently working with a niece to have the stories his father, Henry Young of *SGiida K'aaw,* recorded on reel-to-reel tapes, written.

Remembering the *Tllsda Gaagwii Gina Aahl Juu Gan Xaayda* (Haida Ancient Past)

Although some scholars (Cruikshank 1990:14) would contend that oral traditions are re-created by each generation to fulfill contemporary needs, and others (Mason 2000:249) would charge that remembering events of thousands (or even hundreds) of years ago is impossible, we contend that the *Xaaydas* accurately remember historical events that occurred many thousands of years ago. The *Xaaydas* preserve the *Tllsda Gaagwii Gina Aahl Juu Gan Xaayda* (Haida Ancient Past) so well in their oral histories that western scientists trained in different knowledge production systems are able to recognize the authenticity of some of these narratives.

The *Xaayda* had methods for maintaining accuracy from generation to generation. The methods utilized for transmitting the stories were stringent. The teachers/elders would consider all the children of the clan; out of those numbers, one, or possibly two, were selected to be taught all the oral histories of the clan. Only the very brightest children were selected to receive all the information, and those children would be regularly in the company of elders. The elders would tell the oral history and then the child would repeat it word for word. If the young person got even one word wrong, the teaching of oral history would end for the evening. The next night, the elders would again tell the young person the oral history. The child would have to start over again at the beginning until he or she had the oral history down word for word, including all the correct inflections. One wrong inflection can change a word's meaning. Once that particular oral history had been mastered, the elders would move on to another one. The *Xaayda* protect the integrity of the oral histories by allowing only those who are properly trained and have the right to tell their clan stories to do so. The *tllsda Xaayda k'aaygang.nga* are the intellectual property of the clans.

Stories are used to teach histories. Many of these stories take several hours, if not a day or so, to tell. Some stories also have underlying lessons to teach children about the need to respect all things occupying this earth.

Because the knowledge of the *Xaayda* (and other indigenous peoples) and western knowledge are based upon very different principles and underlying worldviews, it is not always easy to translate knowledge from one system to the other. For example, in the western understanding, everything (essentially) can be categorized as animate or inanimate. In a world in which stones are inanimate, communication with them is not possible. Most indigenous peoples believe that everything is animate, alive, filled with a spirit or life force. In a world in which everything is animate, communication and interaction with stones is possible. We have included some stories in this chapter expecting that some readers will not be able to comprehend them as literally "true." With other stories that we include, namely, those with events that we correlate with western scientific evidence, we hope that readers will come to understand them as factual records of historical events that occurred in ancient times.

These *k'aaygang.nga,* which we suggest can be understood as literally true by westerners, recount events that occurred so long ago that the contention will likely be thought impossible upon first encounter by most readers. Readers might experience skepticism on first encountering these stories, but we hope they will try to suspend judgment while reviewing this evidence. We contend that some oral histories record events that occurred at least as far back as the late Pleistocene, at a time when there were minimal restrictions on and maximum openness to the supernatural. The correlation between oral histories and the geological and archaeological evidence is compelling.

Xaayda k'aaygang.nga

To illustrate our contentions about the *Xaayda k'aaygang.nga,* we provide some examples of stories from the ancient past to demonstrate the kinds of knowledge contained within them. This chapter is not intended to be a comprehensive review of oral history, but to merely suggest and provide examples of what is contained in this body of knowledge. We will outline some of the stories telling about the beginning of time, as they are known, and other stories. We would like to emphasize that different versions of the same event do not necessarily represent inconsistency but may be local variations. Although all the clans are now situated in *Gaaoo* (Old Masset) and *Hl'gaagildallnagaay* (Skidegate), they were once dispersed throughout *Xaayda Gwaayaay* and therefore would have had different experiences of the same event. The most obvious example is the "flood," the rapid rise of sea level that occurred at the end of the Pleistocene. Depending on where the people of the clans originated, their story of the flood differs.

The stories cannot be presented in order according to western science's knowledge of historical timelines, although some connections to western time are apparent. The elders are often aware that some stories are older than others, but may hesitate to tell all the oral histories they know, as some of the stories may not belong to their clan. Some of the *Xaayda* oral histories may have time frames that overlap.

Some of following stories are from a series of *Xuya* (Raven) stories told to Swanton (1905b:72-74) by *Skaay* (John Sky of *K'uuna Kiigawaay* [Those Born at Skedans]), Job Moody of *St'aawaas Xaadagaay* (Saw-whet Owl People), Tom Stevens of *Naayii Kun Kiigawaay* (Those Born at Rose Spit/House Point), and other men. The very fact that most, if not all, of these men were *Lana*

AawGaalang (chiefs) of their village and clan means that they also had to remember all the stories, in total as well as in order. Henry Moody, Mary Ridley, and Henry Edenshaw were the interpreters.

Although meaning and style are filtered and distorted by western writers and some essence is lost in the translation to English (a language based on entirely different concepts) and to written form, we believe that these versions of *Xaayda k'aaygang.nga* give the reader a good idea of how the stories really sound. Some translations of *Xaayda k'aaygang.nga* represent the original poorly, however.

A World Mostly of Water, or *Tl'guuhlga Gan Xaayda Gwaayaay* (Creating Haida Gwaii)

Western science tells us that Haida Gwaii was created by geological processes (Sutherland-Brown and Yorath 1989; Chapter 1).

These stories describe a world mostly of water, and a twilight time. The quotes are taken from the book *Haida Texts and Myths: Skidegate Dialect* (Swanton 1905b). The first story refers to Kil or Flatrock in the area just southwest of the Houston Stewart Channel area.

Over this island [*Xaayda Gwaayaay*] salt water extended, they say. Raven flew about. He looked for a place upon which to sit. After a while he flew away to sit upon a flat rock which lay toward the south end of the island. All the supernatural creatures lay on it like *Genô'* [sea cucumber] from it in this, that, and every direction, asleep. It was light then, and yet dark, they say. [*Skaay,* as told in Swanton 1905b:110]

The Loon's place [dwelling] was in the house of Nañkî'lsLas. One day he went out and called. Then he came running in and sat down in the place he always occupied. And an old man was lying down there, but never looking toward him. By and by he went out a second time, cried, came in, and sat down. He continued to act in this manner.

One day the person whose back was turned to the fire asked: "Why do you call so often?" "Ah, chief, I am not calling on my own account. The supernatural ones tell me that they have no place in which to settle. That is why I am calling." And he said: "I will attend to it (literally, 'make')." [*Skaay,* as told in Swanton 1905b:110]

Skaay related to Swanton how *Xuya* created *Xaadaaga Gwaayaay* and the mainland:

He then stood in front of a house. And some one called him in: "Enter, my son. Word has arrived that you come to borrow something from me." He then went in. An old man, white as a sea gull, sat in the rear part of the house. He sent him for a box that hung in the corner, and, as soon as he had handed it to him, he successively pulled out five boxes. And out of the innermost box he handed him two objects, one covered with shining spots, the other black, saying "I am you. That [also] is you." ... And he said to him: "Lay this round [speckled] thing in the water, and after you have laid this black one in the water, bite off a part of each and spit it upon the rest."

But when he took them out he placed the black one in the water first and, biting off part of the speckled stone, spit it upon the rest, whereupon it bounded off. Because he did differently from the way he was told it came off. He now went back to the black one, bit a part of it off and spit it upon the rest, where it stuck. Then he bit off a part of the pebble with shiny points and spit it upon the rest. It stuck to it. These were to be trees, they say.

When he put the second one into the water it stretched itself out. And the supernatural beings at once swam over to it from their places on the sea. In the same way Mainland [North America] was finished and lay quite round on the water. [Skaay, as told in Swanton 1905b:111-112]

Kaalga Jaad (Ice Woman) and _Scannah-gun-nuncus_

The story of _Kaalga Jaad_ describes a time of climate change, a cooling period, while the story of _Scannah-gun-nuncus_ describes a mass of ice pushing trees and boulders down a valley. According to Deans (1899:3):

Both of these are of great interest to geologists, even though they are traditions of a long past age. Another subject, worthy of notice, is that a large amount of the tales has been taken from the mythology of these people. Others, again, are of great historical value, such as the story of Calcah Jude [_Kaalga jaad_] (Woman of the Ice) and her leadership of the Hidery, when flying before the encroachment of the Ice ...

Also the story of Scannah-gun-nuncus, who fled before the ice coming down the Hunnah [_Xanaa_ or _Honna_], a river on Queen Charlotte Islands.

Kaalga Jaad

Western science describes two periods of intense cold in Haida Gwaii, the Fraser Glaciation and the Younger Dryas cold interval (Chapters 1 and 3).

Long ago ... the climate was warm ... in course of time this Northern climate not only grew colder, but ice began to form, and snow deeply covered first the hill tops, then afterward, the lowlands. Finally the cold became so intense that they had to move farther south. This they did led by a woman whose name was Call cah jude [_Kaalga Jaad_, Woman of the Ice]. They left for a warmer home where they lived for many generations. Afterward, when the climate again got warmer, they moved [should read "returned"] to Alaska and Queen Charlotte's Islands. [Deans 1895:66]

Deans collected a similar story from the Salish people to the south that appears consistent with that of the Haida.

The Story of the Mountain Goats

Salish territory was affected by the same cold intervals as Haida Gwaii. There were also a number of late Pleistocene and Holocene glacial advances in the area (Walker and Pellatt 2003).

> There was a time long ago, our fathers tell us, when our people, the Whull-e-mooch (dwellers on Whull, Puget Sound, State of Washington), lived a long way further south than we their children do now. Northward from the sea coast to the farthest mountains, the whole country as well as the sea was covered with snow and ice, so deep that the summer heat failed to melt it ... After the snow and ice had all gone, the climate became warmer and the land drier, which enabled the Whull-e-mooch to move northward to where we, their children, now live and our fathers lived before us. [Deans 1899:57]

Scannah-gun-nuncus

There was extensive debris-flow (e.g., avalanches) and alluvial fan development during the time of early postglacial landscape stabilization (Clague 1989). This story about *Scannah-gun-nuncus* was recorded in Deans's "Tales from the Totems of the Hidery."

> One day, making a further venture than usual, he sailed up the Hunnah, a mountain stream emptying its waters into Skidegat channel, four or five miles west from the place where he lived.
>
> Tradition says that this river in those days was three times larger than it is nowadays. At present there is seldom water enough to float a canoe, unless at high water ... After pulling up stream, he became tired; so, in order to rest, he pulled ashore and lay down. In those days at the place where he went ashore were large boulders in the bed of the stream, while on both sides of the river were many trees. While resting on the river, he heard a dreadful noise up stream, coming towards him. Looking to see what it was, he was surprised to behold all the stones in the river bed coming toward him. The movement of the stones frightened him so much that he jumped to his feet and ran into the timber. Here he found he had made a mistake, because all the trees were cracking and groaning; all seemed to say to him, "Go back, go back at once to the river, and run as fast as you can." This he lost no time in doing. When again at the river, led by his curiosity, he went to see what was crushing the stones and breaking the trees. On reaching them, he found that a large body of ice was coming down, pushing everything before it. Seeing this, he got into his canoe and fled toward home. [Deans 1899:68]

A few years ago, when the town of Queen Charlotte was drilling for water west of the Xanaa River, they found wood 50 feet underground, and dated it to about 5000 BP (Guujaaw, personal communication).

Grassland and the First Tree
Pollen and macrofossil evidence indicates that the first trees to colonize Haida Gwaii after the Fraser Glaciation arrived about 12,500 BP. Before then, the landscape was characterized by grassy tundra-like vegetation. Cedar probably did not arrive until 5000 to 3000 BP (Chapters 3 and 4).

These stories tell about a time when the sea levels were much lower and grass stood on the land. There were no trees yet.

The Dead Tree

> This island was once all covered with grass, they say. Woodpecker was traveling upon it. He had no feathers. And in the middle of the islands stood a large tree without bark, on which he began hammering. [Swanton 1905b:186]

In *Contributions to the Ethnology of the Haida* (Swanton 1905a) and *Haida Texts and Myths: Skidegate Dialect* (Swanton 1905b), Tom Stevens, chief of Those-Born-at-House-Point, is credited with telling the following two stories, both of which appear to be early ones.

Story of Nâ-iku'n

> At first they pulled grass over themselves for houses, and floated their fishing-lines off from the spit because they had no canoes; but a son of the town chief learned from a supernatural bird (the Redhead) how to make canoes, houses, halibut-hooks, mats and cords, and taught his people. [Swanton 1908:199-200]

Story of the House-Point Families
This story tells how these people learned to make canoes and to use cedar bark.

> After he had pursued it along upon a trail in the ocean for a while, he chased it out in front ... Then it took cedar bark out of its bag. It told him its name was g.a-i. It told him they would use this for houses ... This is how they began to live under cedar barks. And at that time they also began fishing in the ocean. [Swanton 1905b:318]

Raven Travelling
In *Haida Texts, Masset Dialect,* Swanton (1908) writes about Raven finding a

shell that contained people and animals. This portion of the story explains how the black bear, marten, and land otter came to be on *Xaayda Gwaayaay*. It appears to be a story of when the ocean was lower and the islands appeared to be closer together. This story also has *Xuya* (Raven) travelling to many places and setting up how things will operate, not just on Haida Gwaii but in many other areas of the northwest coast. "Walter" told Swanton this story:

> Then he told them to make a town behind the place where they then were. And he told many to go into the mountain. And he told many to go to this island. Then this island was too small for them. He was not pleased with this, and took part of the animals to the other side. Then he told only the Black-Bear, Marten, and Land-Otter to be here. And the strip of ocean between was narrow. The tide flowed back and forth in this, and he pushed the islands apart with his feet ...
>
> At that time there was no tree to be seen. And after they had lived for a while in (the mountain), the weather became bad. [Swanton 1908:324]

The Raven Clan and Families (the First Tree)
This is a story of the first Raven clans and families, and the crests used by those first people. "The order in which these families 'came out' is differently given. An old woman of the Sqoa'ladas and others said that the Xagi-Town-People were the oldest. The latter themselves claim it, and in potlatch time used to wear a small tree or bush fastened to their hair in memory of the first tree upon the islands" (Swanton 1905a:76).

There are no descendants of this clan. The final impact came when Francis Poole was mining in the area and a man with smallpox was dropped off by a sailing ship on its way to Victoria from New Aberdeen (Poole 1872:158, 194-195).

Guustl'as (Tide Coming Over Anything)
Sea level research on Haida Gwaii shows that ocean levels were much lower than today before 9500 BP. From 13,000 to 11,000 BP, Haida Gwaii and the BC mainland were separated by only a narrow stretch of water. A rapid rise occurred after 12,000 BP, and by 9000 BP waters were much higher than today. After 5000 BP, sea levels fell (Chapters 1 and 2).

The following stories relate to the first flood brought about by a supernatural being known as *Rahlln kun* (Cape Ball). They also tell about the end of a flood, which may be the land rebounding after the melting of the glaciers. Two elders, Mrs. Hazel Stevens and Mrs. Kathleen Hans, worked with linguist John Enrico to retranslate and rewrite the following story collected by Swanton in 1900. The story describes the relationship of supernatural beings and early environments to the early *Xaaydas*.

Raḥlln kun (Cape Ball)

He went behind the screen and after a while there was a noise of thunder at the base of this island. Then her husband landed. He asked his wife, "Mother of my darling why was there a noise like the noise when I lie with you?" She laughed and replied, "Maybe I did it with **nang kilsdlaas**-to-be."

The next morning Raven's uncle [the spirit of **rahlln kun**, Cape Ball] was sitting in the ashes. He wore a hat with a column of **sgil**. A large puff of foam was spinning around on top. Raven looked around [to size things up]. Then he went out and got his two skins, put on his two sky skin robes, and came in. Raven's hair was tied up in two bunches. The foam on the top of his uncle's head began to spin around very fast.

And a current began to flow out of the corner. Raven grabbed his mother under his arm, put on the bufflehead skin, and floated here and there in the current ... When the water reached the roof of the house, he was borne out through the smoke hole. Then he put on the raven skin. Immediately he flew up. He ran his beak into this firmament. His tail began to float. Then he kicked the water. "That's enough! It's I who own you." This water stopped right there. The foam started to go down. [Enrico 1995:47]

The Transformer Myth
In *The North American Indian,* E.S. Curtis (1916:154-155) relates a story about *Kéngi* and *Nunkílslās:*

One morning Skóhokona, his wife, and his sister, all sat in the house at the top of the terrace. They saw water spurting out of the four corners of the room. The boy went and put his foot on the streams, and they stopped, but came out again when he removed his foot ... He went out again and got his other bird-skin blanket. The water was now coming out so rapidly and boiling and swelling in the room that he quickly put on the butterball-skin and in the form of a duck he dived repeatedly in the water, bobbing up to the surface just like a duck ... Still the water rose, and he put on the raven-skin, and in the form of a raven he flew quickly up through the smoke-hole; but the rising water touched his tail as he went out. He flew straight up into the sky, and still the water followed him. He reached the next village above, and there he walked about in his human shape.

He began to think about his uncle and his mother, and wondered what they were doing. He looked down and saw the house, and the foam was settling down, all white over it, and smoke was rising from the house. This made him angry. He put on his raven-skin, flew straight down, and settled on the pole in front of the house. The pole split twain ...

After he had gone, word came that he was going to cause a flood ... He said that they should hold to the rings of his great hat, and to this they agreed.

One day Nunkílslãs appeared in a canoe, wearing a hat with a bit of foam on the top of it. From this fleck of foam spurted water, and the level of the ocean rose rapidly. Kéngi put on his high hat, and the others held to it as it grew, upward. Still the water rose, and the hat broke. Those who held to it were drowned, but the ten nephews of Kéngi became small islands. Then the flood subsided. Kéngi was too powerful to be drowned.

Foam-Woman and Djila'qons

Soon after this deluge had abated ... the first cycle or age in Haida mythology extended from the production of the two islands by Raven, as above related, to the flood raised by Cape Ball ... the cycle of human beings began. The picture presented at the commencement of this cycle is very similar to that with which the first started ...

When Xagi emerged from the waters, Foam-Woman was sitting upon it ... but she permitted none of them to come near. If any one attempted it, she looked at him and winked her eyes, when lightning shot forth and drove him back. From this she was also called She-of-the-Powerful-Face. When Djila'qons [Jiilaa Kuns], the grandmother of the Eagles, approached, Foam-Woman said, "Keep away from here before I look at you"; and when she did look, Djila'qons [Jiilaa Kuns], "went down." Others say, perhaps out of respect to the Eagle side, that the latter was one of two beings able to approach. The other was a mouse, which, however, grew smaller and smaller as it came. That is why mice are so small to-day ...

Foam-Woman had many breasts ... When her first child was born, foam came from its mouth and nearly created a second flood. The rock was almost covered again by the waters; but Foam-Woman began to sing. [Swanton 1905a:74-76]

Earthquakes

Haida Gwaii is at the juncture of the Pacific and North American tectonic plates and has experienced numerous earthquakes, including several over magnitude 5.0 and one of 8.1 in the last century (Chapter 1).

The Origin of Carved House-Posts

This story appears to describe an earthquake, subsidence of a grassy delta, and an ensuing tsunami. The town drowned by this event appears to have been at the mouth of present-day Delkatla Slough.

Many people lived in the town of Gî'tAn-q!a-la'na (It stood upon the north shore of Masset Inlet, just where the inner expansion begins.). The east wind blew so strongly that some of the houses were blown down. So they did not care to live there. They went away. And they came to live at Delkatla (a side inlet from Masset Inlet).

Then there was no salt water there. It was all covered with grass. Then they dug the town-chief's house-hole. They finished his first. And all of the people lived in his house. But afterwards they built houses on either side of him. All of these houses were completed. Then all began to live in their own.

One autumn after that, they went to Rose Spit to get food in two big canoes. Very many people were in the canoes. They went for berries.

Then one woman who was not paddling looked into the water. It was very calm. And it was bright sunshine. Then the one who looked into the sea saw something carved at the bottom. It was carved with figures of human beings. And the lower part was carved into the representation of a killer-whale. And the human being stood upon the killer-whale.

They remained a long time above it. They memorized it, they went away. And when they came over to L!ûsk?'ns (Name of the point where the trees end, just back of Rose Spit.), they described it. Some of them said, "We will make the chief's house-posts like it." And some of them were afraid.

And after they were through picking berries, they started off. And they arrived at the town. Then they told those who had stayed at home about it. They were going to imitate it for the chief, when they again built a house for him. And some of them were afraid, and did not want to do it. Still they made the representations. And they completed them. There were two. Then they began to paint them. Then they raised them on something.

At that time this land moved. The Ocean-People were angry on account of it. Then a flood came. And after they had fastened their canoes together, they put the posts upon them. They liked them too much to leave them behind. When the water got far up the side of a small mountain, they put one of them upon that. And they put one into the sea. Then they wept bitterly.

Then they put weasel-skins into their ears as (ear-rings). They also put them into the ears of their wives and children. Then they sang. They sang crying-songs. They sang for themselves, because they thought this would not again dry up. At that time they sang the following crying-song. "The supernatural beings were the ones who made the flood come. The supernatural beings were the ones who made the flood come, made the flood come."

At that time the sea began to move. The canoes began to sink. And after the canoes had sunk they (the people) floated upon the ocean. Now they became birds.

Part of these birds are called Ear-Ring-Wearers. The Ear-Ring-Wearers were once people. And they say that the house-post is now upon Gao (the name of a mountain). People used to see it there when they went up to eat medicine.

Moss grows upon it. Those who were going to be chiefs kicked off the moss from it. When one saw it, he became rich. Near it stands a very big devil's-club. And the chief's house-hole still forms a hole in the sea. When the tide is low, it is still seen. And they also used to pray to the house-post to become wealthy. Those who prayed did become wealthy. [Swanton 1908:457-459]

22 August 1949: Earthquake of Magnitude 8.1
The following is an event that occurred when the first author (Barbara Wilson) was walking with her parents.

It was a bright sunny day in *Kil kun* (Sandspit). *NiisWes* (Ernie Wilson), his wife, *Gwaaganad* (Mary Wesley Wilson), and their three children had travelled there from *HlGaagilda llnagaay* (Skidegate) by boat to visit her maternal family. The couple took their two older children and walked to the store to buy treats for them. The store was approximately a mile away from *Nuni* Nina's house. During their stroll back to *Nuni* (grandma) Nina's home, the earth started undulating like swells on the sea, the tall spruce trees moved like tall blades of grass in a summer wind. *Gwaaganad* ran the remaining distance to the house to save her baby, Harold. She appeared to be jumping from wave to wave as she ran down the road.

Elders living in Skidegate speak of loud noises, a lot of rocking, and not being able to walk – the shaking was very severe. *Nang Kiing.aay7uuans* (James Young, personal communication) relates: "A supernatural being lives under Lawn Hill (on the beach in front of where the road cracks just south of the St. Mary's Spring). When he is 'with' his wife the land rocks and cracks in that area. Sometimes it goes on all night."

Tidal Waves
While there are historic accounts of tidal waves on Haida Gwaii, the geological record for such events has yet to be examined in detail as has been done for the southern BC coast (Chapter 1; McMillan and Hutchinson 2002).

The following stories from Deans and Swanton tell of tidal waves on Haida Gwaii.

Ellzu cathlans coon (Point of the Waves)

In the miniature village in Chicago is a house which has on the ends of its six roof-beams six heads all hanging down; in the original house at Skidegat, each head had hair fixed on it, which waved in the wind. On that account it got the name of six heads house, *cadzo-clou-oonal-n ass* [*Kaajii TlGunuhl Naa*]. The owner of this house and his fore-bears have taken that name but shortened to *clads-ah-coon* [*Kaajii TlGunuhl*]. The family bearing this name was *ellzu cath-lans-coon-hidery* or chief of the point of the waves people. Several generations ago these people chose a beautiful point of land, whereon to build their village, on the east of Queen Charlotte Island [*Xaayda Gwaayaay*], known by the above name Point of the Waves. Some time after they were settled, an immense tidal wave carried off the entire village. Five times it was destroyed and four times rebuilt. Unable to rebuild any longer, the chief, by request of his people, went and bought land from the people of Skidegat, lying at the east end of the village. To this they all removed with their belongings and here they made home for themselves, led by the old chief. In their new home all the houses were arranged as they stood in the old one; following the same order their descendants live to-day still retaining their old tribal name, point of the waves people. [Deans 1899:15]

The people have since all passed away.

T!ç

Before the flood, Qâ'dj?qôk was chief of the Sand-Town-People [Raven clan] at the town of T!ç. After they lived there for a while, they tamed a young sea-otter. At that time they kept laughing at it. When it walked about in the lower part of the house, they laughed at it. It kept calling to its mother ... it sat there during the night. At that time they took it away and began to bring it up. And they also took it to a pond out upon a point. And they put it into this. They put it upon kelp in the middle of this, and threw it in. And after it had swum about in the water for a while, it came out, got on the top of the kelp, and lay down there. Then they took stones and threw them at it. They did not throw straight at it. They only threw near it, because they valued it. The sea-otter was a female. When they threw at it, it got into the sea-water, and swam about there. And when they were about to go home, they took it with them.
   Then they went down to the beach to get mussels for it. And they got mussels. Then they broke them. And they gave it the insides of the mussels to eat. It ate nothing but mussels. But if they were cooked, it did not eat (them). All that time they made fun of it. Because they made fun of it, two big waves came landward. And when the waves got near shore, the young sea-otter ran in. These two waves came for it. At that time came the flood. Then the people of the town of T!ç got into canoes. And the ocean rose very high. And then a little of the top of the mountain was to be seen. That, however, was not covered by the sea. And at that time they came to the dry ground on top of the mountain, and they carried their food and water up there. [Swanton 1908:400-407]

A Second Story of T!ç
A second story of *T!ç* has different characteristics.

When people lived at the town of T!ç, they played with a certain thing. They played with that only ...

One day a certain person won many times. Then those who could run fast got ready for him ... And when he drew near the goal, one of the fast runners caught up with him. He pushed him. His marten-skin blanket lay over his head. Then the players all looked towards him. Then they saw that his back was as if covered with chiton shells lying over one another. And they laughed together. As they laughed, all clapped their hands very much.

Then the chief's son was so much ashamed that he continued to lie there. They were frightened at him, because his vertebrae were not like those of a human being ... While they were watching, the tide came up to him. It came near him ... then the tide came near him, because there was a flat stretch in front of this town. Therefore it came across it rapidly. While they looked at him, the tide reached him. Then it came over him. That was the last they saw of him.

Afterwards the tide did not fall quickly ...

Very early the next day they heard a drumming-sound out at sea ... The waves out at sea were white. When they (the waves) came near them, they saw that this was foam ... Then they saw it was on a level with the houses. They thought it would go down quickly before it reached them. So they were not much troubled. Still it grew bigger. Then however, they collected the things they could save. They also put on their backs the children they borne ...

They got a long distance away, half way up the mountain ... But at that time they blamed one another, because they did not see how they could save their small children. Just so the foam came over some of the children who could not run fast. But they were better able to run for safety with the stronger ones. Not long afterward others became tired. The foam also overwhelmed them ... Before they had gone afar, they said to one another, "There is no way to save our children" ...

Before they had gone far, they looked back. Then the foam was not coming after them again ...

This was really the child of The-One-in-the-Sea ...

Now, all believed it was the son of The-One-in-the-Sea, for who else would have foam come for him in that way? ... Now it is all right.

But when they got through speaking, the women went out of doors to weep. And when they thought of their children and of how they had died, their minds were very sick ... They started back to the same place. There was not a single breaker to be seen ...

Next day they again started away from that place. Then they came again to their own town of T!ç. At that time there was not one house to be seen standing there ... This is a story of what happened to the Sand-Town-People. [Swanton 1908:408-415]

Story of Na-iku'n

Another story tells about a tidal wave being created to punish the Masset people for wanting to kill the chief and his friends.

> Then they (the people who were drowned) went and sat in front of Chief's house. They begged him for a flood. He asked them to come in. They refused. The warriors started home and camped beyond Raven creek. The weather was calm. Toward evening two tidal waves rolled in out of the ocean. The first one came in and broke. The canoes with their skids even drifted away. The last one even washed away the trees by their roots. Half of the warriors were lost. And he (Burnt-forest) escaped along with his copper into the woods and carried it off on his back.
>
> Then by washing away the front of Tow Hill the waves washed dentalium shells to the surface. The Inlet [people] dug them. They paddled north with them to sell them for slaves. They bought slaves.
>
> After that, when they quarreled with one of Those-born-at-House-point, he would say in answer: "Well! Inlet people ceased moving their own bucket handles because my uncles drowned themselves. The Inlet people had plenty of slaves.
>
> And a man of Those-born-at-House-point made figures of the supernatural beings on his house. The ends of the roof poles had images of human beings on them face up. This house was washed away five times. Then he named himself Chief-who-renews-his-property. [Swanton 1905b:319-320]

Scamsum

After 10,000 BP, the climate of Haida Gwaii became warm, much warmer than today, causing major changes in the local vegetation. It was not until after 8000 BP that the cool, wet climate, similar to today's, developed (Chapter 3; Fedje 1993; Pellatt and Mathewes 1994, 1997).

The following story appears to tell of a time of a warmer and wetter climate soon after the flood on *Xaayda Gwaayaay:*

> Long ago, as I have said, the climate was warm and at the same time the land was very moist, and consequently brought forth mosquitos of an enormous size. Their bites were terrible and deadly, many of the people dying from their bites. A sad cry went up to Ne-kilst-luss for relief. He heard their prayer, and sent the Scamsum (mosquito hawk), and gave him the mosquitos for food. This hawk was unable to eat them all. Seeing this, Ne-kilst-luss sent the Dragon Fly (mamma chicka), to help him. So there soon was relief from their tormentors; likewise, the climate growing colder, very much helped to do away with them. [Deans 1895:66]

The Pitch-Town-People

When referring to the "Transitional Complex," Fladmark (1989:219) suggests that stories of the Pitch-Town-People may be "another indication of the perpetuation into late prehistory of an older, simpler way of life."

These stories talk about *Xaaydas* at a time before crests came into existence, before there were male hereditary leaders, and before there were many people living on *Xaayda Gwaayaay*.

Before leaving the Raven families, I must say something of a curious people who formerly inhabited the west coast of Moresby Island. These were called Pitch-Town-People, and were said to have belonged to the Raven side; but I am not convinced that they were entirely exogamic. Although their history is shrouded somewhat in fabulous details, there is no doubt that such a people actually existed. They are said to have been Haida, speaking the same language as the rest, only, in the estimation of the other families, they were somewhat uncultivated, and are said to have lacked a crest system. Their story is as follows: –

They "started" from the neighbourhood of a small lake lying back from a steep part of the western coast, south of Tasu Harbor, called Gambling-Sticks ... They do not remember hearing the name of any chief of these people while they were at this place, but one always hears of a chief woman called Going-to-be-a-Chief's-Daughter, and also of Woman-whom-they-always-think-too-High-to-marry ...

The site of Kaisun [*Kaays7un*] itself is said to have been occupied by one of the towns of the Pitch-Town-People: but, before the new settlers came, all had died out except one man named Taoganat, who was so large that it took two entire bearskins to make his blanket ... Taoganat, used to smell whales, and would direct the people where to go, when they would find at least part of one. All of them are described as strong men of gigantic stature, but barbarous and foolish ...

My informant on the above particulars was one of the Low-Ground People, himself a descendent of the Pitch-Town-People. [Swanton 1905a:90-91]

In the preceding paragraphs, Swanton talks about the girth and height of the Pitch-Town-People. In conversations with *Kwii Aans* (Willis White) of *Gaaoo* (Masset), *Kwii Aans* said that when he and his brothers were preparing the ground for building his house, they found a skeleton of a man and a baby buried together. He said that the baby was cradled in the man's arms. The skeletal remains of the man appeared to be about seven feet tall. *Kwii Aans* said that when he measured the femur against his own leg from the bottom of his foot, the femur went well past his knees. *Kwii Aans* said that he was much younger then, and that he and his brothers stood at least six feet tall. His father, Henry White, told him that the *Xaayda* of old times were much taller and larger than we are today. They built a box and buried the remains in a quiet place. We will leave it here.

Conclusion

We have provided a mere impression of *Xaayda k'aaygang.nga* (oral histories). In spite of the great losses of *k'aaygang.nga,* many, many more still exist in written and recorded forms and in the memories of *Xaayda* elders and the younger family members to whom they are passing their knowledge.

The *k'aaygang.nga* are only one aspect of *Xaayda* traditional knowledge, and the historical aspect of the *k'aaygang.nga* is an important aspect of the knowledge contained within them. The *k'aaygang.nga* show the world the connection between the *Xaayda* and their land and give an idea of the length of their occupation. The stories preserve information about the ancient past that likely cannot be obtained from western sources, but they also store other important kinds of knowledge. The stories can contain information about medicinal knowledge and environmental management. They give roots to the young people of our nation and thereby pride in their connection to *Xaayda Gwaayaay*. This in turn may alleviate the various types of social problems that have become part of the daily lives of many people. The *k'aaygang.nga* hold knowledge that is not only relevant to our people but also of intellectual interest to all people of today. They contain knowledge that could very well contribute to the future survival of not only our own people but also the *iihlgidsii* (other people) with whom we share this fragile planet. That knowledge consists of the values, philosophies, spiritual understandings, and practical knowledge that enabled our people to thrive for millennia. The *k'aaygang.nga* teach the need to have respect for all beings and for the earth itself. The kinds of understandings contained within these stories may assist us all in moving towards a more sustainable relationship with the earth and all its inhabitants.

We are a people living in the twenty-first century but with roots very, very deep in the past and a continuing relationship with the land and sea. We believe we have occupied *Xaayda Gwaayaay* since the beginning of time and have learned much about the land and living on it. In the very recent part of our long occupation, others have come to the shores of *Xaayda Gwaayaay*. The result of that visitation has often been destructive, but the *Xaayda* have struggled to maintain control of their lands and lives, learning what they can from the visitors. Today, we use our time-tested traditional knowledge together with the new tools from western knowledge with synergistic effect.

The end. (But others exist.)

Acknowledgments

Haaw7a to the *Xaayda* elders: *Nang Kiing.aay7uuans* (James Young) for providing us with the story of the origin of the *Xaayda* clans and clarifying several points, and *NiisWes, Laana Aawga Giidaansta* (Chief Skedans), and *Kwii Aans* (Willis White) for their stories and patience in making sure these stories are written as they should be and taking the time to discuss words. To *Guujaaw* and Daryl Fedje, *haaw7a* for your comments and suggestions, which we appreciate. To Skidegate Haida Language Program, *haaw7a* for writing the glossary and the time all of you devote each and every day to teaching those who will listen. Certainly one of the most important acknowledgments is for the guidance you provide to us. *Haaw7a, Haaw7a Kilslaay.* Any mistakes are ours alone.

Note on Intellectual Property

In this chapter, we relate the *k'aaygang.nga* (oral histories), which are the property of *Xaayda* clans or the *Xaayda* collectively. Some clans have completely died out; others have given permission to use their stories.

Note on Orthography

Several *Xaayda* orthographies currently exist. The elders of Skidegate are developing an acceptable one, a glossary and CDs through the Skidegate Haida Language Project (SHIP) and the Skidegate Haida Language Authority to reflect the dialects surviving in *Hl'gaagildallnagaay* (Skidegate). When more than one pronunciation is brought to light, all the variations are recorded and respected. There are different dialects reflected in the words used by the authors. We have chosen to use particular words knowing that there are other versions that can also be used. The *SHIP Xaayda Kil Glossary – September 9, 2003* has been used as the guide for most of the words we have selected to use in this chapter. For the spelling of place names, we have used the *Gwaii Haanas Place Name Map Project – March 16, 2001*.

8

Taadl, Nang Kilslaas, and Haida

Nang Kiing.aay7uuans (James Young)

The following story is an example of what someone engaged in an oral history project could be working with. James Young, the son of Henry Young, one of the last traditionally trained Haida historians from Skidegate, is a student and teacher at the Skidegate Haida Immersion Program (SHIP). James was not fully trained in the traditional way. He had begun the process but then had to go Prince Rupert to go fishing. He remembers some of the stories his father told him, and he has tape recordings of other stories. He says that some of his personal clan stories are three hours long. The story below is a condensed version. James states that he has seen many documentaries "where they have us coming from Asia. And that is wrong. We were here all along. That is why I want to have this story included here."

For SHIP he tells stories in Haida and the program is producing CD-ROMs for the benefit of the Skidegate community and those studying the Skidegate dialect of the Haida language. This story is particularly interesting because it addresses the process of becoming a storyteller.

James Young had requested a tape recorder to record the story at his own convenience. After finishing the recording, he gave the tape to Astrid Greene for transcription. The text of this transcription was returned to James and he clarified some portions. Successive drafts were handed back and forth and the present story was finalized. The original transcript includes frequent shifts between past and present tense. Whenever James described a process, such as the storyteller's apprenticeship, he would recall some portions in the present tense. This would create a feeling of immediacy – and then a shift to the past tense would occur. For ease of reading in English, the story was changed to past tense. To hear the story told is preferable to reading it on paper as not all qualities of delivery can be carried over to written form. We hope that some of the ways of storytelling come through in this rendition.

My name is James Young. I am the son of Henry Young, who was a Haida historian. When my dad was a young man, he was picked as one of the smartest ones in the tribe or in the clan to carry the Haida history. In the wintertime by the bonfire there would be nothing but old grey-haired men sitting around, telling stories. They'd take my dad and sit him among them and tell him a story. The next night, the fire was still going and my dad had to tell the story back to the grey-haired old men. If he missed one word – just one word – the story was over. And the next night they would tell him that same story again. And the next night it is his turn again. When he got it perfectly, word for word, then they would tell him another story. This is the way my dad was brought up. And I am going to try and tell you some of the stories how this island came into being, the North American continent.

A long, long time ago, before this island came out of the water, the loon was swimming around for days and days. Sometimes he'd fly around and there was no land anywhere. Then he'd seen a cloud up in the sky; so he flew up into the cloud. In the cloud there was a native dwelling. The loon went up to the building and the loon was a supernatural being. He went up to the building and took his skin off and changed himself into human form. He went into the house and inside there was a fire going. Two quartz stones were standing in the middle of the house. This is what's burning – it doesn't go out. And beside it was a very old man, lying on his back and sleeping.

The loon walked around the fire and stared at the old man. The old man didn't move at all. So the loon went outside and started calling his loon call, the same as they do today. After a while he went in again, but the old man had not moved. He was still sound asleep. So the loon went out again and called and called and called. Towards evening he went into the house again and the old man was still in the same position. He hadn't moved at all. So the loon went out again – he is in man form all this time – and called again. He called all night long, and in the morning he went back into the house and that old man was still asleep, he hadn't moved at all.

So he went out again and he cried out there all day long. In the evening he went back in and the old man was still lying there and hadn't moved at all. So he went out again and cried all night again. In the morning he went in again and the old man still hadn't moved. And then on the third day, when he was crying, the door opened and the old man came out and said: "What are you crying about? I can't sleep with all this crying."

And the loon answered: "I was down there and there is nothing but water. There is no place for Haida to live." *Haida* in our language means people. We're Haidas. We called ourselves <u>X</u>*aaydaas* before but people around Vancouver, the natives there, could not say <u>X</u>*aaydaas* and they said *Haidas*. "What manner of a people is this that they do not even fear death, these Haidas?" they said. From there we got the name *Haida*.

So the old man called this loon, who was in man form, into the house and he lay down and started rubbing his stomach; pretty soon he pulled a baby out of his stomach. This is a supernatural being that is doing this. When he pulled the baby out, he stood the baby up and stepped on his feet and started to pull him up. He pulled him up and then pushed him higher than himself and then said to this new being that he created: "I'm making you taller than the average man." He made him tall, turned him around several times to see that he was perfect in every detail.

And there was a partition in the house. And he told this being that he created, this human – it is a supernatural being also, which will be later revealed in this story – and told this new being to go behind the partition and get him the box from behind the partition. So he went behind there and got the box and the old man lifted the lid up. And inside it there was another box and he pulled this one out and then there was another box. And this he did five times. Inside the fifth box there were two stones; there is one small stone and another bigger stone. The smaller stone was just black, but the bigger stone had some shiny things running through it, some shiny veins. And the old man gave the smaller stone to this loon and told him: "When you go back down into the water, you place this in the water and breathe on it. But don't breathe on it too long and then let it go. And then you fly away for a day and then you'll put the bigger stone in the water and then you breathe on that one, just for as long as you can – and even longer – before you let it go."

So the loon took the stones, went out, and changed back into the loon, whom we call *taadl,* and then he had this under his wings and he spiralled down; he didn't fly. He put this under his arms because of the stones, he spiralled down, and when he landed in the water, he put the smaller stone down in the water and breathed on it for a while and let it go. He flew away for a day and then put the bigger stone in the water and breathed on it as long as he could and even longer and then let it go. The smaller stone is the Queen Charlotte Islands or Haida Gwaii and the bigger stone, as far as we know, is the North American continent.

After the island came out of the water, this new being that the old man had created turned into a raven and he flew down to this island and his name was *Nang Kilslaas.* He's the one that the raven story is about. Raven that walked the earth. He is the one that taught all the people. When he landed on the island, he changed into human form and he pointed at a rock with one hand and with the other, he pointed at a clump of bushes. And out of the bushes came the first human beings. The life span of these new human beings that he had created wasn't very long. And he had pointed at the rock. Had he created man out of that rock, they said, man would probably have lived longer. But there are no descendants from these people.

The Haidas of today come from what we call *Sgaana Kidiids* – they are sea monsters. They come out of the ocean and in different shapes and forms. On the East Coast there weren't too many, but on the West Coast there were a lot of them. Some were single, others had mates. But in Rose Spit a whole bunch of them came ashore together: they were killer whales.

The bodies of the males that had mates had different designs on them from the females. The reason for this is that the females are of the opposite clans. When they came ashore, they shed their skins and they kept their skins by their dwelling and they could change back into killer whales at any time and go out and hunt for food.

They were killer whales – they changed themselves into human form and the ones that had had mates did not bear any children when they were in human form. So the ones that were single went up to Masset Inlet and they got women from there and they had children from them. These are the ones we call *Naikun Kiigwaay* and they had nothing in those days – absolutely nothing. They had no clothes, nothing to wear. They probably took branches and hung them around themselves, that is all they had. But they had a fire going. When they warmed themselves and they turned around, one side of their bodies would get cold and the other side would get warm. They had absolutely nothing – nothing to wear.

There were a lot of eagles around but they had no way to kill the eagles. So they dug a pit in the sand around above the high-water mark. It's dug so there is a seat in it and they break branches off to cover the pit with. Early in the morning, before daybreak, they would go out, wading in the water, and as soon as a person made some splashes, the dogfish came swirling around and the people that had these pits threw one up – one for each pit. They had a giant clamshell, which I think they call geoducks now, and they sharpened the edge of this by rubbing it against the stone. And with this they cut the dogfish open. And they laid the dogfish beside the pit where they are going to sit. After they had gone in there to sit, they put the branches over the top of the pit and they would sit in there. And all this was done before daybreak.

At daybreak, the eagles saw the dogfish and they landed there to eat the dogfish. And the person sitting in the pit waited for the right time, for the time when the eagle is facing the other way – and they would reach through the branches, grab the eagle by both legs, drag it into the pit, and twist their neck to break them. And they plucked the feathers off the wings and this was interwoven into a blanket. This is all they had. And after they plucked the main feathers off, the fine other down around the breast was left on the skin. And they skinned the eagle with the same clamshell and they turned it inside out and then they dried it. There was a fine feather down on the inside. And when a baby was born, the baby was put in this. This was one of the principal reasons for hunting these eagles. The main feathers were woven into a blanket. They could use it as a cape during the day and as a blanket at night. When a person got two of these, he was considered an *IidXaaydaa,* which means the person is better off than the next guy, who had none or only one blanket. This hunting of the eagles and catching them sounds pretty easy when you talk about it, but is a very hard thing to do. So this is how they lived.

When they had a hook – it is not exactly a hook – it was just a straight piece of board and they would take the bear's penis bone and fasten it on one end and on the other end there are tree roots spliced together and tied to that end. Then there is the sinker in the middle, which is tied on there. And they would take this out to the beach at low water and put it out with the bait on it. I think the bait was clams. And when the tide came in, they had a stick stuck into the ground with a rattle on top of it up by where they lived and then they would tie these spruce roots to the stick, halfway up, and when a halibut bit, the rattle rang – it rattled. Then they run out to the water's edge and grab the line and run up with it as fast as they can. And the halibut fish practically would swim to shore as it was fighting to get away. This is how they caught the halibut – this is how they lived.

Part 3
Haida History through Archaeological Research

Haida Gwaii is well placed to document the human history of the Northwest Coast of the Americas, since it appears that these islands have been occupied for over 10,500 years. Recent work shows that both the environmental and cultural records contain periods of rapid and profound change as well as periods of stability and continuity. While the archaeology of Haida Gwaii has advanced substantially over the past few decades, the culture historical record remains very incomplete.

Archaeology is the science of finding and interpreting the physical remains of past human life. Most commonly, these include tools (artifacts), food remains such as bones and seeds, and the remains of structures such as hearths, posts, depressions, and so forth. Typically, the further back in time, the less remains are preserved. On the Northwest Coast, this is mainly due to bacterial degradation (rotting) of the organic components of the remains, and also to the acidic nature of the forest soils. Fragile, organic-rich remains such as wood, skin, bark, and leather are preserved very poorly at most sites, and may last for only a few years or decades in the ground. Less organic remains such as bone and shell are somewhat more durable, and may last for hundreds or thousands of years, although both are susceptible to acidic and bacterial degradation. When shells build up in enough quantity, such as at a campsite or village site where massive amounts of shellfish were being consumed, a shell midden can form. Shell middens have the happy by-product of reducing the acidity of the immediate soil, which can allow the preservation of bone for many thousands of years. Occasionally archaeological materials are deposited in a waterlogged environment. Such "wet site" deposits can encourage the preservation of wooden artifacts. In the absence of special preservational contexts, only the most durable material will survive in the ground, such as stone tools, highly burnt (calcined) bone, post-moulds (decayed or infilled remains of posts or stakes placed into the ground), and other depression or pit features. Further to this, entire archaeological sites themselves can be destroyed through erosion, sedimentation, reoccupation, or modern disturbances.

In general, then, archaeology tries to tell the story of long-term human history through a highly selective set of material remains of the past. Some sites and some time periods have excellent preservation while others are very poorly represented. For the early period, before 5,000 years ago in Haida Gwaii, most sites contain only stone tools with trace amounts of bone. An exception is the Kilgii Gwaay site in southern Gwaii Haanas, a wet site with a shell midden component. The Cohoe Creek site, at around 5500 BP, is the first known substantial shell midden in Haida Gwaii and it offers much better preservation, especially of bone. Many such sites are known from the last 5,000 years, but ironically fairly few of them, compared with earlier periods, have seen substantial archaeological excavation or reporting. Thus, despite the better preservation of evidence, the more recent past is also poorly known through archaeological research.

When working with these kinds of archaeological remains, some questions are more easily answered than others. Subsistence practices, technology, and settlement leave relatively unambiguous and, to some extent, durable material remains on the landscape, especially at the scale of centuries or millennia. Other aspects of human life do not leave such clear material behind. For example, clan identification, gender relations, and ethnicity are very difficult to discern archaeologically. To set against this selective scope, archaeology can recover quite specific information about everyday life, even thousands of years ago – a hearth, for example, can tell what a small group of people ate during a single day. Thus, Haida history as told through archaeology will always be best considered along with other kinds of history, such as environmental reconstruction and Haida tradition.

History of Archaeological Research in Haida Gwaii

Archaeological investigation in Haida Gwaii dates back to the late nineteenth century, but only in the last few decades has the record been examined in sufficient detail for us to begin to understand the full range of this history. George Dawson (1880) remarked on raised shell midden sites in northern Haida Gwaii as early as 1878 and Harlan Smith (1927) conducted some excavations near Tow Hill in 1911, but the earliest well-documented investigations date only to 1956, when Duff and Kew (1958) conducted limited excavations at Skangwaii village on Anthony Island.

During the late 1960s and early 1970s, a number of broad-ranging surveys and excavations were conducted. Surveys by Fladmark (1971b), Hobler (1976, 1978a), and Gessler and Watney (1976) were preliminary in nature but located a large number of previously unrecorded sites throughout the archipelago. With the exception of Fladmark's work (1973) at the protohistoric Richardson Ranch site and Gessler's essentially unpublished work (1975) at Kiusta, excavations conducted during this period focused on early to mid-Holocene (ca. 2500 to 7500 BP) sites in northern Haida Gwaii, many of which are associated with raised beaches. In 1969 and 1979, Fladmark conducted excavations at the early to mid-Holocene sites of Kasta, Lawn Point, and Skoglund's Landing. These excavations showed that Haida Gwaii had been occupied for close to 8,000 years. Working in the days when access to Haida Gwaii was limited and research budgets were low, Fladmark laid out the basic cultural history of the islands in a way that has since seen only minor revision. In 1973 and 1974, Severs (1974a, 1975) conducted excavations at the mid to late Holocene Tow Hill and Blue Jackets Creek sites, although full analysis of either site has not yet been reported. Blue Jackets, in particular, saw extensive excavation and a large faunal assemblage was recovered that could shed light on the poorly known period between 4500 and 2000 BP.

Between 1984 and 1986, Acheson (1998) led a program of systematic survey and test excavation in southernmost Haida Gwaii. The survey encompassed Kunghit Island and the southern tip of Moresby Island. Test excavations were conducted at twenty archaeological sites, including habitation sites and rock shelters. All sites investigated were late Holocene (post-2000 BP) in age. The results of the archaeological project were integrated with ethnographic data to examine Kunghit Haida settlement pattern dynamics during late prehistoric and early historic time. Collectively, the sites revealed important patterns in Haida subsistence and settlement, although excavations were fairly limited at any given site. Otherwise, only minor, salvage-oriented excavations, such as at Cohoe Creek (Ham 1988, 1990), were conducted during this time.

The past decade has seen a substantial increase in archaeological investigations across Haida Gwaii. Systematic surveys in Gwaii Haanas (southern Moresby Island) and on northern Graham Island have identified many new sites along the modern shoreline as well as a number on raised beaches and in paleo-intertidal context (Zacharias and Wanagun 1993; Eldridge et al. 1993; Mackie and Wilson 1994, 1995; Christensen 1997; Stafford and Christensen 2000). Most of these projects have relied on the long-term sea level histories produced by Fedje (1993) and Josenhans et al. (1997). Most sites excavated during this time are early or mid-Holocene in age, including Arrow Creek (Fedje et al. 1996), Richardson Island and Lyell Bay (Fedje and Christensen 1999), Cohoe Creek (Chapter 13), and Kilgii Gwaay (Fedje et al. 2001; Chapter 11). In the last few years, paleontological and archaeological investigation of karst landscapes has produced exciting new evidence of late glacial to early Holocene animal populations (Ramsey et al. 2004; Chapter 6). Archaeological evidence associated with these early faunal assemblages is limited to a few spearpoints from K1 Cave (artifacts are from a sediment unit with six dates between 10,950 and 10,400 BP) and spearpoints and flakes dating between 10,500 and 10,000 BP from Gaadu Din Cave, but appears to hold promise for the search for the earliest human occupation of the region (Fedje 2003; Fedje et al. 2004b). Limited excavations were also conducted at a few late Holocene sites in southern Haida Gwaii (Sumpter and Mason 1999; Mackie et al. 2001; Orchard 2003). Research-oriented excavation and survey have thus accelerated in recent years, with several projects now coming to fruition and more in the planning stages. A principal impetus for this accelerated work was the creation of Gwaii Haanas National Park Reserve and Haida Heritage Site. Proper management of Gwaii Haanas cultural resources required as full an inventory of archaeological sites as possible, and the testing of a select few. This groundwork attracted archaeologists from the Universities of Victoria and Toronto, who were able to partner with Parks Canada in research-oriented excavation projects.

Current research priorities include the search for pre-10,500 BP human occupation, if any, of Haida Gwaii. The period 5000 to 2000 BP requires further reporting of existing projects and/or new projects to be run, as there is little reliable evidence for the way of life at a time when there is reason to believe that important transformations were occurring in Haida Gwaii. The post-2000 BP period north of Gwaii Haanas is largely unknown. This important time period will shed light on the trends towards the historical Haida way of life, with its monumental architecture and sculpture and wide-ranging interaction with mainland communities. Finally, some preliminary archaeological work in the early historic period shows promise for reconstruction of a pre–fur trade environment and how that trade influenced the natural and human ecology of Haida Gwaii (Mackie et al. 2001; Orchard 2003).

Archaeological Research in Haida Gwaii in Broader Context

The early history (pre-5000 BP) of Haida Gwaii and of the British Columbia coast in general is poorly known as a result of rapid environmental change and a dearth of focused investigation. Prior to the mid-1990s, only three early Holocene sites (Kasta, Lawn Point, and Skoglund's Landing) had been excavated in Haida Gwaii (Fladmark 1989). Although this has begun to be addressed over the past decade (Chapters 9-13), the period is still incompletely known. Elsewhere in British Columbia, only three early Holocene coastal occupation sites – Namu, Bear Cove, and Glenrose Cannery – have been investigated (R. Carlson 1996; C. Carlson 1979; Matson 1996). Of these, only Namu (R. Carlson 1996) has been the focus of multi-year intensive investigations. Other early sites, such as those sampled by Aubrey Cannon (2000) in the Namu area, have yet to be intensively investigated.

In the last decade the archaeological record for the Northwest Coast has been extended to about 10,500 BP with substantial evidence present by 9500 BP (Dixon 2002; Chapter 11). A heightened level of archaeological survey incorporating more precise environmental models has led to increased success in locating and investigating mid to early Holocene archaeological sites in Haida Gwaii (Chapter 10; Fedje and Christensen 1999). Further afield, an increased focus on investigation of ancient coastal landscapes has resulted in the discovery or reinvestigation of a number of early coastal archaeological sites (Dixon 2001; Erlandson 2002; Erlandson et al. 1999; Johnson et al. 2000; Jones et al. 2002; Rick et al. 2001; Sandweiss et al. 1998). Additionally, coastal paleontological sites in British Columbia and southeastern Alaska provide proxy data supporting a human-friendly environment in early postglacial times (Ramsey et al. 2004; Heaton and Grady 2003; Ward et al. 2003; Nagorsen et al. 1995). We now see evidence for fully maritime-capable adaptations as early as 9500 BP, evidence for occupation at 10,600 BP, and evidence for a viable environment perhaps as early as 14,500 BP. It is still not known how or when the first people reached Haida Gwaii, the Northwest Coast, or the Americas, but archaeologists are more optimistic that they will be able to find evidence to answer this important question.

The apparent lack of interest until recently in the early Holocene archaeology of the British Columbia coast is surprising considering the promising pioneering work of archaeologists such as Knut Fladmark (1989) and Roy Carlson (1996). In part this may have resulted from the overarching continental focus of North American archaeology (Bonnichsen and Turnmire 1999; Easton 1992). As recently as the late 1960s, some archaeologists suggested that much of the Northwest Coast, including Haida Gwaii, was probably not inhabited until after 5000 BP (Sanders and Marino 1970). In the 1970s and 1980s, archaeological data showed that initial occupation of the Northwest Coast was of greater antiquity, but most archaeologists held that the earliest populations would be derived from interior people moving down river valleys and adapting to coastal environments, or from a relatively late arrival of a maritime people associated with the Northwest Coast Microblade Tradition (Matson and Coupland 1995; Ames and Maschner 1999; West 1996). In these paradigms, Haida Gwaii, as the most remote west coast archipelago, was thought to be among the last lands occupied by humans. Fladmark's early results, showing early dates of 7500 BP and a clear microblade-based tool kit, appeared to fit Haida Gwaii into its "proper place" in this late-arrival model.

Despite this, Fladmark (1975, 1979a) himself presented a paleoecological model in support of a Pacific coast migration route for the first entry of humans into southern North America, at the end of the last ice age. The central feature of this model was the realization that during the terminal ice age, the sea level would have been much lower than at present, exposing a broad coastal plain along the British Columbian and Alaskan coast. This plain, the characteristics of which were poorly known, could have formed a coastal migration corridor for people prior to 10,000 BP, perhaps rivalling the commonly accepted Alberta "ice-free corridor" as a route for first peopling of the Americas. Fladmark (1975) coined the name "Hecatia" for that part of the plain now drowned by the waters of Hecate Strait. In the 1970s paleoenvironmental evidence for refugia and early deglaciation on the North Coast was building rapidly, although unequivocal evidence for human presence extended no earlier than about 8000 BP. In subsequent decades paleoenvironmental data have confirmed the presence of an early (but now drowned) habitable landscape (see Chapters 2 and 3). Further, methodological advances have enhanced archaeologists' ability to characterize past landscapes and assess them for archaeological site potential. Despite Fladmark's strong calls for increased research on the west coast of North America and a model to aid in the development of this research, little attention was paid to early period archaeology in this area over the following decades. Inattention to the west coast in the investigation of the peopling of the Americas led Easton (1992:35) to suggest that "archaeologists in the Americas are spawned from a continentally-bound culture ... Archaeologists concerned with the field of human migrations to the Americas ... view the sea as an impenetrable barrier over an incomprehensible landscape, a terra incognita." While many still adhere to the interior "Ice-free Corridor" model of human entry into the Americas, the "Coastal Corridor" concept advanced by Fladmark is now being more widely considered. This results in part from a pre-11,000 BP squeeze on the Ice-free Corridor and concurrent relaxation of the Coastal Corridor (Dixon 2002; Fedje 1995, 2002; Mandryk et al. 2000; Wilson and Burns 1999; see discussion in Chapter 3). Arguably, four overarching factors stunted the investigation of the earliest occupation of the Northwest Coast:

1 A deeply drowned landscape produced a pessimistic attitude towards even finding the earliest archaeological material.
2 A prevailing model suggesting that terrestrial adaptation must precede a maritime one directed interest away from the coast.
3 The primacy of the Ice-free Corridor "Clovis-first" model meant that the coast was seen as a backwater of the "peopling of the Americas question."
4 Meanwhile, coastal archaeologists were busy focusing on what was widely considered the "big problem": the development of unique forms of social complexity through the later Holocene.

As noted earlier, the more recent archaeological record for Haida Gwaii is unexpectedly less well known than the earlier periods. For the period from about 5000 to 2000 BP, only the Kiusta, Tow Hill, and Blue Jackets sites have been excavated (Severs 1975) and none have been fully reported. The prehistoric archaeological record for the last 1,500 years is somewhat better known (Acheson 1998), but only for southern Haida Gwaii. To the north, only small salvage and test projects have been reported. Ongoing work by Parks Canada, the University of Victoria, and the University of Toronto is anticipated to fill some knowledge gaps but, again, with a focus on southern Haida Gwaii. The archaeological record for late Holocene Haida Gwaii is summarized by Mackie and Acheson in Chapter 14. Based on research elsewhere on the coast, it is not unreasonable to think that some kinds of semi-sedentary life in plank houses was developed by 3,000 years ago. The transition from a highly mobile way of life to a more settled one may have caused, or been caused by, other social and technological developments, such as extensive food storage, social stratification, semi-sedentism, and the development of a settlement hierarchy: in other words, social complexity. Elsewhere on the coast, resolving this tangled set of interrelated social and subsistence traits has been the primary focus of archaeologists working on late Holocene sites. Haida Gwaii has seen relatively little research on this problem (and little research overall), but Acheson's work is illuminating and cautionary in that it points to different details of Haida subsistence and settlement even in the fairly recent past (Acheson 1998; Chapter 15).

Taken together, archaeology offers one way of knowing the past, based on its material remains. Large questions, such as when and where things happened, are readily answered provided there is good methodology and suitable models. The information produced by archaeologists should be read, as we hope it will be in this book, against the twin backdrops of environmental history (what was the world like?) and oral tradition (what do the people choose to pass down through the generations?). In this manner, a rich and complete human history of Haida Gwaii can be written.

Chapter Organization

In Part 3 of this volume, recent archaeological research is summarized and placed in a broader context. In Chapter 9, Daryl Fedje and Quentin Mackie provide an introductory overview of the cultural history of Haida Gwaii and set this in the context of a more general history of the North Coast. In Chapter 10, Fedje and colleagues summarize archaeological survey method and results for periods when sea level was at the early to mid-Holocene maximum and when substantially lower than at present. Environmental and archaeological information are integrated, showing human responses to a dynamic landscape. In Chapter 11, Fedje and colleagues present preliminary results of recent investigations conducted at earliest Holocene Kilgii Gwaay, a site occupied when sea levels were a few metres lower than at present. Further details about excavations at raised beach sites in both northern and southern Haida Gwaii are given in Chapter 12, by Fedje and colleagues, and Chapter 13, by Tina Christensen and Jim Stafford, which focus on the important Richardson Island and Cohoe Creek sites. Attention then turns to later periods in Chapter 14, in which Quentin Mackie and Steven Acheson synthesize the early and late Graham Traditions, and Chapter 15, in which Steven Acheson examines settlement archaeology of the late Graham Tradition. In Chapter 16, Alexander Mackie and Ian Sumpter outline results of Gwaii Haanas shoreline archaeological surveys and examine the relationship between earliest Holocene and late prehistoric (late Graham Tradition) archaeological sites and their environmental context.

9
Overview of Cultural History
Daryl W. Fedje and Quentin Mackie

The prehistoric record for the northern Northwest Coast has been synthesized by a number of researchers (Fladmark et al. 1990; Carlson 1990, 1996;
Matson and Coupland 1995; Ames and Maschner 1999). Terminology and,
to some extent, interpretation vary widely between researchers. In this chapter, we briefly discuss the regional context of this history and then provide
a summary of the local (Haida Gwaii) record.

Earliest Archaeology of Northwestern North America
The earliest known traces of human occupation in northwestern North
America are the Nenana (ca. 12,000 to 10,500 BP) and Denali (ca. 10,500 to
8000 BP) Complex sites in interior and western Alaska. No antecedents to
these cultural constructs have yet been discovered in Alaska or the Northwest, and Nenana is apparently not ancestral to Denali. It is proposed that
people bearing the Nenana tool kit arrived via the interior of Beringia sometime before 12,000 BP, and the later Denali Complex arrived sometime before 10,500 BP (Hamilton and Goebel 1999).

The Nenana Complex has been defined on the basis of a small number of
open-air archaeological sites in the Nenana and Tanana Valleys of central
Alaska (Powers and Hoffecker 1989; Hamilton and Goebel 1999; Bever 2001).
These sites date from about 11,800 to 10,000 BP. Technology characteristic
of Nenana includes a rich bifacial industry, including small triangular and
teardrop-shaped bifaces ("Chindadn points"); unifacial scrapers; cobble tools;
blade technology; and the apparent absence of microblade technology
(Hamilton and Goebel 1999). Abundant faunal remains from the Broken
Mammoth site components III and IV (11,800 to 10,300 BP) include large
mammal (bison, wapiti, caribou), small mammal, and abundant waterfowl,
and fish remains, possibly salmon (Holmes 1996). The small sample of
Nenana Complex sites constrains full interpretation of human adaptation
at this early time. All sites of this age in Alaska appear to be open-air camps

or lookout sites, although this may reflect archaeological search strategies or inherent site visibility.

The Denali Complex was defined by West (1967) for a number of sites in interior Alaska and the Yukon. More recent work by researchers such as Powers and Hoffecker (1989) and Hamilton and Goebel (1999) has further refined the definition of this early construct. Wedge-shaped microblade cores, blades, lanceolate bifacial points, bifacial knives, burins, and flake tools characterize Denali stone tool assemblages.

The timing and direction of dispersal of early people to the northern Northwest Coast remains poorly understood. Researchers variously propose very early (13,000 to 12,000 BP) movement along the Beringian–Alaskan–British Columbia coast by maritime-adapted people (Fladmark 1983; Dixon 1999, 2002) and somewhat later (11,000 to 9000 BP) movement of terrestrial hunter-gatherers to the British Columbia and southeastern Alaska coasts (with later in situ development of maritime adaptation) either directly from interior Alaska (Borden 1969:260; Carlson 2004) or from the North American interior via major river valleys such as the Skeena, Fraser, or Columbia (Coupland 1998; Matson and Coupland 1995; Workman 2001). Paralleling the Alaskan record, the earliest peopling of the Northwest Coast was characterized as an encounter between two peoples: one bearing microblade technology and the other bearing bifacial technology, although this model is now challenged by new data.

Northern Northwest Coast Culture
Fladmark divides northern Northwest Coast culture history into two very general divisions, a Lithic Stage (Early Period) and a Developmental Stage (Recent Period) (Fladmark 1982; Fladmark et al. 1990). The Lithic Stage includes that part of the prehistoric record dating prior to development of the "Northwest Coast cultural pattern" as expressed by traits that include large shell middens, an emphasis on salmon procurement and storage, extensive woodworking, and development of art.

The Lithic Stage
Early Holocene technological traditions on the Northwest Coast of North America fall into two main categories: those dominated by bifaces and those dominated by microblades. Bifaces are produced from larger cores by soft-hammer percussion and may have been useful either hafted or unhafted. Microblades are produced from small prepared cores and were presumably hafted in relatively complex composite tools. Outside of Haida Gwaii, only two early Northwest Coast sites (Namu and PET-408) are known to contain both these lithic traditions, hence the relationship between them is poorly understood.

Early Coastal Bifacial Tradition

On the British Columbia coast, this early coastal bifacial tradition has been designated as the Pebble Tool Tradition by Carlson (1990) and the Old Cordilleran Tradition by Matson (1996). A small stone tool assemblage from karst caves in southern Haida Gwaii includes leaf-shaped points dating to 10,600 BP and is the earliest known evidence of this tradition (Fedje et al. 2004b; Ramsey et al. 2004; Fedje 2005). It has been suggested that the early bifacial tradition on the Northwest Coast may derive from Nenana or its Beringian antecedents (Dixon 1999, 2002; Carlson 2004; Fedje et al. 2004b; see also discussion in Chapter 12), but there remains a considerable temporal separation (ca. 1,000 years) between initial Nenana Complex dates and the earliest dated bifacial assemblages on the Northwest Coast. Thus, alternate derivations, such as via the Paleoindian or Western Stemmed Point Traditions (Matson and Coupland 1995), need to be explored as well.

Northwest Coast Microblade Tradition

The Northwest Coast Microblade Tradition has been identified at a number of sites along the northern Northwest Coast (Carlson 1979; Fladmark 1982; Fedje and Christensen 1999; Ackerman 1992; Coupland 1988; Magne and Fedje 2004). This tradition is characterized "by a microblade industry; flake cores, including 'pebble tools'; a variety of retouched flake tools; rare crude leaf-shaped bifaces (not always present); rare abrasive stones; rare possible ground or notched sinker stones; and non-shell contexts" (Fladmark 1982). Investigations at Cohoe Creek in the north of Haida Gwaii and on Heceta Island, southeastern Alaska, some 100 kilometres to the north, have identified Northwest Coast Microblade Tradition components associated with small shell-rich middens on raised beaches (Chapter 13; Ackerman et al. 1985). The middens contain marine and terrestrial elements typical of later Northwest Coast middens. Clearly, the "non-shell" context ascribed to the Northwest Coast Microblade Tradition is at least partly a function of preservation. The relatively small sample of archaeological sites presently known for this time period reflects visibility problems relating to factors such as sea level change and mass-wasting.

The Developmental Stage (Recent Period) (ca. 5000 to 250 BP)

The second stage, the Developmental Stage, documents the development of the Northwest Coast cultural pattern. Fladmark (1982) separates this stage into three substages – early, middle, and late – based on degree of development towards the ethnographic cultural pattern.

The Early Developmental Substage (ca. 5000 to 3500 BP) sees the end of the early microblade industry (Fladmark 1982; Coupland 1988) with replacement, in part, by bipolar core technology. The remaining elements of the Lithic Stage continue through the Early Developmental Substage.

Assemblages from the later part of this substage provide the earliest evidence for use of ground stone, including rare ground slate tools. A number of large shell middens with good preservation are known for this time, and as a result the material culture record is much better documented than in the previous stages. Utilitarian artifacts of bone and antler, including points, awls, and wedges, are common. Artistic sculpture of organic objects is rare (predominantly decoration of utilitarian items). Evidence for structural remains from this substage is scanty but points to small dwellings and an absence of housepit features.

The period from about 3500 to 2500 BP is suggested (Fladmark 1982) to be transitional, at least on the South Coast, where it is associated with the Locarno Beach Phase, between the Early Developmental Substage (Charles Phase on the South Coast) and the Middle Developmental Substage (Marpole Phase on the South Coast).

The Middle Developmental Substage (ca. 2500 to 1500 BP) "sees the full attainment of a general Northwest Coast cultural pattern ... the gradual appearance of the complete Northwest Coast woodworking tool kit; large plank houses; numerous art objects, suggestive of complex ideology and craft specialization; frequent ornaments, exotic goods and other primitive valuables indicating a concern with wealth accumulation and display; increased evidence of status differentiation in burials; the full development of complex and diversified fishing and sea-mammal hunting equipment generally similar to that of the ethnographic period; evidence of significant population aggregates, and the first strong indications of warfare" (Fladmark 1982:113). This substage equates to MacDonald and Inglis's "Period II" (1981) for the Prince Rupert Harbour area. They document a substantially expanded material culture record (MacDonald and Inglis 1981:45-47), much increased exploitation of intertidal bivalves and commensurate rapid buildup of shell middens, larger villages, larger houses and house features, as well as social changes such as development of corporate groups (Coupland 1988).

The Late Developmental Substage (ca. 1500 to 250 BP) is applied to prehistoric coastal assemblages that compare closely with those of ethnographic populations of the North Coast area. There is little evidence for any significant shift in adaptive strategy, and changes in the material culture record are not as substantive as between previous substages. Data support a ranked village structure as expressed in structural evidence and associated artifacts, and art styles display close affinity with those documented for the ethnographic northern Northwest Coast (Fladmark 1982).

Haida Gwaii Culture History to about 200 BP

Within the context of North Coast prehistory, the data from Haida Gwaii can be organized into three major chronological units: the Kinggi Complex, the Moresby Tradition, and the Graham Tradition. These cultural constructs reflect significant change in prehistoric technology and, by inference, adaptation. They generally correspond to Fladmark's (1982) Early Lithic, Late Lithic, and Developmental stages, respectively.

Kinggi Complex (> 9500 to 8900 BP)

Pre-8900 BP occupations are assigned to the "Kinggi Complex" (see Chapters 11 and 12; Fedje and Christensen 1999; Fedje et al. 2001). During this time, relative sea levels were rising from a low of about 150 metres below present levels at 12,000 BP. They reached the elevation of the modern sea level towards the latter part of the period, and shoreline-associated cultural resources dating prior to 9400 BP can be expected only in the intertidal zone and on submerged landforms. By 9000 BP the sea level had surpassed current levels and attained the early Holocene stillstand of about 15 metres above modern level. Sites of the late Kinggi Complex are therefore expected on coastal features stranded in the forest. Knowledge of human adaptations at this time remains sketchy, with most information coming from the Richardson Island (Fedje and Christensen 1999; Chapter 12) and Kilgii Gwaay (Fedje et al. 2001; Chapter 11) sites in the south of Haida Gwaii. Richardson Island dates from 9300 to 8400 BP and Kilgii Gwaay is a single component site dating to 9450 BP. Bifacial technology is well represented at this time, while microblade technology appears to be absent. Tools characteristic of these assemblages include leaf-shaped bifaces, large scrapers, scraperplanes or adzes, large unifaces, cobble choppers, gravers, and spokeshaves. These lithic assemblages appear to consist entirely of local materials. This suggests little or no contact with mainland groups at this time. Bone technology is known from Kilgii Gwaay, consisting of bear bone awls, splinter awls, a tabular sea mammal bone percussor, a small unilaterally barbed bone point, and miscellaneous worked bone. Highly fragmentary, calcined bone points have been found in Kinggi Complex hearths at Richardson Island as well. Wooden tools and woodworking debris are also known from Kilgii Gwaay.

The context of Kinggi Complex–age sites implies a maritime adaptation, but only at Kilgii Gwaay is there a significant faunal assemblage. Black bear and a broad range of maritime mammals, birds, fish, and shellfish were recovered from this site. Several species of this fauna could be obtained only by using watercraft (e.g., sea lion, albatross, halibut, and large rockfish). Along with location on a small island in southernmost Haida Gwaii, these data provide strong evidence of a fully capable maritime adaptation. Analysis of calcined bone from numerous hearth assemblages at Richardson Island is revealing a diverse suite of over ten fish taxa, including rockfish, lingcod, dogfish, and salmon. Small archaeological assemblages recovered from cave sites in the south of Haida Gwaii and dating from 10,600 to 10,000 BP likely represent an interior hunting aspect of this early bifacial tradition (Fedje et al. 2004b; Fedje 2005; McLaren et al. 2005).

Kinggi stone tool technology appears broadly similar to that seen at a small number of earliest Holocene archaeological sites along the west coast of North America, exhibiting assemblages characterized by bifaces and cobble tools (Ackerman 1992; Carlson 1996; Dixon 1999, 2001; Erlandson and Moss 2001). Most of these sites are small with few cultural remains. The timing of first appearance of this "early coastal bifacial tradition" on the Northwest Coast is unknown, but, like Nenana, it may have originated in Northeast Asia sometime before about 12,000 BP (cf. Dixon 1999, 2002). This tradition was progressively replaced by a microblade-characterized tradition after about 9500 BP. This replacement appears to pre-date 9200 BP in southeastern Alaska, date to 8900 BP in Haida Gwaii, and postdate 9000 BP in the Central Coast area. South of the Central Coast, microblade technology appears to postdate 8500 BP. Old Cordilleran components, dating from about 8000 to 5000 BP, such as those at Bear Cove, Glenrose, and St. Mungo, may represent the endpoints of a much longer lived early bifacial tradition.

Moresby Tradition (ca. 8900 to 5000 BP)
During this time, relative sea levels remained stable at about 15 metres above current levels. Previously known simply as the Moresby Tradition (Fladmark 1989), separation into an early and late component is now based on an apparent shift away from the use of a bifacial stone technology, as seen at a few key sites in southern Haida Gwaii (Fedje and Christensen 1999).

Early Moresby Tradition (ca. 8900 to ca. 8000 BP)
Microblade technology was added to the Kinggi tool kit about 8900 BP, resulting in lithic assemblages transitional between the earlier Kinggi Complex and the classic Moresby Tradition. This has been assigned the term *Early Moresby Tradition* (Fedje and Christensen 1999). Our understanding of human adaptations at this time is very limited, with most information coming from Richardson Island and Lyell Bay (Fedje and Christensen 1999). Tabular to conical microblade cores and microblades are abundant in these assemblages while other technological elements, including bifacial technology, show little change except in frequency. Recovery of faunal remains from these sites was limited to a small amount of highly calcined marine fish and bird bone. As with Kinggi, the Early Moresby lithic assemblages are composed entirely of local material (Smith 2004). Although there is no evidence of trade with mainland groups, the introduction of microblade technology implies significant interaction at a regional scale. The low number of Early Moresby components is, in large part, a consequence of low visibility and the very limited survey and exploration of raised beaches conducted to date. Sites of this age have not been subject to marine transgression; rather, the sea has fallen away since occupation of these shorelines. Such sites may therefore be relatively abundant and well preserved.

Beyond Haida Gwaii, On Your Knees Cave (49-PET-408) in southeastern Alaska (Dixon 1999) and Namu on the Central Coast of British Columbia (Carlson 1996) exhibit a similar combination of bifacial and microblade technology. The appearance of microblade technology is slightly earlier (ca. 9200 BP) at On Your Knees Cave than in Haida Gwaii, and its appearance is a bit later (ca. 9000 to 8500 BP) at Namu, suggesting a relatively slow southerly expansion along the coast. This tradition appears to be associated with the Alaskan Denali Complex, with ultimate origins in Northeast Asia. Although less well documented, this expansion appears to continue southward, reaching the South Coast of British Columbia by about 8500 BP (Magne and Fedje 2004). The Early Moresby Tradition offers an interpretive challenge to previous explanations of the early Holocene implying that peoples using microblades migrated from the north, meeting peoples using bifaces who were migrating from the south (Matson and Coupland 1995:96; Yesner 1996:271).

Late Moresby Tradition (ca. 8000 to 5000 BP)
The 8000 to 5000 BP archaeological components across Haida Gwaii fit well with Fladmark's Moresby Tradition (1989) and are included here as the "Late Moresby Tradition," which endured until mid-Holocene time. Sites conformable with the Late Moresby Tradition include Kasta, Lawn Point, Skoglund's Landing, Skidegate Landing (Fladmark 1982, 1986, 1989), and Cohoe Creek (Chapter 13) in northern Haida Gwaii and Richardson Island, Lyell Bay, and Arrow Creek in the south of the archipelago (Fedje and Christensen 1999; Mackie n.d.). The sites in this group occupy raised beaches at 12 to 15 metres above current sea level and are "typical" Northwest Coast Microblade sites, with assemblages characterized by microblades, microblade cores, pebble tools, pebble cores, and flakes. Bifacial technology is absent from all Haida Gwaii Late Moresby Tradition components.

Existing data are insufficient to project subsistence and settlement to broad areas, although ongoing research in northern Haida Gwaii (Chapter 13) is shedding considerable new light in this area. Late Moresby site distribution in Gwaii Haanas is limited to about ten sites, with excavation conducted at four of these. Recovery of faunal remains was limited to a very small amount of highly calcined marine fish and bird bone. The geographical location of these sites and data from early periods argue for maritime capacity. Cohoe Creek (Chapter 13) provides evidence of a well-developed maritime adaptation associated with microblade technology. Cultural evidence encompasses structural features, activity areas, and shell midden. The midden contains a diverse assemblage of marine, intertidal, and terrestrial fauna.

Graham Tradition (ca. 5000 to 250 BP)
The Graham Tradition is associated with the Developmental Stage of Flad-

mark et al. (1990). This tradition began about 5,000 years ago and continued to the time of European contact. For the time from about 4500 to 2000 BP, the bulk of our knowledge derives from one site, the Blue Jackets Creek site excavated by Fladmark (1970) and Severs (1974a). Fladmark has divided the Graham Tradition into an early (transitional) and a late component.

The Graham Tradition is marked by the end of the microblade tradition in Haida Gwaii and by association with shell middens and assemblages containing evidence for large quantities of faunal remains, boiling stones, and a variety of ground, pecked, and polished stone and organic artifacts (bone, wood, plant, and shell) (Fladmark 1989). Subsistence resources are strongly dominated by marine and intertidal species.

Early (Transitional) Graham Tradition (ca. 5000 to 3000 BP)
During this time, relative sea level fell gradually, reaching approximately 7 metres above current levels by about 4000 BP. There is insufficient evidence to associate any of the known sites in the Gwaii Haanas area with this time period. In northern Haida Gwaii, the upper levels of the Lawn Point (Fladmark 1986), Cohoe Creek (Chapter 13), Blue Jackets Creek (Severs 1974a), and Skoglund's Landing (Fladmark 1990) sites date to this time. These sites are situated on raised beaches some 7 to 10 metres above the modern sea level and contain midden deposits with a combination of marine, coastal, and terrestrial fauna. Stone tool assemblages contain some ground stone and rare bifacially worked lithics. The microblade technology characteristic of the earlier Moresby Tradition has been replaced by a bipolar technology, often with products morphologically similar to those derived from the former (Fladmark 1975). Until sites excavated in the 1970s (Gessler 1974; Severs 1974a) are more fully reported or additional sites of this age are investigated, this key period in Haida Gwaii prehistory cannot be reliably interpreted.

Late Graham Tradition (ca. 2000 to 200 BP)
At present there are no known sites in Gwaii Haanas dating to the period between 4000 and 2000 BP. After about 2000 BP, a specialized woodworking technology appears in the archaeological record and the developed Northwest Coast culture is evident, including aspects such as large habitation structures, more effective food procurement technology, extensive trade, highly developed monumental and portable art, and more extensive warfare. Some researchers suggest that rapid development of "classic" Northwest Coast adaptation at about 2000 BP resulted from the introduction of a complex of cultural traits from the mainland (Tsimshian) (MacDonald 1983b; Acheson 1998).

Most information on Developmental Stage Haida culture comes from the Blue Jackets Creek site (Severs 1974a), a mid-1980s program of archaeological investigation in the Kunghit Haida territory of southern Moresby Island (Chapters 14 and 15; Acheson 1998; Acheson and Zacharias 1985; Acheson et al. 1986), and the Gwaii Haanas Environmental Archaeology Project (Mackie et al. 2001; Orchard 2002). The Kunghit Haida Archaeological Project investigations support a fully developed Northwest Coast maritime culture oriented to the open coast by about 2000 BP (Acheson 1998). Settlement appears to have been dispersed, with ready access to a wide range of resources negating a need for substantial seasonal mobility. This is the opposite of the situation shortly after European contact, when large aggregated villages and low population density necessitated a "seasonal round." Overall, interpretation supports significant shifts in settlement activity within this time frame, including an intensification of activity in the early part and a substantive shift in adaptation with the introduction of the fur trade in the 1700s (Acheson 1998).

10

Millennial Tides and Shifting Shores: Archaeology on a Dynamic Landscape

Daryl W. Fedje, Tina Christensen, Heiner Josenhans, Joanne B. McSporran, and Jennifer Strang

Investigations conducted in northern Haida Gwaii in the 1970s demonstrated that archaeological sites dating from about 8000 to 5000 BP were associated with shorelines 12 to 14 metres higher than present levels and hinted that pre-10,000 BP coastal occupation sites may have been drowned by rising sea levels (Fladmark 1989). Early work in southern Moresby Island identified several sites suggested to be of early Holocene age (Hobler 1978a). These included a lithic scatter on the 15-metre terrace of Arrow Creek and a number of lithic scatters in the intertidal zone (Figure 10.1). None were dated but the character of the assemblages suggested association with Fladmark's early Holocene "Moresby Tradition" (1989).

Following these lines of evidence, surveys for early Holocene archaeological sites were conducted as part of the Gwaii Haanas basic resource inventory. Several of these surveys were facilitated by the integration of local sea level history with topographic digital elevation models and focused on both stranded and drowned paleoshorelines (Chapter 16; Fedje and Christensen 1999; Fedje and Josenhans 2000).

The first paleoshoreline surveys were undertaken in Gwaii Haanas in the southern part of Haida Gwaii (Figure 10.1). Raised beach, intertidal, and marine surveys were effective in locating early Holocene cultural material. Subsequent raised beach surveys in northern Haida Gwaii more than doubled the number of known mid to early Holocene sites in that area and highlighted site preservation and site visibility differences between northern and southern Haida Gwaii.

Paleoshoreline Survey

Knowledge of the Haida Gwaii archaeological record dating earlier than about 5000 BP has been limited by a lack of familiarity with the paleolandscape, poor site visibility, and poor site preservation. Sea level history research

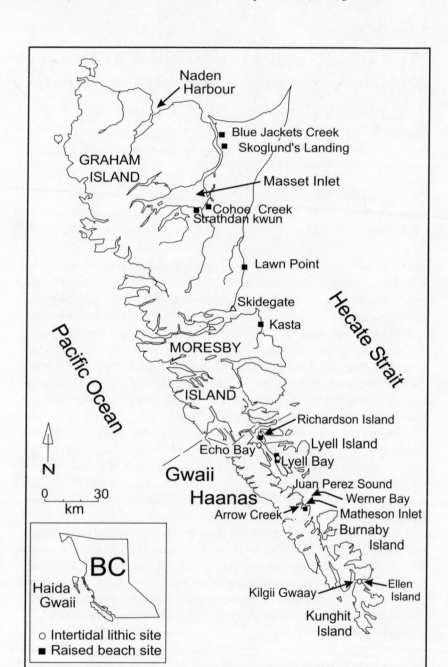

Figure 10.1   Haida Gwaii.

has provided a basis for investigating the early Holocene history of the archipelago (Fedje 1993; Fedje and Christensen 1999). Three areas of applied research have employed this history: systematic survey of raised beaches, survey of drowned shorelines now visible in the intertidal zone, and a more limited survey of deeply drowned shorelines.

Raised beach surveys were carried out in southern Haida Gwaii (Gwaii Haanas) in 1995 (Christensen 1997; Fedje and Christensen 1999) and in northern Haida Gwaii in 1999 (Stafford and Christensen 2000; Young and Eldridge 2001). Prior to these surveys, only eight sites directly associated with the sea level highstand had been recorded in Haida Gwaii (Table 10.1; Ham 1988; Fedje 1993; Fedje and Christensen 1999; Mackie and Wilson 1994, 1995; Fladmark 1971a, 1971b, 1986, 1989; Hobler and Seymour 1975; Severs 1974a, 1974b). Findings from several of these sites were used by Fladmark (1990) to define the Moresby Tradition, a cultural complex dating to between 5000 and 8000 BP and associated with higher sea levels.

Investigations of drowned shorelines include surveys of early Holocene beaches transgressed by rising sea levels at 9400 BP and now exposed in the modern intertidal zone as a result of late Holocene tectonic uplift, and offshore work on deeply drowned landscapes. The 9500 to 9400 BP shorelines were surveyed in the early 1990s (Chapter 16). The surveys of deeply drowned shorelines were conducted in Juan Perez Sound in 1998 and 1999 (Fedje and Josenhans 2000). The latter are the only submarine surveys for late glacial to early Holocene archaeological sites that have been conducted on the Northwest Coast. Similar work is being carried out along the coast of Florida (Faught 2003).

Raised Beach Site Survey: Gwaii Haanas

The sea level history for southern Haida Gwaii identifies a period of relative stability between about 9000 and 5000 BP (Figure 10.2). Sea levels remained within 1 metre of the 15-to-16-metre marine limit during this time. This stability was anticipated to result in a greater concentration of archaeological evidence on that shoreline while the record dating from about 9500 to 9000 BP and about 5000 to 3000 BP would be spread more thinly across the landscape because sea level was moving more quickly. A consequence of swift shoreline changes would be the frequent movement of camps, resulting in limited periods of occupation at one elevation, low densities of cultural materials, and a resulting difficulty in locating sites. In southern Haida Gwaii, terraces intermediate between the 15-metre stillstand terrace and modern shore were not clearly defined, as opposed to the case for northern Haida Gwaii (see below), where two regressive terraces were identified.

Table 10.1

Raised beach sites recorded in Haida Gwaii

Site no.	Site name	Elevation (m aht)	¹⁴C age BP	Lab no.	Diagnostic cultural evidence	Source
Sites recorded prior to 1995 Gwaii Haanas Raised Beach Study						
1127T	Richardson Island site[a]	18-14	9290 ± 50	CAMS-39785	Biface	Fedje and Christensen 1999
			8490 ± 70	CAMS-16199	Microblade	
1131T	Dodge Point[a]	16	5650 ± 70	CAMS-9979	Pebble tools	Mackie and Wilson 1994
FhUa-15	Honna River Bridge site[a]	12	Undated		Microblade technology	Fladmark 1971a
766T	Arrow Creek I[a]	14-16	8200 ± 80	TO-2622	Microblade, hearth	Fedje et al. 1996
			5600 ± 70	CAMS-4111	Stone tools	
922T	Hotspring Island	5	Undated			Fedje 1995
FgTw-4	Kasta[a]	14	5420 ± 100	GAK-3511	Microblade technology,	Fladmark 1986
			6010 ± 95	S-677	pebble tools	
FiTx-3	Lawn Point	14	2005 ± 85	S-678	Pebble tools, microblade	Fladmark 1986
			7400 ± 140	S-679		
FjUb-10	Cohoe Creek[a]	10-12	5750 ± 40	CAMS-50957	Microblade technology	Ham 1988
			4900 ± 80	CAMS-16205	Pebble tools, shell midden	
FhUa-4	Blue Jackets Creek	9	4290 ± 30	GSC-1554	Microblade technology,	Severs 1974a
					pebble tools, shell midden	
FlUa-1	Skoglund's Landing	9	ca. 9000	GX-1696	Pebble tools, shell midden	Fladmark 1989
			4165 ± 80			
FhUa-1	Honna River	10	3300 ± 100	GAK-1870	Shell midden	Fladmark 1971b

Site	Name	Zone	Date	Lab number	Description	Reference
GaTw-5	Tow Hill	6-9	3280 ± 210	GAK-5439	Shell midden, pebble tools	Severs 1975
FhUa-7	Skidegate Landing[a]	15	Undated		Microblade technology, shell midden, pebble tools	Fladmark 1971a
FlUe-3	Naden 1	6	3260 ± 60	CAMS-15372	Shell midden	Fedje et al. 1995
FlUe-4	Naden 2	6	3070 ± 60	CAMS-14436	Shell midden	Fedje et al. 1995

Sites recorded during 1995 Gwaii Haanas raised beach survey

Site	Name	Zone	Date	Lab number	Description	Reference
1351T	Lyell Bay	14	Undated		Microblade technology	Christensen 1997
1352T	Lyell Bay	18	Undated		Pebble tools	Christensen 1997
1353T	Lyell Bay	18	Undated		Stone tools	Christensen 1997
1354T	Lyell Bay	18	5030 ± 40 / 8810 ± 60	CAMS-33910 / CAMS-33913	Microblade technology, pebble tools	Christensen 1997
1355T	Lyell Bay	17	6630 ± 60 / 8450 ± 60	CAMS-26255 / CAMS-33917	Microblade technology, pebble tools	Christensen 1997
1356T	Beresford Inlet	18	3630 ± 50 / 3700 ± 50[b]	CAMS-42479 / CAMS-26258	Microblade technology	Christensen 1997
1358T	Sedgewick Bay	12	Undated		Pebble tools	Christensen 1997
1359T	Poole Inlet	13-16	8270 ± 60	CAMS-26261	Stone tools	Christensen 1997
1360T	Poole Inlet	14	Undated		Pebble tools	Christensen 1997
1361T	Dolomite Narrows	8	Undated		Stone tools	Christensen 1997
1362T	Burnaby Strait	12	Undated		Stone tools	Christensen 1997
1363T	NE Burnaby Island	9	Undated		Pebble tools	Christensen 1997

▼ *Table 10.1*

Site no.	Site name	Elevation (m aht)	¹⁴C age BP	Lab no.	Diagnostic cultural evidence	Source
1364T	Burnaby Strait	18	Undated		Stone tools	Christensen 1997
1366T	Poole Inlet	15-20	Undated		Stone tools	Christensen 1997
1374T	Swan Bay	18	Undated		Pebble tools	Christensen 1997
1375T	Matheson Inlet	17	Undated		Pebble tools	Christensen 1997
Northern Haida Gwaii raised beach sites recorded since 1995						
FhUa-52	Charlotte school site	17	Undated		Microblade technology[c]	Stafford and Christensen 1999
FkUb-16	Strathdang Kwun	10-13	5800-4500	CAMS-19020 CAMS-16203	Shell midden, pebble tools	Fedje et al. 1995
FjUcB16	Begbie Island	ca. 10	Undated		Microblade technology	Young and Eldridge 2001
FkUcB5	Begbie Island	ca. 8	Undated			Young and Eldridge 2001
FkUcA7	Ain River	8-10	Undated		Microblade technology	Young and Eldridge 2001
GaUd-3	Naden Harbour	10-12	5860 ± 60	BGS-2217	Shell midden	Stafford and Christensen 2000
GaUd-10	Naden Harbour	5	Undated		Shell midden	Stafford and Christensen 2000
GaUd-14	Naden Harbour	10	Undated		Shell midden	Stafford and Christensen 2000
GaUd-15	Naden Harbour	8	Undated		Shell midden	Stafford and Christensen

GaUd-17	Naden Harbour	13	Undated	Shell midden	Stafford and Christensen 2000
GaUd-19	Naden Harbour	12	Undated	Shell midden	Stafford and Christensen 2000
GaUd-20	Naden Harbour	9	Undated	Shell midden	Stafford and Christensen 2000
GaUd-24	Naden Harbour	8-10	Undated	Shell midden	Stafford and Christensen 2000
FlUd-20	Naden Harbour	5-8	Undated	Shell midden	Stafford and Christensen 2000
FlUd-8	Naden Harbour	8-10	Undated	Shell midden	Stafford and Christensen 2000
FlUd-6	Naden Harbour	8-10	Undated	Shell midden	Stafford and Christensen 2000
FlUd-1	Naden Harbour	5-7	Undated	Shell midden	Stafford and Christensen 2000
FlUd-14	Naden Harbour	4-5	Undated	Shell midden	Stafford and Christensen 2000
FlUd-3	Naden Harbour	9	Undated	Shell midden	Stafford and Christensen 2000
FlUd-18	Naden Harbour	9	Undated	Shell midden	Stafford and Christensen 2000

▼ Table 10.1

Site no.	Site name	Elevation (m aht)	¹⁴C age BP	Lab no.	Diagnostic cultural evidence	Source
GaUd-7	Naden Harbour	8	Undated		Shell midden	Stafford and Christensen 2000
GaUd-1	Naden Harbour	8	Undated		Shell midden	Stafford and Christensen 2000
GaUd-4	Naden Harbour	8-10	Undated		Shell midden	Stafford and Christensen 2000

a Associated with marine highstand landforms.
b Limiting dates.
c Microblade technology has been found only in sites older than 5,000 years and is used for relative dating purposes.

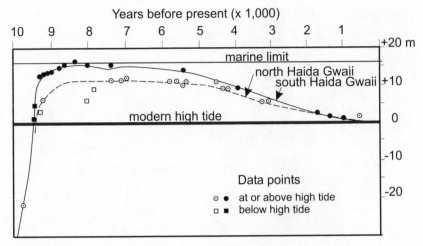

Figure 10.2 Haida Gwaii raised beach history.

Method

In order to find raised beach sites more efficiently, high-resolution digital elevation models were created for select areas. Accurate location of the 15-metre paleoshoreline was important because of poor visibility and topographic variation. Dense forest and deep organic soils are characteristic of this area, severely limiting archaeological visibility. The distance between the modern shoreline and the 15-metre elevation varies between 100 metres and 2 kilometres. By accurately positioning investigation on terrain between 15 and 20 metres elevation, we substantially reduced the area of survey. The initial approach to survey entailed production of digital elevation models and reconstruction of paleoshorelines based on sea level history.

The Gwaii Haanas elevation models were produced using photogrammetry. A vertical accuracy of 0.5 metre was obtained through a 10-metre grid analysis of 1:20,000 air photo stereo pairs. For field use, the data was transformed, using AutoCAD, into 1:5,000 scale 1-metre contour interval maps. With sea level shown at the 15 metres above high tide contour interval, areas with high potential for archaeological sites could be selected.

Three study areas on the eastern shore of Gwaii Haanas were selected for focused raised beach archaeological survey: Lyell Island, Matheson Inlet, and Burnaby Island (Figure 10.1). These areas were selected based in part on protection from the open sea and the location of other early Holocene sites in Haida Gwaii. These sites included known early Holocene intertidal lithic sites and the raised beach aspect of the Arrow Creek site (Figure 10.3). Intertidal lithic sites are lag remnants of early Holocene archaeological sites now exposed in the intertidal zone. The 1-metre contour interval mapped topography around Arrow Creek served as a key example of how early sites

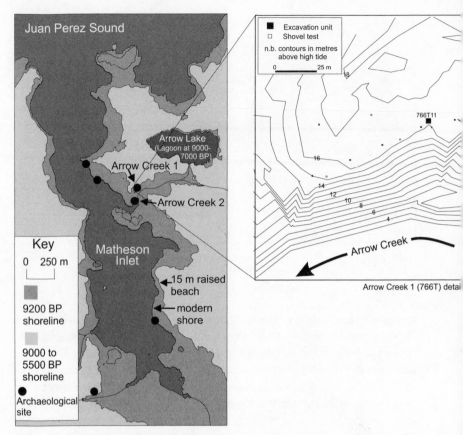

Figure 10.3   Matheson Inlet study area.

could appear on these maps (Fedje et al. 1996). Most prominent was the wide, flat terrace bordering the 15-metre highstand mark of what is now Arrow Creek, but which then would have been a saltwater arm of Matheson Inlet. Also evident was a gently sloping (paleo)intertidal zone. Locations with these characteristics stand out on the 1:5,000 scale 1-metre contour interval maps and were selected for field study.

One-metre contour interval maps were produced for the first two study areas. The maps clearly displayed wide terraces between 15 and 20 metres above high tide in several locations (Figure 10.4). Only 1:20,000 topographic maps were available for the Burnaby Island area, but the survey remained effective as the crew had developed a familiarity with raised beach features following work at Lyell Island and Matheson Inlet.

Two months were spent surveying the three study areas. Teams of two to four persons hiked into the high-potential areas from the modern shore-line. Altimeters, set to zero at the high tide mark, aided in the location of

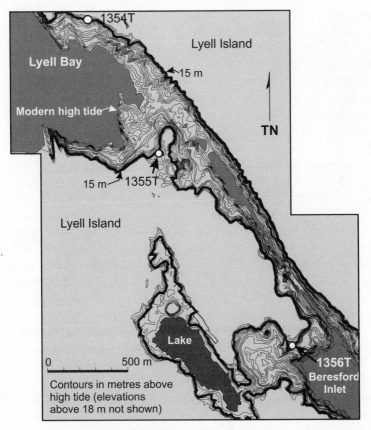

Figure 10.4 Lyell Island study area.

15-metre terraces. When sites were found, hand-levels and stadia were used to verify elevation as the altimeters could give unreliable readings during unstable weather. Besides the selected high- and moderate-potential areas, a large portion of the shoreline thought to have low potential for raised beach sites on the elevation model maps was surveyed to test the validity of the model.

Elevations above and below the 15-metre contour interval (between 10 and 20 metres above sea level) were examined to locate sites back from the highstand shoreline and artifacts eroded from raised beach sites and deposited at lower elevations. Natural exposures were used to locate surface evidence of cultural material, and auger and shovel testing were undertaken to locate subsurface evidence of early deposits. Surveys of stream, creek, and rivulet runoff as well as tree throw matrices were very effective in locating artifacts that were no longer in primary context. These exposures were tracked up to the 15-metre elevation where subsurface testing was undertaken.

Results

This survey located 16 new raised beach sites (see Table 10.1), increasing the raised beach site inventory for Gwaii Haanas to 20. A total of 53 kilometres were surveyed, with a site density of 0.25 sites per kilometre on Lyell Island and 0.35 sites per kilometre in the Matheson Inlet and Burnaby Island study areas (Christensen 1996; Table 10.1).

The majority of these sites were first observed in surface exposures (creeks, rivulets, tree throws) and only a small number ($N = 6$) were located through subsurface testing alone. On Lyell Island, sites were observed only in locations showing high potential on the contour maps, suggesting that the maps were very effective in pinpointing early site locations. Radiocarbon samples taken from charcoal-rich strata in shovel tests at four Lyell Island sites ranged in age from 3600 to 8300 BP.

The 1-metre contour interval maps were not as effective for locating sites in the Matheson Inlet area. Other than the previously recorded Arrow Creek site, only one raised beach lithic site was found. Although the map showed several locations with wide, flat terraces above the sea level highstand, most of these locations proved to be swampy and unsuitable for human occupation.

In the Burnaby Island study area, eight sites were recorded, one of which was dated to 8200 BP. A 1-metre contour interval map was not prepared for this area. Location of several raised beach sites employed 1:20,000 maps and the locational skills developed in the Lyell and Matheson surveys.

Surveyors found that raised beach sites were often situated on early Holocene terraces immediately inland from intertidal lithic and shell midden sites. Half of the raised beach sites are within 200 metres of an intertidal lithic site or a shell midden site, and almost 20 percent are within 200 metres of both. Sites were often associated with small creeks and streams that commonly held artifacts eroded from in situ site deposits.

Raised Beach Site Survey: Northern Haida Gwaii

Following the 1995 raised beach survey of Gwaii Haanas, archaeologists working in Haida Gwaii have focused more resources on locating raised beach sites. Between 1995 and 1999, over twenty new raised beach sites were located in northern Haida Gwaii (Table 10.1; Mason 1995; Fedje et al. 1995; Christensen and Stafford 2000; Stafford and Christensen 2000; Young and Eldridge 2001). Most of these were recorded during surveys initiated by the Council of the Haida Nation and the Ministry of Forests in Naden Harbour and Masset Inlet on northern Graham Island. Shell midden sites were found on several raised beaches on Graham Island, but only one study, at Naden Harbour, was substantive and systematic (Stafford and Christensen 2000). This investigation is detailed below.

Raised Beach Site Survey: Naden Harbour

A survey of Naden Harbour in northernmost Haida Gwaii in 1999 incorpo-
rated raised beach survey along with conventional shoreline survey (Stafford
and Christensen 2000). Previous investigation had identified shell middens
associated with raised beaches in this area (Fedje et al. 1995), but no systematic work was conducted before 1999. Naden Harbour exhibits a long protected shoreline with little relief and few bedrock exposures compared with
the steep, rocky shorelines typical of southern Moresby Island. The sea level
history for northern Haida Gwaii is very similar to that for the southern end
of the archipelago, but with a marine maximum a few metres lower (Figure
10.2). Unlike Gwaii Haanas, at least four beach terraces are readily visible
and suggest a stepping of sea level change.

Method   The investigation of Naden Harbour by Stafford and Christensen
(2000) employed some of the same techniques used in Gwaii Haanas to
locate early Holocene sites, but differences in both terrace and site visibility
and in preservation led to some methodological adjustments. Terrace visibility in Naden Harbour and Masset Inlet enabled the location of extensive
raised beach sites without highly detailed contour maps.

Initially sites were located by a combination of shovel testing, auger testing, and examination of mineral soil exposures. As the survey progressed, it
was determined that the raised terraces contained well-preserved shell
middens and that auger testing, in concert with examination of soil exposures, was the most efficient method for site location. Shovel testing was
discontinued. Auger testing, with tests placed 10 to 50 metres apart, was
carried out on all three terraces. A total of 1,200 auger tests were conducted
along a shoreline length of 15 kilometres. The presence of shell middens
made for easy recognition of cultural matrices.

Results   Extensive and dense raised shell midden deposits were recorded
throughout the study area. Twenty raised beach midden complexes were
identified during the Naden Harbour survey (Stafford and Christensen 2000).
The shell middens' sizes vary between 30 metres and 4 kilometres in length
and encompass a combined midden area of at least 150,000 square metres.
The sites include a total of 48 horizontally discrete components among the
three raised marine terraces. The lowest terrace was at about 5 metres above
sea level and included 27 components, with 7 found in surface exposures
and 20 through testing. The middle terrace was at about 8 metres elevation
and included 8 components, 6 of which were found by subsurface testing.
Thirteen components were located on the upper (10 to 12 metres) terrace.
All were found through subsurface testing. Three of the sites have been
radiocarbon-dated and the results conform to the local sea level record (Table

10.1). Two sites (FlUe-3 and FlUe-4), both about 5 metres above high tide, were dated to between 3000 and 3200 BP, and one site (GaUd-3) on the 10-to-12-metre terrace was dated to 5800 BP.

Distribution of Raised Beach Sites Located in Haida Gwaii

Modelling paleoshorelines based on sea level history has been productive for locating mid to early Holocene raised beach archaeological sites in Haida Gwaii. This was especially true in areas of moderate to high relief such as Gwaii Haanas in southern Haida Gwaii. Although shell-free cultural deposits were located by auger testing in Gwaii Haanas, shovel testing was the preferred method of subsurface testing due to the coarse nature of the sediments. These surveys significantly increased the number of recorded raised beach sites in that area and provided the archaeological community with proven methods for locating these sites in a timely and cost-effective manner.

Subsequent studies in northern Haida Gwaii also used the sea level curve as an aid in locating raised beach sites, although detailed elevation models were generally not required because of the low relief characteristic of much of the area. Intensive auger testing was highly effective in locating raised beach deposits in northern Haida Gwaii, where terraces are more prominent and the highly visible shell midden deposits are preserved. At present it is not known how representative the northern Haida Gwaii site assemblage is, in particular that derived from intensive investigation at Naden Harbour. Early Holocene components may be present but none have been identified. No lithic artifacts, material culture used to identify archaeological sites in Gwaii Haanas, were located in any of the thousands of auger

Table 10.2

Haida Gwaii raised beach site distribution

	No. of sites	Terrace Complex (elevation above high tide)				
		5-6 m	7-9 m	10-12 m	5-13 m	14-17 m
Naden Harbour	20	11	8	7		
Other northern Haida Gwaii sites						
• pre-1995	9		3	6		
• post-1995	5		2	3		
Gwaii Haanas						
• pre-1995	4				1	3
• 1995	16				4	11

Note: A site may extend across more than one terrace complex.
Source: Derived from Table 10.1; Stafford and Christensen 2000; Fedje and Christensen 1999.

tests undertaken in Naden Harbour. More intensive auger or shovel testing would likely be required to locate shell-free cultural deposits.

A total of fifty-four raised beach sites are now known for the archipelago. Examination of the record suggests there are significant data gaps or differences between northern and southern Haida Gwaii (Table 10.2). It is not clear whether this is the result of survey limitations, level of investigation at known sites, environment, site visibility, or a combination of these factors.

In Gwaii Haanas, twenty-two raised beach sites have been located but no shell midden components have been encountered. Nine of these sites have been dated but only one has a component that may be younger than 5000 BP. These sites are situated on rock or diamicton-cored (till or colluvium) promontories, or on small alluvial and debris-flow fans associated with intermittent streams. Associated paleobeaches are generally narrow and rocky.

In northern Haida Gwaii, thirty-four raised beach sites have been located. These include six without shell middens, two of which are dated (ca. 7500 to 6500 BP), and twenty-eight with shell middens. Eight of the raised beach sites with shell middens have been dated. Significant accumulations of shell have not been dated to earlier than about 5500 BP. Only one site associated with the maximum sea level position has been investigated in detail, however, and it is possible that some of the raised midden sites have early Holocene components. Unlike in Gwaii Haanas, there are a number of shell midden sites in northern Haida Gwaii that date to the period between 5000 and 3000 BP. The raised shell midden sites are situated along sand and gravel paleobeaches in very protected inlets. These inlets are rich in shellfish beds and currently contain substantial runs of anadromous fish.

The non-shell sites include two on diamicton-cored terraces and one on a paleoestuary some 500 metres inland from the modern shore (Fladmark 1989).

Drowned Shoreline Survey

Drowned shorelines in the Hecate Strait waters adjacent to Gwaii Haanas date from at least 12,500 to 9400 BP (Josenhans et al. 1997; Fedje and Josenhans 2000). The 9500 to 9400 BP shoreline, drowned about 9400 BP and now visible in the lower intertidal zone because of falling sea levels, was surveyed as part of a multi-year inventory project. The method and results of this survey are presented in Chapter 16 and will not be detailed here. The following will present results of offshore investigations.

Early attempts to model the seafloor entailed associating sea level history with hydrographic data collected in the 1950s. Elevation models based on these data and sea level history provided a very general picture of formerly subaerial lands comprising Haida Gwaii and the Hecate Plain, but lacked resolution for features on this landscape smaller than about 100 metres (see

Figure 10.5). Features such as paleoshorelines, larger lakes, and major fluvial features were defined from this modelling but data were insufficient for accurately targeting features with significant paleoenvironmental or archaeological potential.

The archaeological survey component of the marine program was limited to a few days out of a total of two weeks of ship time over two years, and as such was very preliminary in nature. Sea level history provided no evidence of stillstands in the submarine area. Investigations were thus hampered by the ephemeral nature of coastal shoreline targets and often focused on formerly inland targets such as lakeshores, stream terraces, and confluences.

Method

As with the raised beach surveys, the investigative approach integrated sea level history with elevation models. In 1997 the Canadian Hydrographic Survey conducted swath bathymetry of selected areas adjacent to southern Haida Gwaii. This technology provided very detailed remote data, to a depth of 150 metres, accurate to approximately 10 centimetres vertical and about 1 metre horizontal. The resultant elevation models were used to produce imagery of the paleolandscapes with sufficient detail to define a host of features associated with past sea levels (Figure 10.7). Drowned terrestrial features resolved from the model included rivers, creeks, lakes, ponds, terraces, point bars, deltas, and beaches. Contouring and 3-D imaging with sun shading from various orientations enabled production of maps from which geological and archaeological targets could be identified. The model was tied to GPS (global positioning system) and the team was able to sample points on this landscape, from Coast Guard vessels, with an ultimate accuracy of better than 5 metres.

Results

A number of paleoenvironmental and archaeological targets at 50 to 145 metres water depth were sampled using an approximately 0.5-cubic-metre capacity clamshell bucket. The focus was on transgressive shorelines and associated landforms. Total sampled area was only about 25 square metres but by using the digital elevation model to target likely locations, one archaeological site and a number of significant paleoenvironmental sites were identified (Fedje and Josenhans 2000).

Archaeological targets included stream confluences, terraces, promontories, and beaches. A stone tool was recovered from one of the archaeological targets in Werner Bay (Figure 10.6). The Werner Bay stone tool came from a fluvial gravel lag at 50 metres water depth. The large, glassy basalt billet flake is clearly of cultural origin. It is thin and sharp with one clearly utilized edge, and was recovered in a context of heavily rounded fluvial gravel.

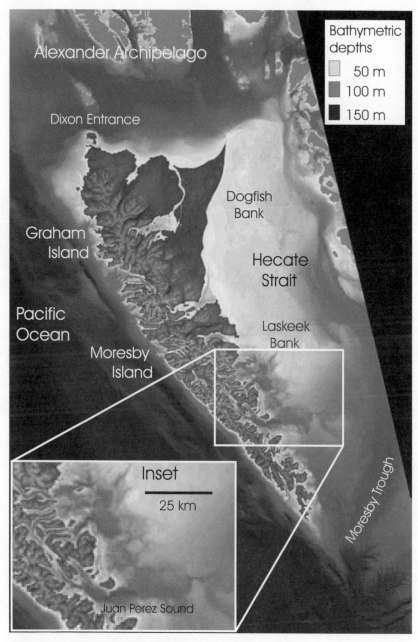

Figure 10.5   Hecate Strait from 1950s bathymetry.

Figure 10.6   Stone tool recovered in Werner Bay.

Only one artifact was recovered and, as such, association with the 10,000 BP (date when sea level rose over the find site; see Figures 10.2 and 10.7b) paleoshoreline is not proven.

Paleoenvironmenal targets from which samples were retrieved include deltas, paleobeaches, lake deposits, forest soils with in situ trees, and till from drumlin fields. Several locations provided in situ evidence of ancient forests. The evidence includes abundant wood, including, at two locations, recovery of tree stumps in growth position. In one location, at 145 metres water depth, a pine tree stump was recovered still rooted in a rich organic forest soil with both the tree and a deciduous twig from within the soil dating to 12,200 BP (Fedje and Josenhans 2000; Lacourse et al. 2003). Preservation appears to be in part a consequence of very rapid marine transgression of these forested lands. The dating and species identification are consistent with sea level history and palynological interpretation (Fedje and Josenhans 2000; Chapters 2 and 3).

Intertidal shellfish were recovered at about 25 percent of the sample sites and several produced abundant shellfish, including species used extensively by prehistoric First Nations peoples on the Northwest Coast. The most productive samples came from paleobeaches at 120 to 135 metres water depth in the eastern part of the swath-imaged study area. The association of a period of relatively slow sea level rise with a well-defined break in slope at about 130 metres (just north of All Alone Stone – Figure 10.7a) and several rich intertidal shellfish sites dated to about 11,000 BP suggests a paleodelta and possible stillstand.

Distribution of Sites Associated with Drowned Shorelines
While intertidal surveys located a large number of sites dating to just before

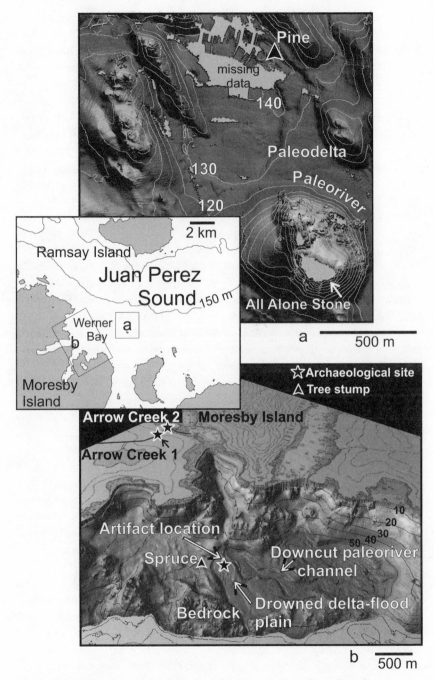

Figure 10.7 Digital terrain models of two locations in Juan Perez Sound.

the approximately 9400 BP marine transgression of the elevation of the modern shore (Chapter 16), offshore surveys located only one site (Fedje and Josenhans 2000). Little can be said about site distribution for the period before 9500 BP although the distribution of the 9500 to 9400 BP paleoshoreline sites may provide some direction in this regard, at least for the preceding few centuries, when environmental conditions were similar (Chapter 16). Before 10,000 BP, the environment and associated resources were shifting rapidly, and the consequences for the location of archaeological sites, if present, are unclear. During that time, Haida Gwaii was dominated by broad plains, large rivers, and lakes, and the climate was much more continental in nature (at least on the east coast). In addition, before 11,000 BP the regional flora was characterized by open pine parkland, and before 12,000 BP, by tundra.

The 9500 to 9400 BP paleoshoreline sites include many ephemeral lithic scatters where a handful of artifacts are distributed across hundreds of square metres of beach and a small number of sites with dense scatters of artifacts, including a broad diversity of tool types (Chapter 16). The former are likely associated with transient activities while the latter may reflect campsite activities. The Kilgii Gwaay site (Chapter 11) is an example of the latter.

The abundance of approximately 9400 BP lithic sites found in the intertidal zone would suggest that earliest Holocene drowned sites should be similarly abundant and visible where lag surfaces have not been buried by recent marine sediment. Exposed lag surfaces were rarely encountered in the late 1990s marine survey, and remote visual survey may be necessary to select targets suitable for effective sampling.

Paleoshoreline Site Location, Environment, and Adaptation
Although the present sample of paleoshoreline archaeological sites is small and surveys are far from comprehensive, the data suggest the possibility of significant temporal and geographic differences between early and mid-Holocene economies, or differences in preservation. In southern Haida Gwaii, only one site, Kilgii Gwaay, contains shell midden dating earlier than about 2000 BP. In northern Haida Gwaii, shell middens are numerous by about 5000 BP (Table 10.1).

The finding of large numbers of pre-2000 BP shell middens in northern Haida Gwaii may be partially a function of the much greater mineral soil visibility resulting from road construction and logging activity. Raised lithic sites (non-shell) include only three examples in the north, dating from 7500 to 6000 BP) (Fladmark 1979b, 1986), but are common in Gwaii Haanas, with several components dating earlier than 8000 BP (Chapter 12). Sea level change, climatic change, and survey limitations may explain part of the observed temporal and geographic differences.

During the early Holocene, rapid sea level rise may have affected some intertidal and anadromous resources in Haida Gwaii (Fladmark 1986). At that time, the availability of mature intertidal clams may have been reduced by continuous drowning of developing habitat and transgressing of maturing beds (six to ten years to maturity in the case of butter clam and littleneck).

In those parts of Haida Gwaii dominated by steep terrain, the development of low-gradient supratidal gravel streambeds and pools needed by some salmon species for spawning and rearing may have been constrained by rapidly rising sea levels prior to maximum marine transgression. The larger creeks and rivers of the archipelago may have provided fewer constraints where these had longer stretches of low-gradient terrain. After about 9000 BP, the paleoshorelines stabilized and the small fans and estuaries characteristic of modern Haida Gwaii began to develop.

Paleoclimate may also be an important factor in the availability of some resources. Between about 10,000 and 6000 BP, the climate in the environs of Haida Gwaii was considerably warmer than today (Pellatt and Mathewes 1997; Chapter 3). Warmer ocean waters may have limited the productivity of west coast anadromous fish because of reduced offshore feed and an increase in predators (cf. Hare and Francis 1995; see also Chapter 13).

This scenario is concordant with present archaeological evidence from Haida Gwaii. Marine fish, including halibut or lingcod, rockfish, dogfish, skate, and herring, dominate the early Holocene components at Kilgii Gwaay, Richardson Island, Ellen Island, and Lyell Bay, with salmon present at Kilgii and Richardson but in relatively low numbers (Chapters 6 and 16). Sample sizes are small, however, and considerably more investigation is needed to substantiate these indications. In this regard, it is noteworthy that salmon are consistently present at Gaadu Din Cave between 12,000 and 10,000 BP (Fedje and Sumpter 2004; Fedje 2005; Chapter 6).

More limited availability of some shellfish and anadromous resources may have necessitated an economy based more on foraging than on collecting, with the possible exception being at major estuaries, where such resources may have been sufficient to permit a greater collecting focus (Fedje et al. 2001). After about 5000 BP, the cooler, wetter climate, stable landscape, and mature forest environment would have resulted in a more productive, predictable, and healthful intertidal and riverine resource base, and thus encouraged sedentism and shell midden development.

Preservation may provide an alternative or supporting explanation for the distribution of early Holocene site types in Haida Gwaii. Lacking sufficient buildup of shell, the edaphic conditions needed for long-term preservation of non-carbonized organics may not have developed for most sites dating before 5500 BP. High rainfall and acidic soils may have contributed to a lack of preservation of shell and other organics at these sites. This would be especially true were shellfish not a key staple or were the economy less sedentary and cultural evidence more thinly spread on the landscape.

This is not to say that sites containing significant shell midden deposits do not date earlier than 5500 BP, but rather that the maritime economy prior to this time may have been based on foraging from logistical camps rather than collecting from semipermanent, or at least seasonal, habitation sites. There may, however, be midden sites preserved in better-drained, more alkaline, or more deeply buried contexts than those investigated to date. For example, shell middens have been preserved in the alkaline soils of the early Holocene Chuck Lake site in southeastern Alaska and in deeply buried context on the California and Oregon coasts (Ackerman et al. 1985; Erlandson 1994; Torben and Erlandson 2000).

Maritime settings imply that sites such as Richardson Island, Arrow Creek, and Kasta must also have had at least scattered organic middens deposited during occupation, and their absence in turn suggests that they were not sufficiently massive to survive seven to nine millennia of acidic soils and high rainfall. Kilgii Gwaay, a drowned (1 to 3 metres below modern high tide) site in southernmost Haida Gwaii, provides support for this interpretation (Fedje et al. 2001; Chapter 11). At Kilgii Gwaay there is a rich maritime vertebrate fauna and poorly preserved invertebrate fauna associated with large numbers of lithic artifacts. Unlike raised beach sites such as Richardson Island, the shell and bone appear to have survived at Kilgii Gwaay because ocean waters flooded the site within a few decades of abandonment. These waters would have maintained the alkaline environment needed for long-term preservation.

Implications and Future Direction for Haida Gwaii and the Broader Context of the Northwest Coast

Raised beach survey results from Haida Gwaii provide direction for site location and research issues in the archipelago, and in concert with paleo-shoreline records suggests approaches for investigation of locations elsewhere on the Northwest Coast.

Although sample sizes are small, the present inventory of raised beach sites suggests change in the nature of site locations between early and mid-Holocene times. Sites older than about 5500 BP may have been generally dispersed across the landscape, with early Holocene foragers focusing primarily on marine and terrestrial rather than intertidal resources. Fishing appears to have focused on marine rather than anadromous species (cf. Torben and Erlandson 2000), at least on the predominantly rocky shored coast of much of southern Haida Gwaii, and to have been part of a mixed maritime and terrestrial economy. There is only limited evidence of caribou hunting but this species may have been a much more significant resource during the drier and more open environment characteristic of the early Holocene and early postglacial period.

After 5500 BP, many sites are found near areas of high anadromous and intertidal productivity. By 5000 BP shell middens were massive and imply a well-developed, and likely sedentary, collecting adaptation. The apparent absence of such sites in Gwaii Haanas may reflect the paucity of significant estuaries and the as yet very limited investigation of the few that are present. After about 2000 BP, sites were adjacent to estuaries and more dispersed along the coast where there was access to offshore fisheries, including halibut, then available in quantity due to development of cedar technology and new fishing techniques.

A number of research questions derive from present results, including adaptation and site location association for the early versus mid-Holocene raised beach sites. Of particular importance is the need to survey the paleoestuaries of larger creeks and rivers for early Holocene sites with potential for heightened preservation of organic remains. From this we may be able to obtain a better understanding of the earliest Holocene adaptations hinted at by site distribution and technology (Chapter 16).

These same approaches could be transferred to surveys in other regions. The paleoshoreline work from Hecate Strait (see Chapter 2) suggests how and where this may be most profitable depending upon research questions being asked. For example, in the search for evidence of earliest postglacial occupation of Northwest Coast shorelines, it appears that the outer mainland coast and the islands immediately offshore may provide the most feasible areas of investigation. There, sea level change is of relatively small magnitude and old shorelines stranded rather than drowned. What is needed is a site-specific focus where paleoshoreline history is well constrained by paleoenvironmental research and a survey focusing on landforms appropriate to specific adaptations (e.g., paleoestuaries for mid-Holocene intertidal-anadromous resource collector sites, and promontories for logistical foragers).

Conclusions

Modelling paleoshorelines is key to the efficient location of archaeological sites on a dynamic landscape such as that of Haida Gwaii. This approach has led to an almost tenfold increase in the number of early Holocene archaeological sites known in the archipelago and resulted in extending the record of maritime adaptations to at least 9500 BP.

The results of archaeological and paleoenvironmental work carried out over the past few years provide clues as to changes in natural resource availability and, as a consequence, coastal economies. A more mobile foraging lifestyle may have been present in most parts of Haida Gwaii during the early Holocene because of rapidly rising sea levels, immature rivers and estuaries, and a warmer climate. In early postglacial time (12,000 to 10,000 BP), the environment would have been even more dynamic (Chapters 2 and 3; Fedje and Josenhans 2000). For both resources and people this would be a time of perpetual recolonization. Stream fans and estuaries would be retreating up steep-gradient shorelines and pockets of more level terrain with sufficient mineral soil accreted from mass-wasting in bedrock-controlled terrain would provide only short-term habitat for intertidal resources. Similarly, appropriate level landforms suitable for human habitation would be both horizontally and vertically constrained by bedrock topography, necessitating a constant shift of habitation sites.

The most significant results of the marine investigations are the detailed imaging of a drowned terrestrial landscape on the continental shelf (as proposed by Fladmark [1979a], Mathewes [1989b], and others) and the evidence for a high degree of preservation of portions of that landscape, including intact, undisturbed soils dating as early as 12,200 BP. While demonstration of human occupation at this time has yet to be established, the data clearly support a biologically productive landscape suitable for humans.

Acknowledgments
The Gwaii Haanas raised beach survey was supported by Parks Canada and the Council of Haida Nations (CHN). The field crew included Allen Brooks, Tina Christensen, Daryl Fedje, John Maxwell, Joanne McSporran, Kevin Robinson, Ian Sumpter, Bert Wilson, Jordan Yeltatzie, and Sean Young. Ernie Gladstone and the Gwaii Haanas staff provided logisitical support for the project. The northern Haida Gwaii raised beach investigations were supported by the CHN and BC Ministry of Forests. The field crews included Heather Barnes, Derrick Belcourt, Vanessa and John Bennet, Tanya and Trish Collinson, Tina Christensen, Morley Eldridge, Jud Jones, John Maxwell, Lisa Rummel, Jim Stafford, James Stanley, Archie Stocker, and Sean Young. The projects were administered by Ernie Collison for the CHN and Julian Wake for BC Forestry. The marine geology/archaeology project was led by Heiner Josenhans with a field crew including the authors, Vaughn Barrie, Kim Conway, Tom Greene, Quentin Mackie, Ian Sumpter, and Jordan Yeltatzie. The project was supported by Parks Canada, the Geological Survey of Canada, and the Canadian Hydrographic Service. Dating was conducted by the CAMS group at Lawrence Livermore National Laboratory, California.

11

Kilgii Gwaay: An Early Maritime Site in the South of Haida Gwaii

Daryl W. Fedje, Alexander P. Mackie, Rebecca J. Wigen, Quentin Mackie, and Cynthia Lake

Kilgii Gwaay is an early Holocene archaeological site containing a rich assemblage of stone tools and organic remains. The site is situated in the intertidal zone of a protected embayment on the south side of Ellen Island in southernmost Haida Gwaii (Figure 10.1). Ellen Island is approximately 20 hectares in area, with a maximum elevation of 25 metres. Haida archaeologist Captain Gold located Kilgii Gwaay in the early 1990s and collected over 1,500 lithic artifacts from intertidal lag deposits. The site was initially assumed to have limited interpretive potential but a detailed assessment carried out in 2000 in response to proposed development identified deeply buried cultural remains, including stone tools and bone. This led to an intensive investigation of the site in 2001 and 2002. The preliminary assessment and results of the 2001 field program were reported by Fedje and colleagues (2001). The site has been dated and faunal analyses are largely complete. Formal analysis of the stone tool and waterlogged artifact assemblages are in progress.

Kilgii Gwaay was occupied from 9450 to 9400 BP, when sea levels were a few metres below modern levels and rising rapidly towards the early Holocene marine maximum. The site was flooded by marine waters about 9400 BP and remained drowned until recent times (see Chapter 2). Between 9000 and 5000 BP, sea levels were 15 to 16 metres higher than at present and terrestrial land at Ellen Island was reduced to two small islets (< 1 hectare). Over the last 5,000 years, tectonic uplift has raised the earth's crust in this area by 15 metres, and as a result Kilgii Gwaay has been re-exposed in the modern tidal zone. The archaeological deposits extend from 1 to 3 metres elevation below the normal high tide line and are distributed in a roughly horseshoe-shaped area surrounding a fossil sediment basin (former pond and lagoon). Erosional processes and bioturbation (burrowing mollusks) during marine transgression and regression have disturbed much of the site, but on the west side of the basin there is a small area of in situ archaeological deposits.

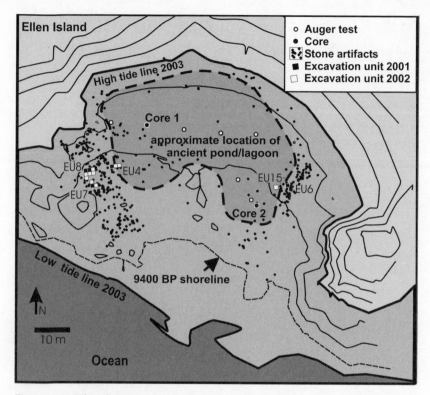

Figure 11.1   Kilgii Gwaay archaeological site.

Investigations

Work at Kilgii Gwaay has included paleoenvironmental investigation of the buried sediment basin (Kilgii Pond) and collection and excavation of archaeological deposits (Figure 11.1). Kilgii Pond was subjected to limited auger testing and recovery of two sediment cores of 10 centimetres in diameter each. Archaeological work entailed surface collection of a lag deposit of stone tools and excavation of a number of shovel tests and block excavations. Most excavation work was carried out on the west side of the site, where exploratory work identified the presence of intact shell-rich cultural deposits.

Site Stratigraphy

Stratigraphy is complex and variable across the site (Figure 11.2). Basal sediment is upper Triassic Karmutsan formation bedrock. Overlying bedrock are a bouldery diamicton, locally derived organics, and clastic sediment to gravel size, cultural deposits, and sediments associated with the early Holocene marine transgression and subsequent regression. Context (terrestrial

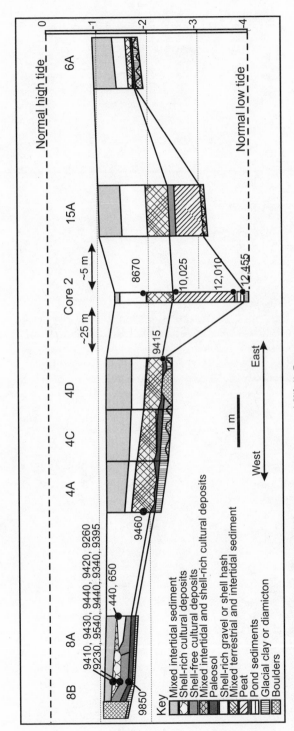

Figure 11.2 Schematic cross-section from representative tests at Kilgii Gwaay.

Table 11.1

Radiocarbon dates from Kilgii Gwaay

CAMS no.	Sample	Material	D¹³C	D¹⁴C	±	¹⁴C age BP	±
Sample overlying archaeological deposits							
77719	1325T8C	Periwinkle shell	0	-121.7	3.6	440	40
77720	1325T8A	Periwinkle shell	0	-143.8	3.6	650	50
Archaeological sample							
70704	1325T3A45	Bear bone	-22.1	-691.4	1.6	9460	50
76666	1325T8B24-1	Charcoal	-25	-691.0	1.6	9430	50
77248	1325T8B24-2	Charcoal	-25	-690.1	1.2	9410	50
76667	1325T8B24-3	Mussel shell	0	-713.3	1.4	9440	50
79681	1325T8B3-31	Mussel shell	0	-712.9	1.7	9420	50
79682	1325T8B3-31	Charcoal	-25	-684.2	1.5	9260	40
76668	1325T8B40-1	Charcoal	-25	-682.9	1.9	9230	50
76669	1325T8B40-2	Mussel shell	0	-717.0	1.2	9540	40
79683	1325T8B4-40	Mussel shell	0	-713.5	1.4	9440	40
79684	1325T8B4-40	Charcoal	-25	-687.2	1.3	9340	40
87641	1325T4D4	Split root wrap	-25	-690.3	1.3	9415	35
87642	1325T8F5	Wood wedge	-25	-689.6	1.4	9395	40

Sample underlying archaeological deposits

76670	1325T8B52-1	Charcoal	-25	-706.5	1.2	9850	40

Pollen core sample

79685	1325TC2-20	Sea urchin	0	-684.5	1.5	8670	40
95557	1325TC2-79	Wood	-25	-712.9	1.3	10,025	40
95558	1325TC2-199	Pine needle	-25	-775.7	1.6	12,010	60
79686	1325TC2-207	*Potamogeton* seed	-25	-787.0	1.4	12,420	60
82214	1325TC2-216	Seed	-25	-780.9	1.6	12,190	60
87243	1325TC2-216	Wood	-25	-784.6	1.0	12,335	40
95559	1325TC2-219	Seed	-25	-787.9	1.0	12,455	40
95560	1325TC2-223	Seed	-25	-766.7	1.3	11,695	45[r]

r CAMS-95560 rejected: date is out of sequence and associated with non-arboreal pollen.

Notes: The quoted age is in radiocarbon years using the Libby half-life of 5,568 years. Radiocarbon concentration is given as D^{14}C. Shell dates have been recalculated using a marine reservoir correction of –600 years (Southon and Fedje 2003).

and lacustrine) and post-depositional processes have resulted in variable preservation of these sediments across the site.

Kilgii Pond: Stratigraphy and Preliminary Analysis

The fossil pond appears to be approximately 50 metres in diameter. It was roughly delineated by auger testing and coring. In the area of the fossil pond, bedrock is overlain, in turn, by glacio-lacustrine clay, gyttja, peat, mixed fresh and marine sediment, and a thick deposit of shell hash and pebble to boulder-sized clasts. The boulders are primarily in the upper part of the shell hash layer and are exposed as an extensive boulder field across the surface of the basin.

A percussion core 10 centimetres in diameter (Core 2 in Figure 11.1) from the east side of the sediment basin penetrated to 3 metres below the modern sediment surface. In order to retrieve this core, the upper 50 centimetres of the shell hash/boulder layer had to be excavated by shovel because of the abundance of large clasts. At the base of this core, there is 0.1 metre of blue-grey clay. The clay is overlain by 0.2 metres of tan to brown organic-rich silt (gyttja). The gyttja is very firm and relatively dry, likely the result of compression by the shell hash/boulder layer. Above the silt layer is 1.2 metres of peat with abundant woody debris in the lower part. Overlying the peat is a thick layer composed mostly of sandy shell hash. The lower part of this layer contains abundant sand to gravel-sized clasts. The upper part contains sand to boulder-sized subrounded rock clasts and occasional complete individual shellfish valves.

Preliminary analysis of the core indicates a long environmental record (Core 2 dates are presented in Table 11.1). The lacustrine record extends from older than 12,500 to 10,000 BP. The diatom record indicates that the basin was freshwater until after 10,000 BP. The basin would have been marine from 9400 to 2000 BP (Fedje and Josenhans 2000). Sediments deposited between 10,000 and 8700 BP have been mixed by bioturbation (e.g., shellfish burrowing) or by a high-energy marine event. The pollen data indicate a largely treeless tundra-like environment from before 12,500 until about 12,200 BP, an open pine forest from 12,200 to about 11,000 BP, a spruce and pine forest from 11,000 to 10,000 BP, and an open alder- and herb-dominated flora in the area of shell-rich cultural deposits (with a hemlock-spruce-pine forest nearby) at 9450 BP (pollen from Excavation Unit [EU] 8 midden deposits).

Stratigraphy in Archaeological Excavations

Stratigraphy in the area of archaeological deposits is variable due to the nature of post-depositional processes. In most areas where archaeological deposits are present, they fall into one of two general sedimentary sequences.

These include one where the cultural sediments are undisturbed and one where they have been mostly mixed by marine processes.

In the first sequence, basal sediment is a clayey diamicton containing unsorted sand and subangular clasts to boulder size. No microfossils were associated with this sediment. Overlying the diamicton is a thin peaty paleosol with occasional artifacts and bone fragments in the upper part. The soil contains some charcoal fragments, one of which was dated to 9850 BP (Table 11.1). A grey-brown gravelly silt that often contains abundant stone tools and bone overlies the paleosol. At lower elevations (near or below the water table), this layer also contains wood debris and wooden artifacts. This artifact-rich gravelly silt grades into a shell-rich layer where faunal recovery is generally greater but that exhibits no obvious difference in distribution of stone tools. In both the shell-rich and the non-shell cultural layers, the distribution of artifacts and bone clearly indicate that they have not been disturbed since the time of deposition. The presence of freshwater diatoms (e.g., *Pinnularia* sp.) and an absence of marine microfossils such as forams and dinocysts suggest these sediments were not deposited or reworked by marine processes. The artifact-rich layer is overlain by a relatively thin, heavily bioturbated intertidal sediment containing occasional complete shellfish, including some in death position and some live.

In the second sequence, marine processes, including bioturbation and/or high-energy wave action, have mixed some or all of the sediment overlying the basal diamicton. In these sequences, the paleosol and lowermost cultural layers can be entirely or partially intact. This appears to relate to the thickness of the cultural sediment and the depth to which burrowing shellfish could mix it (for example, ca. 40 centimetres for butter clams and 20 centimetres for littleneck clams) during marine transgression. Intertidal sediments comparable to those described for the upper part of the first sequence overlie the artifact-rich mixed sediments.

Summary of Sedimentary History

Prior to 9500 BP, the area of the Kilgii Gwaay archaeological site was a small bedrock-and-glacial till (diamicton) constrained terrace facing south to a shallow valley and beyond to the gently rising slopes of what is now Kunghit Island. A small peat-fringed pond was situated near the rim of the terrace. Kilgii Gwaay was used as a campsite from about 9450 to 9400 BP, when sea levels were 2 to 4 metres below modern levels. The site was transgressed by marine waters about 9400 BP.

The boulder-rich diamicton evident at the base of all excavation units and exposed in the intertidal area at several locations around the island was likely deposited during the glacial maximum sometime before 13,000 BP. Glacial clay deposited at the base of the pond and on the surface of diamicton in some areas was transported by slopewash or a small rivulet from a nearby upland source. By 12,500 BP, organic sediments were accumulating in the pond and it is likely that at this time the paleosol encountered in several excavations began to form. Cultural sediment, including stone, bone and wood artifacts, and midden debris were deposited between 9450 and 9400 BP. In most areas of the site, these sediments were mixed with underlying sediment and with sediment deposited during and/or immediately following the marine transgression. There was no evidence of mixing in the western part of EU8 and no shellfish encountered in death position. Survival of undisturbed cultural deposits in this area suggests that post-transgression deposition was sufficiently rapid and massive to prevent intertidal and subtidal shellfish from colonizing the pre-trangressive (cultural) sediments in this area.

By about 8700 BP, shell hash was being deposited in the then deeply drowned embayment. It is unclear whether this was a gradual process or whether the shell hash was deposited by one or more high-energy marine events. The presence of a large number of boulders within and on the surface of the shell hash suggests that at least some of these sediments may have been deposited by tsunami or storm surge. Possibly these large clasts had been winnowed out of diamicton on the low bedrock promontories to the north and south of the site area during the period of higher sea levels and were subsequently strewn across the bay by such an event (cf. Nott 2003).

Live shellfish and specimens in death position were recovered from the muddy sediment in the uppermost part of the excavations. In the area of EU7 and EU8, these were in a 10-centimetre-thick layer, whereas in most of the remainder of the bay they were recovered from a 30-to-40-centimetre-thick layer. It appears that fine sediment, including the shell-rich cultural strata, are being rapidly eroded away in the former area.

Dating

A total of twenty-three radiocarbon dates have been run for Kilgii Gwaay (Table 11.1). These include twelve dates on archaeological deposits, one on an underlying paleosol, two on intertidal deposits capping the archaeological deposits, and a series of eight dates on samples from the pollen core recovered from Kilgii Pond. Nine of the archaeological dates are shell-wood pairs from the shell-rich cultural layer in EU8, two are samples from wooden artifacts, and one is from a spirally fractured bear bone. The distribution of dates on cultural deposits suggests that site occupation occurred between approximately 9450 and 9400 BP. The palynological dates are consistent except for one date (CAMS-79686) that appears to be about 150 years too old and the lowermost date (CAMS-95560), which is considerably younger than overlying dates and inconsistent with the known age (> 12,200 BP) for non-arboreal records in Haida Gwaii.

Table 11.2

Kilgii Gwaay vertebrate fauna, number of identified specimens

Common name	Latin name	NISP
Mammals		
Black bear	*Ursus americana*	83
Harbour seal	*Phoca vitulina*	65
Sea otter	*Enhydra lutris*	20
River otter	*Lontra canadensis*	3
Northern sea lion	*Eumetopias jubatus*	2
Fur seal/sea lion	Otaridae	2
Birds		
Cassin's auklet	*Ptychoramphus aleuticus*	39
Short-tailed albatross	*Phoebastria albatrus*	26
Alcid large, medium, small, v. small	Alcidae	20
Rhinoceros auklet	*Cerorhinca monocerata*	8
Common murre	*Uria aalge*	3
Double-crested cormorant	*Phalacrocorax auritus*	3
Medium duck	Anatidae	3
Medium grebe	Podicipedidae	2
Medium goose	Anatidae	2
Large and small gull	Laridae	2
Pacific loon	*Gavia pacifica*	1
Red-necked grebe	*Podiceps grisegena*	1
Snow goose	*Chen caerulescens*	1
Cackling Canada goose	*Branta canadensis*	1
Surf scoter	*Melanitta perspicillata*	1
Small scoter	*Melanitta* sp.	1
Pelagic cormorant	*Phalacrocorax pelagicus*	1
Shearwater	*Puffinus* sp.	1
Pigeon guillemot	*Cepphus columba*	1
Common raven	*Corvus corax*	1
Fish		
Rockfish	*Sebastes* sp.	622
Dogfish	*Squalus acanthias*	41
Lingcod	*Ophiodon elongatus*	39
Cabezon	*Scorpaenichthys marmoratus*	21
Greenling	*Hexagrammos* sp.	10
Skate	*Raja* sp.	6
Halibut	*Hippoglossus stenolepis*	4
Sculpin	Cottidae	2
Salmon	*Oncorhynchus* sp.	2
Pacific herring	*Clupea pallasii*	1
Irish lord	*Hemilepidotus* sp.	1
Striped seaperch	*Embiotoca*	1
Flatfish	Pleuronectiformes	1

Excavations

In 2001 and 2002, a total of 16 square metres were excavated at Kilgii Gwaay. These included two 1.0-square-metre units on the east side of the pond and three block excavations on the west side (Figure 11.1).

Fauna

Thirty-nine vertebrate and 16 invertebrate taxa are represented within the 2001-2002 excavated assemblage (Table 11.2; Wigen 2003c). The vertebrate assemblage ($N = 4,200$) includes 13 taxa of fish, 6 of mammals, and 20 of birds. Fish are dominated by rockfish, dogfish, and lingcod; birds by auklet and albatross; and mammals by bear, harbour seal, and sea otter. The invertebrates are strongly dominated by California mussel (84 percent of shellfish weight).

Lithic Artifacts

Excavations have recovered some 4,000 lithic artifacts, including abundant debitage and a small number of formed tools (Table 11.3). Cores are mostly unidirectional (Figure 11.3a) and numerous large flakes characterize the flake assemblage. Formed tools are unifacial, with the exception of a single biface fragment, and include scraperplanes, scrapers, denticulates, spokeshaves, gravers, and a small unifacial stemmed point (Figure 11.3b to 11.3f).

Table 11.3

Lithic artifacts from excavated context at Kilgii Gwaay

Type	EU4A	EU5	EU6	EU7A	EU8A	EU15	Total
Unimarginal tool	10	–	5	5	29	–	49
Uniface	1	–	–	–	–	–	1
Unifacial point	–	–	–	–	1	–	1
Scraper	1	–	–	–	3	–	4
Scraperplane	6	–	1	2	5	–	14
Denticulate scraperplane	3	–	1	–	5	1	10
Notch ("spokeshave")	1	–	–	1	2	–	4
Graver	1	–	–	–	8	–	9
Burin	–	–	–	–	1	–	1
Spall tool	1	–	–	–	–	–	1
Chopper	2	–	–	–	–	–	2
Biface fragment	–	–	–	–	1	–	1
Hammerstone	2	1	–	–	1	–	4
Abrader	–	1	–	–	–	–	1
Core	8	–	3	1	13	1	26
Flakes (includes utilized)	799	3	326	503	2,146	24	3,801
Total	835	5	336	512	2,215	26	3,929

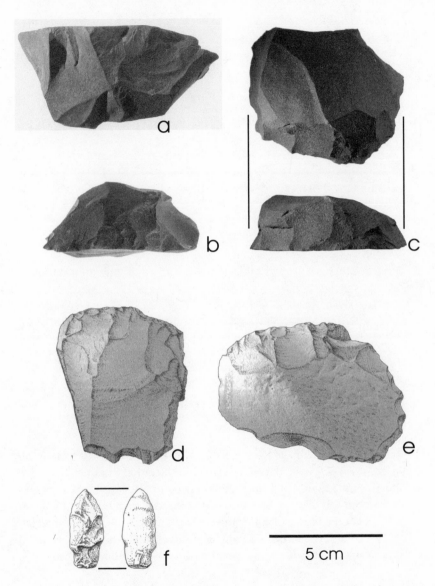

Figure 11.3 Core (a), scraperplanes (b, c), unifaces (d, e), and unifacial stemmed point (f) from Kilgii Gwaay excavations.

Bone Artifacts

Ninety bones from Kilgii Gwaay excavations exhibit evidence of human modification. Formed tools of bone include a unilaterally barbed point, several perforators, and a sea mammal percussor (Figures 11.4 and 11.5b to 11.5c). A number of other pieces of bone exhibit cut marks, chopping marks,

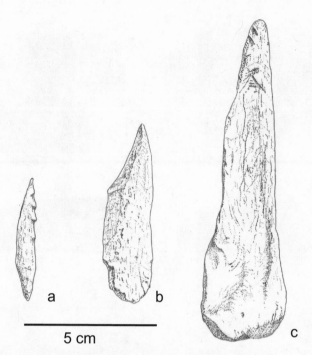

Figure 11.4   Drawings of bone tools from Kilgii Gwaay excavations.

and multiple spiral fractures from butchering and reduction. A bear mandible fragment with chopping and skinning marks is shown in Figure 11.5a).

Wooden Artifacts

Over 100 wooden artifacts were recovered at Kilgii Gwaay (Mackie et al. 2003). Most were recovered from the area of EU8, either in association with or directly underlying the intact shell-rich cultural deposits. Withes and worked wood debitage are the most common artifacts but a number of wooden stakes (Figure 11.6) and formed tools (Figure 11.7) were also recovered. The formed tools include wooden wedges, braided twine, wrapped sticks, a two-part haft, and several small wooden objects that may be points.

Discussion and Conclusion

Kilgii Gwaay contains a remarkably rich archaeological record, considering its antiquity and post-depositional history. The lithic and faunal assemblages are substantial and the preservation of wooden artifacts is unique for a site of this age on the Northwest Coast.

The Kilgii Gwaay lithic assemblage is large despite evidence for an occupation likely no more than fifty years in duration. The abundance of cores and unmodified flakes and the paucity of formed tools suggest that a primary function of the site was core reduction. A low proportion of cortical

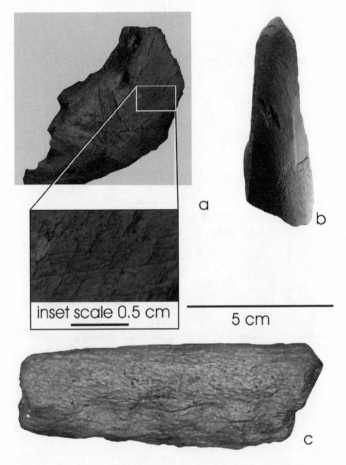

Figure 11.5 Photos of bone artifacts from Kilgii Gwaay excavations.

flakes suggests that most initial core preparation was conducted off-site. The lithics are almost entirely of one type of stone that is available in quantity as beach cobbles and boulders at nearby Benjamin Point.

Well-dated Northwest Coast sites of similar age to Kilgii Gwaay include Namu, Richardson Island, and On Your Knees Cave (Carlson 1996; Dixon 2002; Chapter 12). All contain substantial artifact assemblages but none have the degree of preservation seen at Kilgii Gwaay. The basal component at Namu dates from about 9700 to 9000 BP, but organics are limited to charcoal in components dating earlier than 6500 BP. Richardson Island, the closest to Kilgii Gwaay in age and physical distance, has a large lithic assemblage but a faunal assemblage comprising only small amounts of calcined bone. Although On Your Knees Cave is only about 200 years younger than Kilgii Gwaay, it contains a very different lithic assemblage, including both Early Coast Microblade and bifacial technology (comparable to the post-8900 BP

Figure 11.6   Wooden stake at Kilgii Gwaay.

levels at Richardson Island) (Dixon 2002). The artifacts and fauna are under analysis and cannot be compared with those of Kilgii Gwaay in any detail at this time.

Although Kilgii Gwaay is of similar age to basal Namu and only 150 years older than the earliest levels at nearby Richardson Island, there appear to be significant differences in the respective lithic assemblages. Bifacial technology is strongly represented at Namu and Richardson, while at Kilgii Gwaay only one biface fragment (excavated assemblage of fifty formed tools) and a few bifacial retouch flakes were recovered. Large unmodified flakes are much more abundant at Kilgii Gwaay than at Richardson and Namu. Bifaces are well represented among the 111 intertidal lithic sites recorded in Gwaii Haanas (10 percent of the sites contain one or more bifaces) and a large complete biface was collected from an intertidal lithic site only 200 metres northeast of Kilgii Gwaay. Context and technology suggest these sites date to the same time period as Kilgii Gwaay, but only a few have been directly

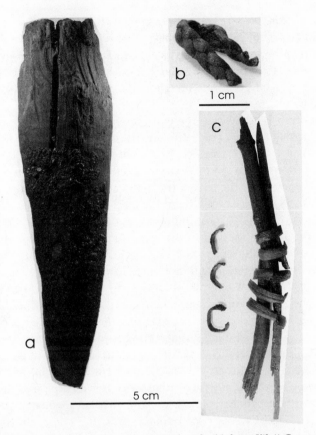

Figure 11.7 Wedge (a), twine (b), and wrapped sticks (c) from Kilgii Gwaay excavations.

dated (Chapter 16). The reasons for the near absence of bifacial technology at Kilgii Gwaay are unclear. Differences may relate to site function and, potentially, less need for curation in the form of bifaces because of the local abundance of high-quality stone.

The Kilgii Gwaay faunal assemblage is rich and contains a broad range of maritime species. Clearly the assemblage indicates a people well adapted to the local environment, particularly the marine resources. Some of the rockfish and halibut specimens weighed over 15 kilograms and are found in fairly deep water. This requires quite sophisticated fishing gear and most likely a boat of some type. The large numbers of harbour seal, as well as the presence of river and sea otter, supports the focus on marine resources of the residents at this site. The birds also tend to be marine species, with the possible exception of the geese. For example, albatross are unlikely to be found on shore and must have been hunted from a boat. Black bears are the only strictly terrestrial resource. Their numbers and large size indicate that they were clearly significant components of the diet. Shellfish are present in the Kilgii Gwaay faunal assemblage, but are proportionately less abundant than in the shell middens typical of mid to late Holocene archaeological sites in Haida Gwaii (Chapter 16). It is unclear to what extent this reflects preservation or adaptation. A foraging rather than collecting focus may be indicated.

In southern Haida Gwaii, there are no excavated sites dating between 9000 and 2000 BP with fauna present that can be compared with those at Kilgii Gwaay. However, a series of 18 sites dating from about 2000 BP to the historic period was tested by Acheson (1998) during a survey of Kunghit Island. At these sites, the bulk of the bones are fish, with salmon and rockfish being the two most important fish species in all but 4 sites. In those 4 sites, salmon is still the most important but herring, halibut, dogfish, and lingcod replace the rockfish in the second rank. The number of mammal bones is substantially less, with 2 sites having none and 6 sites having less than twenty identified mammal bones. In the remaining sites, whales, harbour seal, and sea otter are usually most important. Other species of importance are marten, fur seal, and river otter. The number of bird bones is extremely variable, from none to over 3,000, and a total of fifty-eight different taxa are identified. Seven of the sites have less than twenty bones identified, leaving a group of 11 with a reasonable sample of bird bones. In all of these sites, alcids are the most important bird group, with Cassin's auklet being the single most important alcid. Together these 18 sites show a fairly consistent pattern: salmon, rockfish, whale, sea otter, harbour seal, and Cassin's auklet are the main resources utilized. This pattern is persistent over time and across the varying local environments.

The most significant differences between the older Kilgii Gwaay and the post-2000 BP sites are the strong presence of bear in the older site and the strong presence of salmon in the more recent sites. It is clear that bear hunting was a significant activity at Kilgii Gwaay and not in the more recent sites. This could suggest that there were more bears available at 9400 BP. The more open habitat of the earliest Holocene (see Chapter 3) was likely more suitable for black bear than the current climax rain forest (Heaton 2002). Certainly the recent sites show an extreme maritime focus that is not quite as evident at Kilgii Gwaay. Alternatively, this may reflect a cultural change, with hunting on land being more important to the residents of the older sites. In the case of salmon, local streams may not have been as productive at this early time, as stream gradients were changing significantly and quickly during this period. While salmon were present in Haida Gwaii during this time, the technology for marine interception (e.g., trolling) may not have been well developed or the site may not have been used at the time of year when the salmon were running. Underlying the differences between Kilgii Gwaay and the more recent sites, however, are a great deal of similarities. Despite drastic changes in sea level, climate, and vegetation communities, the people of Haida Gwaii focused on a handful of stable marine resources, including rockfish, harbour seals, sea otters, and Cassin's auklets, for a very long time.

The survival of wooden artifacts and debitage at Kilgii Gwaay is a fortunate consequence of rapid sea level rise and nine millennia of inundation. Although the assemblage of formed tools is small, it demonstrates a well-developed woodworking technology, with many of the elements known for Northwest Coast waterlogged sites of recent age evident among the pieces. The presence of numerous withes suggests production of baskets, nets, or rope. Similarly, the very fine work evident in the cordage demonstrates presence of technological knowledge applicable to the manufacture of a broad range of organic artifacts, such as fibre clothing, basketry, and fishing line. The presence of several wooden wedges and abundant wood chips suggests an ability to split and process large pieces of wood. It also alludes to potential use of wood species other than the spruce, pine, hemlock, and alder known from the pollen record. The wedges could have been used for these woods, but the possibility of more readily split wood such as yellow-cedar (likely present in alpine areas at this time) and drift red cedar from the flooding coastal forests of Washington and Oregon needs to be considered as well. Formal analysis of the wood assemblage (artifacts, debitage, and natural detritus) is underway and is anticipated to provide further information about this early record (Mackie et al. 2003).

Kilgii Gwaay is a unique site on the Northwest Coast in that it contains abundant organic remains, including both bone and wood, dating to earliest Holocene time, and provides clear evidence of a fully developed maritime adaptation in one of the most rugged environments on the coast of the Americas. Present evidence suggests that Kilgii Gwaay was a campsite with a focus on core reduction and also served as a base for maritime foraging activity. The site also contains an excellent paleoecological record from both midden and pond deposits.

Acknowledgments

The Kilgii Gwaay project was funded by Parks Canada's Western Service Centre and by Gwaii Haanas National Park Reserve/Haida Heritage Site. Supplementary funding for student support and analyses was obtained from Social Sciences and Humanities Research Council of Canada and Natural Sciences and Engineering Research Council of Canada grants to Quentin Mackie, University of Victoria. Logistical support was provided by Gwaii Haanas. The Kilgii Gwaay crew included the authors, Helene Chabot, Alan Davidson, Bryn Fedje, Marty Magne, Trevor Orchard, Ian Sumpter, and Barb Wilson. Faunal analysis was conducted by Becky Wigen (vertebrates) and Ian Sumpter (invertebrates). Preliminary lithic analysis was carried out by Cynthia Lake with the assistance of Marty Magne. Dating was conducted by the CAMS group at Lawrence Livermore National Laboratory, California. Artifact drawings were prepared by Joanne McSporran.

12

Test Excavations at Raised Beach Sites in Southern Haida Gwaii and Their Significance to Northwest Coast Archaeology

Daryl W. Fedje, Martin P.R. Magne, and Tina Christensen

This chapter presents results of work carried out at four raised beach archaeological sites in Gwaii Haanas and examines these results in the broader context of Northwest Coast archaeology. Gwaii Haanas is an archipelago in the southern part of Haida Gwaii consisting of southern Moresby Island and adjacent smaller islands (Figure 12.1). The archaeological sites documented here include Richardson Island (1127T), Arrow Creek 1 (925T), and two sites in Lyell Bay (1354T and 1355T).

Site 1127T, Richardson Island

The Richardson Island site is situated on the west side of Richardson Island in southeastern Haida Gwaii (Figure 12.2). The site is on a small debris-flow fan that flows into Darwin Sound and is about 1 kilometre east of Moresby Island. The fan encompasses about 3 hectares.

This site was first recorded as an intertidal lithic scatter (Mackie and Wilson 1994). Subsequently, lithic artifacts were observed in the bed of a small intermittent stream and traced up to an eroding terrace situated approximately 15 metres above high tide (Fedje and Christensen 1999). Some 30 lithic artifacts, including one microblade core, were observed in situ in a finely bedded gravelly soil in a vertical exposure positioned 15 to 17 metres above the modern tidal limit. In 1995 Parks Canada and Haida archaeologists returned to the site and conducted systematic auger testing and excavation of a 1-by-1.5-metre test unit (1127T10) adjacent to the stratigraphic exposure. Some 3,300 lithic artifacts and a small amount of calcined bone were recovered. Although successful in yielding a significant archaeological record, the 1995 excavation failed to reach the bottom of the cultural deposits. In 1997 a 1-by-1-metre unit (1127T12) was excavated into the bed of the intermittent creek adjacent to the 1995 excavation. Unit 12 provided direct stratigraphic continuation of the archaeological deposits. Some 4,000 lithic artifacts, charcoal, and a small amount of bone were recovered from this excavation. In total, 5 vertical metres of stratified deposits were excavated.

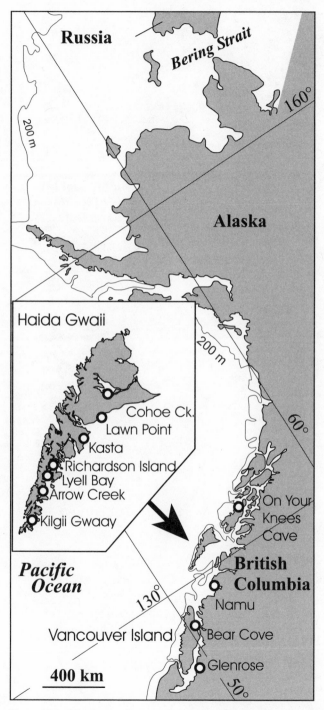

Figure 12.1 Northwest Coast and Alaska with Haida Gwaii inset.

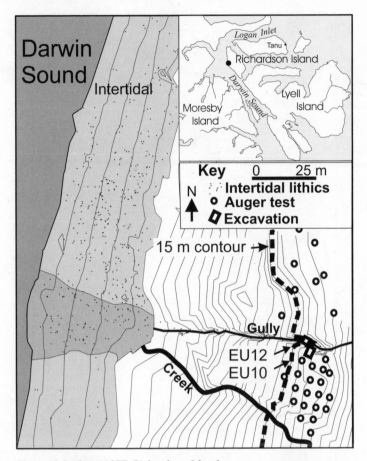

Figure 12.2 Site 1127T, Richardson Island.

Further excavations were conducted by the University of Victoria under the direction of Quentin Mackie in 2001 and 2002. Analysis and reporting on this work is underway.

Stratigraphy

Site stratigraphy is complex as a result of relative sea level rise and associated marine processes, and concomitant terrestrial processes, including mudflow, rain-wash, and alluvial deposition. Three major stratigraphic units are evident from the excavation (Figure 12.3), including a diamicton, a stratified, interdigitated terrestrial and marine sediment sequence, and an overlying layer of recent debris-flow and organic soil. Separation of these units and their component strata is based on imbrication, gross physical difference in sediment, and microfossil analysis.

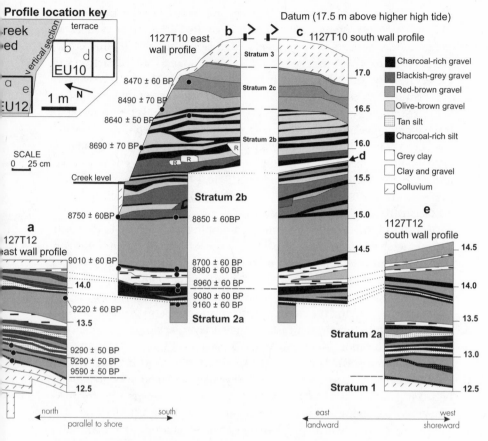

Figure 12.3   Stratigraphy at Site 1127T, Richardson Island.

The lowermost unit (Stratum 1) is a massive diamicton or debris-flow deposit with little evidence of stratification. A paleosol, defined by abundant charcoal and stone tools, is present on the surface of this deposit.

The middle unit (Stratum 2) encompasses a minimum of thirty-three distinct depositional layers. The structure of this stratum is complex, and it appears to include materials deposited by both terrestrial and marine processes. Paleosols characterized by black greasy A horizons are present within twenty-three of these layers. The layers can be separated into three groups based on depositional environment.

Stratum 2a is dominated by level to gently shoreward dipping sediment at elevations of 12.5 to 14 metres. A high silt/clay fraction in the paleosols likely reflects a significant rain-wash or aeolian component deriving from upslope debris-flow deposits. Several of the layers are characterized by a silty B horizon overlain by a black greasy artifact-rich gravel A horizon.

Provenance of the gravel in these upward coarsening layers is unclear. Possibly the gravels represent alluvial washes or are culturally derived as, for example, the prehistoric (Ackerman 1996b; Christensen 1998) and ethnographic (Deans 1899) practice of lining activity areas with beach gravel. Preservation of intact horizontally continuous charcoal-rich layers with in situ features argues against deposition in the wave-active intertidal zone. Within Stratum 2a, at 13.5 metres, there is a massive gravel unit underlain by clay-rich gravel. This appears to represent very rapid deposition, possibly a single event resulting from a severe storm, tsunami, or rapid aggradation following a submergence (e.g., subduction earthquake) event (Mathewes and Clague 1994; Hutchinson and McMillan 1997). There is no stratification within this 50-centimetre deposit and approximately 10 percent of the artifacts within the layer are water-worn.

Deposits in Stratum 2b are landward-dipping and appear to represent marine overwash (berm) deposits. A grey clay at base of this stratum contains a diatom assemblage with marine, brackish, and freshwater species. The clay layer is likely the toe of a small terrestrial mudflow or rain-wash from one upslope. Charcoal and stone tools are present in the clay layers. Immediately overlying the clay is a charcoal and artifact-rich gravel paleosol and, at about 14.0 metres, a massive gravel layer lacking any evidence of internal stratification. Approximately 10 percent of the artifacts from this layer are water-worn. The deposits likely derive from a short-term event (e.g., tsunami). A ^{14}C span of almost 200 years from about 9000 to 8800 BP between paleosols at 14.2 and 15.0 metres and an associated ^{14}C inconsistency may represent an erosional disconformity (Table 12.1; Figure 12.3). The surface of the gravel is approximately level, suggesting complete infilling of the berm depression. Above this are a series of berm deposits to about 16 metres. Some of the gravel interpreted as berm deposits may have been culturally introduced, as suggested for layers in Stratum 2a. Berm construction would account for horizontal to gentle shoreward slope sedimentation and provide backshore depressions where rain-wash–derived clay could precipitate into ponded water.

Stratum 2c includes shoreward-dipping alluvial sands and gravels to about 17.0 metres. These sediments were deposited during the transgressive maximum and are associated with a sea level position of about +16 metres.

Stratum 3 includes clay-rich colluvium and the modern organic forest soil.

In sum, the sediment data suggest that initial occupation was on a supratidal debris-flow landform with gradual rain-wash and alluvial and cultural deposition. Subsequently, occupation was on an aggrading berm. By the time deposition switched from berm to alluvial, the area of the site coinciding with the excavations was no longer occupied. The timing of the transgressive maximum indicated by the Richardson Island data is consistent with that from the sea level record recovered from the study of isolation

Table 12.1

Richardson Island radiocarbon dates (radiocarbon years BP)

CAMS no.	Sample no.	Material	Datum m(aht)	Depth (cm)	Age (BP)	±	Comment
Richardson Island, Site 1127T							
Stratigraphic exposure 1							
16199	1127T6A#10	Charcoal	18	50	8490	70	Raised beach
16200	1127T6A#29	Charcoal	18	100	8690	70	Raised beach
16201	1127T6A#9	Charcoal	18	200	8750	60	Raised beach
16202	1127T6A#13	Charcoal	18	300	9010	60	Raised beach
Excavation Unit 10							
26262	1127T10J3-61	Charcoal	18	61	8470	60	Raised beach
26263	1127T10N-108	Charcoal	18	108	8640	50	Raised beach
26264	1127T10N-251	Charcoal	18	251	8850	60	Raised beach
26265	1127T10S-325	Charcoal	18	325	8700	60	Raised beach
26266	1127T10S-329	Charcoal	18	329	8980	60	Raised beach
26267	1127T10S-347	Charcoal	18	347	8960	60	Raised beach
26268	1127T10S-354	Charcoal	18	354	9080	60	Raised beach
26269	1127T10S-374	Charcoal	18	374	9160	60	Raised beach
Stratigraphic exposure 2							
26270	1127T11A-348	Charcoal	18	348	9220	60	Raised beach
Excavation Unit 12							
39875	1127T12T18	Charcoal	18	404	9290	50	Raised beach
39876	1127T12T20	Charcoal	18	421	9290	50	Raised beach
39877	1127T12R21	Charcoal	18	434	9590	50	Basal charcoal layer

Note: m(aht) = metres above high tide. All dates are corrected for isotopic fractionation ($^{13}C/^{12}C$).

basins in the Moresby Island area (Fedje 1993). Dated strata at Richardson Island are assumed to approximate maximum tide position due to the nature of berm deposition. Total rise was approximately 4 metres over the 1,000 years of site occupation identified.

Dating

Sixteen accelerator mass spectrometric (AMS) dates were obtained on charcoal from the excavations and directly associated adjacent stratigraphic section (Table 12.1). A date of 9590 BP from the surface of Stratum 1 provides an approximate age for this debris-flow as there is no significant soil development or evidence of a disconformity (i.e., lag deposit) at its surface. The dated charcoal and associated artifacts may relate to initial occupation, but at 9590 BP high tides would have been at least 15 metres below the sampled site (Fedje and Josenhans 2000). Alternatively, the charcoal may be from old wood. The earliest unequivocal occupation, at 12 metres above modern high tide, dates to shortly before 9290 BP. The dating supports rapid, steady relative sea level rise between 9300 and 8800 BP. The date of 8700 BP at 14.2 metres is out of sequence. This may represent a statistical outlier as it overlaps with adjacent dates at two sigma, but sedimentology suggests a possible disconformity.

Cultural Layers

For purposes of analysis, the stratigraphic record was collapsed from the thirty-five observed depositional strata to twenty-six cultural layers (Figure 12.4). This is because some layers were either discontinuous or were inseparable during excavation, and because the uppermost and lowermost strata were non-cultural.

Richardson Island Flora and Fauna

Nine millennia of acidic soils, oxidation, and soil microfauna have removed all but the inorganic carbon at the site. Floral and faunal preservation is limited to charcoal and calcined bone. Flotation of soil samples from charcoal-rich layers produced a small assemblage of plants. Preliminary identifications include pine, western hemlock, rose family, sedge, blueberry/huckleberry, saskatoon, goosefoot, and grass (Jackman 1998).

Faunal remains were recovered from most levels but were largely limited to tiny fragments of calcined fish bone. The greatest concentration was associated with a hearth feature from layer 25, which dates to 9290 BP. The site assemblage includes bird (number of identified specimens [NISP] = 8), fish (NISP = 383), large mammal (NISP = 10), and small mammal/bird (NISP = 17) (Wigen 1998). Only a few bones could be identified to genus or family. These include rockfish, lingcod or halibut, and caribou (tentative identification).

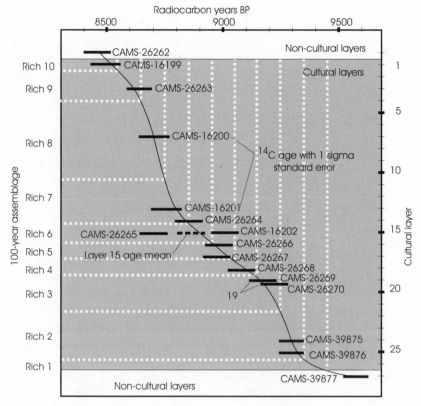

Figure 12.4 Plot of 100-year assemblages and cultural layers by radiocarbon age for Richardson Island.

Features

The 1-square-metre area of excavation at Richardson Island limited the potential to distinguish features, but several concentrations of lithic detritus and partial hearth features were recorded. Lithic features included dense clusters of microblade manufacturing detritus in upper levels and bifacial reduction detritus in lower levels. Hearth features were shallow charcoal concentrations often with associated calcined bone.

Sites 1355T and 1354T, Lyell Bay

The Lyell Bay South and East sites (1355T and 1354T) are located on the western shore of Lyell Island, at the head of Lyell Bay in southeastern Haida Gwaii (Figure 12.5). During the early Holocene, higher sea levels would have flooded the physically prominent Beresford Fault, which runs through Lyell Bay and south to Beresford Inlet. The sites are situated at either side of the northern end of this narrows, likely to access the rich marine sea life that would have inhabited the fault when sea levels were higher. Thick deposits of intertidal shellfish are present in raised intertidal sediments exposed along the Beresford Fault. These sites were first identified in 1995 when artifacts, including microblades, were located on the surface and in shovel and auger tests (Christensen 1996). The shovel tests demonstrated a minimum of 1 metre of cultural deposits at both sites. Test excavations were conducted in 1996 and 1997 (Christensen 1998).

Site 1355T, Lyell Bay South
The Lyell Bay South site is located on a small alluvial fan and on an adjacent rock-cored ridge (Figure 12.5). Both landforms are at the elevation of the early Holocene high sea level position. A small depression behind the ridge contains organic soil underlain by clay. The clay contains marine diatoms and scattered charcoal dated to about 9000 BP (Table 12.2).

Stratigraphy
Investigations at Lyell Bay South revealed complexly stratified deposits (Figure 12.6). Nineteen stratigraphic layers were identified in Excavation Unit (EU) 3, an excavation unit placed on the 15.5-metre terrace on the west side of the small creek that bisects the site, and fifteen layers were identified in EU6. At both excavation units the cultural strata dip towards the modern shoreline. Strata orientation and the sediment analyses (Christensen 1998) indicate that the deposits are alluvial in nature and that the creek was probably extant at the time of site occupation. The stratigraphy of EU3 consists of three major units: a basal unit consisting of sand, cobbles, and fine clays; an intermediate unit consisting of thick alluvial gravel deposits; and the overlying humic layer deposited during the late Holocene.

The basal unit encompasses layers 17 to 19 and consists of olive-grey clay overlain by sand and gravel. These sediments likely represent a former beach. Cultural material was present only in the uppermost part this unit. The middle unit includes layers 16 through 2 and contains the bulk of the cultural material. These layers consist primarily of gravel, ranging from 1 to 5 centimetres in size, in a matrix of silt. These sediments display many of the characteristics of alluvial fan deposits: poorly sorted subangular to subrounded gravel matrices with a paucity of fine sediment, evidence of in situ pedogenic weathering (particularly red iron oxides), and local sorted lenses (Lewis 1984:26). It is likely that the gravel was deposited seasonally and that people were living on these surfaces and incorporating cultural material into the gravel.

The base of cultural deposition is at 13.3 metres above high tide and dates to about 8400 BP. At this time, sea levels were at the early Holocene maximum of about 15 metres above high tide (Fedje and Josenhans 2000). This discrepancy suggests that the small terrace into which EU3 was excavated has slumped as a block from its original location. Earthquake-induced slumping

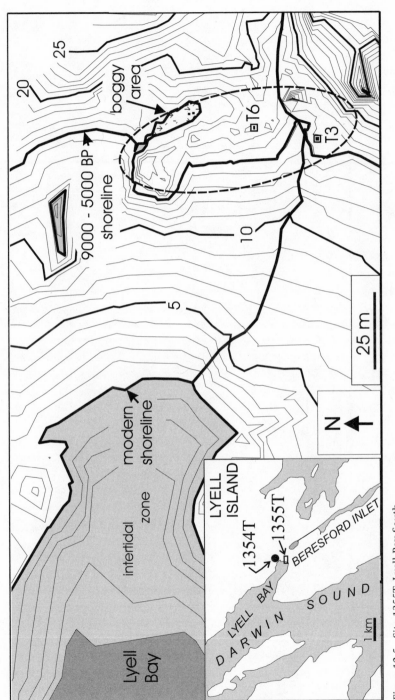

Figure 12.5 Site 1355T, Lyell Bay South.

Table 12.2

Lyell Bay South radiocarbon dates (radiocarbon years BP)

CAMS no.	Sample no.	Material	Datum m(aht)	Depth (cm)	Age (BP)	±	Comment
Lyell Bay South, Site 1355T							
Test T2							
26255	1355T2-65	Charcoal	15.5	65	6630	60	Raised beach
26256	1355T2-85	Charcoal	15.5	85	8110	60	Raised beach
Excavation Unit 3							
33914	1355T3-94	Charcoal	15.5	94	7940	60	Raised beach
33915	1355T3-143	Charcoal	15.5	143	8060	60	Raised beach
33916	1355T3-193	Charcoal	15.5	193	8170	60	Raised beach
33917	1355T3C-218	Charcoal	15.5	218	8450	60	Raised beach
Excavation Unit 6							
42480	1355T6-104	Charcoal	17.5	104	8230	50	Raised beach, hearth
Test B2							
42481	1355TB2-86	Charcoal	14.5	85	9070	50	Marine clay

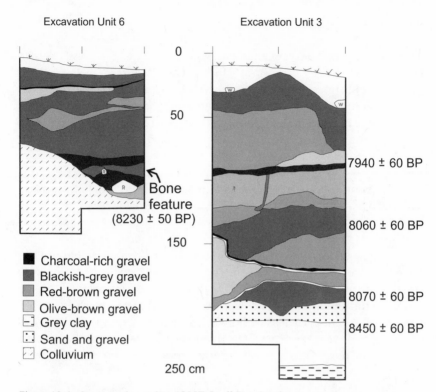

Figure 12.6 Stratigraphy at Site 1355T, Lyell Bay South.

of a portion of the paleo-terrace may account for the sea level and time period discrepancies, as it is only a few hundred metres from the Beresford Fault, along which recent earthquakes have been recorded (Clague 1989:67).

Excavation of EU6, on the 17.5-metre terrace east of the small creek that bisects the site, exposed three main stratigraphic units: a diamicton, a stratified alluvium, and a humic layer.

The basal unit consists of a sloping deposit of angular pebbles suspended in clay-rich silt. The large percentage of fine-grained material, lack of internal organization, and unsorted nature of the larger clasts are consistent with a debris-flow. Cultural material, particularly a large number of microblades of the same material type, was found spread throughout the upper 10 to 20 centimetres of these deposits. Next in sequence, the middle unit deposits consist of alluvial gravel in organic-rich sediment. This unit includes a hearth feature, a concentration of fire-cracked rock, and a thin lens of calcined bone. A culturally sterile humic layer overlies the alluvial gravel.

Dating

Seven charcoal samples were dated for this site (Table 12.2). Stratigraphic integrity of the site, despite the evidence for slumping, is suggested by the correlation between radiocarbon age and depth of samples.

The earliest date from the cultural deposits is 8450 ± 60 BP (CAMS-33917), taken from the beach deposits at 218 centimetres distance below surface (dbs). The uppermost date from EU3 is 7940 ± 60 BP (CAMS-33914), taken from 94 centimetres dbs. A charcoal sample from 85 centimetres depth in a shovel test (T2) adjacent to EU3 was dated earlier, to 6630 ± 60 BP. Charcoal from the base of a hearth feature in EU6 was dated to 8230 ± 50 BP.

Fauna
Calcined bone collected from the hearth feature in EU6 includes a dense concentration of herring (NISP = 119) and unidentifiable fish.

Features
No definable features were excavated in EU3, but two were found in EU6. These include a microblade concentration (*N* = 157) within the upper 20 centimetres of the debris-flow matrices and a 20-centimetre thick hearth feature in the middle unit. The hearth consists of charcoal, black greasy silt, and gravel. A lenticular lens of brown gravel with concentrations of calcined fish bone caps the feature. Overlying the bone lens is another layer of black silt, charcoal, gravel, and fire-cracked rock.

Site 1354T, Lyell Bay East
Excavation Unit 3 at Site 1354T was placed on a small rise on the east side of the Beresford Fault (Figure 12.5, inset). The rise is surrounded on all but the west side by seasonal runoff channels. Approximately 10 metres behind the rise is a small creek.

Stratigraphy
Fifteen layers were identified in EU3 within three major stratigraphic units: a basal colluvium, an alluvial sequence, and the overlying humic deposit. The basal layer is artifact-rich and consists of light brown unsorted sand with pebbles and cobbles. Overlying the basal strata are alluvial gravel deposits (layers 14 through 8) containing the bulk of the archaeological record. The upper stratigraphic unit consists of silty sand and humic deposits.

Dating
Table 12.3 lists the dates on charcoal for selected samples taken from this site. Due to time constraints, sterile matrices were not reached in the excavations. The date of 8810 ± 60 BP is a minimum age for initial occupation.

Site 766T, Arrow Creek 1
Arrow Creek 1 is situated on a stranded alluvial fan overlooking Arrow

Table 12.3

Lyell Bay East radiocarbon dates (radiocarbon years BP)

Lyell Bay East, Site 1354T

CAMS no.	Sample no.	Material	Datum m(aht)	Depth (cm)	Age (BP)	±	Comment
Test T1							
26257	1354T1-95	Charcoal	15	95	7540	50	Raised beach
Excavation Unit 3							
33910	1354T3D5-65	Charcoal	15	65	5030	40	Raised beach
33911	1354T3D5-117	Charcoal	15	117	5350	60	Raised beach
33912	1354T3D5-169	Charcoal	15	169	8610	60	Raised beach
33913	1354T3D5-192	Charcoal	15	192	8810	60	Raised beach

Creek in Matheson Inlet, Juan Perez Sound (Figure 12.7). The general location of the site, 200 metres upstream from the creek mouth and 15 to 17 metres above the modern tidal limit, was first recorded by Hobler (1976; 1978a).

Systematic shovel testing was carried out in 1991 and 1993 (Fedje et al. 1996), followed by excavation of a 2-square-metre block in 1996 (Fedje and Christensen 1999). The 2-square-metre excavation, EU11, was positioned adjacent to the terrace edge. Archaeological material recovered included some 900 lithic artifacts and several charcoal concentrations. No faunal remains or clearly defined features were encountered. Eight radiocarbon dates have been run on archaeological deposits from the site. Of these, four are from the area of the block excavation, two at each of two test units (Table 12.4). Stratigraphic separation of the archaeological deposits at the block excavation is limited. These have been analyzed as a single component.

Stratigraphy
Site stratigraphy reflects rapid estuarine and alluvial aggradation followed by several millennia of landform stability. Interpretation is based upon gross sedimentology and paleobotany (Fedje et al. 1996). Four major stratigraphic units are evident in the excavation and adjacent stratigraphic exposures.

The lowermost unit (Stratum 1), evident in a creek bank exposure at 2 to 6 metres elevation, comprises stratified clay and sand layers rich in intertidal shellfish. Stratum 2, at 6 to 15 metres elevation, contains stratified alluvium, from sand to cobble size. These sediments derive from high-energy fluvial sedimentation and represent the aggrading fan of Arrow Creek. EU11 extended down to the top of this unit (Figure 12.8). Stratum 3 includes a thin sand layer and overlying sequence of charcoal-rich sand to pebble-sized sediments (natural layers 3 to 6 in Figure 12.8) from which cultural remains were recovered. The pea-gravel in layer 5 is similar in character to the berm and culturally introduced gravels at Richardson Island. The moderate to dense concentrations of charcoal and artifacts in a greasy black soil reflect attenuation of alluvial sedimentation and heightened cultural activity. Artifact concentration (dense microblades and cores) and excellent condition indicate primary deposition.

Dating
Four AMS dates were obtained on charcoal from EU11 and four from shovel tests (Table 12.4). A date of 8800 BP marks the surface of Stratum 2. A few pieces of lithic debitage and rare fragments of charcoal were recovered from this level. The black greasy charcoal and artifact-rich sediments in levels 3 to 6 date from about 8100 to 7000 BP. The inversion of the two uppermost dates likely indicates some post-depositional mixing.

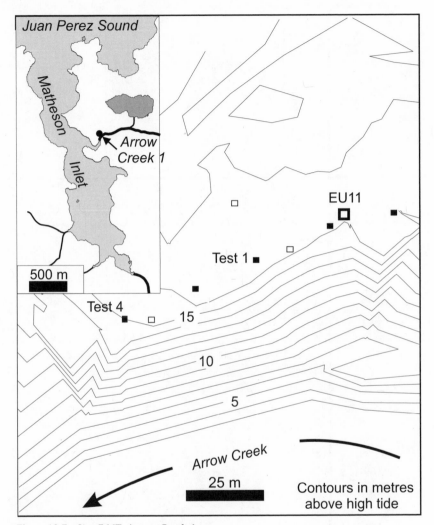

Figure 12.7 Site 766T, Arrow Creek 1.

Features
Features encountered included two shallow, basin-shaped hearths and dense clusters of microblade manufacturing debitage.

Artifacts
Artifacts recovered from the Gwaii Haanas raised beach sites described here include only those recovered from stratified context with good radiocarbon control. This assemblage includes 8,748 pieces of chipped stone and 3 pieces of ground stone. The artifacts have been sorted into twenty-seven tool classes and three debitage classes: platform remnant-bearing flakes (PRB), shatter, and biface reduction flakes (BRF) (Table 12.5).

Table 12.4

Arrow Creek 1 radiocarbon dates (radiocarbon years BP)

CAMS no.	Sample no.	Material	Datum m(aht)	Depth (cm)	Age (BP)	±	Comment
Arrow Creek 1, Site 766T							
Excavation Unit 11							
33906	766T11D3-49	Charcoal	16.5	49	7410	60	Raised beach
33907	766T11D5-78	Charcoal	16.5	78	7000	50	Raised beach
33908	766T11D5-80	Charcoal	16.5	80	8150	60	Raised beach
33909	766T11D8-119	Charcoal	16.5	119	8880	50	Raised beach
Test Units							
TO2622	766T1/1	Charcoal	16.5	35	8200	80	Raised beach
TO2622	766T1/2	Charcoal	16.5	40	8200	90	Raised beach
41111	766T4/1	Charcoal	15	90	5650	70	Raised beach
41112	766T4/2	Charcoal	15	100	5650	70	Raised beach

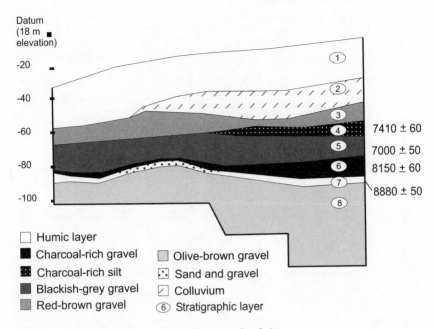

Figure 12.8 Stratigraphy at Site 766T, Arrow Creek 1.

The tool classes consist of three core types (unidirectional, multidirectional, and core fragments), four classes related to microblade core technology (microblade cores, microblade core preforms, microblade core facial rejuvenation flakes, microblades), three formal bifacial classes (bifaces, biface ends, biface fragments), bimarginal tools (flakes with non-invasive flaking on both faces), two unifacial tool classes (unifaces, uniface fragments), unimarginal tools, scrapers (flakes with continuous unifacial flaking on a rounded end), core tools (unifacially worked pebble fragments), spall tools (unifacially worked flake spalls), utilized flakes (continuous utilization along one or more edges), utilized biface reduction flakes (utilized flakes retaining bifacial platform remnants), spokeshaves (flaked concavities), gravers (utilized graver spurs), spokeshave/gravers (both occurring on single pieces), denticulate scraperplanes (domed scraperplanes with denticulate projections), denticulate scraperplane fragments, scraperplanes (domed scraperplanes, exhibiting use-wear), scraperplane fragments, and flake scraperplanes (thick flakes with steep-angled scraperplane edges). In total, there are 878 tools at Richardson Island (371 microblades), 167 tools at Arrow Creek 1 (91 microblades), 416 tools at Site 1355T (377 microblades), and 79 tools at Site 1354T (60 microblades).

All lithic materials appear to be of local origin. Although no quarries have been located, comparable material for most lithologies is present on fans and beaches throughout the area. These include siltstone, basalt, rhyolite,

Table 12.5

Raised beach lithic assemblages in Gwaii Haanas

	Richardson 1 9400	Richardson 2 9300	Richardson 3 9200	Richardson 4 9100	Richardson 5 9000	Richardson 6 8900	Richardson 7 8800	Richardson 8 8700	Richardson 9 8600	Richardson 10 8500	Arrow Cr 1 ca. 7500	1355 Lower ca. 8400	1355 Upper ca. 7200	1354 Lower ca. 8600	1354 Upper ca. 5500
PRB	40	177	522	177	196	158	345	277	45	119	215	85	31	27	25
Shatter	76	273	1374	238	283	355	462	415	37	261	409	255	78	37	65
BRF	15	10	52	7	11	13	32	9		2					
Total debitage	131	460	1948	422	490	526	839	701	82	382	624	340	109	64	90
Unidirectional core			1	2	1	4		3	1		8	4			2
Multidirectional core				1	1			2	1	1	10				
Core fragment									1	1	6				
Microblade core							1	1	1	1	11		1		
Microblade core preform							2	2	2		3				
Microblade core flake							4	6	2		1	1		1	
Microblade						5	31	194	47	94	91	314	63	38	22
Biface	1	1	1		3	3	1			1			1		
Biface end	1	6	2	5	3		2	1		1					

Biface fragment				1				3	3	3	3	2	5	4	2
Bimarginal tool								3	3		1				1
Uniface			2				1	1	1	3		2	2	1	
Uniface fragment			1	1	2		1	1	1	2	2	1	1	1	
Unimarginal tool	1		1	1			1	2	4	4	1	2	2		1
Scraper	2			1	1		1						2		
Core tool		1	2	3					1	1					
Spall tool			4				1								
Utilized flake	5	2	4	9	4	12	13	22	10	18	16	5	3	2	
Utilized biface reduction flake										3	3	9			
Spokeshave	2		1	1	1		2	6	4	6	4	2		1	
Graver		1	3	3	1	1	7	16	3	3	9	3	3	5	
Spokeshave/graver	1		1	1			1	12	3	2	1	4	1		
Denticulate scraperplane	1		2	2	1	1	2	5	10	13	14	13	4	3	
Denticulate scraperplane fragment	2	1	2	3	1		1	2		1	2	8	1		
Scraperplane				4	1	1	2	6	4	2	14	5	4	2	
Scraperplane fragment				4		2	2		3	1	1	7	4		
Flake scraperplane					1	1	2	1		3		2			
Total tools	36	43	75	341	167	109	75	253	117	59	62	77	66	40	20

andesite, and dacite. Small amounts of chalcedony (agate), also locally available, are also present.

Debitage (7,208)
This debitage category includes platform remnant-bearing flakes (PRB), biface reduction flakes (BRF), and shatter.

Unidirectional Cores (26), Multidirectional Cores (16)
Unidirectional cores show flakes or blades removed in one direction from one platform surface. These cores are ubiquitous in raised beach sites. Flake removal on multidirectional cores is not restricted to a single platform.

Microblade Cores, Preforms, and Rejuvenation Flakes (41)
The Moresby Tradition microblade cores in Gwaii Haanas are similar to those from Chuck Lake (Ackerman et al. 1985; see also Fladmark 1986). They are flat-topped, are not rejuvenated by platform tablet removals, may be rejuvenated by flute-face removals, are relatively wide, bear crushing at their bases and some lateral platform crushing, and range in form from "boat-shaped" to "conical" to "bullet-shaped" (Figure 12.9). The cores are very different from the Campus cores except for the basal crushing, but are very similar to microblade cores from Hidden Falls, and Ground Hog Bay 2 in southeastern Alaska (Ackerman 1985, 1992).

Microblades (899)
Microblades are small blades or specialized flakes, made by a pressure technique, with parallel lateral edges. Microblades are one of the defining characteristics of the Moresby Tradition and comprise the single most common formal tool in the raised beach assemblages. Blade lengths range from 0.5 to 2.75 centimetres and widths from 0.2 to 0.8 centimetres. This artifact class is present in all raised beach components postdating 9000 BP. These blades were likely hafted on the end of a shaft for cutting purposes (Croes 1995; Hutchings 1996) or set in the side of slotted bone points and used as knives, spears, or projectile points (Chapter 13).

Bifaces, Bimarginal Tools, and Fragments (61)
Bifacial technology was present only in the Richardson Island assemblage. Richardson bifaces are leaf-shaped except for some that are extensively reworked (Figure 12.10). Complete bifaces from the lower component include two teardrop-shaped bifaces reminiscent of Chindadn points (Goebel et al. 1996) and an oval specimen. A large side-notched biface was recovered from the upper component at this site. All other bifaces are fragmentary but conformable with the leaf-shaped specimens. These biface forms are very similar to the "foliate" bifaces from Namu (Carlson 1996).

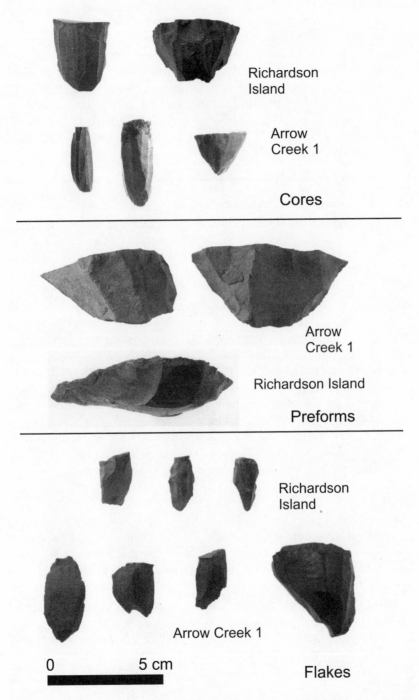

Figure 12.9 Microblade cores, preforms, and rejuvenation flakes flakes from Gwaii Haanas raised beach sites.

Biface reduction is generally initiated from flake or tabular blanks. This can be seen from bifaces broken during manufacture and from refitting of reduction detritus to bifaces. There is extensive use of soft hammer technique and little or no evidence of edge grinding either during manufacture or on completed tools. This is in contrast to the approximately 10,000 to 9000 BP Stemmed Point Tradition, where lanceolate and leaf-shaped points were produced by reducing discoidal cores with constant grinding of edges during manufacture and extensive grinding of the stem on completed tools (Fedje et al. 1995).

Cobble Chopper/Core Tool and Spall Tools (15)

This class includes large, unifacially flaked cobbles or cobble spalls, probably used for woodworking, felling trees, or butchering.

Scraperplanes, Flake Scraperplanes, and Fragments (75)

Scraperplanes are large planar to dome-shaped tools with working edges at about 80° to 90° (Figure 12.11). These are most often manufactured from tabular igneous or metamorphic rock, with the tabular surface left unmodified as the "ventral" plane of the tool. A few have been prepared from large, thick flakes. A number of these tools exhibit considerable edge rounding from use, probably on soft material. Projections may be highly rounded without any use microflaking, while non-working edges are pristine with manufacturing flake scars. This is a very distinct class of tools that is common in sites of similar age on the BC and Alaska coast. This same type of tool is also associated with earlier interior Alaskan Denali and Nenana Complexes (11,500 to 10,500 BP). It is noteworthy that small end scrapers typical of Paleoindian components are absent except for one thumbnail end scraper-like specimen from the upper levels at Richardson Island.

Denticulate Scraperplanes and Fragments (96)

These are morphologically similar to scraperplanes but with one or more pronounced projections along the working edge (Figure 12.11). Edge rounding is not as prevalent but is present on some specimens. This class of tool appears to have been utilized in the same fashion as the scraperplanes. It is possible that the denticulate edge is designed to remove mass from the worked object in a more aggressive manner, as would a rasp. Some specimens exhibit use rounding and use microflaking on adjacent edges. This type of tool, along with scraperplanes generally, are fairly common in pre-8000 BP assemblages such as Namu (Carlson 1996) and Glenrose (Matson 1976), then decline in relative importance in later components (e.g., Matson 1976, table 17-1).

Figure 12.10 Bifaces from Richardson Island.

Richardson
Island

Denticulate
scraperplanes

Richardson
Island

Arrow
Creek 1

Plan view

Profile view

0   5 cm

Scraperplanes

Figure 12.11   Scraperplanes and fragments.

Unifaces, Unimarginal Tools, and Scrapers (45)

Unifaces are artifacts that have flake removal on one surface only. The unifaces in the raised beach sites include artifacts that could be labelled side-scrapers.

Spokeshaves, Gravers, and Spokeshave/Gravers (120)

Spokeshaves exhibit one or more unifacially flaked concavities and are presumably used to scrape, smooth, and shape wood or bone implements. Gravers are characterized by small projections, usually isolated by unifacial flaking and often exhibiting microflaking edge damage and/or polish. Spokeshaves and gravers commonly co-occur on a single item, thus the spokeshave/graver class. (See Figure 12.12.)

Utilized Flakes (138)

This artifact type consists of flakes and shatter with use wear on one or more flake margins. These flakes do not show intentional modification but do show evidence of use in the form of edge rounding, edge nibbling, or step fracturing. Material type and weathering likely results in this tool class being significantly underrepresented.

Abraders (2)

Two sandstone abraders (including one in two pieces) were recovered from Lyell Bay excavations. One is from radiocarbon-dated context. Abraders of varying sizes have been excavated from other Moresby Tradition sites in Haida Gwaii, including Kasta (Fladmark 1986) on Moresby Island and Skoglund's Landing on Graham Island (Breffitt 1993). Fladmark (1989) sees abraders as evidence for the presence of organic cultural items in early deposits despite the fact that tools manufactured from organic materials have not been preserved.

Technological Trends and Transitions

Quantitative Analysis of the Raised Beach Assemblages

Interpretation of temporal patterning at Richardson Island is complicated by the fact that some levels were deposited relatively quickly, others more slowly. Therefore when the data are plotted against all twenty-six cultural layers, the time factor is represented unevenly. Fortunately, the site is very thoroughly dated so that 100-year approximations can be extrapolated for the levels (Figure 12.4), and then the artifact data can be presented at intervals of 100 years. In this way the time intervals are properly scaled, so that, for example, layers 4 through 10 are all included in the 8700 BP level (Figure 12.4). Arrow Creek 1 (one component), Lyell Bay South (two components) and Lyell Bay East (two components) are added to the Richardson

Figure 12.12 Spokeshaves and gravers from Richardson Island.

Island levels in the same manner, these assemblages representing the later periods of about 8800 to 5000 BP.

The analytic data set was created by compressing entire tool classes with their associated fragmentary classes (e.g., bifaces + biface ends + biface fragments = Bifaces) and collapsing some of the other tool classes as well (e.g., cobble tool + spall tool = Large Tools). This makes the data easier to manipulate and reduces analytic biases that may result from low frequencies in certain categories. These data then consist of three debitage classes (PRB, shatter, BRF) and twelve tool classes (cores, microtechnology, bifaces, unifaces, marginals, large tools, utilized flakes, spokeshaves, gravers, spokeshaves/gravers, denticulate scraperplanes, scraperplanes). Table 12.6 shows the analytic data set employed, consisting of the fifteen artifact tool classes across

Table 12.6

Analytic data set of twelve tool classes and three debitage classes

Assemblage	Date (BP)	PRB	Shatter	BRF	Total debitage	Cores	Microblade tech.	Bifaces	Unifaces	Marginal	Large tool	Utilized flakes	Spokeshaves	Graver	SPK/GRV	Denticulate scraperplanes	Scraperplanes	Total tools
1354 Upper	8000-5000	25	65	0	90	2	22	0	0	0	2	5	0	2	0	3	0	36
1354 Lower	8800-8000	27	37	0	64	1	38	0	0	0	0	2	0	1	0	1	0	43
1355 Upper	8000-5000	31	78	0	109	1	65	0	1	0	1	1	0	3	1	2	0	75
1355 Lower	8800-8000	85	255	0	340	4	315	0	1	2	2	4	0	8	1	4	0	341
Arrow Creek 1	8000-7000	215	409	0	624	24	106	0	3	1	7	9	1	3	0	5	8	167
Richardson 10	8500	119	261	2	382	1	96	3	3	0	0	4	1	0	0	1	0	109
Richardson 9	8600	45	37	0	82	2	52	0	3	2	0	12	0	1	0	1	2	75
Richardson 8	8700	277	415	9	701	5	203	4	4	4	1	13	2	7	1	3	6	253
Richardson 7	8800	345	462	32	839	0	38	6	2	0	1	22	6	16	12	7	7	117
Richardson 6	8900	158	355	13	526	4	5	6	2	4	1	10	4	3	3	10	7	59
Richardson 5	9000	196	283	11	490	2	0	6	5	1	0	18	6	3	2	13	6	62
Richardson 4	9100	177	238	7	422	3	0	7	1	3	0	19	4	9	1	15	15	77
Richardson 3	9200	522	1374	52	1948	1	0	8	3	2	0	14	2	3	4	15	14	66
Richardson 2	9300	177	273	10	460	0	0	11	3	0	0	3	0	3	0	12	8	40
Richardson 1	9400	40	76	15	131	0	0	4	0	1	0	2	1	5	1	4	2	20

ten temporally scaled assemblages at Richardson Island, the one component from Arrow Creek 1, and upper and lower components at each of 1354T and 1355T at Lyell Bay, for a total of fifteen assemblages. As at Richardson Island, the Arrow Creek and Lyell Bay assemblages have been assigned dates for the purpose of temporal comparisons.

Several of the artifact classes show strong tendencies through time and inter-relationships. Calculating a Spearman's rho correlation matrix (Figure 12.13) using the artifact frequencies and 100-year age demonstrates that microblade technology (–0.76) and bifaces (0.85) exhibit the strongest association with time (Figure 12.13 highlights correlations $p < .05$ and $p < .01$). That is, in a linear manner, microblades are abundant in late assemblages and bifaces are abundant in early assemblages. Both denticulate and "normal" scraperplanes are more common in early levels than in late ones, although less strongly (0.64, 0.62).

In Figure 12.13, large tools increase sharply in frequency through time (–0.67) and although the frequencies of large tools in individual levels are low, they are concentrated in the more recent levels. This may simply be an indication that these large tools replaced the scraperplane varieties in function, or in slightly changed function. This patterning is reflected in the microblade-biface pattern, so it could be argued that biface functions were largely replaced by microblades.

Meaningful relationships in this fifteen assemblage/fifteen class tool set within the tool classes themselves are apparent in two main areas: the strong negative associations of microblade technology with bifaces (–0.71) and denticulate scraperplanes (–0.64), and the strong positive association of bifaces with the scraperplanes (0.80, 0.76). Perhaps not surprisingly, denticulates and scraperplanes are strongly positively associated (0.83), as are spokeshaves and spokeshave/gravers (0.74) and gravers and spokeshave/gravers (0.63). Spokeshaves are also strongly associated with utilized flakes (0.77) and moderately associated with bifaces (0.62). Spokeshaves, gravers, and spokeshave/gravers are more frequent in the lower levels,

R-mode cluster analysis is a clear way to show the principal artifact types in graphic fashion. Using SPSS 10 (SPSS 1999), the tool class frequencies (complete + fragments, etc.) were clustered using a chi-square distance (SPSS default) and Ward's dendrogram, producing Figure 12.14. Not surprisingly, this mirrors the correlation results above. Cores and large tools form a clear cluster of all large tools; bifaces and scraperplanes of all kinds group strongly into a strange cutting/scraperplane group; a good cluster of small tools is represented by unifaces with marginals, utilized flakes, and spokeshave/gravers; and microblade technology forms its own distant group.

Taking these four major tool groups and plotting their proportions through time yields Figure 12.15. Bifaces and scraperplanes decline through time while microblade technology increases rapidly starting at 8900 BP. The small

	DATE	PRB	SHAT	BRF	CORES	MBTCH	BIF	UNIF	MARG	LRGTO	UTIL	SPOKE	GRAV	SPKGR	DENT	SCPL
DATE	1.00															
PRB	0.43	1.00														
SHATTER	0.28	0.92	1.00													
BRF	0.81	0.62	0.63	1.00												
CORES	-0.39	0.14	0.15	-0.39	1.00											
MBTCH	-0.76	-0.10	0.00	-0.61	0.46	1.00										
BIFACES	0.85	0.65	0.57	0.84	-0.30	-0.71	1.00									
UNIFACES	0.19	0.71	0.61	0.27	0.24	0.09	0.35	1.00								
MARGINAL	0.29	0.36	0.28	0.21	0.66	0.02	0.23	0.28	1.00							
LARGETOOL	-0.67	-0.01	0.21	-0.36	0.54	0.61	-0.47	-0.15	0.04	1.00						
UTILFLK	0.28	0.72	0.56	0.45	0.28	-0.20	0.48	0.48	0.47	-0.03	1.00					
SPOKESHAVE	0.48	0.71	0.67	0.72	0.11	-0.33	0.62	0.39	0.39	-0.11	0.77	1.00				
GRAVER	0.35	0.47	0.43	0.42	0.10	-0.06	0.39	-0.07	0.37	0.26	0.40	0.48	1.00			
SPK/GRV	0.43	0.54	0.60	0.74	-0.06	-0.29	0.53	0.12	0.38	0.02	0.53	0.74	0.63	1.00		
DENT	0.64	0.65	0.59	0.65	0.04	-0.64	0.80	0.24	0.34	-0.10	0.55	0.62	0.56	0.59	1.00	
SCPLN	0.62	0.77	0.62	0.57	0.10	-0.49	0.76	0.40	0.42	-0.16	0.62	0.59	0.44	0.38	0.83	1.00

sig. > .01 $p > .05 < .01$

Figure 12.13   Spearman's rho correlation for Gwaii Haanas raised beach site artifact classes.

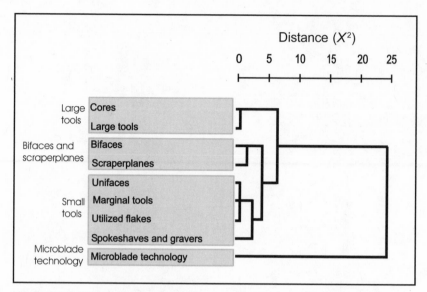

Figure 12.14 Cluster analysis for Gwaii Haanas raised beach site tools.

tools play a role of "filling in" while bifaces decline in the early levels, and sustain greater occurrence than bifaces in the later levels. Large tools are essentially background noise through all levels, so this graph shows that they grouped together in the R-mode cluster analysis because they do not trend strongly through time as do the other classes. Significantly, bifaces do not disappear completely once microblades make their appearance; in fact, at 8800 BP, both microblades and bifaces alone each comprise 26 percent of the tool assemblage at Richardson Island. In the early, pre-9000 BP levels, the small tools usually make up 40 to 50 percent of the entire tool assemblage. Scraperplanes alone exhibit a pattern very similar to that of the bifaces, although they decline in importance somewhat earlier. Through the Richardson sequence, bifaces drop from 54 percent of the tool assemblage at 9400 BP to 5 percent at 8500 BP; denticulates drop from 40 percent at 9300 BP to 1 percent at 8500 BP; and microblade technology rises from zero at 9000 BP to 86 percent of the tool assemblage at 8500 BP.

A cluster analysis was used to test the internal integrity of the Richardson Island sequence and to examine similarities of the Arrow Creek 1 and Lyell Bay assemblages to Richardson. The assemblage data from Table 12.6 were first standardized, mainly to reduce the effects of the abundant microblade technology class. This means that artifact class frequencies were given a range of +1 to –1. For each artifact class, the level with most frequent occurrence was given a frequency of +1 and the lowest a frequency of –1, then the intervening level frequencies were calculated (–0.33 or +0.74, for example) to fit. This is a calculation that weighs all classes equally, yet allows

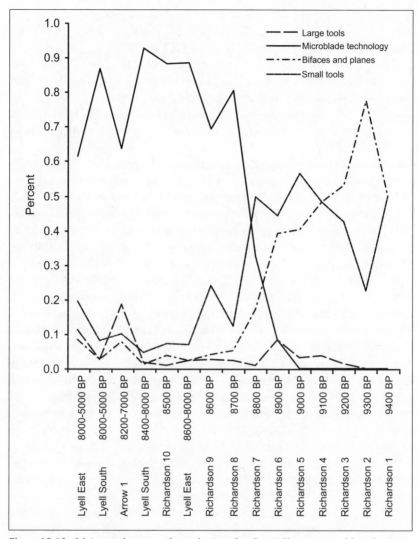

Figure 12.15 Major tool groups through time for Gwaii Haanas raised beach sites.

proportional relations between classes to be compared (see, for example, Matson and True 1974:55).

The standardized data were then subjected to a Ward's Method Cluster Analysis employing a chi-square distance measure (SPSS 1999). This analysis resulted in the dendrogram shown in Figure 12.16. Overall, the Richardson sequence is highly internally consistent from earliest to latest levels, and the Arrow Creek 1 and Lyell Bay assemblages relate to Richardson almost exactly as they should, given their later periods of occupation. The dendrogram shows a very strong upper/lower dichotomy to the Richardson levels, and there are two very distinct clusters overall. Richardson levels 1 through 7 group very strongly, as do Richardson levels 8 through 10 with Arrow Creek and Sites 1354T (Lyell East) and 1355T (Lyell South). Interestingly, the "transitional" low-frequency microblade-bearing levels of 8800 and 8900 BP link clearly to the earlier non-microblade levels. This may in fact be evidence of washing in and mixing of these few microblades into earlier levels. The later Richardson assemblages from 8700 BP, 8600 BP, and 8500 BP group together, as do each of the lower and upper assemblages from 1354T and 1355T.

Perhaps the most enlightening feature of the cluster analysis is that the presence of microblades in the 8800 and 8900 BP Richardson components does not override the overall similarity of those to the earlier non-microblade components. This finding, combined with the near-linear decline of bifaces and scraperplanes, strengthens our notion of a transitional period at Richardson Island at the time when maximum sea levels were stabilizing. Alternatively, the entire Richardson sequence can be seen as a transition period of about 1,000 years in total length, showing a continuing decline of major tool classes ("cutting" – bifaces; "heavy scraping" – scraperplanes), while microblades rather quickly come to dominate over a span of about 200 years. Why would this be? What caused the inhabitants to start making microblades and to sharply curtail their use of bifaces and scraperplanes? There could be several reasons: microblade manufacture is a way of obtaining a large amount of straight edge from a small amount of stone, so perhaps preferred stone sources were drowned and inaccessible; perhaps certain environmental conditions, such as stream gravel beds, were being formed that would be beneficial to certain fish species such as salmon, which can be processed efficiently with sharp, straight edge tools.

These quantitative analyses do not consider some technological characteristics of the lithic assemblages that may be significantly patterned through time and that may be better indicators of what the inhabitants were actually doing at these locations. For example, the denticulates and scraperplanes at Arrow Creek 1 are generally much smaller than those from Richardson Island, although they are otherwise morphologically very similar. Other aspects of the technology may also have correlations with size factors and with stone raw material factors. Stone raw material selection appears to have changed markedly through time at Richardson Island, from a strong preference in early levels for a hard, black and white metamorphic stone to a softer argillite in the later levels, a trend that appears to continue at the Arrow Creek 1 and Lyell Bay assemblages (Magne 2000). These types of technological trends will be examined carefully in future analyses.

The period from 9000 to 8800 BP is when sea level at the Richardson Island site was stabilizing at its peak height of about 15 metres above today's

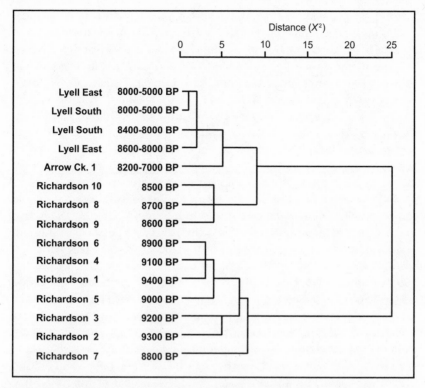

Figure 12.16 Cluster analysis of fifteen debitage and tool classes (chi-square distance on standardized frequencies, Ward's Method Cluster Analysis).

mean sea level, so it is interesting that this is also the period of time when microblade technology was appearing and bifaces and scraperplanes were only moderately represented and then declined substantially. This period of time appears to be a transitional period for which the artifact classes may be providing clues regarding the kinds of subsistence and settlement changes that the populations were undergoing.

Bifacial Tradition

It is apparent from the lithic assemblages recovered from the four raised beach sites that significant technological change occurred in this area during early to mid-Holocene times. Basal cultural components are characterized by a bifacial technology, large scrapers, and associated simple flake tools. The bifacial elements are gradually supplanted by microblade technology beginning about 8900. By about 8000 BP, bifacial technology has been entirely replaced. The earliest raised beach assemblages, present only at the Richardson Island site, date from about 9300 to 8900 BP and lack any evidence of microblade technology. The non-microblade assemblage includes teardrop-shaped bifaces, other foliate bifaces, predominantly unidirectional blade cores, large scraperplanes, and a variety of simple flake tools. These have been assigned to the Kinggi Complex (Fedje and Christensen 1999).

There are more than 100 early Holocene intertidal lithic sites recorded in southern Haida Gwaii, many with bifacial technology evident. Most of these are suggested to date from 9500 to 9400 BP (Fedje and Christensen 1999), but only two intertidal components, at Arrow Creek 2 (925T) and Kilgii Gwaay (1325T), are securely dated to earlier than 9000 BP (Fedje et al. 1996, 2001; Chapter 11). Microblade technology is not present at either site. Both sites have associated faunal and floral remains, although it is only at Kilgii Gwaay on Ellen Island that these appear to be in primary context (Fedje et al. 2001; Chapter 11). This site has a large (> 2,000) lithic assemblage and has been radiocarbon-dated to about 9450 BP.

The evidence for a pre-NWCMT (Northwest Coast Microblade Tradition) bifacial tradition in Haida Gwaii prior to 8900 BP is consistent with that seen elsewhere on the central and northern Northwest Coast (Ackerman 1996b; Carlson 1996; Dixon 1999). The non-microblade component Period 1A (ca. 9500 to 9000 BP) tool kit at Namu is characterized by foliate bifaces, denticulate and core scrapers, and simple flake tools. At On Your Knees Cave (49-PET-408) in southeastern Alaska, Dixon (2002) has identified a non-microblade component stratigraphically beneath a NWCMT component dating to about 9200 BP. Further south, C. Carlson (1979) and Matson (1996) recovered substantial non-microblade assemblages from maritime sites dating between 8000 and 8500 BP. On the west coast of the Americas south of the Northwest Coast region, there is evidence for early non-microblade (and non-Clovis) bifacial technology using maritime occupations on both continental and island locations (Erlandson 1994; Erlandson and Moss 1996; Dillehay 2000).

Although the absence of microblade technology in pre-8900 BP components in Haida Gwaii is consistent with Pebble Tool Tradition technology, samples are small and the Kinggi assemblage may not be fully representative. It is possible that both microblade and non-microblade tool kits are present at this time, at sites with differing function or season of use, as has been suggested for Denali (microblade) and Nenana (lacking microblades) complexes (West 1996; Cook 1996).

The non-microblade assemblages from the Northwest Coast as seen at Richardson Island and Namu appear technologically quite distinct from Paleoindian assemblages but do present a number of similarities to Nenana Complex assemblages, including leaf-shaped bifaces, focus on cobble tools, expedient flake tools, and large core tools such as scraperplanes (Pearson 1999; Hoffecker et al. 1996; Goebel et al. 1996). Dixon (1999) suggests a common early postglacial West Beringian origin for early bifacial technologies, including Nenana and Paleoindian. However, the issue of site function versus lithic industry (e.g., non-microblade versus pre-microblade) has yet to be fully resolved (Ackerman 1996b; West 1996; Dixon 1999). Lithic technology at Denali sites is broadly similar to that of Nenana except for the exchange of Chindadn bifaces for microblade technology. The two complexes may overlap and have been suggested to be part of or derive from a larger, "more ancient" Denali tradition (West 1996; Cook 1996).

Transition from Biface to Microblade Focus

The upper component at Richardson Island (8900 to 8400 BP) and lower component at the Lyell Bay sites (8800 to 8000 BP) have been assigned to the Early Moresby Tradition (Fedje and Christensen 1999). The assemblages from these components compare favourably with the NWCMT as seen in the 9000 to 6000 BP assemblages at Namu (Carlson 1996) and the 9200 to 8800 BP components at On Your Knees Cave (49-PET-408) (Dixon 2002).

Richardson Island is distinguished from Fladmark's Moresby Tradition (1989) in that bifacial technology is represented. Microblade technology appears at Richardson Island at 8900 BP, and during the period from 8900 to 8400 BP, both microblade and bifacial technology are well represented. At a few intertidal lithic sites, microblade technology is present but, where dated, is in a context indicating secondary deposition (associated with post-9000 BP radiocarbon-dated estuarine sediments or situated directly downslope of eroding raised beach sites). Other than the addition of microblade technology to the tool kit, there appears to be little change in the lithic assemblage at Richardson Island. By about 8000 BP, however, bifacial technology no longer appears to be a significant part of stone tool technology in Haida Gwaii. Only rare biface fragments have been recovered from excavated context beyond Richardson, and these date to later than 4000 BP.

At Namu microblade technology also appears shortly after 9000 BP (Carlson 1996). There, Carlson (1996) notes no essential differences between pebble tool (non-microblade) and microblade assemblages except the addition of the microblades, and suggests that the earlier technology simply added them. Personal comparison of the Namu technological sequence with the one at Richardson Island has shown that the artifacts in the cobble tool–biface–scraperplane classes are highly similar. Many could be interchanged. In addition, although the term *pebble tool* has precedence, it is apparent that domed, flat-faced scraperplanes are also dominant tool types, along with foliate or leaf-shaped bifaces (see Fedje and Christensen 1999; Carlson 1996). The microblade technology of Namu and Richardson Island differ in that the Namu microblade cores are exhausted and battered, although they are clearly non-Denali, and one of them as well as many microblades are of Edziza obsidian. In Haida Gwaii all microblade cores from excavations and beach collections are non-Denali, and no exotic materials are present anywhere in the assemblages.

The assemblages from Arrow Creek 1 (8200 to 7000 BP) and the upper components at the Lyell Bay sites (8000 to 5000 BP) have been assigned to the Late Moresby Tradition (Fedje and Christensen 1999). These assemblages fit well into the NWCMT and Fladmark's Moresby Tradition. Microblade technology dominates the assemblages but the remainder of the tool kit is little changed from that of the Kinggi and Early Moresby components. There is no evidence of bifacial technology among the approximately 1,500 artifacts recovered from these assemblages. This is consistent with the results of excavations in northern Haida Gwaii at Lawn Point, Kasta, and Cohoe Creek (ca. 7500 to 5000 BP – Fladmark 1989; Chapter 13), where bifacial technology is not evident within the (ca. 7,000 artifacts) combined assemblages. Similarly, in southeastern Alaska at Chuck Lake (8200 BP – Ackerman et al. 1985), Ground Hog Bay component 2 (ca. 8900 to 4200 BP – Ackerman et al. 1979, 1996b), and Hidden Falls (< ca. 9500 BP – Davis 1989, 1996), the NWCMT components exhibit no evidence of bifacial technology (Ackerman et al. 1985, 1996b; Davis 1989).

In one sense, there appears to be considerable continuity in lithic technology through the thousand years of human occupation at Richardson Island and on into the occupation at Arrow Creek 1 a thousand years later. That is, there is gradual replacement of bifaces with microblade-armed tools but other elements of the early Holocene tool kits are little changed except in relative frequency. There are notable changes in raw material use over time, but there is no evidence that lithic procurement was anything but insular. These changes are likely a result of sea level change and landscape maturation and the concomitant visibility and availability of bedrock sources and fluvial or beach cobbles.

A similar pattern of non-microblade-to-microblade traditions is seen in the Alaskan interior, but at earlier times. Dry Creek, Moose Creek, and Broken Mammoth (Hamilton and Goebel 1999; Pearson 1999) perhaps best demonstrate this, with dates of about 11,800 BP for the initial non-microblade Nenana Complex to about 10,500 BP for the beginning of the Denali Complex. In terms of technical characteristics, there are definite distinctions in microblade technology as it occurs in interior and coastal regions. The early Alaskan assemblages are very dominantly "Denali" in manufacturing, with extensive platform rejuvenation and rare "Shirataki" or biface-splitting manufacturing, and are often associated with burins. On the other hand, the NWCMT sites do not contain burins, and the microblade cores are almost always plain-platformed with a smattering of flute-face rejuvenation. However, the significance of the distinction between Denali and NWCMT microblade cores is unclear as both types co-occur in the early microblade components at Groundhog Bay and Hidden Falls (Davis 1996; Ackerman 1996b) and in Denali Complex sites such as Whitmore Ridge (conoidal cores on marine chert and wedge-shaped cores on fine-grained lustrous chert –

West et al. 1996). This is suggested to relate to material types or knapper competence. Similarly, in Siberian assemblages both types of manufacturing occur, although the "Denali" technique is prevalent by far (Derev'anko 1998).

The ultimate origin of the NWCMT is unclear. Goebel and Slobodin (1999) describe a "western Beringian Mesolithic" adaptation that demonstrates many commonalities with the NWCMT. The associated lithic technology includes prismatic to conical and pencil-shaped microblade cores, segmented microblades hafted into slotted bone and antler points, and a variety of cobble tools. This construct is proposed to derive from the broadly distributed Sumnagin Complex, possibly arriving in western Beringia from Yakutia about 9000 BP.

Magne (2000) suggests that the NWCMT technology may have developed on the Northwest Coast through the application of Denali-derived technology to existing early coastal bifacial technology, with the latter possibly related to the Nenana Complex of central Alaska (see also Dixon 1999). The precedence of the NWCMT, with dates of 9200 BP in southeastern Alaska and 8900 BP in Haida Gwaii (Dixon 1999; Fedje and Christensen 1999), tends to support the interpretation of independent development and the possibility of a west-to-east movement of aspects of this technology.

Discussion

The driving mechanisms for the sequence of Northwest Coast technological manifestations from bifacial to microblade and "shell midden/developmental" are unclear, but both cultural and environmental factors may be operating. Upper Paleolithic blade and bifacial technology is present in central Siberia and possibly in Japan (where extensive use of obsidian hydration dating lowers confidence in the dates received) by about 20,000 BP and in Alaska, as the Nenana Complex, at about 12,000 BP (Goebel and Slobodin 1999; Goebel et al. 2000). Archaeological evidence from Asia and Alaska suggests that the change from early bifacial to microblade tradition may represent a "gradual" spread of technology and, perhaps in part, movement of people, from central Asia to Alaska and south along the west coast of America. Microblade technology, with wedge-shaped cores, is first evident about 18,000 BP in the Transbaikal region of southern Siberia, 14,000 BP in the Russian Far East, about 11,000 BP in western Beringia, and about 10,500 BP in central Alaska. A variant of this technology, the Northwest Coast Microblade Tradition, characterized by tabular to conical microblade cores, was present in southeastern Alaska by 9200 BP (Dixon 1999) and by about 8900 BP in Haida Gwaii and Namu (Carlson 1996).

Recent linguistic studies have shown strong correspondence between the North American Na Dene and the Yenesian people of central Siberia (Ruhlen 1998). These data are consistent with other linguistic and genetic data, which present evidence for physical migration of people from Northeast Asia into the Americas (Greenberg et al. 1986; Greenberg 1996; Wallace et al. 1999). Together with the evidence from stone tool technologies, these data can be viewed as support for the thesis of a Na-Dene microblade-using people moving into the Americas at approximately 10,500 BP (Carlson 1990; Dumond 1969, 1998; Yesner 1996).

This period of time was also one of significant environmental change (see Chapters 2 and 3). From about 12,000 to 9,000 BP, the west coast and most associated resources were in a constant state of flux because of rapidly shifting shorelines (Chapter 2). Significant climatic change also occurred at this time (Chapter 3). Between about 10,700 and 10,000 BP (Younger Dryas), the climate was significantly colder than today and the ocean waters of the Hecate Strait area both colder and more brackish (Mathewes 1993; Patterson et al. 1995). The ramifications of these changes are not fully known but it is likely that they would have altered the productivity and, to some extent, the viability of some aspects of maritime adaptation in the North Pacific. Rapid climatic amelioration occurred at 10,000 BP, with warmer and drier conditions than today enduring until about 6500 BP (Pellatt and Mathewes 1997). After this time, climatic deterioration ensued and the cool, wet conditions characteristic of modern Haida Gwaii and environs were established. In Gwaii Haanas the arrival of the NWCMT occurred very near maximum marine transgression, after which sea levels remained 15 metres higher than at present for some 4,000 years. The NWCMT continued through this environment and then disappeared about the same time that sea levels began dropping and climatic cooling commenced.

Although recent geological research suggests the possibility of human occupation of the Northwest Coast prior to 10,500 BP, there is still no physical evidence. From before 12,000 BP up to 11,000 BP, climate was moderate and maritime conditions were similar to those of today (Mathewes 1993; Patterson et al. 1995). The Younger Dryas cool period may have made some early Amerind adaptations less viable and presented an opportunity for Na-Dene expansion into the Americas. It may be that if there were two successive groups of people arriving in the Americas in early postglacial times, their basic technological adaptations were highly similar but that they also had particular specializations. A microblade-using group may have been better adapted to more marginal, more seasonally extreme interior and maritime environments (Fladmark 1975), such as, for example, late glacial Siberia, Younger Dryas Beringia, and early Holocene Zhokov Island (Goebel et al. 2000; Pitul'ko and Kasparov 1996). On the other hand, the biface–pebble tool people (cf. Nenana, Old Cordilleran) may have been adapted to more open landscapes with greater resource abundance and diversity. Certainly the Old Cordilleran (Pebble Tool Tradition) components at Bear Cove and Glenrose are diverse in subsistence resources, as revealed in the faunal assemblage of marine and terrestrial mammals as well as fish and minor shellfish utilization (Matson 1996).

The relatively late addition of microblade technology into southeastern Alaska and Haida Gwaii technologies may represent efficiencies in adaptation to a still marginally productive coastline during the period of rapid environmental change that endured until mid-Holocene time. The stone tool assemblages in Haida Gwaii record substantial, technological shifts, but we do not know what adaptive advantages these changes held. It is also unclear whether changes were carried by people (i.e., migration and replacement or assimilation of populations) or introduced as a concept by diffusion, or whether microblade technology was a technology that the Haida Gwaii people were already familiar with and resurrected for environmentally driven reasons. To answer the question of adaptation, we need to reconstruct in greater detail the environment and resource base available to the Haida and their ancestors during early postglacial time and track changes through to the mid-Holocene.

Conclusions

Recovered data from the Gwaii Haanas sites and those investigated by Fladmark in northern Haida Gwaii suggest that significant technological change occurred during early Holocene times. Some elements of the lithic technology remained constant (scraperplanes, spokeshaves, gravers) but declined in abundance, but the important new element of microblades was added. Yet there is still a potential for technological patterns to relate to factors such as site function and seasonality; that is, microblades may be present in other areas of the pre-8900 BP Richardson Island site or at sites that we have not yet investigated. A larger sample of sites from this key period will be needed for more unequivocal interpretation. The location of the sites on islands in an isolated marine archipelago and the recovery of sea mammals, marine fish, and birds enable us to infer a maritime adaptation, including offshore hook-and-line fishing. Efficient watercraft would have been necessary on a daily basis to travel from the Richardson Island campsite to the resource-rich estuaries on nearby Moresby Island. Recent excavations at the site of Kilgii Gwaay support these interpretations. This site has produced a rich and varied maritime fauna in association with a non-microblade lithic assemblage dating to 9450 BP (Fedje et al. 2001; Chapter 11).

The assemblages from these raised beach sites compare well with those of comparable age from southeastern Alaska and the Central Coast. The Kinggi assemblage is similar to the lowermost (Pebble Tool/Old Cordilleran) components at Namu and Bear Cove. Ultimate origins may derive from an early bifacial industry coming out of Beringia (cf. Nenana). The Early Moresby Tradition assemblages compare well with components 1b and 2 at Namu and the microblade component at On Your Knees Cave (49-PET-408) in southeastern Alaska, where microblade technology is associated with leaf-shaped bifaces, large stone tools, and expedient flake tools. The Late Moresby Tradition assemblages from Gwaii Haanas fit well with the Moresby Tradition assemblages from northern Haida Gwaii and other NWCMT sites, such as the southeastern Alaskan sites of Chuck Lake, Groundhog Bay, Hidden Falls, and Thorne River.

Depending on investigators' perspectives, recovered data from Haida Gwaii can suggest significant technological change or significant technological continuity during these early Holocene times. It is to us no coincidence that the Haida Gwaii pattern mirrors the Nenana-Denali switch, which occurred when maximum postglacial warming had occurred and the environment cooled, leading to the interior Alaskan and Yukon intermontane landscapes of today. It remains to be demonstrated that Denali and Nenana are not simply technological or functional variants of the same tradition, as questioned by West (1996) and West and Robinson (2000). Our inclination for Haida Gwaii is to perceive technological continuity in the broad sense, and to suggest that microblade manufacturing was an option available at any time in the early Holocene, to be employed as circumstances dictated.

Acknowledgments

Parks Canada and the Council of Haida Nations supported the investigations presented here. Fieldwork was carried out by a crew including the authors, David Archer, Derek Belcourt, Tanya Collinson, Bryn Fedje, Edana Fedje, Freia Fedje, Tom Greene, Joanne McSporran, Archie Stalker, Ian Sumpter, Barb Wilson, and Jordan Yeltatzie. Dating was conducted by the CAMS group at Lawrence Livermore National Laboratory, California. Marty and Tina carried out the lithic analyses. Becky Wigen of Pacific Identifications conducted faunal analyses. Joanne McSporran prepared artifact illustrations.

13

Raised Beach Archaeology in Northern Haida Gwaii: Preliminary Results from the Cohoe Creek Site

Tina Christensen and Jim Stafford

The excavation described in this chapter was initiated in response to concerns expressed by members of the Haida community and archaeologists regarding ongoing damage to the Cohoe Creek site, a mid-Holocene midden in Masset Inlet, Haida Gwaii. The project addresses data gaps in the archaeological record regarding Haida subsistence, landscape use, and the use of organic artifacts during the Late Moresby and early Graham Traditions.

The Cohoe Creek site was first investigated in 1987 by Leonard Ham (1990) during an archaeological impact assessment of the Juskatla Gravel Pit for the British Columbia Ministry of Transportation and Highways. This assessment and later visits by others (Fedje et al. 1995) determined that a rare intact mid-Holocene shell midden component was present at the site. It was not until 1998, however, that intensive investigations were initiated by the Old Masset Village Council.

Study Area

The Cohoe Creek site is located on the eastern shore of Masset Inlet, Graham Island, Haida Gwaii, approximately 2 kilometres south of Port Clements, near the mouth of the Yakoun River (Figure 13.1).

As sea levels fell over the last 5,000 years (see Chapter 2), the alluvial fan on which the site is located was stranded over 100 metres back from the tidally controlled Yakoun Bay estuary and approximately 12 metres above high tide today. The site is bounded to the south and east by Cohoe Creek, to the north by a terrace of approximately 30 metres, and to the west by the Yakoun Bay estuary. Cohoe Creek supports a limited coho salmon run today. The nearby Yakoun River, the largest river in Haida Gwaii, supports coho, pink, sockeye, spring, and steelhead (Northcote et al. 1989).

Methodology

Excavation focused on Locality A, at the southeast corner of the gravel pit, at the edge of the highstand terrace, where the largest concentration of

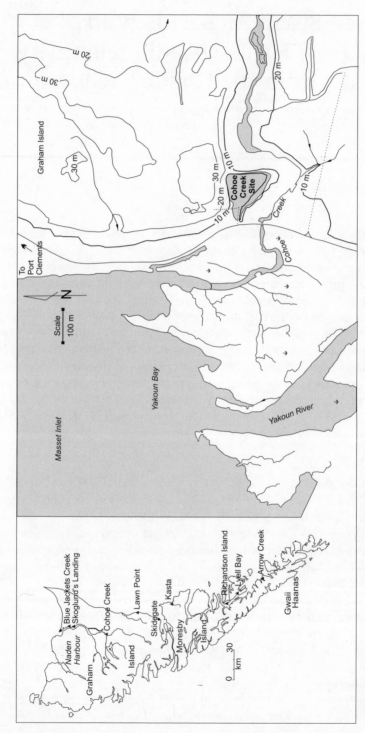

Figure 13.1 The Cohoe Creek study area at Graham Island.

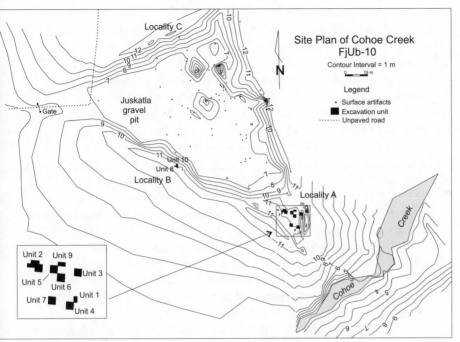

Figure 13.2   Map showing site elevation and the distribution of excavation units at Cohoe Creek.

intact shell midden deposits were recorded (see Figure 13.2). A grid system was set up over Locality A, and eight excavation units and fourteen auger tests were distributed along the grid (see Figure 13.2). Two additional units (Units 8 and 10) were placed in Locality B, situated north of Locality A along the front edge of the 12-metre terrace.

Units were excavated in 10-centimetre arbitrary levels. Natural layers and lenses within each arbitrary level were excavated separately. All artifacts and faunal remains were described for natural layers within an arbitrary level when possible. Artifacts found in situ were given vertical and horizontal provenience. Excavation matrices were wet-screened through 1/8 inch mesh.

Artifacts found on the disturbed surface were flagged and later mapped by total station, collected, bagged, and labelled. The high level of disturbance within and around the gravel pit suggests that surface artifact provenience is poor.

Stratigraphy

Locality A
Locality A is situated on a point of land created by the meeting of Cohoe Creek and Yakoun Bay 5,000 years ago. During the 1998 excavations, four

major cultural components (1-4) were identified at Locality A (see Figure 13.3). Five discrete stratigraphic layers, Layers A, A4, B, C, and D, were placed into these four components based on unique matrices, artifacts, and radiocarbon dating.

The Layer D sediments, which overlie a culturally sterile basal layer of loose brown pea gravel with trace amounts of shell, are assigned to Component 1 (ca. 6000 to 5600 BP). Layer D is the oldest discrete cultural stratum identified in Locality A.

This layer consists of alternating lenses of loose, well-sorted gravel and sand with occasional localized lenses of compact black carbon stained gravel and charcoal. The few artifacts found in this layer are water-worn and likely redeposited from another location through natural processes.

Component 2 (ca. 5600 to 5200 BP) incorporates Layers C and B in Locality A. These layers consist of rich organic sediments with high concentrations of lithics, two hearths, stratified living surfaces, and a pit feature.

Layer C consists of compact gravel, sand, and pebbles with extensive carbon staining extending across the main site area. No shell is present in this layer but small and large fragments of bone are present. Lithic artifacts, including microblades, are found throughout.

The Layer B deposits, localized in Unit 2, are a concentration of numerous stratified living surfaces of approximately 9 square metres (see Figure 13.4). The layer consists of scattered and lensed, broken, and crushed shell (largely mussel), in compact black silt and grey-green coarse sand. Several fire-cracked rock (FCR) hearths were excavated in this layer, which also contains a high concentration of small lithic debitage. Although no structural features, such as postholes, were identified, thin stratified surfaces composed of relatively fine matrices suggest that this discrete layer may be associated with a dwelling or specific activity area at the site.

Layer A4, assigned to Component 3 (ca. 5200 to 5000 BP), underlies Layer A across most of Locality A. The Layer A4 matrix is characterized as a dense layer of rich gravelly organic sediments with small pockets and lenses of whole or large fragments of clamshell, and lithic material. The surface of A4 is littered with large cobbles and scattered fire-cracked rock and is rich in lithic material and features. Hearths and lithic production activity areas were documented in this component and are described in the "Features" section below. The interface of this component and Component 4 marks the end of the use of microblade technology at the site.

A thick stratified accumulation, or low mound, of loose whole and fragmented shell with FCR is present in Layer A4. The mound exhibits layering with depositional episodes separated by relatively thick and well-defined carbon-stained bands and lenses that may represent paleosols formed during episodes of area abandonment or times of minimal shell deposition or erosion. This discrete refuse pile represents the initial large buildup of shell

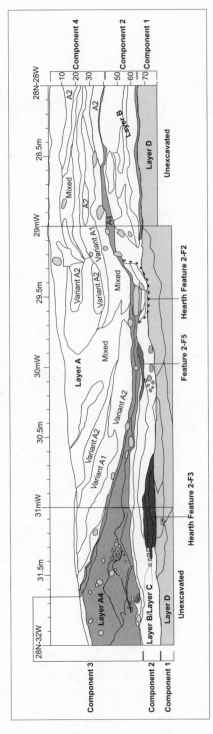

Figure 13.3 North wall profile of Unit 2, Cohoe Creek.

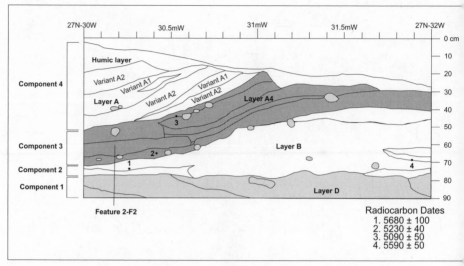

Figure 13.4   South wall profile of Unit 2-1, Cohoe Creek.

at the site, beginning about 5200 BP. Within 200 years, this distinct 50-centimetre-thick stratified shell deposit is overlain by the largely undifferentiated thick accumulations of shell typical of the Graham Tradition.

This component constitutes the upper shell-rich matrices at the site (Layer A), represented by alternating bands of midden (Variant A1 and A2), which likely represent different activities within the same component. In many cases they are separated only by thin carbon-stained lenses.

Variant A1 is distinguished from A2 by a predominance of crushed mussel with other shellfish species represented (butter clam, dire whelks, barnacle fragments, and limpets). This matrix is tightly compacted and crushed and has a higher concentration of organic sediment than Variant A2. An abundance of small pebbles (< 5 centimetres) also characterize this variant. Variant A1 was found in all tested portions of the site.

Variant A2 is characterized by loosely compacted butter clam (large fragments) with extensive deposits of large cockle and small amounts of mussel, whelk, and green sea urchin. These differences in matrix composition may relate to season of use of the site. Variant A2 occurs across the site in Layer A.

Locality B

The 20-centimetre-thick cultural deposits from Locality B consist of black greasy sediments and an underlying shell midden composed of whelks, sea urchin, blue mussel, cockle, clam, and fish bone. The deposits were buried beneath about 1 metre of bulldozer overburden and are the youngest deposits investigated at the site, dating to about 4300 years BP (see Table 13.1).

Table 13.1

Radiocarbon dates from the Cohoe Creek site

Lab no.	Sample no.	Material	Elevation	Age (BP)	±	Comments	Component
Locality A							
CAMS-16205	Cohoe A#2a	Charcoal	11.74	4900	80	Locality A midden (Fedje et al. 1995)	4
CAMS-50958	CC2/0-6	Charcoal	10.50	4930	50	Unit 2 midden (south wall)	4
CAMS-16206	Cohoe A#3a	Charcoal	11.84	4970	60	Locality A midden (Fedje et al. 1995)	4
RIDDL-1227	–	Charcoal	ca. 11.50	4990	110	From column sample B3 Ham trench (Ham 1990)	4
CAMS-16207	Cohoe A#4a	Charcoal	11.92	5000	70	Locality A midden (Fedje et al. 1995)	4
CAMS-50954	CC2/1-4	Charcoal	10.50	5090	50	Unit 2-1 midden (south wall)	3
CAMS-50950	CC2/1-2	Charcoal	10.60	5230	40	Unit 2-1 midden (south wall)	3
CAMS-50962	CC7-1	Charcoal	ca. 11.50	5260	40	Unit 7 midden	2
CAMS-50960	CC5-1	Charcoal	ca. 11.40	5290	40	Unit 5 midden (south wall)	2
CAMS-16204	Cohoe A#1a	Charcoal	11.55	5320	60	Locality A midden (Fedje et al. 1995)	2
CAMS-19017	Cohoe A2	Charcoal	11.60	5370	70	Locality A2 midden (Fedje et al. 1995)	2
CAMS-50952	CC2/1-3	Charcoal	10.60	5380	40	Unit 2-1 midden (south wall)	2
CAMS-50956	CC2/1-5	Charcoal	10.50	5590	50	Unit 2-1 midden (south wall)	2
CAMS-50948	CC2/1-1	Charcoal	10.00	5680	100	Unit 2-1 midden (south wall)	1
BETA-25179	Area A	Charcoal	ca. 11.50	6150	70	1987 AIA trench (Ham 1990)	1
Locality B							
CAMS-16208	Cohoe B#1a	Charcoal	9.70	4390	70	Locality B midden (Fedje et al. 1995)	4
CAMS-16209	Cohoe B#2a	Charcoal	9.70	4420	60	Locality B midden (Fedje et al. 1995)	4
Locality C							
CAMS-54599	Locality C	Charcoal	12.00	6980	50	Exposure west end of gravel pit (Fedje et al. 1995)	1

The deposits were assigned to Component 4, given the age and the lack of microblade technology.

Locality C

A cultural deposit was identified in an exposed bank at the far northern end of the site. The exposed bank was created by road construction and is set back from the front of the raised beach terrace. Artifacts could be seen eroding from a charcoal-stained deposit dated to 6980 ± 50 BP (CAMS-54599). No shell or faunal material was noted. The cultural deposits at Locality C were not excavated and the data are insufficient for further classification.

Dating

Eighteen dates have been processed from the site, eight from excavated contexts, two from a backhoe trench, and the rest from stratigraphic exposures. The dates are listed in Table 13.1.

The earliest date from the site, 6980 ± 50 BP, comes from the shell-free deposits in Locality C. Fifteen samples date Locality A to between about 6150 and 4900 BP. It is likely that younger deposits were once present at Locality A but were destroyed when the top layers of the midden were bulldozed off. Two samples from Locality B, taken in 1995, date these deposits to between about 4300 and 4400 BP. Altogether, the radiocarbon samples date the site to both the Late Moresby Tradition and the early Graham Tradition.

Faunal Analysis

All vertebrate material collected in situ and in the screens was analyzed from Units 5, 6, 9, 2, 2-1, 2-2, and 2 at Locality A and Units 8 and 10 at Locality B.[1] The bone material was identified using the faunal collection of the Department of Anthropology, University of Victoria, as well as the Royal British Columbia Museum. Analysis of the Cohoe Creek faunal assemblage is preliminary but a list of vertebrates identified to date, compiled from 8,007 analyzed bones, includes forty-six different fish, birds, and land and sea mammals. A total of 2,018 elements were identified past the basic bird, fish, or mammal categories. A wide variety of invertebrates are also present but a formal study of the column samples has not been completed. The numbers of individual specimens (NISP) are presented in Tables 13.2 to 13.5.

Land Mammals

Only seven land mammals (shrew, deer mouse, ermine, marten, river otter, black bear, and caribou) are listed as indigenous to Haida Gwaii (Foster 1965); five of these were identified in the Cohoe Creek faunal assemblage. Caribou (*Rangifer tarandus*), black bear (*Ursus americanus*), dog (*Canis familiaris*), river otter (*Lutra canadensis*), shrew (Soricidae), and deer mouse (*Peromyscus* sp.)

Table 13.2

Mammal remains from the Cohoe Creek site

Common name	Latin name	NISP
Caribou	*Rangifer tarandus*	79
Black bear	*Ursus americanus*	34
Dog	*Canis familiaris*	21
River otter	*Lutra canadensis*	12
Shrew	Soricidae	1
Deer mouse	*Peromyscus* sp.	1
Carnivore species	Carnivora	6
Ungulate species	Artiodactyla	6
Unidentified mammal	Mammalia	2,773

NISP = number of identified specimens

as well as unidentified mammal, carnivore, and ungulate elements were excavated from the site. Taxa identified from bones, as well as the number of individual specimens of each taxon, are listed in Table 13.2. A total of 2,933 land mammal bones and fragments were recovered during the 1998 excavations, of which only 160 were identified to taxon.

Seventy-nine caribou bones were recovered during the excavation of Locality A. Thirty-one of these came from within a concentration of caribou bone in a small pit at the base of Unit 5, Component 2, but caribou was also found in Components 3 and 4. References to the hunting of caribou in the Haida ethnographic literature are virtually nonexistent (Spalding 2000). Cannon (1991:22) points out that for the central mainland coast there is a quantity of ethnographic data suggesting that deer were valued for their skin and bones for tool manufacture. At the same time, the composition of the faunal assemblage from the Namu excavations indicates that the whole deer was brought back to camp and that deer made a "terrestrial based contribution" to the diet (Cannon 1991:27). Representative elements from almost the entire caribou skeleton were found at Cohoe Creek, suggesting that caribou were used as food. At the same time, the presence of modified caribou bones also indicates that the animal remains were also being used for tool manufacture (see "Artifacts" below).

Bear and dog elements were found in similar numbers to each other, 34 and 21, respectively. The bear elements were excavated from Components 3 and 4 and all except two of the dog elements were recovered from Component 3.

The oldest directly dated dog remains on the Northwest Coast come from Namu and date to 5400 ± 50 BP (Beta-87709) (Cannon et al. 1999:402). Dog bones have also been recovered from Period 2 (7000 to 6000 BP) deposits at the same site (Cannon 1991:85) and from deposits dating to between about

Table 13.3

Sea mammal remains from the Cohoe Creek site

Common name	Latin name	NISP
Harbour seal	*Phoca vitulina*	15
Sea otter	*Enhydra lutris*	9
Pinnepedia sp.	Mammalia	1
Unidentified sea mammal	Mammalia	4

NISP = number of identified specimens

8000 and 4000 BP at Bear Cove, Vancouver Island (C. Carlson 1979:188). The Cohoe Creek dog remains date to between 5600 and 5000 years BP.

Twelve river otter elements were recovered from Components 3 and 4, with the majority from Component 4. The two other mammal species recovered were the shrew and deer mouse, their small numbers indicating that they were not food sources.

Sea Mammals

Twenty-five sea mammal bones were identified to the species or family level, including harbour seal (*Phoca vitulina*), sea otter (*Enhydra lutris*), and a pinneped (see Table 13.3). Four of the sea mammal bones were unidentified elements.

Harbour seal was recovered from Components 2 and 3, sea otter from Components 3 and 4, and the pinneped from Component 3. Masset Inlet today supports a population of seals (Prince Rupert Interagency Management Committee 1999) and probably would have in the past.

Fish

A minimum of 12 fish species are present in the Cohoe Creek faunal assemblage (see Table 13.4). A large proportion of the total number of fish bones (N = 4,668) were unidentified fish elements. The numbers of elements identified to taxon are listed in Table 13.4.

Jack mackerel, salmon, and flatfish are the most abundant fish in the assemblage, with jack mackerel making by far the greatest contribution (85 percent of identified remains), with 1,466 bones and bone fragments. Jack mackerel remains were found in Components 2, 3, and 4, with the largest number in Component 3.

Salmon were found in significantly smaller numbers (5 percent of the fish assemblage). Salmon was present in Component 2 but significant numbers do not appear at the site until Component 3.

Flatfish were the third most common fish in the assemblage but made up only 4 percent of the entire Cohoe Creek identified fish bone assemblage. All but ten of the flatfish remains (84 percent) were found in the Graham

Table 13.4

Fish remains identified at Cohoe Creek

Common name	Latin name	NISP
Jack mackerel	*Trachurus symmetricus*	1,466
Salmon	*Oncorhynchus* sp.	81
Flatfish sp.	Pleuronectiformes (family)	62
Pacific herring	*Clupea pallasi*	26
Gadid (not hake)	Gadidae, not hake (family)	21
Pacific cod	*Gadus macrocephalus*	19
Myoxocephalus sculpin sp.	Cottidae (family)	13
Dogfish shark	*Squalus acanthias*	12
Staghorn sculpin	*Leptocottus armatus*	9
Great sculpin	*Myoxocephalus polyacanthocephalus*	7
Halibut	*Hippoglossus stenolepis*	5
Sculpin sp.	Cottidae (family)	4
Skate	*Raja* sp. (unident)	2
Plain sculpin	*Myoxocephalus jaok*	2
Pollock	*Theragra chalcogramma*	1
Rock sole	*Lepidopsetta bilineata*	1
Three-spine stickleback	*Gasterosteus aculeatus*	1
Unidentified fish		2,936

NISP = number of identified specimens

Tradition deposits (Component 4) at Locality B. This could indicate a change in fishing practices following 5000 BP.

Birds

Over 21 different taxa of birds were recovered from the archaeological deposits at Cohoe Creek and are listed in Table 13.5. Of the 358 bird bone and bird bone fragments recovered, 83 could be identified to the species or family level.

Fifty-nine (72 percent) of the bird bones identified to taxon were ducks. Grebes and loons were the next most common taxa, with 6 percent each. Scoters made up 5 percent of the assemblage and cormorants 2 percent. Only one element of each of the other bird taxa was recovered and identified. Modern studies in Haida Gwaii show that waterfowl (ducks, geese, and swans) numbers increase in the winter, peaking in February (Hamel 1989:190), but are available year-round. Waterfowl prefer settings such as the Yakoun estuary to the southwest of the site.

Invertebrates

Invertebrates comprise a large portion of the cultural matrices at Cohoe Creek. A preliminary list of the invertebrates include butter clam (*Saxidomus*

Table 13.5

Bird taxa identified at the Cohoe Creek site

Common name	Latin name	NISP
Medium duck	Anatidae (medium)	30
Large duck	Anatidae (large)	15
Diving duck	*Aythya* sp.	10
Hooded merganser	*Lophodytes cucullatus*	2
Mallard	*Anas platyrhynchos*	1
Small duck	Anatidae (small)	1
Common loon	*Gavia immer*	5
Pacific loon	*Gavia pacifica*	1
Grebe sp.	Podicipedidae	5
Red-necked grebe	*Podiceps grisegena*	1
Scoter	*Melanitta* sp.	2
Surf scoter	*Melanitta perspicillata*	2
White-winged scoter	*Melanitta fusca*	1
Cormorant sp.	*Phalacrocorax pelagicus/pen.*	1
Pelagic cormorant	*Phalacrocorax pelagicus*	1
Canada goose	*Branta canadensis*	1
Medium alcid	Alcidae (medium)	1
Blue grouse	*Dendragapus obscurus*	1
Small songbird/sparrow	Passeriformes	1
Common murre	*Uria aalge*	1
Unidentified bird elements		142
Unidentified medium bird		128
Unidentified large bird		5

NISP = number of identified specimens

giganteus), littleneck clam (*Protothaca staminea*), bent-nose clam (*Mocoma nasuta*), horse clam (*Tresus capax*), cockle (*Clinocardium nuttalli*), blue Pacific mussel (*Mytilus edulis*), green sea urchin (*Strongylocentrotus droebachiensis*), Lewis moon-snail (*Polinices lewisii*), as well as crab, barnacle, limpet, sea urchin, and chiton. Dense accumulations of shellfish remains occur mainly in Component 4, the basal layers of which postdate 5000 BP. There are large lenses and thick pocket accumulations of butter clam in Component 3 and pockets of sea urchin and crushed mussel in Component 2.

Discussion of Faunal Assemblage

In summary, a total of 8,007 faunal bones were analyzed from the Cohoe Creek excavation, including 4,668 fish bones, 2,933 mammal bones, 358 bird bones, 29 sea mammal bones, 18 bones that were either small mammal or bird bones, and 1 reptile bone. The most common fauna, based on the number of bones recovered, are jack mackerel, salmon, caribou, flatfish, duck, black bear, dog, harbour seal, sea otter, loon, and scoters. This order is based on number of individual specimens and not on minimum number of individuals, so it is premature to generalize regarding the relative importance of each species represented. Many of the principal fauna used by the ethnographic Haida (halibut, salmon, other fish, sea mammal, shellfish, sea urchin, bear, wapiti, water fowl, and birds eggs) (Fladmark 1975:51) are present in the Cohoe Creek assemblage.

The Cohoe Creek faunal assemblage appears quite distinct in some respects from those of other Early Period sites in Haida Gwaii, such as the Kilgii Gwaay site, Richardson Island, and Lyell Bay sites. The paucity of faunal material from most Moresby Tradition sites and the diverse environments of the few that have been recovered limits meaningful comparison. However, the abundance of caribou and mackerel at Cohoe Creek is noteworthy compared with other sites in Haida Gwaii. Cohoe Creek shares some similarities, especially the presence of caribou, with some early Graham Tradition sites (Wigen 1990).

Fedje and colleagues (2001) suggest that the 9400 BP faunal assemblage from Kilgii Gwaay was very similar to the fauna being utilized by the Southern Haida in the last 2,000 years, and while Cohoe Creek shares the presence of caribou with some Graham Tradition sites, the majority of the Cohoe Creek species list is different from recent assemblages. Some of the differences between Kilgii Gwaay and Cohoe Creek can be attributed to their local microenvironments. The difference in birds, fish, and sea mammals represented at the two sites is at least partly a function of environment. For example, the high incidence of albatross and auklet at Kilgii Gwaay is likely due to its outer coast location, as albatross are found offshore and auklets nest on outer coast islands whereas the birds at Cohoe Creek are typical of inland protected estuarine environments. The absence of caribou remains at Kilgii Gwaay and their presence at Cohoe Creek can tentatively be explained with ecological arguments. The only excavated sites with significant quantities of preserved faunal remains in South Moresby, other than Kilgii Gwaay, postdate 2000 BP and have no caribou remains. Sites on Graham Island dating to about 4,000 to 3,000 years ago have significant numbers of caribou remains in their assemblages, in some cases accounting for 20 percent of the identified mammal remains (Savage 1971:19). Caribou remains predating 6000 BP include a mid-Wisconsin fossilized caribou antler from Graham Island[2] (R.W. Mathewes, personal communication) and ungulate remains, tentatively identified as caribou, excavated from sediments dated between 12,000 and 10,500 BP in K1 Cave on Moresby Island (Chapter 6). The Holocene-age landscape of Moresby Island may not have had enough caribou habitat to support viable populations compared with Graham Island with its extensive areas of muskeg.

Calcined bone from the Kinggi Complex/Moresby Tradition Lyell Bay South and Richardson Island sites in Gwaii Haanas, dating to between 9000 and 5000 BP, include species not present in the Cohoe Creek assemblage (lingcod) and species found only in small numbers at Cohoe Creek (herring, rockfish, and halibut) (see Chapter 12; Wigen 1998).

The early cultural layers of the Blue Jackets Creek site, which dates to between 4300 and 2000 BP and is also located on Masset Inlet, are contemporaneous with the upper layers at Cohoe Creek. While a detailed analysis of the Blue Jackets Creek site material is not available, Severs (1974a) indicates that salmon and halibut are the most common fish and that elements of dog, marten, bear, and caribou are also present. Jack mackerel is not present at Blue Jackets Creek. Mammals present at the two sites are comparable and, like aspects of the artifact assemblage, suggest similar subsistence practices.

Savage's preliminary analysis (1971) of 304 bones collected at the 3,300-year-old Honna River site on Skidegate Inlet (Fladmark 1970) resulted in the identification of 10 fish bones, 83 bird bones, and 211 mammal bones representing twenty-six taxa of fauna. The most common fish were dogfish at 86 percent and salmon with 14 percent.[3] Fish representations are likely a result of screening techniques and are therefore not useful for comparison. The most common bird bones in the assemblage were the bald eagle and scoters (33 percent and 24 percent, respectively). Bald eagle is not present in the Cohoe Creek assemblage, while scoters are present in small numbers. The greatest numbers of bones at Honna River come from mammals. Sea mammals were the most common: sea otter at 43 percent and harbour seal at 27 percent. Caribou was the third most important taxon, with 10 percent of the identified mammal remains. This order of abundance is almost the reverse of that found at Cohoe Creek, which could be attributed to recovery techniques, environment, or seasonality.

Salmon, rockfish, and halibut were found to be the dominant fish in an analysis of eighteen sites postdating 2000 BP in southernmost Haida Gwaii (Wigen 1990; Acheson 1998). Harbour seal and sea otter dominate the mammal assemblage in that study. Again the difference from Cohoe Creek may be due to the inland nature of Cohoe Creek as opposed to the outer coast nature of the Kunghit Island sites.

One curious difference between Cohoe Creek and all other reported sites is the significant presence of jack mackerel at Cohoe Creek. Jack mackerel, to the best of our knowledge, has not been recorded in any other archaeological sites on the Northwest Coast except one unexcavated site in Naden Harbour, Haida Gwaii (Stafford and Christensen 2000). Mackerel is not found in the list of fauna important to the diet of the Haida at contact, and although Dawson (1993:104) observed mackerel during his 1878 visit to Haida Gwaii, he noted that the fish was not "specially sought after by the Indians [Haida]." Not only is jack mackerel present at Cohoe Creek but it is present in significant numbers and would have contributed greatly to the diet of the population 5,000 years ago.

Mackerel have not been recorded in Masset Inlet in modern times and are considered largely an offshore fish that sometimes travel inshore when mature (Eschmeyer and Herald 1983). The presence of this largely offshore fish in the Cohoe Creek deposits is intriguing as the site is located on Masset Inlet, about 50 kilometres inland from the north coast of Haida Gwaii. Although the inhabitants at Cohoe Creek may have been travelling out of Masset Inlet to catch these fish, it is possible that the mackerel were attracted to Masset Inlet by the presence of the Yakoun River, a large salmon spawning stream, as mackerel have been observed feeding on salmon fry in Haida Gwaii (Alexander Mackie, personal communication).

Ham's (1990) initial investigation provided some interesting comment on the seasonal occupation of the Cohoe Creek site. Ham (1990:216) concluded that Cohoe Creek was a "shell midden and lithic quarry site occupied during the late winter for harvesting shellfish and other intertidal resources, and fishing." His seasonal conclusion is based on a shellfish seasonality study. The presence of mackerel in a winter setting was taken as evidence that the winter climate was warmer than at present or that El Niño conditions were in effect. Wigen and Christensen (2001), using the recorded range of mackerel, concluded that "it is not necessary to have warmer marine temperatures for the jack mackerel to be present." Provided that marine temperatures were not significantly different from today, the presence of mackerel may indicate that people inhabited the site in the late summer and early fall, when the mackerel range as far north as Haida Gwaii. Salmon, herring, and waterfowl in the Cohoe Creek faunal assemblage are further indicators of seasonality: salmon spawn in the Yakoun River between the early spring and fall, herring spawn in Haida Gwaii in the late winter and early spring, and waterfowl are abundant in Haida Gwaii in the winter but can be found year-round. The range of fauna found in the Cohoe Creek assemblage suggests the possibility of year-round occupation.

Features

Features recorded at Cohoe Creek include hearths, lithic concentrations, bone concentrations, and postholes. Features were observed only in Components 2, 3, and 4.

Component 2

In Component 2, four features were recorded, including a bone-filled depression, two hearths, and a concentration of microblades. Feature 5-F2 is a rough depression or pit dug into the basal sand and gravel (see Figure 13.3) containing a concentration of caribou bone, including a piece of worked caribou antler that appears to have served as a tool blank.

Within the Component 2 living surfaces, several hearths were identified, including a stratified hearth (Feature 2-F3) without associated fire-cracked rock and a hearth (Feature 2-F4) consisting of a circular concentration of rocks about 2 to 5 centimetres in size and FCR (see Figure 13.3). The sand and gravel surrounding these features is highly oxidized.

A concentration of fifty-three microblades, a microblade core, and associated debitage were recorded adjacent to the western wall of Unit 6, between 72 and 74 centimetres dbd (depth below datum) (Feature 6-F2). Most of the microblades were oriented in an east-to-west direction reminiscent of the sorted microblade piles excavated at Lawn Point (Fladmark 1986).

Component 3

Several features were observed in Component 3, including two hearths, a concentration of FCR, and a posthole. Feature 2-F2 is a cluster of flat cobble-sized rocks arranged at the edge of a hearth composed of ash, burnt clam shell, and oxidized gravel and sand. The profile of this hearth indicates that it was dug into the charcoal and artifact-rich gravel and sand of Component 2.

To the west of Feature 2-F2, at the same level, is an extensive (ca. 90 by 110 centimetres) complex hearth feature (Feature 2-F5) composed of a thin lens of coarse uniform red/brown sand, large butter clam shell fragments, scattered charcoal, lenses of burnt perishable material, and a dense concentration of fire-altered lithic debris (see Figure 13.3).

Within Unit 5, Component 3, a large cluster of FCR and lithic flakes was recorded (Feature 5-F1). The FCR pieces are large and unusually dense, and together are outlined by a distinct black loam matrix.

During the removal of column samples, a posthole (Feature 6-F3) was exposed in the west wall of Unit 6. The posthole begins in Component 3 deposits and extends 24 centimetres into Component 2 matrices.

Component 4

Two features, a possible posthole and a pit feature, were observed in Component 4. Feature 5-F1, recorded in Unit 5, is a possible posthole that begins near the top of the excavation unit and extends down 72 centimetres, indicating that it is either associated with the last occupation at Locality A or is a historical feature such as a fence posthole.

Feature 6-F1 is a semicircular outline of shell-free organic sediments in the southwest corner of Unit 6. The "pit" feature begins about 35 centimetres below surface and continues to about 65 centimetres below surface. The top of the feature is about 120 centimetres wide and tapers to about 100 centimetres wide. It contains a dense concentration of large crude pebble cores and choppers.

Discussion of Features

The features recorded at Cohoe Creek are mainly found in Components 2 and 3 (ca. 5600 to 5000 BP) and reveal that a wide range of activities were being undertaken at the site over several hundred years.

Until recently, very few features have been recorded in sites dating to the Moresby Tradition, and most are limited to simple hearths and lithic concentrations. At the Lyell Bay South, Arrow Creek, and Lawn Point sites, only simple hearths of charcoal and concentrations of lithic debris were noted (see Chapter 12; Fladmark 1986). Although this lack of complex features was one of the defining characteristics of the Moresby Tradition, recent excavations at the Richardson Island site and Cohoe Creek reveal that a wide variety of features are associated with pre-5000 BP sites. During the 2001 and 2002 excavations at Richardson Island, approximately fifteen hearths, a variety of post moulds (single-stake and four-stake composite), a possible living structure in the form of a pit, and a tool-use activity area were observed in the pre-8900 BP Kinggi Complex deposits (Q. Mackie, personal communication).

In the two years of excavation at the early Graham Tradition Blue Jackets Creek site, over 100 features were recorded, including burial pits with associated burial inclusions, open and excavated hearths, postholes, and living floors with structural remains (Severs 1972, 1974a). Similar feature types predating Blue Jackets Creek by several hundred years, with the notable exception of burials, were recorded at Cohoe Creek. It is likely that a wider variety of features exists at Cohoe in association with Component 4 and located beneath and beyond the bulldozed midden located at the edge of the terrace. As sea levels fell following 5000 BP, activity area locations and associated features would have shifted to new shoreline locations, now between the raised beach terrace and the modern shoreline.

Artifacts

Ham (1990) recorded pebble cores, pebble core reduction flakes, microblade cores, microblades, anvil stones, chipped bone points, and worked antler during his impact assessment of the Cohoe Creek site in 1988. A further 170 formed tools, 278 microblades, and thousands of fragments of debitage were excavated in 1998. A large number of artifacts were also mapped and collected from the gravel pit surface during the 1998 study. Analysis at this time is preliminary and the discussion of artifacts and total artifact numbers should be viewed as very preliminary. The artifacts recovered from the 1998 excavations will be presented here.

The artifact assemblage includes chipped, ground, and pecked lithics and chipped and ground bone tools. These are listed by component in Table 13.6. Many of the chipped stone artifact types are defined in Chapter 12.

Chipped and Pecked Stone

Only one chipped and pecked stone artifact was recovered from the 1998 excavations at Cohoe Creek, in Unit 10, Locality B. The artifact, a wedge or adze, is half moon in shape in cross-section with a rough rounded poll. The sides taper towards the poll and the bit is chipped and flaked. The cobble cortex remains on one surface, a portion of it pitted in an attempt to

Table 13.6

Preliminary typology of formed tools, cores, and microblades from 1998 excavations at Cohoe Creek

	Component			
	1	2	3	4
	?-5600 BP	5600-5200 BP	5200-5000 BP	5000-4300 BP
Bone, antler artifacts				
Slotted point	–	–	1	–
Simple points	–	2	1	4
Unilaterally barbed point	–	–	–	1
Needle	–	4	4	2
Antler wedge	–	–	–	1
Cut and ground bone	–	3	1	5
Wedge	–	–	1	–
Splinter awl	–	–	1	–
Bone tool total	0	9	9	13
Lithic artifacts				
Abrader	–	1	–	2
Adze	–	–	–	1
Anvil stone	–	2	3	–
Hammerstone	–	4	2	–
Bipolar core	–	7	1	2
Core	–	9	3	2
Multidirectional core	–	7	–	2
Unidirectional core	1	5	2	1
Microblade core	1	13	4	–
Spokeshave	1	17	1	4
Graver	–	3	1	–
Scraper	–	12	1	2
Spall tool	–	–	1	1
Bifacial chopper/core	–	1	1	–
Unifacial chopper/core	1	2	1	–
Retouched flake	–	9	1	4
Utilized flake	–	1	1	1
Microblade	5	203	70	–
Stone tool total				
(excluding microblades)	4	93	23	22
All Tools Grand Total l				
(excluding microblades)	4	102	32	35

remove some of the thickness of the spall. This artifact was removed from Graham Tradition deposits and was the only adze recovered from Cohoe Creek.

Pecked and Ground Stone
The pecked and ground stone at the site consists of tools used in the production of other tools: anvil stones, abraders, and hammer stones.

Five flat cobbles were recovered from Components 2 and 3 in Locality A. These cobbles exhibit pitting on at least one surface and may have functioned as *anvil stones* in the production of bipolar flakes and microblades.

Two *abraders* were excavated from Component 4 and one from Component 2 in Locality A.

Six *hammerstones,* cobbles with pitting on either end, were excavated from Components 2 and 3.

Chipped Stone Artifacts
The chipped stone assemblage includes microblades and cores, bipolar cores and flakes, multidirectional and unidirectional cores, spokeshaves, scrapers and gravers, bifacial and unifacial choppers, spall tools, and retouched and utilized flakes (see Figure 13.5).

Eighteen *microblade cores* were excavated from the Cohoe Creek site deposits. The cores are produced from a variety of materials (rhyolite, basalt, chalcedony) from which a number of blades were removed. The flake scars on many of the cores are limited to one face, are few in number, and are short and irregular. Many of the cores exhibit basal crushing.

Ten *bipolar cores* were recovered from Components 2, 3, and 4 at Locality A. Seven of the cores were found in Component 2, where the majority of the microblades and microblade cores were recovered.

Unidirectional cores are found in all Locality A components at Cohoe Creek but are most common in Component 2 deposits.

Multidirectional cores are present in the Component 2 and 4 deposits at Locality A. In addition to the microblade, unidirectional, and multidirectional cores, fourteen unclassified cores were excavated from Components 2, 3, and 4.

Microblades, small parallel-sided flakes of stone struck from a prepared core, are the most common artifact type at Cohoe Creek other than debitage, and were found in Components 1 through 3. The microblades ($N = 278$) are made from fine-grained basalts, rhyolites, and andesites. Microblades are present in Component 1 but in very small numbers ($N = 5$). In Component 2 there are 203 microblades. In Component 3 there are 70 microblades. No microblades were recovered from Component 4 at Cohoe Creek or in other post-5000 BP cultural deposits in Haida Gwaii. A large number of microblade-like flakes were found in microblade-bearing deposits.

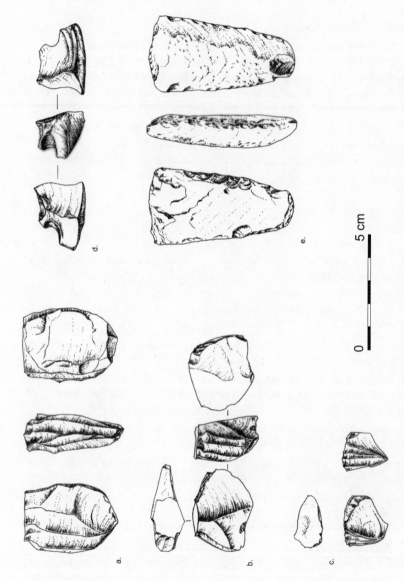

Figure 13.5 A selection of stone artifacts from Cohoe Creek: (a) to (c) microblade cores, (d) spokeshave, (e) ground and pecked adze.

Scrapers are one of the most common non-microblade-technology arti-facts found at Cohoe Creek. These unifacially flaked tools were abundant in Component 2 (N = 12). Two scrapers were excavated from Component 4 and one from Component 3.

Twenty-three *spokeshaves* and four *gravers* are found within the Cohoe Creek assemblage. These two artifact types, like scrapers, are most commonly found in Component 2.

Both *bifacial* (N = 2) and *unifacial* (N = 3) *choppers* were found in small numbers in Components 1, 2, and 3 at Cohoe Creek.

Two *spall tools* were excavated from Components 3 and 4.

The complete count of the number of *retouched and utilized flakes* is not available but both types are found in Components 2, 3, and 4.

The *Qay'llnagaay* Museum in Skidegate, Haida Gwaii, has in its collection *bifacial points and knives* catalogued as having been collected from surface deposits at Cohoe Creek (Natalie McFarlane, personal communication). Bi-facial technology, in the form of bifacial choppers, is present at Cohoe Creek but no formed bifaces were found in excavated deposits in 1998.

Bone and Antler

A variety of organic artifacts were recovered from Components 2, 3, and 4 at Locality A, dating to between 4,300 and 5,600 years ago. Artifact types within the assemblage include needles, a unilaterally barbed point, a vari-ety of simple points, a slotted point, splinter awls, and worked bone.

Several examples of long, thin worked bone fragments (N = 10), likely used as *needles,* were excavated from the three upper components at Local-ity A. These range from bone splinters ground to form flat, symmetrical tapered shafts to tapered fragments that are ovoid in cross-section. A num-ber of these examples have remnants of the needle eye.

A fragment of a *barbed point,* measuring 4.2 centimetres long, 1.45 centi-metres wide, and 1.0 centimetre thick, was excavated from Component 4 (see Figure 13.6b). In cross-section the artifact is teardrop-shaped with one round surface and one sharply bevelled surface. The bevelled surface has one tang along its edge.

Three varieties of simple *bone points* were recovered from Components 2, 3, and 4. One variety, represented by one point fragment, is broad and oval to flat in cross-section, with one end tapering to a point; it was recovered from Component 4 deposits. The artifact measures 9.7 centimetres long, 1.6 centimetres wide, and 0.95 centimetre thick, and is very similar to the bone point collected by Ham (1990:215) from Cohoe Creek in 1988, which he suggests may be a fragment of a large harpoon point.

Another point, represented by two fragments, is narrow, long, and ovoid in cross-section, and tapers to the distal end.

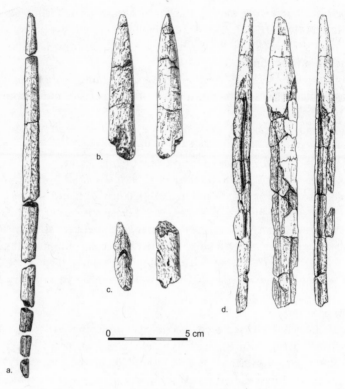

Figure 13.6   A selection of bone artifacts from Cohoe Creek: (a) type 3 point, (b) type 1 point, (c) unilaterally barbed point, (d) slotted point.

Seven fragments of a long and thin point were also recovered (see Figure 13.6a). The lateral sides of the point have been ground flat and one face has been ground into a gentle bevel visible in cross-section. Four of the fragments have been slightly burned.

One fragmentary *slotted point* was recovered from Component 3, Locality A (see Figure 13.6d) in microblade-bearing deposits. A long groove, V-shaped in cross-section, was cut into both lateral sides of a piece of antler, likely to accommodate the insertion of microblade sections.

Ham (1990) identified 15 fragments of bone from Cohoe Creek that he categorized as *splinter awls*. These long bone fragments were bifacially chipped at one end to form a point or to enhance a pointed end. One long bone fragment, which may be a splinter awl, was recovered from Component 3 deposits during the excavation of Locality A. This split mammal long bone, probably caribou or bear, has a point at one end, which is smooth and slightly polished.

Several fragments of *sawn, cut, and ground bone and antler,* representing different stages in the manufacture of bone artifacts, were recovered. Several long bone fragments show deep, wide linear cuts clearly meant to split the bone for tool blanks. A large section of caribou antler, with one antler tine cleanly removed using the methods just described, was excavated from a concentration of caribou bone in pit feature 5-F2 in Component 2. The antler also shows a shallow incised line on one surface that may indicate where the next tool blank was to be removed. Another fragment of worked antler was cut and ground to form a flat wedgelike end.

Discussion of Artifacts
A preliminary analysis of the artifact assemblage from Cohoe Creek includes five core types, eight formed tool types, modified flakes, and several artifacts modified by use (abraders, hammerstones, and anvil stones). All of the lithic artifact types have been found in excavated sites in Haida Gwaii. Eight categories of organic artifacts were excavated at Cohoe Creek, all of which, except the slotted point, have been observed in other sites in Haida Gwaii.

Abraders have been found at other Moresby Tradition sites (Skoglund's Landing, Kasta, Lyell Bay South and East, and Richardson Island), and Fladmark (1989:207) theorized that they were used in the production and maintenance of bone and antler tools, based on their association with bone tools in Graham Tradition sites. At Cohoe Creek, the abraders were found in deposits where ground bone and antler tools were recovered, supporting this assumption.

Unidirectional and multidirectional cores are common in Moresby Tradition and Kinggi Complex sites in Gwaii Haanas (Fedje and Christensen 1999), and unidirectional cores are found in the artifact list produced for the Late Moresby Kasta site (K. Fladmark, personal communication) and the early Graham Skoglund's Landing site (Breffitt 1993). The abundance of spokeshaves in Component 2 is comparable to that observed in Moresby Tradition sites in Gwaii Haanas (see Chapter 12). Hammerstones, spall tools, and scrapers are common in Moresby Tradition (Fladmark 1989, 1986) and early Graham Tradition deposits (Severs 1974a).

Both chopper types present at Cohoe Creek are characteristic of Moresby Tradition sites in Gwaii Haanas (see Chapter 12), and both types are present at Skoglund's Landing, Kasta, and Lawn Point (Breffitt 1993; Fladmark 1986).

Summarizing the progression of microblade technology in Haida Gwaii, Fladmark (1989:208) wrote that "the latest microblade cores seem to suggest a 'deterioration' of the highly organized prepared core technology, in favour of increased use of more random 'bipolar' percussion to produce microblades and microblade-like flakes." Fladmark also suggests that "the cores from [Kasta] present an appearance of haphazard workmanship when compared with the finely regular cores from Lawn Point. The flutes are shorter on the whole, and there is a much greater incidence of hinge fracturing. Likewise the bases of the Kasta cores are usually heavily battered, suggesting that in some cases direct percussion, perhaps on an anvil stone, may have been employed for blade removal."

These "deteriorated" microblade cores are found at Cohoe Creek and are very different from the Early Moresby Tradition cores excavated from Gwaii Haanas, which are described as flat-topped and boat-shaped to conical (see Chapter 12; Magne 1996). The Late Moresby Tradition and Gwaii Haanas Early Moresby microblade cores do share the presence of basal crushing, suggesting that anvil stones were employed throughout the Moresby Tradition. The conical water-worn microblade core recovered from the early Component 1 deposits at Cohoe Creek is more characteristic of the Early Moresby microblade cores from Gwaii Haanas and Lawn Point than the later Kasta cores. The presence of this core suggests that Early Moresby Tradition deposits are present in the area, likely at the dated but untested Locality C.

Bipolar cores were excavated from the Graham Tradition Skoglund's Landing (Breffitt 1993) and Blue Jackets Creek (Severs 1974a) sites and from the Late Moresby Kasta site, but are not noted at the Late Moresby Lawn Point site (Fladmark 1986) or at Moresby Tradition and Kinggi Complex sites in Gwaii Haanas (see Chapter 12). Bipolar technology appears to be a Late Moresby Tradition development that influences the prevalent microblade technology and then replaces it following 5000 BP.

During the 1988 impact assessment of the Cohoe Creek site, Ham (1990:213) recovered a microblade of dark green obsidian that he suggests was similar to obsidian sources in the Mt. Elias Range, but the obsidian sources in Haida Gwaii have yet to be fingerprinted. No obsidian was recovered during the 1998 excavations.

The absence of bifaces at Cohoe Creek is consistent with Late Moresby Tradition assemblages in Haida Gwaii. Formed bifaces are diagnostic of the Early Moresby Tradition and are common in the Richardson Island lithic assemblage dating to between 9000 and 8400 BP (see Chapter 12), but no bifaces have been recorded at any Moresby or Early Graham Tradition sites dating to between 8400 and 2000 BP. Bifaces have been found at several undated sites in Haida Gwaii (Fladmark 1969, 1971b; Acheson 1995; Stafford and Christensen 2000) and at Blue Jackets Creek, obsidian chipped points were found in the upper levels of the site that were dated to 2008 ± 110 BP (Severs 1974a:2). The absence of bifaces from excavated contexts at Cohoe Creek despite their presence in surface collections suggests that bifaces, like the water-worn microblade core and other artifacts, may have come from redeposited matrices.

The variety of organic artifacts in the upper layers at Cohoe Creek is limited compared with the contemporaneous Blue Jackets Creek matrices (Severs 1974a) but more diverse than the earlier Kilgii Gwaay site (Fedje et al. 2001). As at Cohoe Creek, needles, barbed harpoon points, and awls were found at Blue Jackets Creek, but the assemblage also included punches, leister prongs, channelled harpoon valves, fishhook shanks, and modified teeth (Severs 1974a). From Kilgii Gwaay, Fedje et al. (2001:107) recovered bone splinter awls, bone awls, a bone percussor, and a small unilaterally barbed bone point – a small bone tool assemblage compared with Cohoe Creek.

The slotted point from Cohoe Creek is similar in shape and size to the one from Namu that dates to the millennium prior to 5000 BP (Carlson 1996:101). In Alaska several early Holocene sites have produced slotted points that are commonly associated with ungulate remains (West 1996:482; Ackerman 1996a:471). The Cohoe Creek specimen and those from Namu and Alaska also compare closely with the early Holocene slotted knives and points with intact flint insets recovered from Zhokhov Island, Russia (Pitul'ko and Kasparov 1996).

There does appear to be a clear association between slotted point technology and ungulate remains, particularly caribou, possibly indicating that the points were either used to hunt ungulates or that ungulate bone or antler was particularly suited to the manufacture of slotted points. The importance of large mammal remains in the manufacture of tools on the Northwest Coast, as described by Hodgetts and Rahemtulla (2001), is clearly demonstrated at Cohoe Creek. Preservation is likely a factor in the absence of slotted point technology at the microblade-rich Early Moresby Richardson Island deposits (see Chapter 12). Although bone technology was preserved in the shell midden deposits at Kilgii Gwaay (Fedje et al. 2001), these matrices are microblade-free, explaining the absence of slotted points.

The organic artifacts excavated from the Moresby Tradition deposits at the site provide clear evidence of the use of bone and antler for tool manufacture earlier than 5,000 years ago in Haida Gwaii and provide some sense of the organic tool forms that were utilized. The Cohoe Creek assemblage shows a greater diversity of tools than previously known for the Moresby Tradition and begins to fill in the blanks regarding tools made from organic materials in Haida Gwaii.

Summary

Cohoe Creek is a midden approximately 4,000 to 6,000 years old containing gross shell accumulations characteristic of some large habitation sites, overlying relatively shell-free deposits with localized dense lenses of shell and a variety of features. In Haida Gwaii, only Cohoe Creek and the unexcavated Strathdang Kwun site have significant cultural deposits dating to both the Graham and Moresby Traditions and therefore provide a unique look at the transition between the two traditions. Preliminary findings from the site provide new insight into the composition of the Moresby Tradition and provide evidence of a degree of technological continuity between the Moresby and Graham Traditions.

Some aspects of the faunal assemblage from Cohoe Creek contrast sharply with Kinggi Complex, Moresby Tradition, and Graham Tradition sites, while other aspects of the assemblage are common to all Holocene-age adaptations on the archipelago. The differences are likely due to the inland nature of Cohoe Creek, the resources available in protected versus exposed microenvironments, and the millennia being investigated. As mentioned previously, the most striking difference at Cohoe Creek is the abundance of mackerel, which may be explained through further analysis of the Late Moresby deposits at Cohoe Creek.

Cohoe Creek is situated on Masset Inlet and represents a maritime adaptation despite being located approximately 50 kilometres inland from the outer coast. At the time of occupation, because of higher sea level, Masset Inlet would have been significantly larger. Although the dominance of fish at Cohoe Creek suggests that the diet was marine-based, the faunal assemblage indicates that land mammals contributed significantly to the diet. The site location provides some unique subsistence opportunities not readily available to people living in outer coast settings. The people at Cohoe Creek had access to seals, marine fishes, shellfish, and other intertidal species available on the outer coast while benefiting from immediate access to the largest salmon spawning stream on the islands, concentrations of waterfowl that flock to the Yakoun estuary, and populations of caribou, black bear, and other mammals that inhabit Graham Island.

The Cohoe Creek tool kit dated to the Moresby Tradition includes microblade, bipolar and flake, and core technology; a variety of processing tools, including scrapers, spokeshaves, gravers, and utilized and retouched flakes; and organic artifacts. The lithic technology in the pre-5000 BP deposits closely resembles the Late Moresby Tradition as defined by Fedje and Christensen (1999), with the main addition of a bone and antler tool assemblage. Bone and antler tools are not abundant but have been preserved in significant numbers and include a rare example of a slotted point demonstrating one purpose for the abundant microblades recovered at the site. Slotted tools were likely common in other microblade-bearing Moresby Tradition sites in which organic artifacts have not been preserved.

The majority of the bone and antler artifacts from Cohoe Creek suggest that hunting and processing activities occurred at the site. The pit of caribou bone and modified antler illustrates that caching of bone for tool manufacture took place. The presence of hammerstones, anvil stones, abraders, lithic and bone debitage, and artifact preforms also shows that tools were being manufactured and maintained at the site. A variety of raw materials were used for tools at Cohoe Creek, including bone, antler, basalt, rhyolite, andesite, chert, chalcedony, sandstone, and granite, all locally available on Graham Island. Evidence for trade with mainland groups is absent from Cohoe Creek as well as at other Moresby Tradition and Kingii Complex sites.

At Cohoe Creek the tool kit dated to the Graham Tradition component differs from the Moresby Tradition component in two ways: the absence of microblade technology and the presence of chipped and pecked technology in the form of one adze. The stone adze directly links the site to the ground and pecked woodworking technology abundant at Blue Jackets Creek. An increase in the number of bone artifacts in the Graham Tradition component is evident but likely due to preservation factors.

The nature of the Transitional Complex and its relationship to both the Moresby and Graham Traditions can be evaluated using the preliminary findings from Cohoe Creek. The Transitional Complex was originally defined using what was considered a unique assemblage from the Skoglund's Landing site (Fladmark 1989; Breffitt 1993; Chapter 14). The assemblage was characterized by chipped stone debitage, cores and unifacially retouched flakes, bipolar core reduction, few features, and a paucity of organic remains (Breffitt 1993:1). Breffitt (1993:149) concluded that the Skoglund's Landing assemblage contained items found in Graham Tradition deposits at other sites and could not be used as the type-site for a separate cultural complex in Haida Gwaii. The Cohoe Creek matrices document the gradual change from the "typical" Moresby Tradition assemblage to the "typical" Graham Tradition assemblage. The Skoglund's Landing site tool kit can be found within the Graham Tradition matrices at the Cohoe Creek assemblage but lacks the preservation of organic remains that is found at Cohoe Creek. The Skoglund's Landing site is either a "special use site" where limited activities were undertaken or it is a product of preservation.

Cohoe Creek spans the Moresby/Graham Tradition boundary and suggests technological continuity between these two traditions and an apparent gradual increase in population at this location, as manifested in thicker and denser shell midden deposits.

Conclusion

A preliminary analysis of the data collected from Cohoe Creek suggests that it is primarily a maritime-adapted semi-sedentary camp or village dating to the Late Moresby Tradition, with continued occupation through the early Graham Tradition. A wider range of activities is visible at Cohoe Creek than was previously identified in other Moresby Tradition sites. This enables us to extend our limited understanding of the Moresby Tradition from a "simple mobile hunting-fishing-gathering way of life" (Fladmark 1989:210) to include a variety of settlement types, including semi-sedentary camps or villages. The processing of food, the manufacture and maintenance of tools, the caching of faunal material, and the presence of stratified hearths and shell midden indicate that a wide range of activities took place at Cohoe Creek earlier than 5,000 years ago.

Cohoe Creek demonstrates the importance of shellfish, as well as mammals, birds, and fish, in the diet of the Late Moresby Tradition peoples. Dense lenses of whole and crushed clam shells in association with microblade technology, and firmly dated to between 5,200 and 5,000 years ago, were excavated at Cohoe Creek, and thin deposits of crushed clam and mussel were excavated from matrices dated to between 5,600 and 5,200 BP. It is clear from this excavation that shell accumulations occurred in amounts sufficient to begin preservation of shell "heaps," "mounds," or "middens" as well as other perishable materials 5,200 years ago. These shell accumulations are associated with the presence of features and activity areas not identified in Early Moresby Tradition sites, as well as with a diminishing microblade industry.

The Cohoe Creek site exhibits a tool kit very similar to Late Moresby sites in southern Haida Gwaii, with the addition of bipolar technology. Cohoe Creek also provides some idea of the range of bone and antler tools likely present in many Moresby Tradition sites and the function of the abundant microblades. Insight into the subsistence practices of Moresby Tradition peoples is also provided, given that micro-environmental differences are taken into consideration. The bone and antler assemblage as well as the early stone adze display continuity with the Graham Tradition Blue Jackets Creek site. The Cohoe Creek site demonstrates the initial stages of technological transformation that later become established in the Graham Tradition, including the replacement of microblade technology with bipolar reduction and the addition of pecked and ground stone tools. A gradual transition from the Kinggi Complex (non-microblade) to the Early Moresby Tradition (microblades and bifaces) at Richardson Island has been identified, suggesting the diffusion or addition of cultural ideas rather than a cultural population replacement. A similarly gradual transition between the Late Moresby and early Graham Traditions is evident at Cohoe Creek.

Acknowledgments
The Cohoe Creek excavation project was administered by the Old Masset Village Council (OMVC) and was funded by the BC Heritage Trust, the BC Ministry of Transportation and Highways, the Gwaii Trust, MacMillan Bloedel, and Student Summer Works. Al Mackie was instrumental in helping to acquire funding for the project. This project would not have been possible without the support and interest of Lucille Bell, Heritage Officer for Economic Development and Heritage Resources, OMVC. A good portion of the field equipment was kindly loaned by Parks Canada. Daryl Fedje provided guidance throughout the project, and with Ian Sumpter volunteered archaeological expertise on site. The excavation crew included the authors as well as archaeologists Joanne McSporran, Bob Muir, Tommy

Greene, Jordan Yeltatzie, and summer students Shannon White, Belinda Humphries, Mathew Brown, and Rodney Brown. Site dates were kindly provided by Daryl Fedje and John Southon. Peirre Peltier of MacMillan Bloedel created the project site maps. Joanne McSporran kindly provided the artifact drawings and Rebecca Wigen of Pacific Identifications lent her expertise in Northwest Coast fauna to the project.

Notes
1 Faunal material collected from units 1, 2, 3, 4, and 7 have not yet been analyzed.
2 The earliest dated caribou remains from Haida Gwaii were found at the head of Kliki Damen Creek (White Creek) on the northeastern shore of Haida Gwaii. This antler was dated to ca. 47,000 BP (R.W. Mathewes, personal communication).
3 The frequency of salmon and dogfish bones at Honna River may reflect the highly identifiable nature of these taxa.

14
The Graham Tradition
Quentin Mackie and Steven Acheson

The Graham Tradition is a long-term archaeological culture complex in Haida Gwaii, dating from approximately 5,000 years ago to the early historical period after contact in AD 1774. Covering the period when Haida culture is thought to have assumed much of its complex social organization, ceremonialism, and elaborate material inventory, it is the most recent of four sequential cultural stages now defined for the islands. By conventional definition, the tradition includes all shell midden sites containing pecked and ground stone and bone artifacts, among other items, and coincides with the period of declining sea levels in Haida Gwaii (Fladmark 1989; Fladmark et al. 1990). In this chapter, we define the early Graham Tradition as the period 5000 to 2000 BP, and the late Graham period from 2000 BP onward. The reason for this distinction is primarily evidential: although substantial work has been performed at some earlier sites, they differ in ways that prevent reliable synthesis with late Graham materials. While the focus of this chapter is on the later periods, we begin with an overview of archaeological research, followed by a review of the early Graham Tradition.

History of Archaeological Research on the Graham Tradition
Considerable effort has been expended on the early periods in Haida Gwaii, and it fair to say that at least as much, if not more, is known from archaeological sources about the pre-5000 BP Moresby Tradition than about the more recent times. Following the early work of Harlan I. Smith, George MacDonald (1969, 1973) examined several sites, including a shell midden at the Honna River and three burial sites dating to the historical period: Skungo cave on North Island, a burial shelter on Gust Island in the vicinity of Skidegate Channel, and subterranean burial chambers at the historic village of *T'anuu,* off the southeast coast of Moresby Island. This work was primarily salvage-oriented in response to threatened or actual destruction of these sites. In addition to MacDonald's investigation, Wilson Duff and

Michael Kew (1958) conducted test excavations at "Ninstints" (*SGang gwaay*) village and at a nearby habitation cave on Anthony Island in 1957. Duff and Kew's work in 1957 and Donald Abbott's 1981 investigations at Anthony Island (Abbott and Keen 1993), and MacDonald's later work at *T'anuu*, were early excavation of sites assigned to the Graham Tradition in Gwaii Haanas. Duff and Kew's excavations yielded a "paucity of artefacts" (1958:53), allowing the authors to speculate only on the affiliation of the assemblage to Drucker's "Northern Aspect." Abbott's investigation was confined within the "well-defined historical horizon" as first identified by Duff and Kew (1958:54). Nicolas Gessler's work (n.d., 1974, 1975, 1988) at the historical village of Kiusta on the north shore of Graham Island has not been fully reported, making it hard to assess the conflicting basal dates of 2400 and 4380 BP. Similarly, only brief reports account for the large-scale excavations conducted in the early 1970s at the important Blue Jackets Creek (Severs 1974a), although the human remains from this site have been well analyzed (Murray 1981; Cybulski 2001). Severs also conducted minor excavations at Tow Hill (Severs 1974b) and at the Council Site in Masset (Severs 1975). Philip Hobler of Simon Fraser University conducted survey of sites in southern Haida Gwaii in the 1970s (Hobler 1976), presciently noting the relationship of intertidal sites to changing sea levels (Hobler 1978a). Hobler (1978b) also reports on an interesting cache of fishing gear from western Moresby Island, noting that it shows a sophisticated late pre-contact bottomfishing technology.

The most comprehensive early investigations were by Knut Fladmark of Simon Fraser University. Fladmark, perhaps best known for excavating at Moresby Tradition raised beach sites such as Lawn Point and Kasta (Fladmark 1986), also worked on Graham Tradition sites in the course of formulating his pioneering culture history for the islands. Fladmark excavated an important "Transitional Complex" site at Skoglund's Landing (Fladmark 1970, 1973, 1975, 1979b; Breffit 1993), and also an early nineteenth-century Haida house at Richardson Ranch near Tlell (Fladmark 1973).

It is only in the last two decades that some late Graham Tradition sites have received concerted attention. Steven Acheson conducted extensive excavations at a series of sites in Kunghit Haida territory, in southernmost Haida Gwaii (Acheson 1998). A project now under the direction of Trevor Orchard (Mackie et al. 2001; Orchard 2003) is aimed at recovering both cultural and environmental responses to European settlement and has also focused on late Graham Tradition sites in Gwaii Haanas National Park Reserve and Haida Heritage Site (hereafter Gwaii Haanas). Apart from these focused research programs, recent archaeological research on the Graham Tradition has been the domain of consulting and salvage-oriented projects, often consisting of only one or a few excavation units. To these, one must add several large-scale survey and mapping projects, notably the Gwaii

Haanas inventory (e.g., Mackie and Wilson 1994) and a smaller-scale effort at Naden Harbour (Stafford and Christensen 2000). Finally, in common with the rest of British Columbia, the past decade in Haida Gwaii has seen huge effort and expense put into recording and sampling culturally modified trees (CMTs), all of which necessarily date from the late Graham Tradition. Indeed, some of the earliest such projects provincewide were carried out in Haida Gwaii in the early 1980s by Michael Nicoll (1981) and Kathryn Bernick (1984)

The Graham Tradition: Overview

Prior to about 5,000 years ago, a long-standing example of the North Coast Microblade Tradition was the dominant cultural expression at archaeological sites in Haida Gwaii. Termed the Moresby Tradition (Fladmark 1989), this period coincided with a period of stable sea levels some 15 metres higher than at present. Sea level drop began about 5,000 years ago and slowly but steadily declined towards modern levels. Coinciding with this decline was technological change. Most notably, microblades disappear from the tool kit, while ground stone becomes much more common. The exact reasons for this change are not known. Some sites contain enigmatic lithic components dominated by bipolar reduction and convex-edged retouched flakes, collectively known as the "Transitional Complex." As discussed below, this complex may relate to task-specific tool kits rather than represent a culture-historical phenomenon.

The Graham Tradition owes its origins as a concept to work conducted at four Graham Island sites. The most important of these is the Blue Jackets Creek site on Masset Sound (Severs 1974a); indeed, the characterization of the Graham Tradition by Fladmark (Fladmark 1989; Fladmark et al. 1990) comes almost entirely from Blue Jackets Creek data. There were doubts early on about how representative the components from these few sites were for the rest of the archipelago, particularly as there was little evidence from the past 2,000 years. Subsequent excavations in southern Haida Gwaii (e.g., Acheson 1998) have filled in this gap, but a regional bias remains: investigated early Graham Tradition sites are mainly from northern Graham Island, while their late Graham Tradition counterparts are almost entirely from southern Moresby Island (Table 14.1). Geographically the gap is in central Haida Gwaii from northern Gwaii Haanas to Tlell. Temporally the gap centres on the period 4000 to 2000 BP (Figure 14.1). Hence, a persistent complication exists in trying to understand the full scope of the Graham Tradition across the archipelago and through time. This limitation in fact underlies much of the current debate in the literature about the nature of the relationship between the Graham Tradition and the Transitional Complex, which overlap chronologically as well as share a number of lithic traits (Fladmark et al. 1990). Recent excavations at a late Moresby Tradition shell

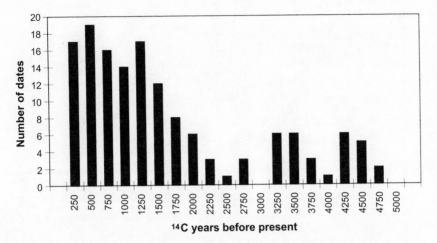

Figure 14.1 Post-5000 BP radiocarbon age estimates from Haida Gwaii assigned to Graham Tradition (*N* = 146) (based on Table 14.1).

midden at Cohoe Creek (Chapter 13) has shown that some of the traits, such as ground stone, ground bone, and shell-rich deposits, once described as distinctive of Graham Tradition sites, are present in earlier periods as well. Indeed, the recently discovered Kilgii Gwaay site pushes ground bone technology and shell-rich deposits back to the earliest Holocene and establishes the presence of woodworking and cordage at about 9400 BP (Fedje et al. 2001; Chapter 11).

In general, the Graham Tradition presents the following distinctive traits compared with the previous period: predominant association with shell middens, increase in the pecked stone and ground stone technology, increase in the expression of ground bone and antler technology, first evidence for decorative items, absence of microblades, general reduction in the importance of flaked stone, and first evidence for large houses and pole structures. At least some of these traits must be considered as the result of differential preservation between older sites and more recent ones. For the above reasons, in the following sections, the early (5000 to 2000 BP) and late (2000 BP onward) Graham Traditions are dealt with separately.

Early Graham Tradition Sites

Blue Jackets Creek (FlUa 4)
A total of twenty-eight units were excavated in several field seasons, amounting to approximately 52 square metres of deposits that ranged up to 270 centimetres deep and included at least 110 features. A series of eleven radiocarbon age estimates puts occupation between approximately 5200 BP and

Table 14.1

Radiocarbon dates within last 5,000 years and assigned to Graham Tradition components

Region[a]	Site name or location	Site no.	Lab no.	[14]C Age[b]* (1 S.d.)	±	Reference
South	Arrow Creek 2	925T	CAMS-8383	2750	80	Fedje et al. 1996
South		925T	CAMS-8379	1810	60	Fedje et al. 1996
South	Matheson Weir	1221T	CAMS-10840	1520	60	Fedje, pers. comm.
South	Bag Harbour	751T	CAMS-2328	390	70	Fedje, pers. comm.
		751T	CAMS-2329	270	80	Fedje, pers. comm.
South	Blood Fort	794T	CAMS-15394	310	60	Southon and Fedje 2003
South	*Xagi* Town	714T	CAMS-33901	1000	60	Southon and Fedje 2003
		714T	CAMS-33902	1020*	50	Southon and Fedje 2003
		714T	CAMS-33903	1160	50	Southon and Fedje 2003
		714T	CAMS-33904	1090*	50	Southon and Fedje 2003
		714T	CAMS-33905	1700	60	Fedje, pers. comm.
South	Beresford N. High	1356T	CAMS-26258	3700	50	Fedje, pers. comm.
		1356T	CAMS-26259	3630	60	Fedje, pers. comm.
		1356T	CAMS-42479	3230	50	Fedje, pers. comm.
South	East Copper Island	740T	CAMS-70707	490*	40	Mackie et al. 2001
		740T	CAMS-70708	390	50	Mackie et al. 2001
South	Darwin Sound	1134T	CAMS-70705	370*	40	Mackie et al. 2001
		1134T	CAMS-70706	190	40	Mackie et al. 2001
		1134T	CAMS-14421	160	60	Southon and Fedje 2003
		1134T	CAMS-14422	240	60	Southon and Fedje 2003
		1134T	CAMS-15357	140*	60	Southon and Fedje 2003
		1134T	CAMS-15358	430*	70	Southon and Fedje 2003
		1134T	CAMS-15359	350*	90	Southon and Fedje 2003
		1134T	CAMS-15360	60*	60	Southon and Fedje 2003

South	Echo Harbour	1160T	CAMS-14426	880	50	Southon and Fedje 2003
	– Gil Islet	1160T	CAMS-15365	790*	60	Southon and Fedje 2003
South	Hlgaedlin	798T	CAMS-14419	150	60	Southon and Fedje 2003
		798T	CAMS-15394	310*	60	Southon and Fedje 2003
South	Darwin Sound Shuttle Bay	1165T	CAMS-15366	250*	70	Fedje, pers. comm.
South	Hotspring Island Gunlai Kin	922T	CAMS-10842	110	60	Southon and Fedje 2003
		922T	CAMS-10873	1820	60	Southon and Fedje 2003
		922T	CAMS-10843	1850	60	Southon and Fedje 2003
		922T	CAMS-62511	1170	40	Fedje, pers. comm.
		922T	CAMS-62512	1450	40	Fedje, pers. comm.
		922T	CAMS-10873	1820*	60	Southon and Fedje 2003
South	Murchison Islet	1233T	CAMS-14430	720	50	Southon and Fedje 2003
		1233T	CAMS-15369	730*	50	Southon and Fedje 2003
		1233T	CAMS-14431	820	50	Southon and Fedje 2003
		1233T	CAMS-15370	670*	60	Southon and Fedje 2003
South	Kunga Island	1191T	CAMS-14429	540	60	Southon and Fedje 2003
		1191T	CAMS-15368	730*	60	Southon and Fedje 2003
South	Lyell Bay N1	1142T	CAMS-14424	730	60	Southon and Fedje 2003
		1142T	CAMS-15361	220*	60	Southon and Fedje 2003
		1142T	CAMS-15362	630*	60	Southon and Fedje 2003
		1142T	CAMS-15363	1210*	60	Southon and Fedje 2003
South	Lyell Bay N2	1443T	CAMS-14421	160	60	Southon and Fedje 2003
		1443T	CAMS-15364	300*	50	Southon and Fedje 2003
South	Moore Creek	1133T	CAMS-10864	180	80	Fedje, pers. comm.
South	Qla'dadja'ns	661T	CAMS-14418	210	50	Southon and Fedje 2003
		661T	CAMS-15356	300	90	Southon and Fedje 2003
		661T	CAMS-10870	240*	60	Fedje, pers. comm.

▼ *Table 14.1*

Region[a]	Site name or location	Site no.	Lab no.	¹⁴C Age[b]* (1 S.d.)	±	Reference
South	Sedgwick	1358T	CAMS-26260	740	60	Fedje, pers. comm.
South	*Tlgunghung*	803T	CAMS-14420	100	50	Southon and Fedje 2003
South		798T	CAMS-15394	310*	60	Southon and Fedje 2003
South	Tanu Passage	1179T	CAMS-14428	430	60	Fedje, pers. comm.
South		1179T	CAMS-15367	400*	70	Fedje, pers. comm.
South	Ramsay Island	923T	CAMS-75532	150*	50	Mackie et al. 2001
South	*Xe-uda'o*	FaTr 3	BGS-1327	500	130	Acheson 1998
		FaTr 3	BGS-1328	1300	100	Acheson 1998
		FaTr 3	BGS-1355	1650*	70	Acheson 1998
South	NW Kunghit Island	FaTs 1	BGS-1324	1210	90	Acheson 1998
		FaTs 1	WAT-1622	1210	90	Acheson 1998
South	*Ta'dasL'in*	FaTs 3	BGS-1352	740	70	Acheson 1998
South	Gilbert Bay	FaTs 17	BGS-1330	850	110	Acheson 1998
		FaTs 17	BGS-1331	1730	70	Acheson 1998
South	Bowles Point	FaTs 20	BGS-1332	930	130	Acheson 1998
		FaTs 20	BGS-1333	2050	270	Acheson 1998
South	Houston Stewart Channel	FaTs 27	WAT-1711	50	60	Acheson 1998
South	Moore Head	FaTs 31	BGS-1334	900	70	Acheson 1998
South	*SGang gwaay*	FaTt 1	SFU-352	1590	160	Acheson 1998
		FaTt 1	SFU-366	1430	160	Acheson 1998
		FaTt 1	SFU-367	1320	200	Acheson 1998
		FaTt 1	SFU-360	660	300	Acheson 1998
		FaTt 1	SFU-359	170	100	Acheson 1998
South	*Tclu'uga*	FaTt 9	BGS-1320	390	100	Acheson 1998
		FaTt 9	BGS-1321	730	80	Acheson 1998

Region	Site	Site No.	Lab No.	Date	±	Reference
		FaTt 9	WAT-1624	570	70	Acheson 1998
		FaTt 9	WAT-1625	300	75	Acheson 1998
		FaTt 9	WAT-1637	980	65	Acheson 1998
		FaTt 9	BGS-1322	890	120	Acheson 1998
		FaTt 9	WAT-1699	670	65	Acheson 1998
		FaTt 9	WAT-1626	770	65	Acheson 1998
		FaTt 9	BGS-1325	630	70	Acheson 1998
		FaTt 9	BGS-1326	600	70	Acheson 1998
South	Xil	FaTt 16	BGS-1335	850	180	Acheson 1998
		FaTt 16	BGS-1353	1240*	70	Acheson 1998
		FaTt 16	BGS-1354	2520*	70	Acheson 1998
South	Cape Freeman	FaTt 22	WAT-1621	1140	80	Acheson 1998
		FaTt 22	WAT-1640B	1420	80	Acheson 1998
South	Cape Freeman	FaTt 23	BGS-1338	1000	100	Acheson 1998
South	Ta'gil	FaTt 28	WAT-1631	1400	90	Acheson 1998
		FaTt 28	WAT-1933	1180	70	Acheson 1998
		FaTt 28	BGS-1318	1000	110	Acheson 1998
		FaTt 28	WAT-1644	840	80	Acheson 1998
		FaTt 28	BGS-1319	1030	100	Acheson 1998
		FaTt 28	WAT-1612	1120	70	Acheson 1998
		FaTt 28	WAT-1645	1040	70	Acheson 1998
		FaTt 28	WAT-1690	300	65	Acheson 1998
		FaTt 28	WAT-1652	590	70	Acheson 1998
South	Qayjuu	FbTs 4	BGS-1296	1370	400	Acheson 1998
		FbTu 5	BGS-1356	1360*	125	Acheson 1998
South	Hair-seal Low-Tide Town	785T	TO-10888	630	60	Orchard, pers. comm.
		785T	TO-10889	850	60	Orchard, pers. comm.

▼ *Table 14.1*

Region[a]	Site name or location	Site no.	Lab no.	^{14}C Age[b]* (1 S.d.)	±	Reference
		785T	TO-10890	570	50	Orchard, pers. comm.
		785T	TO-10891	1810	60	Orchard, pers. comm.
Central	K1 Cave	FgUc 6	CAMS-75558	1750*	40	Ramsey et al. 2004
Central	*Qay'llnagaay*	FhTx 19	CAMS-10871	1150*	60	Southon and Fedje 2003
		FhTx 19	CAMS-10598	1180	60	Southon and Fedje 2003
Central	Visitor Centre	FhUa 58	Beta-76788	1540	70	Mackie 1994
		FhUa 58	CAMS-16556	1300	60	Mackie 1994
Central	Kagan Bay	FhUa 57	TO-5766	1380	50	Wigen, pers. comm.
		FhUa 57	TO-5767	1910	50	Wigen, pers. comm.
Central	Honna River	FhUa 1	GAK-1871	3300	100	MacDonald 1969
		FhUa 1	GAK-1870	3040	100	MacDonald 1969
North	Lepos Bay Midden	Unknown	CAMS-14437	1700	60	Southon and Fedje 2003
		Unknown	CAMS-15376	1680*	70	Southon and Fedje 2003
North	Strathdang Kwun	FkUb 16	CAMS-16203	4520	60	Fedje et al. 1995
North	Cohoe Creek	FjUb 10	CAMS-16208	4390	50	Fedje et al. 1995
		FjUb 10	CAMS-16209	4420	60	Fedje et al. 1995
		FjUb 10	CAMS-16961	4290*	70	Fedje et al. 1995
		FjUb 10	CAMS-16962	4420*		Fedje et al. 1995
North	Blue Jackets Creek	FlUa 4	GSC-1554	4290	130	Severs 1974a
		FlUa 4	S676	4155	115	Severs 1974a
		FlUa 4	S4591-M420	2008	110	Severs 1974a
		FlUa 4	GAK-4883	2270	85	Severs 1974a
		FlUa 4	GAK-4884	3750	145	Severs 1974a
		FlUa 4	S935	3815	115	Severs 1974a
		FlUa 4	S2338	4100	170	Severs 1974a

Region	Site	Provenance	Lab no.	Date BP	±	Reference
North	Kiusta	FlUa 4	S936	4150	90	Severs 1974a
North	Skoglund's Landing II	FlUa 4	S2776	4160	140	Severs 1974a
		FlUa 4	S2349	4675	145	Severs 1974a
		GbUg 1	2721Axx	4175	55	Gessler 1988
		FlUa 1	GX1696	4165	80	Fladmark 1969:19
		FlUa 1	GSC-1290	1930	140	Fladmark 1969:19
		FlUa 1	GX1628	1145	80	Fladmark 1969:19
		FlUa 1	S675	2510	90	Fladmark 1969:19
North	Naden River 1	FlUe 3	CAMS-14434	3340	50	Fedje et al. 1995
		FlUe 3	CAMS-14433	3260	60	Fedje et al. 1995
		FlUe 3	CAMS-14435	3250	70	Fedje et al. 1995
		FlUe 3	CAMS-15372	3260*	60	Southon and Fedje 2003
		FlUe 3	CAMS-15373	3240*	60	Southon and Fedje 2003
		FlUe 3	CAMS-15374	3210*	60	Southon and Fedje 2003
North	Tow Hill	GaTw 5	GAK-5439	3280	210	Severs 1975:15
		GaTw 5	GAK-5440	2050	115	Severs 1975:15
North	Naden River 2	FlUe 4	CAMS-14436	3070	60	Fedje et al. 1995
		FlUe 4	CAMS-15375	3300*	60	Southon and Fedje 2003
North	Council Site	GaUb 7	S934	1425	70	Severs 1975
North	Masset	GaUa 11	BGS-2189	1310	50	Christensen & Stafford 2000
North	Masset	GaUa 2	Beta-11056	1230	60	Skinner 1983

a   South = within boundary of Gwaii Haanas National Park Reserve and Haida Heritage Site; Central = from north boundary of Gwaii Haanas up to and including north shore of Skidegate Channel; North = the north, west, and east shores and interior of Graham Island, and Masset Inlet.

b   Due to inconsistent reporting, we cannot establish that all dates have been corrected for delta ^{13}C; normally this results in a variance of a few decades. Some dates can be checked via the online Canadian Archaeological Radiocarbon Database.

Note: Dates on shell or marine organisms are marked with an asterisk, and have been corrected in this table for the marine reservoir effect by subtracting 600 years (Southon and Fedje 2003). Shell dates from Acheson 1998 are marked with an asterisk and have been recalculated in this way. Dates have not been calibrated to a dendrochronological curve.

3700 BP. An additional date of 2270 BP was obtained from the upper layers, with two obsidian hydration dates also suggesting occupation about 2000 BP (Severs 1974a:169, 199). It thus appears that the site was probably occupied from about 5000 BP to 2000 BP. No final tabulation or description of artifact types, materials, or proportion is yet available, nor are there full descriptions of faunal materials and stratigraphy. Approximately 75 percent of the assemblage of more than 2,000 artifacts were stone, predominantly flakes, unifacial cobble choppers and unifacially worked flakes, cortical spall tools, and "modified cores." Ground and pecked stone tools are present in numbers, especially celts and abraders. Two obsidian biface fragments were found, but otherwise bifacial working is very rare. Most of the varied raw materials are thought to be local, apart from the obsidian. Of the organic artifacts, most are made of land mammal, sea mammal, and bird bone, with lesser utilization of antler and other materials. Curiously, the relatively low percentage of bone artifacts is seen despite generally favourable faunal preservation, suggesting that there may actually be a lower proportion of bone artifacts in this early period compared with later ones. Distinctive artifacts include bilaterally barbed harpoon points, unilaterally single- and multiple-barbed/tanged "leister" fixed points, and bone and antler composite fishhook shanks similar to those from Vancouver Island's "West Coast Culture Type." Unusual or decorative objects include a single-piece bone fishhook, beads made of bone, shell, and teeth, comb fragments, decorated incised bone, "ribbed" stones, and a ground jet frontal labret. Many of these are illustrated in Fladmark et al. (1990:236) and Severs (1974a). The site is, however, best known for the well-documented remains of twenty-eight human burials (Cybulski 2001; Murray 1981), mainly dating from the pre-4000 BP layers. As discussed below, these remains show certain physical traits that appear to set them apart from historical-era Haida. Cybulski (2001) gives a good summary account of the important skeletal population from this site, including a variety of multivariate measures of similarity with other coastal populations. Full integration of this site into Haida Gwaii culture history awaits publication of the results of Severs's excavations. Sadly, the site has been almost completely destroyed by a recent housing development. One of the authors (Mackie) observed several microblade cores at the remains of the site in 2002, suggesting that a Moresby Tradition component was also present.

Other Early Graham Tradition Sites
Early Graham Tradition and/or Transitional Complex components are also present at Skoglund's Landing (FlUa 1) (Fladmark 1990), only a few kilometres from Blue Jackets Creek. The Honna River site (FhUa 1) near Skidegate, a large shell midden site with dates from 3300 and 3040 BP (Table 14.1), is reported (Fladmark 1989:216) to have no flaked stone technology. The Tow Hill site (GaTw 5) has dates of about 3000 and 2000 BP

(Severs 1974b), although there are few published details of what was found. At Kiusta (GbUg 1), Gessler (1975) oversaw major excavations amounting to almost 200 square metres, including near-complete excavation of a house platform. Regrettably, as at Blue Jackets Creek, these excavations have been reported in only the most preliminary fashion. More recently, excavations at Strathdang Kwun (FkUb 16) and renewed work at Cohoe Creek (FjUb 10), both on southern Masset Inlet, have produced dates ranging from the later Moresby Tradition to as recently as 4520 and 4390 BP, respectively (Tables 13.1 and 14.1), although the assemblages assigned to these most recent dates are small and inconclusive and thus may represent terminal Moresby Tradition occupation.

Early Graham Tradition: Discussion

Little is known of the period between the end of the Moresby Tradition around 5,000 years ago and the start of the later Graham Tradition. Fladmark (1989) has proposed two contemporaneous archaeological units of analysis: the (early) Graham Tradition and the Transitional Complex, so named because it contains elements of both Moresby and Graham Tradition tool kits. The Transitional Complex, with dates from about 4500 BP to as recently as 2500 BP (Fladmark 1989:212), is known for its distinctive lithic assemblage consisting of simple unifacially retouched, convex-edged basalt flakes and a system of bipolar core reduction. The Transitional Complex has been viewed variously as a contemporaneous cultural form distinct from the Graham Tradition, perhaps even representing different social or ethnic groups (Fladmark 1989:217), or as evidence of special use sites or activities associated with the early Graham Tradition. It has been found at both non-shell midden (e.g., Skoglund's Landing, FlUa 1) and shell midden (e.g., Blue Jackets Creek, FlUa 4) sites. In a recent analysis, Breffitt (1993) suggests that the term *Transitional Complex* is ambiguous and inappropriate, and, since the complex is known only as an isolated assemblage at a single site, Skoglund's Landing, that inferences should not yet be drawn about its place in Haida culture history. It may well turn out to be a specialized tool kit or some other functional variant of the early Graham Tradition rather than being in a meaningful sense "transitional" between the Moresby and Graham Traditions themselves. While Fladmark (1989:216) states that it can be seen as a "linear technological descendant" of the Moresby Tradition, partly on the basis that very late Moresby Tradition sites such as Kasta show a trend from microblade manufacture towards its near-functional equivalent, bipolar reduction, the relationship between the Transitional Complex and the early Graham Tradition must remain unresolved until further representative sites are found and reported.

The issue of the Transitional Complex aside, early Graham Tradition tool types and technologies include pecked and ground stone, and a minor component of bifacially flaked stone – all traits that were originally credited to a mainland origin or influence. Noticeably absent from the assemblage is the older microblade industry of the Moresby Tradition. A degree of continuity with earlier lithic technologies is maintained, however, with the presence of cobble and cortical spall tool forms, unifacial tools, and *pièces-esquillées*. Bifacial tools had been thought to occur relatively late in the Graham Tradition as part of a mainland influence, with some reportedly made from mainland obsidian. Recent work at Richardson Island and on a series of 9,400-year-old intertidal sites in Gwaii Haanas, has revealed the much earlier presence of this tool type (Chapters 12 and 16). As for the source of the obsidian, there is now believed to be a local source, although four pieces of obsidian from the Skoglund's Landing and Blue Jackets Creek sites are from Mount Edziza on the northwestern BC mainland (Carlson 1994:314). A bifacially flaked and ground stone blade similar to ones from Prince Rupert that date to after 4,500 years ago has also been recovered from Clonard Bay on the west coast of Graham Island (Acheson 1995). Small flaked adzes or chisels, finished by pecking and grinding, unique in form to the islands, are common to the period.

Bone and antler tools include barbed harpoons, harpoon values, fishhook shanks, a variety of awls and punches, needles, leister barbs, and rare single-piece fishhooks. Items of personal adornment complete the assemblage and include bone combs, pendants, and beads of bone, tooth, ivory, and shell, as well as labrets made of stone. The importance attached to the preponderance of bone and antler tools for this period must be tempered in light of the context in which they occur. Preservation as much as cultural practice may account for their numbers, given the buffering effect that shell middens have on the normally deleterious acidic conditions of forest soils. Abraders used in the manufacturing of bone implements, for example, do occur in earlier assemblages from non-shell sites such as Richardson Island, while a small assemblage of wooden and bone tools is now known from the 9,400-year-old Kilgii Gwaay site near Kunghit Island (Chapter 11). Thus, firm conclusions should not yet be drawn about the role or development of woodworking, bone working, or resource procurement patterns in this part of the cultural historical sequence.

The emphasis on flaked stone technologies, the unique form of woodworking tools, and the higher relative frequency of stone tools to bone and antler than found at Prince Rupert tend to differentiate the early Graham Tradition from mainland developments. The early Graham Tradition sees the disappearance of microblades from Haida Gwaii, apparently functionally replaced by bipolar technology. At Cohoe Creek, these technologies coexist in the terminal Moresby Tradition. A ground stone industry becomes more prominent, again with antecedents at Cohoe Creek. The overall trend is towards a typical developed Northwest Coast assemblage of prominent ground bone and stone industries, supplemented by flaked stone. Presumably wooden artifacts would have formed a major constituent of the tool kit. Casting the early Graham Tradition into its longer temporal context, we see antecedents of the ground bone industry and a shell midden feature at Kilgii Gwaay, 9400 BP. Bone and antler technologies are also present at Cohoe Creek between 5000 and 6000 BP.

Little is known of early Graham Tradition subsistence, but again at Kilgii Gwaay a fully maritime-capable adaptation is in place very early during the Kinggi Complex, so the capacity for one is presumably retained in later periods. Certainly at Cohoe Creek there is a strong marine component to the diet. At Blue Jackets Creek, Severs (1974a:197) notes that fish, sea mammals, birds, and land mammals (especially caribou) are present, in approximately that order, in a shell matrix dominated by butter clam, cockle, blue mussel, littleneck clam, and sea urchin. At Tow Hill, Severs (1974b:12) briefly notes that salmon, halibut, and seal are present in a matrix that includes butter clam, littleneck clam, razor clam, cockle, and blue mussel, among other invertebrates. Both these faunal assemblages point to a strongly maritime adaptation.

In summary, there appear to be many points of similarity between the early Graham Tradition and the Moresby Tradition, and many of the apparent differences may stem from the better preservation of shell-bearing deposits in the more recent periods and the subsequent preservation of organic artifacts in these deposits themselves. As discussed in a subsequent section, there appears to be as much distinction between early and late Graham assemblages as there is between Late Moresby and early Graham ones. While this may reflect the Kunghit-centric nature of the late Graham assemblages, this observation also highlights a gap in data for the period between about 3250 BP and 2000 BP. As illustrated in Figure 14.1, only 9 of the 146 total radiocarbon dates on archaeological material from the last 5,000 years fall into the this mid-Graham period, and none of these are from well-excavated, properly reported contexts with a significant artifact assemblage. In fact, assemblages from reasonably well-reported sites are effectively absent between 4000 and 2000 BP. Acheson's oldest reliable date is 1725 BP. While Figure 14.1 highlights this gap, we also note that some archaeological sites of this age are known, such as Tow Hill, Honna River, and several in Naden Harbour (Chapter 10), and only await investigation. The probable reason for the gap is that so much research has focused on either raised beach sites, at the well-defined 15-metre highstand, or on sites on the current shoreline that almost exclusively date within the last 2,000 years (intertidal lithic sites excepted). Sites associated with the slowly regressive shoreline after 5000 BP but significantly back from the current shoreline (i.e., those between about 10 and 3 metres above sea level that would probably date to mid-Graham times) are underinvestigated. Research on these might also shed light on the Transitional Complex, which at present we suggest be set aside as a culture-historical organizing concept until it can be better understood. Filling the mid-Graham data gap is certainly a research priority in Haida Gwaii.

Until this data gap is filled, it will be very difficult to reconcile the anomalous Blue Jackets Creek skeletal population. Cybulski (2001) and Murray (1981) have performed detailed analyses of the Blue Jackets Creek skeletons, which were recently repatriated to Haida Gwaii. In virtually every one of these, the Blue Jackets Creek skeletons are the outliers compared with other Northwest Coast groups. Where they do group closely, they do so mainly with populations from the Tsimshian area. In one analysis (Cybulski 2001, figure 3b), Blue Jackets Creek joins with both North Coast peoples and with another Haida skeletal population. The primary distinction can be characterized as a trend towards long-headedness (dolichocephaly), as opposed to the more round-headed (brachycephalic) historic Haida. Cybulski also notes other seemingly anomalous results, such as the marked separation between the Namu and Waglisla (Bella Bella) populations despite their presumed close cultural relationship, and the tight clustering on some measures of Tlingit populations and those from Namu. In addition, the Haida skeletal sample as a whole is the most heterogeneous of all the populations he analyzes.

The Blue Jackets Creek population, however, is not large enough nor does it cover sufficient time depth or geographic scope to allow us to draw any firm conclusions. It is not clear whether the variation from past to present in Haida Gwaii arises from a biological evolutionary process within a single cultural group across the intervening 4,000 years, or from different populations arriving on the islands that could, in turn, have played a role in some of the apparent technological changes associated with the Graham Tradition. Cybulski suggests that the burials could all be from a single related lineage and that this might account for their internal similarity and unique appearance relative to present-day Haida, a situation he believes also shapes the physical relationships among the Gust Island (Skidegate Channel) skeletal population excavated by MacDonald (1973). Cybulski (2001:137) cautions that one should not be too quick to conclude that "Blue Jackets Creek is not ancestral to the historic Haida and that, logically, the Haida cannot trace their archipelago roots back 4000 years ... there does not appear to be a close biological association of the Haida, Tlingit and Tsimshian in this study." Rather, many questions are unresolved about this skeletal sample. At present, then, too much emphasis on the apparent biological singularity of this skeletal population is unwarranted; concomitantly, it is premature to speculate on the ethnic affiliations of the peoples responsible for the early Graham Tradition and/or the Transitional Complex.

In summary, the early Graham Tradition is poorly known. While caution must be used when we consider the different environmental niches that the best-known sites occupy, it is nonetheless striking that the early Graham Tradition sites may, with the exception of microblades, be coming to look more like Late Moresby Tradition sites. When we consider the possible functional similarities between microblades and bipolar technology, the difference between the two traditions is again reduced. Fladmark's (1990) distinction that Graham Tradition sites are associated with shell middens, and Moresby Tradition sites are not, still holds as a general pattern. However, the recent finds of shell-rich deposits or small shell-midden components at the Moresby Tradition sites of Strathdang Kwun and Cohoe Creek (Chapter 13) and the Kinggi Complex site of Kilgii Gwaay (Chapter 11) means that this Graham-Moresby distinction needs closer examination. Relatively stable sea levels during the Moresby Tradition suggests that sites could have been repetitively used for long periods and that shellfish beds would have time to develop. Does the pattern arise from taphonomic issues, whereby earlier sites are less likely to have preserved shell deposits due to long-term acid leaching? Or were early occupants less interested in shellfish exploitation, perhaps because of lower population densities or because of higher rates of paralytic shellfish poisoning (PSP) (Chapter 16)? More data will be necessary to resolve the meaning of this pattern, which is also seen elsewhere on the Northwest Coast. At present there is no compelling reason to believe in a major cultural shift or external influence more pronounced than those that appear elsewhere across the Northwest Coast around this time.

The Late Graham Tradition

The regional and temporal data gap noted above for the Graham Tradition as a whole is also relevant to the later periods. Between the early and late Graham Tradition, the archaeological assemblages appear to have undergone considerable change, perhaps more than can be reconciled within a single culture-historical unit of analysis. Flaked stone declines, as does ground stone. The assemblages become dominated by bone tools, especially bird bone. This pattern is probably skewed by the most reliable excavations having been undertaken in the most remote southern area of the archipelago, where a regional variation of the late Graham Tradition may hold. Elsewhere in the archipelago, late Graham assemblages have included more flaked stone than in Kunghit territory. The following discussion of the later Graham Tradition deals only with sites from the last 2,000 years. The focus is on Acheson's Kunghit Haida archaeological research, as it is the most fully complete in terms of subsistence, settlement, and material culture.

The Kunghit Haida Prehistory Project

In the early 1980s, Acheson undertook a multi-year settlement archaeology project in the Kunghit Haida traditional territory of southernmost Gwaii

Haanas (Acheson 1998; Chapter 15). Chronometric dates obtained for fourteen of the eighteen sites investigated in 1985-86 firmly place their occupation in the latter part of the Graham Tradition. Irrespective of their elevation, all but one of the dated sites from the Kunghit sample postdate 1750 BP (Table 14.1). The earliest reliable date of 1725 ± 70 years BP was obtained from the base of a rather unassuming rock shelter site (FaTs 17) located on the west coast of Kunghit Island at an elevation of 6 metres above present sea level. Several sites cluster around the mid-1400s, but the general pattern is one of more or less continuous occupation of the region for the last two millennia. Seven sites have historical components.

Detailed analysis of column samples collected from sixteen of the eighteen sites demonstrates a strong correlation between layer type and the distribution of the component elements (Keen 1990:10-11). Two principal depositional sequences were identified, distinguished from one another by the number and density of shell layers and by the frequency of pit and hearth features. At FaTr 3 and FaTs 17, for example, alternating dense, massive shell deposits gave way in the upper levels of these sites to mixed, compacted humus and shell layers along with a noticeable increase in the number of features, characteristic of living floors. Examination of the relative frequency of different types of deposits revealed statistically significant variations (after Wigen and Stucki 1988). The number of living floor, hearth, refuse, and noncultural deposits for thirteen of eighteen tested sites showed a decrease in the frequency of non-cultural layers with a comparable increase of floor-type deposits, suggestive of increased cultural activity around 800 BP.

The combined artifact assemblages from the Kunghit area are notable for the nearly complete absence of stone tools. Abraders, presumably used in the manufacture of other implements, are the most common of the few stone artifacts recovered from the Kunghit sites. This absence is particularly noteworthy since stone tools were common enough among the Kunghit in 1787 for Colnett (n.d.) to comment on their use of "the Rocks of the shore, & the common stone," as well as the use of "green stone" for adzes. Within the year, he observed the near universal use of iron by the Kunghit, noting "their stone tools are laid aside, & Iron substitute in their Room" (see also Acheson 2003). All the indigenous artifacts recovered during the Kunghit project, including the strand of native copper wire from FaTt 9, have a wide distribution on the coast, and show a strong material similarity with neighbouring groups. Subsistence implements include variously shaped bone barbs for hooks, unilaterally barbed harpoons, and composite toggling harpoon elements.

The intra-site artifact distributions for a number of Kunghit sites are particularly telling. The largest concentration of artifacts was retrieved from the series of floor deposits and associated pit features representing the middle occupational period at *Tc!u'uga* (FaTt 9). This assemblage consists mostly of whole, curated items such as bone drinking tubes, barbed points, dentalia shell beads, and one example of a bone comb and the fragment of copper wire. Despite their co-occurence, there is variation in the functional categories represented by these artifacts. In the three cases where test units were judged to be towards the rear of a house (FaTr 3, FaTt 9, FbTs 4), the artifact yield was generally greater and more varied, with an increased frequency in personal adornment and decorated items. Thirty-five percent of the artifact assemblage of *Xe-uda'o* (FaTr 3) falls into this category and includes a variety of pendants. A number of items are of European materials or manufacture and include miscellaneous worked pieces of sheet copper, a rolled copper bead, and a glass trade bead. From the one test unit placed in the central back area of a house at *Qayjuu* (FbTs 4), an assortment of iron and two glass trade beads were recovered. A similar pattern is suggested at the Richardson Ranch site on Graham Island (Fladmark 1973). In contrast, the artifact yield from the smaller habitation sites was negligible. While European goods recovered from *Qayjuu* (FbTs 4) and *Xe-uda'o* (FaTr 3) indicate a historical component, neither site yielded the kind of goods, such as patented medicine bottles, window or bottle glass, percussion caps, and ceramics found at *SGang gwaay* village to suggest an intense, prolonged historical occupation (Abbott and Keen 1993; Acheson 1982).

A total of 165 animal taxa were identified from the eighteen sites examined in the Kunghit project (Acheson 1998; Keen 1990; Wigen 1990). The overwhelmingly dominant shellfish is the sea or California mussel (*Mytilus californianus*), which totals 95 to 100 percent of the shell weight for thirteen of the sixteen sites analyzed. The small midden site at the head of Balcom Inlet (FaTs 35) and two cave sites (FaTs 27 and FaTt 20) are the exceptions. Clams occur at only four sites in weights of greater than 0.5 percent of the total shell weight. Interestingly, three of these four three sites, *Ta'dasL'in, Tc!u'uga,* and *Ta'gil,* are towns. Among the clams, littleneck dominated with 56 percent, followed in descending order by butter (37 percent) and horse, cockle, polluted macoma, razor, and mud clams with 1 percent or less. Chiton and barnacle are also occasionally present but never constitute more than a moderate constituent of the shellfish assemblage.

Salmon, rockfish, and halibut are the major fish species represented, but their relative contribution is difficult to establish since halibut is most likely to be severely underrepresented because of poor preservation as well as butchering practices (Wigen 1990). Sablefish, found only occasionally in a few sites outside of Gwaii Haanas, is also present in low but persistent numbers and again is likely underrepresented due to poor preservation.

An overall increase in salmon is also evident in the later occupation period of many of the sites. This pattern is sufficiently widespread, occurring at eight sites of varied type, to discount sampling bias or taphonomic factors as an explanation. Where cultural deposits are seen to shift from refuse to

living floor–type deposits, salmon emerges with few exceptions as the dominant species. For refuse deposits, salmon is either matched or eclipsed in
numbers by rockfish. The pattern is most evident at FaTt 9 and FaTr 3 and
suggests observable differences in butchering and discard practices for these
two species. At FaTs 20 and FaTt 23, rockfish remain dominant throughout
the deposits, although in both cases salmon show a measurable increase in
the upper levels.

The fact that halibut and rockfish numbers of identified specimens (NISP)
actually drop in the more recent levels, even though the bones are in noticeably poor condition in the lower levels, tends to rule out taphonomic
processes, such as differential preservation, to account for the pattern. While
the exact proportion of rockfish to salmon bone is affected by the their
different deposition environments, the sudden influx of salmon indicates
other changes, corresponding in time with the projected increase in size
and complexity of a number of sites, including *SGang gwaay* (FaTt 1) and
Ta'gil (FaTt 28). The other three sites, FaTt 31, FaTs 27, and FaTt 20, have
too few bones to exhibit any patterns other than that salmon and rockfish
are the dominant species.

The relative frequency of bone elements of the two most common species
of fish, salmon and rockfish, compared with expected ratios further demonstrates different handling procedures for these species (see Wigen et al.
1990). The dominance of salmon vertebrae in these sites, particularly in
association with living floor deposits, indicates that most of the salmon
were processed before reaching the site, further implying a somewhat sedentary settlement arrangement. In the case of rockfish, on the other hand,
whole fish were brought to the site, whether a camp or a village, for processing, and the remains were deposited in outside refuse areas.

The two dominant mammal species recovered are harbour seal and sea
otter. Given their larger size, harbour seal was probably the more important
of the two in the diet. Seal and sea otters of various ages were recovered. The
large amount of whalebone recovered from FaTt 22 suggests that whales
made a significant contribution to the subsistence base at this site, whether
hunted or salvaged (Acheson and Wigen 1989). The presence of whalebone
in the house floor deposits at FaTt 9 is possibly linked to tool manufacture,
an interpretation consistent with that for the historic Haida house of
Richardson Ranch near Tlell (Fladmark 1973:70). The lack of whalebone in
the refuse deposits, in turn, is likely the result of the practice of butchering
whales on the beach, although the excavation sample size is insufficient to
confirm this interpretation.

A wide variety of bird species are represented in the eighteen sites, but
again no clear distributional pattern emerges. The dominant group consists
of the small alcids (murrelets and auklets), which were undoubtedly hunted
while nesting during the early spring. No other single group or species stands

out, although the persistent and sometimes high numbers of songbirds is unique for coastal sites. Other summer resident species found at many of the sites are albatross and shearwater. Also present are swans, a winter resident on the islands. Ducks, including marine ducks, are very uncommon.

The seasonal range and variety of fauna found at many sites suggests a substantially more fluid subsistence-settlement pattern during the late Graham Tradition, with little distinction between winter and summer site use. Several of the larger village-like sites may well have been occupied year-round, with some of the larger sites standing apart in terms of the sheer volume and range of faunal remains present at these sites. This aside, there is little inter-site variation among the various sites regardless of size in terms of the faunal assemblage, with rockfish, salmon, sea otter, harbour seal, alcid, and California mussel being the dominant species for most sites.

As discussed by Acheson (1995, 1998; Chapter 15), the Kunghit Haida project showed evidence of a marked change in settlement pattern in the historical era. This emphasizes the caution with which ethnographic information, as vivid and detailed as it may be, must be used by archaeologists interested in even the most recent pre-contact periods.

Other Late Graham Tradition Sites

Outside of Kunghit Haida territory, several sites in Haida Gwaii dating to the late Graham period have seen testing or minor excavation. The following sections outline the more important of these, with the intention of adding some regional balance to the Kunghit data presented earlier.

Gunlai Kin (Hotspring Island) (922T)

Results of test excavations at this site in Juan Perez Sound in 1993 (Sumpter and Mason 1994; Crockford 1994) and 1998 (Wigen 1999a; Sumpter 1999) are combined together in this summary. The total NISP is 6,461 vertebrate elements, of which fish compose almost the entire assemblage; bird accounts for only 0.01 percent (65 elements) and mammal for 0.03 percent (161 elements). In both years, NISP for salmon is higher or highest in the lower layers or levels, being replaced in upper levels by rockfish, red Irish lord, and prickleback. This pattern is opposite to that observed in the Kunghit project (above), although it must be stressed that this is a limited spatial sample with only relative temporal control established to date the faunal remains. Salmon comprises the highest percentage of fish elements overall, at 28 percent of the total. Fewer than 10 non-vertebral remains of salmon, out of 715 total identified salmon elements, may suggest storage of this taxon. The 1993 project differs slightly in having somewhat fewer prickleback, probably due to a lack of analyzed column samples. Of the mammalian elements, the identified remains are limited to river otter, beaver, dog, sea otter, fur seal, northern sea lion, and harbour seal.

Forty-two different taxa of invertebrates were identified from the 1998 project (Sumpter 1999). Of these, "by far the most common are undifferentiated Veneridae, barnacle, Venus and little neck clams, California mussel, sea urchin, horse clam and blue mussel. The shellfish assemblage indicates people collected material from a variety of habitats, both protected inside bays and estuaries, and from outside, exposed rocky shores" (Sumpter 1999). The faunal remains indicate a similarly diverse set of exploited ecosystems (see Crockford 1994).

All five radiocarbon estimates from *Gunlai Kin* fall within the last 2,000 years. In this regard, it is of interest that fifteen of the twenty-five artifacts recovered at *Gunlai Kin* are made by flaked stone technology, in contrast to the near absence of this technology in the Kunghit project.

Gwaii Haanas Environmental Archaeology Project (GHEAP) Sites
Four late Graham Tradition sites have been test excavated during a project designed to recover environmental information for management purposes in 2000 (Mackie et al. 2001) and 2002 and 2003 (Orchard 2003). A total of only 10 square metres were opened at sites 740T (East Copper Island, Skincuttle Inlet), 923T (Ramsay Island, Juan Perez Sound), 785T (Lyell Island), and 1134T (Darwin Sound). Material culture from these sites is primarily historical, as the project was targeted towards immediate pre-contact contexts. At 740T no artifacts were found. The 923T assemblage includes several examples of stone tools, while at 785T and 1134T a small assemblage of Haida manufacture includes a flake and two rounded pebbles similar to the ones found at *Gunlai Kin* (Table 14.2). Other pre-contact artifacts include miscellaneous ground bone, an abrader stone, and a bird-bone awl. A plain stone elbow pipe, possibly argillite, was found at 1134T and is probably of Haida manufacture. Similarly, testing at site 923T near Hotspring Island discovered 7 non-historical artifacts, of which 5 are stone (one unifacial chopper, one abrader, two hammer stones, and a sinker stone) and the other 2 are a bone awl and miscellaneous worked bone (Mackie et al. 2001). A single date of 150 ± 50 BP (CAMS-75532) was obtained from 923T, which, combined with the less than 1 metre above sea level elevation, argues for the inclusion of these deposits with the late Graham Tradition. The unifacial chopper is somewhat water-rolled, a condition it shares with a possible cortical spall tool. While a limited sample, it is worth noting again that Acheson's more extensive series of excavations to the south in Kunghit territory revealed a total of only two examples of flaked stone technology: a graver and a unifacial scraper (Acheson 1998:45). A comparison with Acheson's major classes of "Bone" and "Stone" (includes ground stone) is instructive: Acheson recovered 235 bone and 13 stone artifacts (a ratio of 18:1). At Hotspring Island the corresponding figures are (discounting the 4 enigmatic "round

Table 14.2

Summary of small artifact assemblages from the later Graham Tradition sites *Gunlai Kin* (922T, Hotspring Island), Ramsay Island (923T), and Hairseal Low-Tide Town (785T, Lyell Bay)

		922T	923T	785T
Stone	Unifacial chopper	2	1	0
	Bifacial chopper	1	0	0
	Flakes and flake shatter	10	0	1
	Cores	2	0	0
	Hammerstones	1	2	0
	Round pebbles	4	0	1
	Abraders	0	1	1
	Pecked sinker stone	0	1	0
Bone	Self-armed composite toggling harpoon valve	0	0	1
	Ground bone point/awl	2	1	5
	Miscellaneous worked sea mammal bone	3	1	2
	Miscellaneous worked mammal bone	0	0	5
Totals		25	7	16

pebbles" thought [Sumpter 1999] to be gaming pieces or manuports) 5 bone and 16 stone artifacts, a ratio of 0.3:1. As discussed below, when combined with the different faunal pattern between Hotspring Island and the Kunghit area, it may be premature to extend too widely the area covered by a Kunghit-defined late Graham Tradition.

While the sample size is relatively small, with a NISP of 6,622, the GHEAP did recover a diversity of faunal remains, representing sixty-seven taxa in total. The sites were chosen to represent protected, semi-protected, and exposed conditions, and the faunal assemblages reflect these local conditions in both diversity and kind of species (Mackie et al. 2001). Taken together, fish dominate the assemblages, with salmon making up over 40 percent of the fish at all sites. Rockfish contribute the bulk of the other fish, although herring, greenling, dogfish, and halibut are also present in numbers. Alcids are by far the most important bird taxon. The most important mammals by NISP are sea otter and harbour seal, while harbour porpoise, fur seal, and black bear are also found. Invertebrate species are unsurprisingly diverse, but the only taxa to record greater than 1 percent by weight of the assemblage are California mussel, purple-hinged rock scallop, butter clam, and other clam, barnacle, and chiton.

Phase II of the GHEAP was started by Trevor Orchard in 2001, and included fieldwork in 2002 (Orchard 2003) and 2003, research that will form the basis of a PhD dissertation at the University of Toronto. Site 785T, on the west side of Lyell Island in Darwin Sound, was test-excavated, including deposits dating up into the protohistoric period. Radiocarbon age estimates are pending. From relatively modest excavations, 74 faunal taxa were identified, 63 to genus or species level, from over 20,000 identified specimens. Sea otter and harbour seal dominate the mammal assemblage, alcids dominate the bird assemblage, and salmon are the most important fish, followed by rockfish. Orchard (2003:26) notes a slight increase in salmon relative abundance through time, which is in agreement with Acheson's findings (1998) further south. Invertebrate remains are not yet quantified, but mussel, littleneck clam, and butter clam are all important. Artifacts of Aboriginal manufacture include a self-armed toggling harpoon valve, similar to those found in Kunghit territory by Acheson and on the west coast of Vancouver Island (Mitchell 1990), as well as bird-bone points, abrader stones, and cortical spall tools. The self-armed variety is characteristic of the West Coast Culture Type of Vancouver Island (Mitchell 1990). In 2003, three more sites in Juan Perez Sound were excavated (T. Orchard, personal communication).

Second Beach – Qay'llnagaay (FhTx 19)
Christensen and colleagues (1999:76) describe various formed artifacts, mainly made of bone. No lithics are recorded. However, the majority of the artifact assemblage is not known to have been reported for this site near Skidegate. Test excavations here have recovered 1,557 vertebrate bones, of which 91 percent are fish, 2 percent bird, and 7 percent mammal, spanning thirty-two separate taxa. These come from three main stratigraphic layers, from each of which an approximately equal volume of material was analyzed. On average, flatfish are dominant in fish NISP, followed by dogfish, Pacific cod, and salmon, in percentage order, although salmon ranks first in the uppermost layer (Wigen 1999b). The assemblage of the uppermost Layer B is split fairly evenly between salmon, flatfish, and dogfish, while the lower layers are dominated by dogfish and Pacific cod. Salmon essentially disappears in the lower layers. This follows the general temporal trend in salmon-versus-rockfish use reported by Acheson (1998), except that rockfish are lacking, apparently "replaced" by flatfish. If so, the pattern probably reflects the locally favourable flatfish habitat of Skidegate Channel. Mammals are limited to small numbers of dog, sea otter, harbour seal, black bear, and, unusually, Pacific white-sided dolphin. Birds are a minor contributor, being a mix of sea and shore species. The fish remains suggest utilization of two major habitats: shallow sandy or muddy areas, and deeper waters. A large number of mainly non-articulated burials are known from this site. Two dates of about 1200 BP have been obtained from this site (Table 14.1), consistent with its context, which suggests a later Graham Tradition occupation.

The Richardson Ranch Site (FjTx 1)

The Richardson Ranch Site is located 5 kilometres north of Tlell on Graham Island, and consists of several house depressions, a shell midden component, and two human burials (Fladmark 1973). Approximately 36 square metres of deposits were excavated in a trench running the length of one of the housepits. Fladmark (1973:73) estimates that the house was occupied between AD 1810 and 1840. While the assemblage cannot be truly assigned to the later Graham Tradition, given that it has a strong component of historical-era materials, the materials obviously shed light on the late pre-contact period as well. It must be realized, however, that these artifacts and faunal remains are all from intra-house or grave-proximal context and may not be completely comparable with other assemblages. Thus, Fladmark notes the presence of bird-bone tubes, sawn bird-bone epiphyses, miscellaneous worked bone, a perforated bone disk similar to a spindle whorl, and several other bone artifacts. Stone is represented by hammer stones, abraders, and a number of pigment stones and their associated grinders. There is also a considerable quantity of ground argillite, including decorative objects and pipes. Perhaps of most interest is the large number ($N = 50$) of flaked stone pieces, mostly crudely chipped and battered chalcedony, again placing this assemblage at odds with the Kunghit data.

Faunal remains from Richardson Ranch include some 1,490 specimens of twenty different taxa, mostly coarsely identified. More than 40 percent of the NISP are unidentified bird; Fladmark (1973:84) notes that this count refers to large birds, probably Canada geese. Butter clam dominates the invertebrate assemblage, with large numbers of barnacle and whelk, while sea otter and "whale" are prominent mammals. The sea otter remains suggest a pre-1820s occupation. No caribou remains were found, suggesting that this species had already become rare, as the site is located in apparently favourable caribou habitat. Fladmark does not discuss his faunal recovery and identification methods, but it is fair to assume that fish, at 7 percent, are probably underrepresented. Indeed, this entire faunal assemblage, which appears to have been only partially identified, could be the subject of further fruitful analysis. In the meantime, recovery and identification uncertainty, its historical period context, and its position close to burials make it best not to draw overly firm conclusions about dietary patterns from this faunal assemblage.

Gwaii Haanas Visitor Reception Centre Site (1248T/FhUa 58)

A small shell midden site in central Queen Charlotte City was test-excavated in 1994, before construction of the Gwaii Haanas Visitor Reception Centre (Mackie 1994). Radiocarbon dates of 1300 and 1540 BP place occupation in the later Graham Tradition. Excavation was limited to systematic recovery of column and soil samples. Only one artifact, an early-stage basalt flake, was recovered. Analysis of the various column samples gives some useful data about later Graham subsistence outside of Gwaii Haanas, albeit from a very small sample. California mussels comprise up to 73 percent of the invertebrate assemblage by weight, while clams, especially butter clams, are also important. Very little bone was recovered, mostly salmon bone with some herring, flatfish, and mammal bone also found (Mackie 1994:25-28). At another nearby site, FhUa 57, two radiocarbon dates of 1380 and 1910 BP are known (R. Wigen, personal communication; cf. Christensen 1995).

Masset Department of National Defence Site (GaUa 11)

A small inland shell midden near Masset on Department of National Defence property was test-excavated as part of an impact assessment in 1999 (Dady and Christensen 2000). A single radiocarbon date of 1310 BP was obtained from 56 centimetres below the surface (Table 14.1). No artifacts were found, but a very small faunal assemblage (vertebrate NISP = 55) was collected and identified by Rebecca Wigen. Fish included some dogfish and greenling, but sculpin dominated this small assemblage. A large goose, sea otter, and, notably, caribou were also identified. No quantified shellfish component is recorded, but butter clam, littleneck, cockle, and whelk are all noted.

Hiellen River (GaTw 7)

This site on the northeast corner of Graham Island was test-excavated with a single unit by Christensen (2000). A ground bone wedge, bird-bone awl/needle, and worked sea mammal bone were found. A good faunal assemblage of 417 elements was recovered, the most important of which are sea otter and halibut. Salmon is relatively uncommon. A variety of birds are present, but only a judgmental sample of shellfish was taken.

Discussion

The best and most complete data for the late Graham Tradition are from the Kunghit Haida project. These enable us to describe an archaeological culture type consisting of very little flaked stone, considerable ground bone, and only a little ground stone, mainly abraders. However, we must set against this the presence of more flaked stone artifacts at non-Kunghit late Graham sites; for example, there is as much flaked stone at 922T and 923T as there is in all of the Kunghit project excavations. The prominence of flaked stone at Richardson Ranch shows that it was known further north and into the historical period as well. It would be surprising if there were not regional variation in technology across Haida Gwaii, although we truly do not yet have the data to evaluate the nature and kind of this variability. With present knowledge, however, it is best to treat the Kunghit data as a southern variant of a later Graham Tradition that elsewhere included a flaked stone industry.

Unilaterally barbed and composite toggling harpoons, although varying in material, barb shape, and type of line attachment, again have a wide if not universal distribution on the Northwest Coast. Similar unilaterally barbed harpoons occur in all horizons of the Prince Rupert assemblage dating from 3000 BC to AD 1830 (MacDonald 1969; MacDonald and Inglis 1981). They appear at the Central Coast sites of Grant's Anchorage (Simonsen 1973:47-48), McNaughton Island (Carlson 1976:103, 110, 111), Namu dating to 4550 BP (Luebbers 1978:62), and Roscoe Inlet (Drucker 1943:91), as well as at Yakutat Bay, Kachemak Bay, and Angoon of southeastern Alaska (de Laguna et al. 1964:131-132; de Laguna 1934:80, 1956:164, 1960:111). Composite toggling harpoons, although considered rare on the northern Northwest Coast (Drucker 1943:123), occur infrequently after AD 500 in the Prince Rupert sequence (MacDonald and Inglis 1981:52), and are reported by Drucker (1943) for nearby Schooner Passage. They also occur at the Grant's Anchorage site (Simonsen 1973:49), McNaughton Island after 200 BC (Carlson 1976:103), and Roscoe Inlet and "Kilkitei Village" (Drucker 1943) on the Central Coast. Composite harpoons are found at nearby Namu by AD 1470 (Luebbers 1978:56), and both harpoon types occur at Kwatna after AD 480 (Carlson 1972).

Bird-bone tubes, a common element of Drucker's Northern Aspect (1943:123), are also typical of the Kunghit assemblage. Again, these are found throughout the coast and are common at Yakutat Bay, Kachemak Bay, Angoon (de Laguna et al. 1964:164; de Laguna 1934:97, 1960:121), the Prince Rupert Harbour sequence (Macdonald 1969:23; MacDonald and Inglis 1981), Schooner Passage (Drucker 1943:104), and the Hecate Strait–Milbanke Sound area (Simonsen 1973:57). A number of worked bird-bone tubes have been categorized as bone drills. The serrated working tip is typically polished, with the outer surface showing fine encircling striations under magnification. These occur in all three components of the Prince Rupert Harbour sequence (MacDonald and Inglis 1981). Awls, and notably the ubiquitous bird-bone splinter awl, represent another common Northwest Coast tool type prevalent in the Kunghit assemblage. The number of awls in the Kunghit assemblage finds agreement with Hoskins's remark (n.d.) in 1791 on their use of "sharp bone of various sizes, according to the fineness of the work [in making] their garments, which are sewed together." Also, several examples of bone wedges and chisels from the Kunghit sites are comparable with those from Kachemak Bay (de Laguna 1934:100), the Prince Rupert Harbour sequence (MacDonald 1981), Roscoe Inlet, Schooner Passage (Drucker 1943:97, 104), and Grant's Anchorage (Simonsen 1973:57). Harpoon points can be unilaterally or bilaterally barbed, or can be composite, including self-armed types. These examples point to the presence of a broad sphere of interaction across the northern coast at least in the later Graham Tradition, although Sutherland (2001) also points to less detailed evidence for similar social interaction in the early Graham Tradition.

Intriguing parallels can also be noted between the late Graham Tradition as known from southernmost Haida Gwaii and the West Coast Culture Type (Mitchell 1990) of Vancouver Island. From Kunghit Island to Cape Scott on Vancouver Island is about 200 kilometres, the same distance as to Waglisla (Bella Bella). Both the west coast of Vancouver Island and Kunghit Haida territory are extremely exposed environments on the open Pacific, and share a similar resource regime of abundant flatfish, rockfish, and sea mammals, and relatively poor salmon runs. In general, both archaeological cultures are characterized by an extreme bias towards bone technology, especially bird bone, and a near absence of flaked stone. Unusual artifacts in common include self-armed composite toggling harpoons and ground bone and stone fishhook shanks of similar styles. The subsistence base is similar and there is a strong signature of whale use present in both areas. Indeed, there is a possibility that the Haida may have hunted whales in common with their Nuu-Chah-Nulth neighbours (Acheson and Wigen 1989). The late Graham Tradition is also the time when the West Coast Culture Type starts to expand into Queen Charlotte Strait, and it may be the time when the Central Coast Nuxalk people become isolated from other Coast Salishan speakers (Mitchell 1988; McMillan 1999). This pattern of Wakashan expansion may have had a peripheral effect on the southernmost Haida. It is interesting to note the account of the burning of the Kunghit Haida village of *SGang gwaay* by the Koskimo and/or Ditidaht people from Vancouver Island around 1892 (Acheson 1998:94), suggesting some history of antagonistic relations to the south. At the least, we feel that when considering the cultural relations of the late Graham Tradition, Vancouver Island should be considered a potential source of substantial interaction and mutual influence.

The Kunghit faunal remains point to the importance of salmon and rockfish. Halibut is also important but almost certainly underrepresented for taphonomic reasons. A temporal trend towards increased salmon and fewer rockfish in more recent times is apparent in the Kunghit area, but the more limited evidence so far available from elsewhere is equivocal on this point. Invertebrates are heavily weighted towards California mussel, with littleneck and butter clam also occasionally important. Alcids are an important food everywhere, as are sea otter and harbour seal. Caribou remains are very rare or absent in Gwaii Haanas, which probably represents habitat differences, not a real change from its earlier pattern of exploitation as known from Graham Island. In the absence of a good late Graham Tradition sample from central and northern Haida Gwaii, however, the possibility of declining caribou numbers towards the present must be kept in mind – it is certainly present in quantity at Blue Jackets Creek and in the terminal Moresby Tradition component of Cohoe Creek (Chapter 13). The Blue Jackets Creek and Cohoe Creek caribou are of normal size (Severs 1974a; R. Wigen, personal communication), suggesting that Dawson caribou became dwarfed sometime in the past 4,000 years. This may be because the spread of dense red cedar climax forests presented an adaptive challenge to this species.

Referring back to the 4000 to 2000 BP data gap (Figure 14.1), the differences between early and late Graham assemblages are accentuated. Flaked stone declines markedly, while ground bone becomes dominant. By the late Graham period, there is evidence for most of the hallmarks of the historic Haida way of life, some aspects of which, such as the large consolidation villages, are actually historical developments. However, technological development, subsistence, and settlement are poorly known and equivocal across the Graham Tradition. While the data present the appearance of cultural change between the early and late Graham Traditions, the patchy nature of the evidence leads us to conclude that the overall culture history of Haida Gwaii is one of long-term continuities with occasional technological innovations and inflections. These may be instigated by environmental changes such as sea level rise and forest succession, or by contact with neighbours to north, south, and east. We suspect that it is only with more knowledge of organic technology, and more research designed to fill the middle Graham Tradition data gap, that it will become possible to clearly sketch the outline of Haida culture history through the developmental phases to its historical expression.

Summary

The Graham Tradition remains a broad concept. Causal explanations for the appearance of shell middens, along with the accelerated growth in the number of sites and material inventory remain fundamentally ecological, stressing greater resource availability and/or extraction capabilities on the part of the people of the Graham Tradition. The nature of this relationship remains vague, however, in view of the general lack of detailed faunal data needed to decipher Graham Tradition subsistence behaviour. There is an apparent broadening and greater emphasis placed on marine resources on the islands during this period (Fladmark et al. 1990), which is supported by the Gwaii Haanas data for the late Graham period. At present, the lack of a better distribution of sites, both temporally and spatially, precludes overly firm conclusions about reasons for cultural change during this time period.

Material culture from Graham Tradition sites suggests a pattern of both cultural continuity and regional differences. Other Northwest Coast groups see some cultural change around 5000 BP and 2000 BP (see Clark 2000;

Coupland 1988; McMillan 1999; Mitchell 1988; Maschner and Reedy-Maschner 1998; Simonsen 1973). There is increasing evidence for heightened cultural interaction, growing conflict, and change throughout the coastal region to indicate that this is, for whatever reason, a pan-coastal phenomenon. Further research in Haida Gwaii should help resolve how, and to what extent, this isolated archipelago was part of the larger Northwest Coast system.

Evidence of personal adornment, including the use of labrets and grave inclusions, indicative of growing social stratification, occurs at Blue Jackets Creek after 5000 BP. There is greatly increased shell midden accumulation and/or preservation and increased evidence of intergroup trade, both elements that may be traced to the earlier period. Site content becomes increasingly similar to that found on the mainland coast, supporting the concept of a broad co-tradition for the region, but hardly suggests an upheaval or supplanting of the preceding cultural form. These trends do correspond in time with when the materially important red cedar (*Thuja plicata*) became regionally abundant (Hebda and Mathewes 1984). While this is an ecological event, one of its possible material outputs – larger, more seaworthy canoes – might well have instigated greater social interaction across the North Coast.

The Haida are the most geographically isolated group of people on the Northwest Coast. There is a tremendous story of how the historical Haida cultural pattern, with its complex social structure and material culture, sedentary winter villages with large plank dwellings, ranking, and elaborate ceremonialism, arose in this remote and challenging archipelago. Haida oral histories tell this story in vivid terms. Archaeology has the potential to tell the story of everyday life across the millennia. While only preliminary conclusions can be drawn from the modest amount of archaeology done so far, we believe that Haida culture history can be characterized by long-term in situ development, with important but intermittent external influences from their neighbours.

Acknowledgments
We thank Daryl Fedje for the invitation to contribute to this book, and for sharing his catalogue of radiocarbon dates. We also thank Tina Christensen for sharing unpublished data and her own compilation of radiocarbon dates. Rebecca Wigen contributed miscellaneous faunal reports and an unpublished radiocarbon date. Trevor Orchard provided access to recent unpublished data from the Gwaii Haanas Environmental Archaeology Project. Nicole Smith kindly assisted at the editorial stage.

15
Gwaii Haanas Settlement Archaeology
Steven Acheson

Settlement archaeology has long been seen as a way of gaining insight into the social and otherwise intangible aspects of an archaeological culture. Arguably, embedded within the material considerations of resource availability, procurement technology, and the matter of safety in settlement patterning are the social considerations. For the Haida, as for other Northwest Coast groups, settlement distribution and form served to channel the complex interplay of kin, locality, and class affiliation for its members. Settlement patterns thus serve as a record of past social form and of cultural change available to archaeological inquiry and scrutiny.

The late 1700s were a period of intense economic activity for the Haida and other Northwest Coast groups, with European economic advances to the Northwest Coast. This encounter has garnered considerable attention, though hardly agreement, in the scholarly literature about its effect on these societies. This chapter focuses on the settlement archaeology of Gwaii Haanas to show that the onset of European contact and the subsequent maritime fur trade had an immediate and far greater impact on Haida settlements for reasons that take into account not only the agents of change but also the process. Among the Kunghit Haida for example, two exceptionally large settlements emerged within the historical period, *SGang gwaay,* located on the eastern shore of Anthony Island, and *Qayjuu,* a lesser-known settlement at Benjamin Point. Bordering on Kunghit territory, and within the park boundary of Gwaii Haanas, is *T'anuu* village. Although *T'anuu* is not a Kunghit village, its settlement history is closely intertwined with that of the Kunghit and will form part of the discussion.

A decidedly more complex settlement history is emerging, owing largely to a growing body of archaeological data for the region not available to earlier researchers (Blackman 1990; Cole and Darling 1990; Drucker 1965; Duff 1964; Fisher 1977). This chapter explores the timing, scope, and implications of this trend towards large multilineage settlements in light of recent archaeological survey findings for Gwaii Haanas (Chapter 16). Arguably, large, seasonally occupied multilineage winter villages did not typify the late pre-contact settlement pattern among the Kunghit, as observed historically on the islands and elsewhere on the Northwest Coast (e.g., Blackman 1990:244-245; Fladmark 1975:70, 292; MacDonald 1983a, 1989; Mitchell and Donald 1988:309-312; Swanton 1905b:71). The implications of this shift to large, seasonally occupied multilineage villages are multifaceted and far-reaching, and include such basic themes in Northwest Coast research as the seasonal or annual round, ranking and political authority, ownership of resources, wealth distribution, and trade.

Background and Setting

Haida, or "people," as they collectively refer to themselves, are a distinct language family whose members historically recognized four dialectic-territorial divisions. The other divisions – "People of Skidegate Inlet," "Inlet People" of Masset Inlet and Sound, and "Separate Island People," otherwise known as Central, Northern, and Kaigani Haida (Murdock 1934b:355) – survive to this day. The Kunghit Haida, or "island end people," inhabited the southern end of Haida Gwaii, corresponding closely to the boundaries of Gwaii Haanas National Park Reserve/Haida Heritage Site (Figure 15.1). Their territory extended along the west side of Moresby Island to a point just below Tasu Sound, and on the opposite shore the northern reaches of Juan Perez Sound, including part of Lyell Island (*Lgakungwa-I*) (Brown 1869:390; Newcombe n.d.a, n.d.b; Swanton 1905a:277-278), all of Kunghit Island, and surrounding smaller islands. Bordering on the Kunghit were the "People of Skidegate Inlet" or Central Haida, whose closest major settlement to the Kunghit was *T'anuu*, located inside the northern boundary of Gwaii Haanas.

The region is exceedingly rich in marine resources, including the halibut and salmon that are all-important in Haida subsistence behaviour, which provided for a level of settlement stability uncharacteristic of small-scale or kinship-based societies. The ethnographic and historical literature depicts Haida settlements as having functioned primarily as a winter residence for a number of lineage groups residing in large, cedar-plank houses. Historically, these groupings formed dense, socially stratified population aggregates, which customarily dispersed through the spring, summer, and autumn months to take advantage of seasonally available resources. What has been missing from this depiction of Haida settlement behaviour is an appreciation of how widespread and long-lived this pattern was.

Methods and Sources

Diverse lines of evidence were considered for this study and include detailed archaeological survey data compiled over the last two decades, with a review of the historical and ethnographic literature on the cultural area. A working premise for integrating these data is that, when critically assessed,

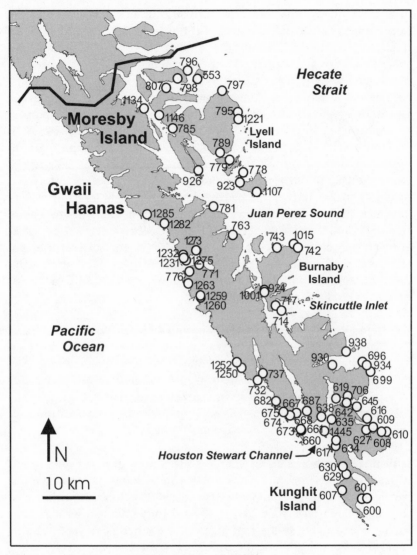

Figure 15.1 Study area showing towns in Gwaii Haanas.

they offer a historical perspective on the ways in which the Native community met and adjusted to changing social and economic conditions, which then enables us to consider both the possibilities and content of pre-contact conditions (see Wylie 1985).

Primary archival sources included the journals, logs, and charts of early traders, and later accounts and records of government agents, missionaries, travellers, and ethnographers to the region. Ethnographic works consulted date mostly from the late 1800s and the first half of the twentieth century

(Boas 1889, 1898; Curtis 1916; Dawson 1880; Murdock 1934a, 1934b, 1936; Newcombe n.d.a, n.d.b; Swanton 1905a, 1905b, 1905c, 1912). More recent studies include those of Blackman (1979, 1990), Boelscher (1989), and Stearns (1984), but with few exceptions (see Newcombe n.d.a, n.d.b), these were conducted among Haida groups other than the Kunghit.

Archaeological data include the original findings of a three-year archaeological survey and testing program conducted in the 1980s for the purpose of reconstructing the history of *SGang gwaay* (Acheson and Zacharias 1985; Acheson 1987). Recognized as the finest surviving in situ example of Northwest Coast architecture and monumental art, the village was designated a World Heritage Site in 1981 when little was known about its history and that of its inhabitants. That study covered the immediate shoreline of all of Kunghit Island, surrounding smaller islands, and the southernmost part of Moresby Island within a 20-kilometre radius of *SGang gwaay* village. Subsequent survey coverage was expanded in the 1990s, with the establishment of Gwaii Haanas, resulting in detailed site inventory data for all of the Kunghit traditional territory and that of the neighbouring *T'anuu* people on the east coast to as far north as Tangil Peninsula.

The Haida Village: Size, Distribution, and Composition

> The single-clan [lineage] village appears to represent a more static and rudimentary socioeconomic situation, not in some hypothetical scheme of social development but within the actual boundaries of our reconstruction of Northwest Coast society on the basis of historical and traditional accounts. (Wike 1957:309)

Settlement form is a defining feature of the Northwest Coast cultural pattern, but for all its importance it is not well understood. The study of Haida settlement form faces a number of challenges common to settlement archaeology. Swanton (1905b:268) recognized early on when recording the names of Haida village sites that many were not necessarily contemporaneous settlements. Without the benefit of an established chronology, he realized that some had undoubtedly been abandoned for extended periods or had otherwise reverted to seasonal camps, while others were never more than campsites despite their designation of *'Ilnagaay* (town). To complicate matters, towns could be known by several names (Swanton 1905b:120). Acknowledged but not fully appreciated by the ethnologists of the day was the apparent restructuring of Haida settlements due to historical factors.

Both Boas (1898:25-26) and Swanton (1905b:66) had reasoned that the Haida multilineage village was originally the dwelling place of only one lineage, since many lineage and sublineage names were derived from a mythical or actual place. The village community, Boas concluded, was the "constituent element" of the moiety, and "each family formed originally a local unit, so that each village would seem to have been inhabited by one family only" (1898:21, 25). Curtis (1916:187) shared the view that the unilineage village was the earlier form. While both he and Murdock (1936:16) saw the development of multilineage communities as a historical phenomenon, only Murdock attributed their development to population decline. Central to the Kunghit's story, and which illustrates in unequivocal terms this evolution in settlement form, is *SGang gwaay* town. On the Kunghit's northern frontier was the village of *T'anuu*, belonging to an amalgamation of Central Haida and which similarly shares a central place in their story.

SGang gwaay Town (660T)

The earliest historical reference to *SGang gwaay* village appears in the Hudson's Bay Company census of 1835-41 reporting a population of 308 living in twenty houses at "Quee-ah," a derivation of the leading Raven chief "Xo'ya" (Douglas n.d.; see Swanton 1905b:295). A less likely identification by Newcombe (n.d.a) was that of *Lk!iä'*, a former *T'anuu* town. Not until 1853 was the village location charted with the Kunghit name of "Shangoi" (*SGang gwaay*) (Inskip n.d., vol. 2:39-42).

Kunghit oral accounts, compiled by Newcombe and Swanton around 1900, report a complex settlement history culminating at *SGang gwaay* village (Newcombe n.d.a; Swanton n.d., 1905b). Collectively known as *GA'ñxet Xa-idAga-i* ("Island End People") or alternatively as "Ninstints people" in recognition of the reigning chief, nine Kunghit lineages resided at *SGang gwaay* village (Swanton 1905a:268, 272).

All the Kunghit Raven lineages traced their origins to one of two towns, *Xaagyah* ("Stripped") Town (714T), situated within Skincuttle Inlet, or *7a tana* ("House"; 778T) located on the northern boundary of Kunghit territory (Swanton 1905a:75-79). The Eagle lineages of the opposite moiety were founded at *Lga'dAn*, a village on the south shore of Moresby Island near Louscoone Inlet (Swanton 1905a:92-93).

By their own accounts, the leading *Sa'ki* lineage of Gowgaia Bay led by Ninstints settled at *SGang gwaay* before the end of the 1700s (Swanton 1905a:94), joining an already established Raven settlement (Newcombe n.d.a). The timing of their resettlement was within just four generations from the time of Swanton's study in 1900, which finds compelling support in both historical and ethnographic accounts (Colnett n.d.; Haswell n.d.; see also Howay 1941:327). Following the *Sa'ki* Eagles' lead to *SGang gwaay* were two chiefs from Louscoone Inlet, and members of *Naagaas* village (732T) at Nagas Point. Another former village chief to settle at *SGang gwaay* was

Q!Anxawa's (juicy grass), a *Xa'gi* Raven from *Q'adajaans* (661T), a small village located on the northwest shore of Anthony Island. Other Kunghit lineage chiefs' names later associated with *SGang gwaay* include *Wada'* of Skincuttle Inlet and *Kiä'nskina-i* of Juan Perez Sound.

The *Ta'dji* Ravens led by *Kiä'nskina-i*, who was both lineage head and village chief of *Qayjuu* village, were the last group to join *SGang gwaay*. At its height, *Qayjuu* consisted of some sixteen houses at Benjamin Point. Historical records place their move to Anthony Island before 1853 (Cooper n.d.; Newcombe n.d.b; Trevan n.d.:293).

Supporting evidence of the historical merger of these family groups, as well as an indication of their relative status within the community, comes from both the house and associated monumental poles at *SGang gwaay* itself. According to Swanton's list (1905a:283) of houses, one of the largest houses, measuring 13.6 by 13.7 metres, is assigned to the leading *GA'ñxet* Eagles. The scale of this house, with its large excavated floor and prominent central location within the village, meets all the criteria for having been the residence of a high-ranking chief (Curtis 1916:129). Another, measuring 14.1 by 14.85 metres and the second of only two with an excavated floor, was owned by one of several generations of *Sa'ki* Eagle lineage chiefs with the name Ninstints (Swanton 1905a:282). The two most prominent houses then included that of Chief Ninstints, located near the south end of the village, and the other belonging to members of the opposite moiety, the *GA'ñxet* Eagles. The southern section of the village was then dominated, but not exclusively inhabited, by Eagle lineages, while the a northern section "belonged" primarily to Raven families.

Despite all the outlying Kunghit groups having joined *SGang gwaay* by the mid-1800s, the town's future was short-lived. Although Dawson (1880:170B) reported sight unseen that there were still "a good many" people living at the village in the summer of 1878, the Canada 1881 census lists just thirty-one Kunghit, the eldest going by the name of *Xo'ya*. Three years later Newton Chittenden (1884:24) landed at *SGang gwaay* to find among "20 houses, 25 carved poles, and 20 burial columns" just "30 inhabitants." The Methodist missionary G.F. Hopkins (1885:175), established at Skidegate, wrote in October 1885 that the Kunghit numbered only "20 or 25" and resided mostly with the *T'anuu* people. One account has the village being abandoned shortly thereafter, with their former enemies, the Skidegate, assisting with their move to Skidegate Mission (Duff and Kew 1958:62). Church records, however, reveal that the move northward by the various southern groups to join the Skidegate was a more protracted affair. Many Kunghit, as well as Skedans people, first moved to New Klue (Duff n.d.). New Klue, named after the *T'anuu* chief *Xe-u*, was a new settlement consolidating the few surviving southern communities at Church Creek on the south shore of

Cumshewa Inlet in 1887 through the encouragement of the Methodist Church (Henderson 1985:4).

For the Kunghit, their extinction as a community came in the winter of 1887-88, when the few remaining families abandoned *SGang gwaay* for New Klue and Skidegate (United Church of Canada 1888).

T'anuu Town (796T)

For all its size, little is known of *T'anuu's* apparently short history. At its height about 1840, there were perhaps as many as 40 houses and over 500 inhabitants at *T'anuu* (Work 1945), although Swanton (1905a:283) managed to solicit only 26 house names in 1898. The National Museum of Man survey in 1968 identified 25 house sites (MacDonald 1983b:89), while the more recent Parks Canada inventory confirmed 24 house sites with the likelihood of more along the shoreline that have since eroded out (A. Mackie, personal communication).

Located on the eastern shore of an island of the same name on Laskeek Bay, the village of *T'anuu*, like *SGang gwaay* to the south, became a formidable settlement, serving to attract members from the region's many surrounding towns in the early 1800s. Relations between these two settlements also evolved in step with their changing fortunes, from one of enmity to eventually sharing a common village. Swanton (1905a:105) described the *T'anuu* people as the Kunghit's greatest enemy, a view supported by Newcombe (n.d.b), who wrote in 1901: "The waters here seem to have been kind of debatable ground between the rival chiefs of the Ninstints and Gitkûn [i.e., Kloo or *T'anuu*] districts."

Lineages from both moieties were also present at *T'anuu*, including two closely aligned, senior ranking Eagle families, Those Born at Skedans and the Djigua Town People. Acknowledged as founding members of *T'anuu*, these two Eagle lineages traced their origins to Cumshewa Inlet by way of another major settlement, *Hlk'yaah 'llnagaay* ("Chicken Hawk Town"; 795T), at Windy Bay on Lyell Island. Fourteen of the twenty-four named houses belonged to this moiety. The Ravens were represented by just the one lineage, Those Born at Qadasgo Creek, who owned the other ten houses.

From all accounts (Newcombe n.d.b; Swanton 1905a), *Hlk'yaah 'llnagaay* appears to have been a major settlement. Abandoned sometime before the mid-1800s, at least ten house sites have been confirmed archaeologically, the largest and most imposing measuring 15 by 13 metres (Chapter 16).

T'anuu, or *Klue* village after the name of the ruling Eagle chief, appears to date no earlier than 1735, according to MacDonald (1983b:89), which places its beginnings within the proto-historical period. Abandoned shortly after 1885, its inhabitants moved to Cumshewa Inlet, settling New Klue on Church Creek. New Klue was a short-lived community, lasting only ten years.

The Settlement Archaeology of Gwaii Haanas

The concept of settlement archaeology consists of three structural components: the individual house, the arrangement of houses within a settlement, and the distribution of settlements. Each of these offers some insight into the social forces at work in settlement form. Relative size and structural complexity of houses can serve as a reliable measure of social differences and of settlement permanency. The layout of a settlement can further reveal differences in status, as well as kin and class affiliations. And at the regional level, such factors as trade networks and personal safety can influence settlement distribution. Having already described briefly what is known about the ownership and timing of occupation of key villages and individual houses, we now expand the discussion to characterize and explain discernible patterns in the settlement archaeology of Gwaii Haanas. Particular attention is paid to several variables, including house size, the number of houses per town, and shoreline setting.

Wave exposure is the single most important consideration in all classification schemes used to define shoreline setting. Over half (54.39 percent) of the entire Gwaii Haanas shoreline is defined by Harper and colleagues (1994) as protected waters whereas just 14.93 percent is described as exposed or very exposed. Wave exposures vary greatly between the four established coastal subregions, West Coast Outer, Hecate North Inner, Hecate North Outer, and Hecate South Outer, each with their distinctive geomorphology, biota, and wave exposure levels. Significantly, the West Coast region, according to Harper and colleagues (1994), is probably the highest-energy coast in Canada, with much of the region being categorized as very exposed. For the purposes of this analysis of settlement distribution, a modified scheme based on Harper and colleagues' (1994) model (see Chapter 16) is used to categorize the macro-setting of individual towns, rather than their immediate environment, as either exposed, semi-protected, or protected. The reason for this modification is that while sites occur within small, enclosed bays or small archipelagos, which afford some protection from an otherwise extremely exposed shoreline, the macro-setting has the greatest influence on the kinds and amount of resources available, and also meets the need for defensive sites. It is no coincidence that defensive sites, which are typically isolated, steep-sided islands, pinnacles, or headlands, occur mostly within an exposed coastal setting. Aside from offering unrestricted views of the surrounding waters, the degree of exposure itself made an attack that much more difficult. Both were strategic considerations in settlement location.

Newcombe (n.d.b) reported that there were as many as 35 "permanent villages" within the extreme southern region alone, of which 28 town names survive in the ethnographic literature. Another 33 town names complete the tally of settlements cited for the Kunghit (Table 15.1). Although this

Table 15.1

Tally of settlements cited for the Kunghit Haida

Number	Name	Post-contact component	Exposure	Number of houses/town	Average house area	Max. house area	Min. house area	Standard deviation	Coefficient of variability	Lineage affiliation/chief Comments
553T	Q'angru 'llnagaay		E	5	189.55	300	120	59.80	0.32	Owned by the Q'una qiirawaay, Chief Qayts'iid (Swanton 1905a:278).
600T	Sqaay 'llnagaay ("the village that faces south")		E	1	35.00	35	35	0	0	Qayiuu Ravens, Chief Tc'la'nu al qola'i (Swanton 1905a:277). Also known as Rangxiid 'llnagaay and appears on a number of maps as "Cape St. James village."
601T	Sdasraaws 'llnagaay		E	1	40.00	40	40	0	0	"A camping place ..." (Newcombe n.d.b).
607T	S7waanaay 'llnagaay	y	E							Camp or village (Newcombe n.d.a), owned by the Rangxiid qiirawaay (Swanton 1905b:288). Known also as Kundi 'llnagaay (after Enrico n.d.:16).
608T	Saawdan gwaay 'llnagaay	y	SP	2	56.00	63	49	7	0.13	Early historical component; northern boundary of the Kunghit on the west coast.
609T	Sindaas kun 'llnagaay ("village on a point always smelling")		E	7	53.75	76.5	37.5	13.77	0.26	Qayiuu Ravens (Newcombe n.d.a; Swanton 1905a:277).

▼ *Table 15.1*

Number	Name	Post-contact component	Exposure	Number of houses/town	Average house area	Max. house area	Min. house area	Standard deviation	Coefficient of variability	Lineage affiliation/chief Comments
610T	Xyuu daw 'Ilnagaay ("the village that fishes toward the south")	y	E	1	144.00	144	144	0	0	Qayjuu Ravens, Chief Xo'ya (Swanton 1905a:277; n.d.). Early historical component.
616T	Hlaagi 'Ilnagaay		SP	5	104.10	120	82.5	15.91	0.15	Qayjuu Ravens (Swanton 1905a:277).
617T	Tada stl'hng 'Ilnagaay ("shimmering point town")		E	1	35.00	35	35	0	0	
619T	Gwaay 'Ilnagaay (island town)	y	P	1						Sa'ki Eagles, Chief Ninstints (Newcombe n.d.a). No house data available; used by Ninstints as a fishing camp.
627T	(Unknown)		P	1	24.00	24	24	0	0	
629T	Dang7un 'Ilnagaay		E							
630T	Saawdan gwaay 'Ilnagaay ("Place of Ooligans")		E							
634T	gaydu 'Ilnagaay		E							
635T	7awggadids kun 'Ilnagaay ("no wind point town")		E							
638T	Sthuugin		E	1	300.00	300	300	0	0	
642T	Nawdaas 'Ilnagaay		SP							Qayjuu Ravens, Chief Xo'ya (Newcombe n.d.a).
645T	SLlndadji		SP							"An old village" (Newcombe n.d.a, n.d.b).

				n						
660T	*SGang gwaay 'llnagaay* ("Red Cod Island Town")	y	E	17	111.83	215.93	35.2	43.50	0.39	*Qayjuu* Ravens, Chief *Xo'ya* (Newcombe n.d.a), Sa'ki Eagle, Chief Ninstints (mid-1800s) (Swanton 1905a:277). Extended historical occupation abandoned 1887-88.
661T	*Q'adajaans 'llnagaay* ("one who gets angry with another and talks against him behind his back")		E	2	156.50	160	153	3.5	0.02	*Xaaqyah 'laanaas* Ravens, Chief *Q!Anxawa's* (juicy grass) (Swanton 1905a:277).
667T	*Hlradan 'llnagaay* ("he will suffer for it" [as from overwork]		E	4	120.00	120	120	0	0	*Sgidaay 'laanaas* Eagles, a branch of *Rangxiid qiirawaay*, chief unknown (Swanton 1905a:277, 1905b:208). Estimates only.
668T	*Xuud jiihldaa 'llnagaay* ("to go for cedar")		E	4	120.00	120	120	0	0	*GA'ñxet qe'gawa-i* Ravens of *Tc!a'al* (Gold Harbour) and Kunghit *GA'ñxet qe'gawa-i* Eagles, Chief *Xi'liñas* (Thunder) (Swanton 1905a:270, 277).
673T	*Qayjuuxaal 'llnagaay*		E							*Rangxiid qiirawaay* Ravens, Chief *Cillngaas* (Swanton 1905a:277).
674T	*Ts'uura 'llnagaay*		E							
675T	*Cil 'llnagaay* ("leaf"/ "medicine" town)		E							*Xaaqyah 'laanaas* Ravens, Chief *Sgyaamsin hltanwaad* or *Skiä'msm ltA'nwat* (hawk-feathers) Newcombe n.d.a; Swanton 1905a:277) or *gawsgid* (T. Tait in Newcombe n.d.a).
682T	*Stl'lndagwaay 'llnagaay* ("the village deep in the inlet")		E							
687T	*Taaji 'llnagaay*		SP					0		Chief *Ninsgunilgas* (?) (Newcombe n.d.a).

▲

▼ *Table 15.1*

Number	Name	Post-contact component	Exposure	Number of houses/town	Average house area	Max. house area	Min. house area	Standard deviation	Coefficient of variability	Lineage affiliation/chief Comments
696T	Hlaaýi 'lhagaay		E	2	36.00	45.6	26.4	9.6	0.27	*Ta'dji* Ravens, Chief *Kiä'nskina-i* (Swanton 1905a:268, 277) or *Klu-iya'ns* (Newcombe n.d.a).
699T	Qayjuu 'lhagaay ("Songs-of-Victory-Town")	y	E	16	94.36	132	42	26.60	0.28	
706T	Styuu jin 'lhagaay	y	E							
714T	Xaagyah 'lhagaay	y	SP	18	56.18	93	32.5	20.61	0.37	*Xaagyah 'laanaas* raven town, Chief *Waadaa*. No data on 9 houses; "old Indian settlement" (Poole 1872:163).
717T	7aydi 'lhagaay	y	SP	1	45.00	45	45	0	0	
732T	Naagaas 'lhagaay ("town inhabited")		E	4	120.00	120	120	0	0	*Xaagyah 'laanaas* Ravens or Slaves, a sublineage of the *Xaagyah 'laanaas* Ravens (Swanton 1905a:199), Chief *Ga-i'ns* (the dead shellfish, cod, etc., drifted ashore by the waves) (Swanton 1905a:277) or *LagEne'nigodEn* (Newcombe n.d.a). Estimates only.
737T	Jidralraay 'lhagaay		SP	2	80.00	80	80	0	0	
742T	Srwaay kun 'lhagaay	y	E							Chief *Giid 7ang gasdlaas* (T'anuu people) (Newcombe n.d.a). A town of sufficient size to accommodate "20-30 houses," according to Newcombe (n.d.a), bordering on Kunghit territory.

ID	Name		Type							Notes
743T	(unkown)		SP	1	12.00		12	0	0	
763T	Raduu 'lnagaay		SP	1	63.00		63	0	0	Possibly a T'anuu town although identified as belonging to the Kunghit (Curtis 1916a; Swanton 1905a:278)
771T	Yahgu 'laanaas 'lnagaay		SP							
776T	Juu q'yuu 'lnagaay		E							Owned by the *Saahgi qiirawaay*, Chief *Nang sdlaana gaws* (Swanton 1905a:277).
778T	7a tana 'lnagaay		SP							*Taaji 'laanaas* Ravens, Chief *Kyaansginaay* (Swanton 1905a:277). Small village on House Island.
779T	(Unknown)	y	SP	3	50.00	63.75	30	14.47	0.29	Early historical component.
781T	(Unknown)	y	SP							
785T	Xuud tsixwaas 'lnagaay	y	P	4	82.00	143	48	36.70	0.45	*Xaagyaj 'laanaas*, Chief *Gitiqo:nai* (Swanton 1905a:277). Early historical component; Kunghit town on the northern border with the T'anuu.
789T	Raysigaas q'iid 'lnagaay	y	SP	6	47.46	89.25	30	19.98	0.42	Chief *Kisdlaay qwaan* (Kunghit) (Newcombe n.d.a). Early historical component; "Place where there is no surf town."
795T	Hlk'yaah 'lnagaay ("Chicken Hawk Town")	y	E	10	195	195	0		0	Described as a Kunghit town by Swanton, although assigned to *Xe-u* of the *Q'una qiirawaay* Eagles (Those Born at Skedans) (Swanton 1905a:97, 278). Data available for only 1 house; early historical component.
796T	T'anuu 'lnagaay	y	E	24	112.50	244.9	60	43.35	0.39	Belonged to *Q'una qiirawaay* Eagles, Chief *Gid qun* (Swanton 1905a:278). Extended historical occupation abandoned after 1885.

▲

Number	Name	Post-contact component	Exposure	Number of houses/town	Average house area	Max. house area	Min. house area	Standard deviation	Coefficient of variability	Lineage affiliation/chief Comments
797T	Tllgang xang 'llnagaay	y	P	14	209.59	306.25	60	73.23	0.35	Owned by Jiigu7ahl 'laanaas Eagles, Chief Xe-u (Swanton 1905a:278). Hudson's Bay Company era; reverted to a fishing station after abandonment in mid-1800s.
798T	Hlraaydlln 'llnagaay		P							Suus xáaaydaraay, a branch of Q'una qiirawaay, Chief Qayts'id (Swanton 1905a:278).
807T	Sk'udas 'llnagaay	y	P	8	51.28	110	25	26.87	0.52	Owned by Jiigu7ahl 'laanaas Eagles, Chief Gina skilaas, brother of Xe-u (Swanton 1905a:277). Largest house centrally located.
923T	Rayran kun 'llnagaay	y	SP							Southernmost T'anuu town (Swanton 1905a:278). Early historical component.
924T	Q'iid 'llnagaay	y	P							Owned by Q'iida 'laanaas, a branch of the Xaagyah Ravens, Chief T'aaru 7un kingaang (Swanton 1905a:277), or possibly Taarun qina ("Heavy Spring Salmon") or T'aarun qina ("Heavy Feather") (Newcombe n.d.b). Early historical component.
926T	(Unknown)	y	SP	1	160.00	160	160	0	0	
930T	Uccah's village	y	SP					0	0	
934T	(Unknown)		E	1	120.00	120	120	0	0	

938T	*T'awts'i s'nalaa*									
1001T	*'Laanaa darangaa*		P	1	126.00	126	126	0	0	Owned by the *Saahgi qiirawaay*, Chief *Gid qun*.
1015T	*'Laanaay gwaas 'Ilnagaay*		E							
1107T	*Xiina t'awts'iraay*	y	E	3	33.33	50	25	11.79	0.35	
1134T	*Huulaagwaans 'Ilnagaay?*	y	P	4	48.19	76.5	21	21.35	0.44	"A Ninstints town." Dates to around the mid-fur trade period.
1146T	(Unknown)		P	1	25.00	25	25	0	0	
1221T	*Qayjuudaal 'Ilnagaay?*	y	E	10	84.05	169	36	40.51	0.48	Owed by the *Xaldaangrads sils*, Chief *Ran darungaay* (Swanton 1905a:278). Known also as *Sgaama q'yuu 'Ilnagaay* (Swanton 1905b:404).
1231T	*Srilgi 'Ilnagaay*		E	3	76.00	98	60	16.08	0.21	Owned by the *Saahgi qiirawaay*, Chief *Nan sdins* (Ninstints) (Swanton 1905a:277).
1232T	(Unknown)		E							
1250T	*Xa jihldaa 'Ilnagaay*	y	E	2	58.13	60	56.25	1.88	0.03	Chief *Nang q'ulaas*. "Still several houses here when Ninstints was a young man" (Newcombe n.d.a).
1252T	*Gwaayaay qan jins*		E							"Once a fair-sized town"; "inner part was a touts [fort] of old" (Newcombe n.d.b).
1259T	*K'in.gi'Ilnagaay*		E							
1260T	*T'awjiugins*		E	1	40.00	40	40	0	0	
1263T	*Kaawdaas 'Ilnagaay*	y	E	2	68.38	94.5	42.25	26.13	0.38	Chief *Nang q'ulaas* (Newcombe n.d.a).
1273T	*Ruusgi*		SP							
1275T	*K'ayhlaan*		E	10	102.35	153	38.25	38.98	0.38	Abandoned at contact.
1282T	*Sq'iin 'Ilnagaay*		E							
1285T	*K'iijaa raws*		E							"Camping place" (Newcombe n.d.b).
1445T	*Sin7id 'Ilnagaay*	y	E	8	44.81	100	15	31.54	0.70	

Note: E = exposed; SP = semi-protected; P = protected.

tally was based on the fieldwork of Charles Newcombe, Swanton (1905a:277-278) later listed just 24 "towns" for all of Kunghit territory. Associated with many of these were fort sites (Newcombe n.d.a, n.d.b).

Substantially fewer ethnographic town names are documented for the *T'anuu* people, with just nine listed in the published literature (Swanton 1905a). Of the seventy-three town sites identified in Gwaii Haanas, forty-four sites (about 60 percent) show evidence of houses in the form of timbers, posts, and/or berms and ridges that delineate house floors. With few exceptions, these sites appear in the ethnographic or historical literature as towns (Table 15.1). The remaining entries (N = 29; about 38 percent) include sites listed as towns in the ethnographic literature and, while lacking surface features that would indicate the presence of houses, do contain cultural deposits. Excluded from the analysis are those sites assigned only as possible house sites where there is no supporting ethnographic or historical documentation, and those locations having a name but no supporting archaeological evidence.

Five of the six named Kunghit village sites test-excavated in the earlier study, including *Xyuu daw* (610T), *Tada stl'lng* (617T), *Xuud jihldaa* (668T), *Cil* (675T), *Taaji* (687T), and *Qayjuu* (699T), also revealed the stratigraphic signature of well-used living floors over time. Deposits indicative of living floors typically consisted of humus-rich sediments with traces of shell, charcoal, ash, sand, and/or pebbles as secondary constituents (B. Stucki, personal communication; see Wigen and Stucki 1988).

Setting

Irrespective of town size, the majority of settlements occur on or very near the exposed outside coasts (Figure 15.2). Figure 15.2 shows the distribution of the seventy-three towns according to size (large, >5,000 square metres; medium, 1,000 to 4,999 square metres; small, <1,000 square metres) and coastal setting. Only ten of the seventy-three are found within fully protected waters, and of these just three (619T, 785T, 924T) measure greater than 1,000 square metres. *Gwaay* (619T) is situated on the strategic waterway of Houston Stewart Channel at the entrance to Rose Inlet, a setting not dissimilar to those sites found on the outside coast. The other two, *Q'iid 'llnagaay* ("Strait Town" on Burnaby Narrows; 924T) and *Xuud tsixwaas 'llnagaay* ("Hair-seal Low-Tide Town" on Darwin Sound; 785T), are situated adjacent to waters rich in marine resources. Forty-four of the town sites are found on the exposed outer coast, including equally exposed smaller offshore islands. Nineteen towns occur within the transition zone between the exposed and protected shoreline, typically within small sheltered coves at or near the entrance to large inlets and bays. No correlation exists between the location of town sites and salmon spawning streams in the area,

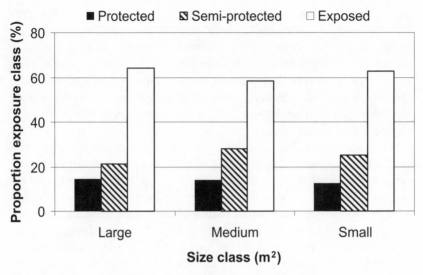

Figure 15.2   Size and exposure of Gwaii Haanas towns (*N* = 73).

despite the well-documented dietary importance of salmon among the Haida (see Dawson 1880:110B).

Another line of evidence supporting a pre-contact pattern of small, widely dispersed settlements is the faunal record. Key to the large multilineage winter village model is the seasonal round. As late as 1878, Dawson (1880: 117B) observed the relationship of settlement distribution and resource activities:

> The Haidas reside in these permanent villages during the winter season, returning to them after the close of the salmon fishery, about Christmastime. A portion of the tribe is, however, almost always to be found at the permanent village, and from time to time during other seasons of the year almost the whole tribe may be concentrated there. The villages differ somewhat in this respect. When the territory owned by its people is not very extensive, or does not lie far off, *they live almost continually in the village.* When it is otherwise, they become widely scattered at several seasons. [emphasis added]

The seasonal range and variety of fauna from the larger sites sampled on the extreme south end of Gwaii Haanas in fact reveal little distinction between winter and summer site use. For the eighteen sampled sites, there is little inter-site variation in the faunal assemblages. Rockfish (*Sebastes* sp.), salmon (*Oncorhynchus* sp.), sea otter (*Enhydra lutris*), harbour seal (*Phoca vitulina*), alcid, and California mussel (*Mytilus californianus*) are the dominant species for most sites, followed by herring (*Clupea pallasii*), northern sea lions (*Eumetopias jubata*), and whales (Cetacea) (Wigen 1990). Although the Haida salvaged drift whales, the possibility of their having hunted this mammal has until recently been largely discounted. Some ethnographic and historical sources (see Blackman1979:51, 1981:9; Colnett n.d.; Collison 1915: 244; Deans 1888:42), however, along with the number of whale bones recovered from some Kunghit sites (Wigen 1990), do indicate the existence of a modest whaling tradition.

At the other end of the food spectrum, the large California mussel totals 95 to 100 percent of the shell weight through time for thirteen of the sixteen sites analyzed (Keen 1990). Known as *táaxáaw* (sweet food), this extremely abundant food source was exploited by the Kunghit Haida throughout the year, contrary to ethnographic claims (see Boit in Howay 1941:373; Colnett n.d.; cf. Dawson 1880:112B). "The great salmon harvest of the Haidas," on the other hand, occurred only from the middle of August to October in the southern Queen Charlotte Islands with the arrival of the chum salmon (Dawson 1880:110B). Although poorly represented in the faunal assemblage due to taphonomic processes, a significant food fish was the halibut (*Hippoglossus stenolepis*). Halibut were fished year-round (Dawson 1880:109B), although they were most abundant and accessible in spring and summer. Northern sea lions were also hunted throughout the year (Blackman 1979:51; Newcombe and Newcombe 1914:133), while alcids were sought in the spring when nesting in burrows along the outer coast (Niblack 1890:278; Newcombe n.d.b; Poole 1872:283-284).

The distribution and availability of these resources placed a premium on locating a settlement along the outside coast. Well-established settlements such as *Naagaas* (732T), *Qayjuu* (699T), *SGang gwaay* (660T), *Xuud jihldaa* (668T), *Taaji* (687T), *Xyuu daw* (610T), and *Srilgi* (1231T) were located on key points near the entrances to the large inlets and Houston Stewart Channel. The inhabitants had the added advantage of controlling and intercepting important food sources, including herring, salmon, and the seals and sea lions that pursued them, as they became seasonally available in these waters. Another advantage was the ability to monitor the movement of others from these vantage spots.

The Matter of Protection: Defensive Sites

Personal protection was second only to access to resources in determining settlement location. Fortifications, or *t'awts'is*, dot the coastline of Gwaii Haanas and references to fortified or defensive sites in the region appear throughout the ethnographic and historical literature (e.g., Colnett n.d.; Fleurieu 1801:295, 353; Haswell n.d.; Ingraham 1971; Table 15.2). So prevalent are fortified sites on the North Pacific that many see it as one of the defining traits of Northwest Coast cultures (see Moss and Erlandson 1992). Joseph Ingraham, who traded extensively in Haida Gwaii in 1791, remarked that "their villages are always near some high land which affords places of safety when attacked by their enemies" (1971:112).

Typically, defensive sites occupy small, precipitous islands, or "stacks" and headlands on the open coast where access could be both easily monitored and defended against surprise attacks. Newcombe (n.d.a, n.d.b) recorded no fewer than fifteen such sites, located on small, precipitous islands, stacks, or headlands within the southern reaches of Gwaii Haanas, adding that "there were eight or nine isolated forts sometimes occupied for months." A strong correlation exists between defensive or fort sites and the type of coastline. For all of Gwaii Haanas, some thirty-two fort sites are documented, based on ethnographic and/or archaeological data, with most (75 percent) occurring along the exposed coastline although this shoreline type represents only 32 percent of the entire coastline (Table 15.2). Defensive sites occur at or in the vicinity of *SGang gwaay* (660T), *Qayjuu* (669T), *Naagaas* (732T), *Xuud jihldaa* (668T), *Taaji* (687T), *Xyuu daw* (610T), *Tada stl'lng* (617T), *Jidralraay* (737T), *Stl'lndagwaay* (682T), and *Sindaas kun* (609T). The fortification at *Naagaas* includes substantial earthworks with associated houses, while others appear to have been simply suitable landforms used on an intermittent basis.

Fortifications appear to be a relatively late phenomenon on the Northwest Coast, coinciding with apparent growth in village size and in the size of individual households within the last 2,000 years. Viewed as a proxy measure of both population growth and increasing status differences along with this trend in settlement and house size, these trends coincide with the evidence for conflict (see Maschner and Reedy-Maschner 1998). Warfare appears most intensive at times of material change in the archaeological record, marking a new phase or period, an observation that would also describe the contact period.

With a few notable exceptions, settlements appear strategically located on the outside coast to meet the mutual needs of resource availability and security. Two of the largest Kunghit sites, *SGang gwaay* and *Qayjuu*, are situated at each entrance of Houston Stewart Channel. Aside from having a well-defined historical component, both sites are characterized by discontinuous cultural deposits. The pattern is consistent with ethnographic accounts of the late arrival of the *Ta'dji* Ravens from *Qayjuu*, who settled the northern half of *SGang gwaay* village. Cultural deposits within this area of the village are noticeably sparse (Acheson 1982). *T'anuu* differs in this regard only in the fact that sparseness of deposits characterizes the entire site. *SGang gwaay* served as a nucleus to which other communities gravitated during the historical period, whereas *T'anuu* appears to owe its very origins to the process of amalgamation.

Table 15.2

Identified fort sites in Gwaii Haanas

Parks Canada site no.	Place name	Site type	Comments
660T	*SGang gwaay 'llnagaay*	TOWN	Ninstints village; also associated with a fort located "on a fair-sized island between Anthony Island and a group of 'bare rocks'" (Newcombe, n.d.a).
682T	*Stl'lndagwaay 'llnagaay*	TOWN	Associated with a fort (DM).
732T	*Naagaas ('llnagaay)*	TOWN	Associated with a fort (DM).
794T	*Ray t'awts'is*	DM	"Blood Fort" (Swanton 1905a:278; 1905b:418-424).
938T	*T'awts'i s'nalaa*	DM	"Fort on Bluff Point" (Jimmy Jones in Newcombe n.d.b).
1107T	*Xiina t'awts'iraay*	DM	Located on southeast corner of Ramsay Island.
1173T	*Q'axada t'awts'is*	DM	On an islet northwest of Murchison Island; possibly Flowerpot Island; south of Dog Island.
1217T	*Tllga kun t'awts'iraay*	DM	South of *Hlk'yaah 'llnagaay* (795T).
1250T	*Xa jihldaa 'llnagaay*	TOWN	Associated with a fort (DM).
1260T	*T'awjuugins*	DM	Associated with *K'in.gi 'llnagaay* (1259T).
1270T	*Gweek'aa gwaas t'awts'l*	DM	Fort; may also apply to the town of *Ts'iihllnjaaws* (1272T) (Newcombe n.d.b).
1278T	*Nang gwaay t'awts'l*	DM	"Many small houses used in time of war" (Elijah Ninstints in Newcombe n.d.b).
1498T	*Laanaa t'awts'is*	DM	On an islet off the north shore of Tanu Island, midway between the east and west ends; just inside Selwyn Inlet (Swanton 1905a:278; 1905b:408, 412).
	Ji7arang t'awts'iraay	DM	Defensive site on the Kerourard Islet, closest to Kunghit Island.
	Tyuuxans	DM	St. James Island.
	Tada stl'lng t'awts'iraay	DM	Fort, presumably associated with site *Tada stl'lng 'llnagaay* (617T).

Styuu t'awts'is	DM	Fort, possibly located on Annette Island.
K'ildaga t'awts'iraay	DM	Fort; located "at N. side of entrance to Luxaena" (Newcombe n.d.a).
Cil t'awts'iraay	DM	Described as "a small island fort about 2 miles within the inlet [Flamingo Inlet]" (Newcombe n.d.b).
Gan̄gahlda t'awts'iraay	DM	Fort; "visible through N. channel opp. Ninstints; near *Taaji* (687T); island fort on E side of entrance to Louscoone Inlet; pillar-like rock" (Newcombe n.d.a).
T'awts'i radgins	DM	Fort; outside Houston Stewart Channel, just to the north.
Q'al t'awts'iraay	DM	Fort; supposed to be in Rose Inlet.
Quxan t'awts'is	DM	Fort; supposed to be on the east side of Rose Inlet.
Sq'aws t'awts'l	DM	"Small island fort in front of *Sqaws giidawaay 'llnagaay* (931T)" (Newcombe n.d.b).
Q'una t'awts'iraay	DM	Southeast corner of Burnaby Island; "a rock fort on the point just to the south of Blue Jay Cove" (Newcombe n.d.b).
Jaats'aad t'awts'iraay	DM	Fort on Howay Island; "on the island in Granite Bay" (Newcombe n.d.b).
Qal q'uhlgi t'awts'iraay	DM	
T'awts'is xiillaa	DM	"Clearly there was a fort on the islet just off the north of Alder Island" (Enrico n.d.:52).
?	DM	
7a tana t'awts'iraay	DM	Fort located on a small peninsula at the south end of House Island. May be 1002T, but is likely further to the southwest.
Cay t'awts'is	DM	Fort; near Hotspring Island (Swanton 1905b:428).
Tlldaraaw t'awts'is	DM	Fort; on an islet between Dog and Lyell Islands (Swanton 1905a:278; 1905b: 402); one of the Stansung Islets (Enrico n.d.:60).

Note: DM = defensive midden

House and Home

Of all the towns identified in Gwaii Haanas, *SGang gwaay, Qayjuu,* and *T'anuu* are the largest, having the greatest number of houses, some of the largest houses, and the greatest ranges in house size (Table 15.1; Figure 15.3). The pattern with smaller settlements is for greater intra-site uniformity in house size, as shown in Figure 15.3. More striking, however, is the strong correlation that exists between the coefficient of variation in house size for individual towns with two or more houses and the presence of a historical component. Excluded from the analysis were fourteen single-house "towns," a form observed by George Dixon (1789:205) at Hippa Island on the west coast of Graham Island in the summer of 1787. Of these fourteen towns, only three have an identified historical component.

Twenty-eight of the seventy-three towns have a historical component, indicating their occupation or reoccupation within the contact period. They include the two largest Kunghit settlements, *SGang gwaay,* which has the distinction of being the last and the largest (Acheson 1985), *Qayjuu* at Benjamin Point, and the Central Haida village of *T'anuu.* More telling is that without exception, the largest settlements have a well-defined historical horizon, as do a number of intermediate-sized towns. The process of amalgamation has all the appearance of proceeding in measured stages, from small to intermediate to very large multilineage settlements.

An earlier judgmental survey of Moresby Island supports just such a trend (Hobler 1976). Twenty-four of 36 identified villages had fewer than 5 houses per site, 6 settlements contain 5 to 9 houses, and the remaining 6 villages

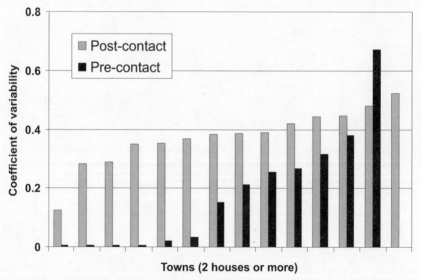

Figure 15.3   Variability in house size in Gwaii Haanas (*N* = 192 houses, 27 towns).

(17 percent), all with a well-defined historical horizon, have 16 or more houses. For Gwaii Haanas there are nearly twice as many pre-contact towns, 45, as there are those found to have a historical component ($N = 28$), whereas the average number of houses per town more than doubles in the case of historical settlements from 2.73 to 7.63. Coinciding with this trend, the average area of post-contact settlements jumps nearly threefold, to 6,953 square metres from 2,659 square metres (Tables 15.3 and 15.4).

Arguably, village size and the size of individual houses provide a relative measure of the wealth, and by inference the status, of a community and of individual house groups (see Blackman 1981; Coupland 1988:271-280). The highly visible exception to the pattern is *K'iijaa raws* (1285T), the town at Puffin Cove on the west coast, which has a coefficient of variability of 0.70. One possible explanation for this anomaly is that the site may in fact have been occupied within the early contact period so that the high coefficient is really an indicator of a historical component. Another consideration may have to do with its setting, situated as it is within one of very few protected locations on an otherwise extremely exposed coast, which required a larger number of family groups than usual to share the site.

Table 15.3

Town size pre- and post-contact based on site area

Data for towns with recorded dimensions	Exposure code			
	1	2	3	Total
Pre-contact				
Count of number of towns	4	10	29	43
Average number of houses per town	0.5	1.11	1.90	1.58
Average of area (m sq)	1,378	3,782	2,448	2,659
Max. of area (m sq)	3,600	15,000	9,350	15,000
Min. of area (m sq)	70	36	130	36
Post-contact				
Count of number of towns	6	9	13	28
Average number of houses per town	5.17	3.44	6.39	5.18
Average of area (m sq)	7,784	4,161	8,501	6,953
Max. of area (m sq)	33,600	16,200	42,500	42,500
Min. of area (m sq)	1,500	375	600	375
Total count of towns	10	19	42	71
Total average of number of houses per town	3.3	2.28	3.23	3
Total average of area (m sq)	5,122.43	4,078.06	4,011.69	4,182.56
Total max. of area (m sq)	33,600	16,200	42,500	42,500
Total min. of area (m sq)	70	36	130	36

Table 15.4

Town size pre- and post-contact based on number of houses

| Data for towns | Exposure code | | | Grand |
with recorded house feature	1	2	3	Total
Pre-contact				
Count of number of towns	2	5	19	26
Average number of houses per town	1	2	3.11	2.73
Average of area (m sq)	347	1,682	2,796	2,393
Max. of area (m sq)	625	2,700	9,350	9,350
Min. of area (m sq)	70	264	130.5	70
Post-contact				
Count of number of towns	5	6	8	19
Average number of houses per town	6.2	5.17	10.38	7.63
Average of area (m sq)	2,422	4,505	9,233	5,947
Max. of area (m sq)	5,500	16,200	42,500	42,500
Min. of area (m sq)	1,330	375	600	375
Total count of towns	7	11	27	45
Total average of number of houses				
per town	4.71	3.73	5.26	4.8
Total average of area (m sq)	1,829	3,222	4,703	3,894
Total max. of area (m sq)	5,500	16,200	42,500	42,500
Total min. of area (m sq)	70	264	130.5	70

Five town sites with between 4 and 10 houses, and all exhibiting a well-defined historical component, have the next highest coefficients, clustering between 0.42 and 0.52. These are followed by *SGang gwaay* and *T'anuu*, which have strikingly similar coefficients of 0.389 and 0.385, respectively, although *T'anuu* village is nearly a third larger. It is another historical *T'anuu* settlement, though, located near Dodge Point on Lyell Island, that has the largest house. One of 14 houses identified at *Tllgang xang* (797T) measures 306 square metres. The next largest houses, measuring 300 square metres, are found at the pre-contact sites of *Q'angru* (553T) and *Stluugin* (638T). Whereas *Stluugin* has just the 1 house, *Q'angru* has 5, but the coefficient of variability falls to 0.315.

In general, the pattern implies growing material disparities between house groups within the larger multilineage towns, indicating a realignment of wealth and political authority among senior ranking families. The pattern is also consistent with the interpretation accounting for the proliferation of defensive sites on the Northwest Coast and their prevalence in Gwaii Haanas. How this was realized is the subject of the following discussion on the structure of Haida relations.

Haida Polity and the Politics of Change

As a kin-based society, all Haida relationships were legitimized and regulated by kinship ties and stratified by rank. The division of Haida society into two exogamous matri-moieties, Raven and Eagle, governed marriage and property exchanges. This division functioned as a regulatory device that underpinned reciprocal social obligations and material exchanges between individuals, families, and lineage groups. Kin groups were structured by rules of exogamy and matrilineal descent with avunculocal residence (see Bishop 1967:83; Murdock 1934b:358, 361; Swanton 1905a:66, 1912:32). The lineage consisted then of individuals genealogically linked through the mother.

Marriage was the single most important means of securing advantageous alliances upon which the strength of the kin group and one's social rank within the group depended. Cross-cousin marriage was the preferred arrangement, with moiety exogamy the only marriage prescription. The tendency was for both females and males to marry into their father's lineage, with cross-cousin marriages effectively combining uxorilocal and virilocal residence, which allowed for the consolidation or maintenance of both property and lineage members within the same household (Curtis 1916:120; Murdock 1934a:250; 1934b:364; Swanton 1905a:68; see Fox 1967:53, 187). This arrangement could conceivably result in the two highest-ranking chiefs of a multilineage village being father and son.

Haida society was also stratified according to a historically well-defined socioeconomic class structure. The unilineal descent group itself was cross-cut by three strata: *yahit* (nobility or chiefly class), *'sa'gida* (commoners), and *xAda'ngats* (slaves), who were attached as property. Chiefly authority was dependent on the relative wealth and number of followers at a chief's disposal and in turn sanctioned by public opinion and notions of generosity, honour, and obligation on the part of nobles – to be "fit for respect" (Boelscher 1989:70-71).

A hierarchical order was also recognized among the chiefs, who with their families made up the nobility. House chiefs, whose authority was near absolute within the confines of the household, according to Swanton (1905a:69), were the owners of the large cedar-plank dwellings that constituted the village (Boas 1889:36). House groups were the fundamental unit of production and consumption (see Mitchell and Donald 1988:313, 328) and were largely autonomous, with house chiefs orchestrating the economic activities of the household. According to Swanton, "each Haida household was so complete in itself that all it required was a name and a certain amount of isolation to develop into an entirely independent family, and there was a constant tendency in that direction" (1905c:333).

At the head of the lineage or sublineage was a "chief," who as trustee for the lineage's territory and resources, coordinated the political and ceremonial affairs of the lineage group. Their position, like that of the house chief, was inherited through the practice of primogeniture, although it was also partly personal and was achieved through the ability to display and redistribute wealth. A lineage chief's authority, Swanton concluded, was "a varying one, dependent on, and at the same time, limited by, the number and power of his house chiefs" (1905a:69). Above lineage heads were "town" chiefs (*lána-ôka*, or people's mother [Curtis 1916:119]), a position usually accorded to the highest-ranking, wealthiest house chief of the lineage that owned the town site. That women could also hold the title conforms both with the notion of the segmentary martrilineage and with Durlach's explanation (1928) for the derivation of the term *clansman* (i.e., those of one's mother's village) (see Bishop 1967:63; Haswell n.d.; Hoskins n.d.; Murdock 1936:16).

While this hierarchical arrangement appears straightforward enough, there is little agreement in the ethnographic literature concerning the nature and boundaries of political authority between the respective offices of town, lineage, and house chiefs. In noting the relative autonomy of lineage chiefs compared with that of town chiefs, Murdock (1936:16) concluded that the existence of multilineage villages prior to European contact was "quite exceptional," writing in 1934 that "no chief wields any actual authority outside the clan" (Murdock 1934a:238). Furthermore, lineage chiefs could not "command their obedience or punish insubordination" of house chiefs (Murdock 1934a:237; see also Dawson 1880:118-119B). Dawson (1880:118-119B) took the opposing view, claiming that the influence of the lineage chief, although far from absolute, "was doubtless very much greater in former times" than that observed in 1878. Both Swanton (1905b:69) and Curtis (1916:119, 187) felt that issues affecting the townspeople as a whole were decided by the town chief.

The historical record is not much clearer on the role of chiefs. While trading with the Haida in 1787, Dixon found that "every tribe ... is governed by its respective Chief, yet they are divided into families, each of which appear to have regulation and a kind of subordinate government of its own" (1789:227). Two years after Dixon's venture, Captain Douglas found the authority of Blakow-Coneehaw at Kiusta on northern Haida Gwaii "superior to that of any other chief whom we saw on the coast of America" (Meares 1790:367). That same year, traders credit Skidegate of the Central Haida "to be the Great Chife [sic] at the Queen Charlottes Islands" (Bartlett n.d.; see also Ingraham 1971:129). Later still, Poole (1872:108) observed in the early 1860s that chiefs of the southern region of the islands deferred "to the great Chief of the Siddans [Skedans] tribe." That Chiefs Blakow-Coneehaaw, Skidegate, and Skedans should represent the three recognized dialectic-territorial Haida divisions in Haida Gwaii – the Northern, Central, and Kunghit Haida, respectively – does imply, although it does not prove, a level of political authority beyond that of lineage and village emerging within the historical period.

The apparent ambiguity surrounding the authority of Haida town chiefs in the ethnographic and historical literature led Stearns (1984:198) to conclude that their function was largely symbolic, since she believed that the apparent overlapping and duplication of political roles with those of lineage and house chiefs would have been unworkable. Town chiefs, however, were not prevented from seeking greater authority at the expense of either lineage or house chiefs. A town chief's position was based on the same principles and involved the same groups and intergroup ties that ordered social relations generally. Given that the village, as an organizational unit, effectively both channelled and defined socioeconomic associations, the large multilineage village presented new opportunities for senior ranking chiefs to forge lucrative alliances and increase their status. The apparent ambiguity over the respective authority and responsibilities between town, lineage, and house chiefs may be best understood as a shift towards hereditary political unification with the establishment of multilineage villages (see Sahlins 1961:326; Earle 1989).

An Ethnographic Perspective

Support for this interpretation is found in the language itself. Haida residential associations, according to Durlach's detailed linguistic treatment (1928:163, 164) of kinship terms, appear to have cross-cut social relationships. The term *taxu* for "clansman," for example, denoted residential association, referring to the people of one's mother's village in contrast to *qe'gawas* (those born with you) from one's father's village. In effect, kinship relationships extended among descendants whose fathers were lineage mates (Boelscher 1989:105). Further, Durlach (1928:112) claimed that the clan system was a late development arising from a family system organized along village lines. Murdock agreed with Durlach's reconstruction, noting that the terms for grandfather, grandmother, and grandchild showed no cleavage along moiety lines and concluding that "the division into moieties is antecedent to, and more fundamental than, that into clans seems beyond all question. In origin the clan appears to be merely the localized segment of a moiety settled in a particular village" (1934b:383-384).

The distinction between "clansman" and those "born with you" introduces the question of residence patterns. Of relevance here is Murdock's observation (1949:183) that the rule of residence is normally the first aspect of a social system to undergo modification and kinship terminology is the last. While many factors influence choice of residence, the choices are few and each, in turn, dictates specific kinds of changes in the social structure that lead to the recognition of non-localized kin groups (Murdock 1949:

202-203, 209-210). Durlach's definition of *qe'gawas* implies virilocal residence, a practice that prevailed among the Haida in olden times, according to Swanton (1905a:66; see also Stearns 1984:192-193). Coupled with avunculocal residence, the Haida local group would ideally consist of matrilineally related men with their wives and dependent children. Curtis, on the other hand, found that "sometimes the bride's father would declare that he wished the couple to remain with him ... but more often the couple went to live with the husband's people, and if he were a chief ... she was compelled to accompany him" (1916:120). Similarly, Murdock declared that a married daughter lived with her father "unless her husband is a house chief or the heir apparent to a chiefship" (1934b:362).

The vulnerability of both unilineal groups and single-lineage villages to falling populations places renewed importance on the role of disease within the contact period (see Fox 1967:120). The late 1700s saw the first in a number of devastating smallpox epidemics that had a direct and immediate impact on the Native community. Six decades after European contact and the smallpox epidemic(s) of the late 1700s (see Bishop 1967:70-71, 83, 91-92; Fleurieu 1801:294; Green 1915:39; Swanton 1905a:105), a census commissioned in 1836 by the Hudson's Bay Company tallied 8,342 Haida, which included 308 Kunghit at *SGang gwaay* (Douglas n.d.), a decline of nearly 6,000 from a projected pre-contact population of around 14,500 Haida. The Haida in Haida Gwaii numbered only a tenth of that in 1881 (Canada n.d.), reaching a mere 588 individuals in 1915 (Duff 1964:39).

Dawson (1880:134B) cited a practice used by the Haida to cope with a rapidly declining population, in which children were transferred to a paternal aunt to effect descent through the father's lineage, which according to Niblack (1890:248) was in "danger not only of loss of prestige but of extinction" (see also Boelscher 1989:38). Curtis may have been referring to this practice when he stated that "generally a boy of good family went, even at a very early age, to live with a *paternal uncle,* where he was treated with considerable austerity and at the same time was taught what a man should know – fishing, hunting, speech-making, accumulating of property" (1916:126, emphasis added).

Swanton was unaware of the custom, but did find that a "chief's sons were ... sometimes adopted by other chiefs of the same side as their own fathers" (1905c:328). Boelscher, in turn, found little evidence of such forms of adoption among the Masset Haida, but they did "legitimate successions by extending lineage ties and even resorting to bilateral ties" (1989:109-110). Another practice was for a father to provide his son and wife with a house in the father's town (Swanton 1905a:66). The introduction of the son's wife's lineage in this manner was one way of establishing multilineage towns, but in Swanton's own mind (1905a:67) this practice alone could not account for the prevalence of multilineage villages.

For single-lineage communities, settlement distribution is critical to maintaining relations with one's natal lineage, the avunculocal matrilineal descent group (see Schneider 1961). Murdock (1949:215) concluded that the single-lineage community was unworkable in a matrilineal society, which prescribed a rule of uxorilocal residence requiring all male kin to leave the community (see also Fox 1967:103). Avunculocal "tribes," according to Murdock's cross-cultural survey (1949:74), consisted typically of single-lineage communities, the "clan-community," whereas the "clan-barrio" or multilineage village typified uxorilocal societies. In the case of multilineage villages, an uxorilocal residence pattern could effectively offset, or at least lessen, the threat to the community's survival at a time of demographic decline. Moreover, the importance of younger male and female labour to a house chief's ability to maintain an independent, viable household could be met by retaining married daughters within the household or acquiring another, younger wife, both of were at a premium during the historical period.

Cultural Contact and Village Structure
Kinship ties within Haida society functioned to control, among other things, both the amount of labour a chief could mobilize for collective purposes and the amount of political power he could exercise. With the advent of the maritime fur trade, new socioeconomic opportunities to enhance the political stature of chiefs, and by association their communities, were realized. Although they still adhered to the form and idiom of kinship (see Wolf 1982:96), the social and material content of this exchange, coupled with changing conditions of warfare, enabled successful chiefs to recast this relationship and consolidate and extend their authority beyond traditional bonds of kinship. Countering the inherent centrifugal tendencies of kinship and segmentary groupings, chiefs could move towards a new political order – the chiefdomship.

There can be little doubt that European contact and the subsequent pursuit of the maritime fur trade by indigenous communities affected settlement form, but in what way has not been given balanced treatment. One of two diametrically opposed interpretations of the impact of the maritime fur trade is the enrichment thesis, an interpretation that ostensibly embraces an ethnocentric material bias where initial contact had little impact on traditional conditions (see Drucker 1939, 1955:33, 1965:193-198; Duff 1964:57-58; Wike 1951:92). Here the trade resulted in little more than "an elaboration of existing culture patterns" (Fisher 1977:21), bringing "prosperity, an increase in wealth in a society already organized around wealth" (Duff 1964:57). The exploitation thesis or "decadence model," first posited in the detailed historical works of Howay (1925, 1932), saw a darker side to these events. Accompanying the influx of material wealth were the demoralizing effects of an ailing and increasingly dependent indigenous population on external trade goods. While possessing bargaining skills that gained enormous respect among maritime fur traders, Native participation in the trade meant more than a simple exchange of material goods for these communities. The extent to which the Haida came to rely on the trade in their mistaken belief "that the supplies furnished them would continue to be as liberal as at present" was remarked upon by Sturgis (n.d.b) in 1799. For the Kunghit, their growing reliance on trade goods, ranging from iron for weaponry and tools to muskets, clothing, and foodstuffs, could not be sustained with the rapidly declining fur resources of the region. Nor were they in a position to exploit the highly lucrative middleman role available to their mainland neighbours (see Acheson 1998).

Trade relations also proved exceedingly volatile. Revenge for real and supposed transgressions (see Acheson 1985, 1991), added to the growing Haida dependency on trade, contributed to a volatile mixture of suspicion, avarice, and violence. Continual renegotiation and increased demands by Haida and maritime traders alike were a constant source of friction. Also, the drive for a profitable venture in a highly competitive and increasingly unsure market encouraged desperate measures among some maritime fur traders. Nefarious practices such as holding chiefs hostage to force trade or to simply extort furs were all too frequent, as were attempts to cheat on the quality or quantity of goods exchanged for furs (Furgerson n.d.; Haswell n.d.; Sturgis n.d.a, n.d.b).

Accompanying these practices was the temptation on the part of the Native community to gain wealth by seizing a ship. By the beginning of the nineteenth century, no fewer than ten violent altercations had occurred between the Haida and maritime fur traders, of which four involved the Kunghit. They succeeded in capturing one of two ships lost on the islands before the end of the 1700s, but the cost in Kunghit lives was enormous (see Bartlett n.d.; Boit 1981:49-50; Haswell n.d.; Hoskins n.d.; Ingraham 1971: 204). Aside from these disastrous encounters negatively affecting an already declining population, trade was effecting change of another kind.

Groups strategically located to exploit trade now had the material, if not the military means, to expand and consolidate their sphere of influence. Chiefs Skidegate and Blakow-Coneehaw and the latter's successor, Edenshaw of Kiusta, made enormous political gains during this period, while other chiefly lines such as *Xo'ya* (Raven) and Ninstints (the one who is [equivalent to] two) of *SGang gwaay* were effectively extinguished. Those who gained access to arms and wealth outside of indigenous productive relationships were able to extend their authority over lesser leaders in other communities. The literature talks of "territorial chiefs" such as Coneehaw who had influence over neighbouring villages (MacDonald 1983b:188). This trend, coupled with the deadly virulent effects of infectious diseases, most notably smallpox, and chronic diseases such as scrofula, brought about the consolidation of surviving, and many unrelated, groups into one settlement. An inevitable outcome of this process was the realignment of property relations between corporate members and their chiefs. Niblack drew this inescapable conclusion, writing at the close of the nineteenth century that "the ownership of a tract of land by a family ... through being vested in an individual or in the head of that family, [amounted to] individual ownership" (1890:335).

For the Kunghit, the strain of heightened conflict, population loss, and the growing importance of the maritime trade, which could not possibly be sustained, worked to dissolve their many settlements. In spite of reconstituting themselves in the large multilineage villages of *SGang gwaay* and *Qayjuu*, circumstances and geography worked against them as they became increasingly isolated. The Kunghit were infrequent participants in the lucrative coastal trade after 1800, following the failure of the sea otter population in Gwaii Haanas. In startling contrast to the volume of trade conducted on the Northwest Coast between 1785 and 1825, involving some 230 to 236 vessels (Elliot 1957; Howay 1930, 1931, 1932, 1933, 1934), few ventured to southern Haida Gwaii after 1800 (see Cross n.d.; Ebbits n.d.; Furgerson n.d.; Gale n.d.; Haskins n.d.; Martain n.d.; Meek n.d.; Peirce n.d.; Porter n.d.; Reynolds 1938; Suter n.d.a, n.d.b; Walker n.d.). The bloody conflicts with Europeans in the late 1700s undoubtedly contributed to the decline and isolation from which the Kunghit were never able to recover.

Adding to their growing isolation, and likely a factor in their selection of *SGang gwaay* as a major village site, was the Kunghit's reputation for slaving. The economic value of slaves, who could be exchanged through Native middlemen for European goods, was not lost on the Kunghit, their neighbours, or the Europeans. The entry of 7 September 1842 in the Fort Simpson journal, days after an attack on the Tsimshian by a Haida raiding party, remarked:

It is said to be two tribes towards the South end of Queen Charlottes that commit all these depridations [sic]. These people never visit this place or other forts except a few of them in company with the other Haidars. They are said to obtain what scanty supplies they get by the sale of slaves taken in these plundering excursions, they are represented as being badly supplied with arms and ammunition but have themselves fortified on a rocky island which is very difficult of access and easily defended against a strong party and that the enmity of the other tribes which they have injured they keep a most vigilant watch and are not easily surprised. (Hudson's Bay Company n.d.a)

Table 15.5

Population of Haida villages, 1836-41

Village	Population	Houses
Lu-lan-na (Kiusta/Yaku)	290	20
Nigh-tan (Kung)	280	15
Massette (Masset)	2,473	160
Nee-coon	122	5
H-se-guang (Hiellan)	120	9
Skid de gates (Skidegate)	658	48
Cum-sha-was (Cumshewa)	286	20
Skee-dans (Skedans)	439	30
Quee ah (*SGang gwaay*)	308	20
Cloo (*T'anuu*)	545	40
Kish a win (Kaisun)	329	18
Kow-welth (Chaatl)	561	35
Too (Tian)	196	10
Total	6,607	430

Source: Douglas n.d.

Being frequently singled out for their role in trafficking slaves in this manner, the Kunghit must have been exceedingly wary of retributive raids as their numbers declined and felt that *SGang gwaay*'s remote setting surely offered them an enormous degree of security from surprise attack.

Before the last smallpox epidemic struck the islands in 1862, the Kunghit were already reduced to just the one village of *SGang gwaay* on Anthony Island. *Qayjuu* had been abandoned a decade earlier. Shortly after 1862 the Kunghit began their exodus northward to join the Skedans and *T'anuu* people within central Haida Gwaii. Their extinction as a community was complete by 1888, when the few surviving Kunghit at Anthony Island settled among their former enemies at Skidegate (United Church of Canada 1888).

Circumstances were not dramatically different for their former enemies, the *T'anuu*. Although closer to the centres of trade, they fared little better, abandoning their town on Tanu Island for New Klue shortly after 1885. They, along with remnant populations from *SGang gwaay* and Skedans, would fall in with the Skidegate before the turn of the century. The pattern was repeated among the Northern Haida until only two villages, Masset and Skidegate, survived at the close of the nineteenth century, from the thirteen villages enumerated for all Haida Gwaii in the years 1836-41 (Table 15.5).

Conclusion

Site inventory data collected in Gwaii Haanas in the last few decades have enabled a level of analysis in settlement archaeology rarely possible. Integration of these data with detailed historical and ethnographic observations relevant to the Kunghit, the original inhabitants of the region, reveals a decidedly more complete and complex picture of the region's settlement archaeology. In being able to track the continuities, shifts, and struggles within this one community following historical contact, the findings, while specific to this group, have important implications for our handling and understanding of settlement form and social structure well beyond Gwaii Haanas.

Although destined to become the last and largest of the Kunghit villages, *SGang gwaay* was only one among a number of small, nucleated year-round settlements within the region prior to historical contact. Initial comparisons between the survey results from the southern and the northern subregions of Gwaii Haanas suggested possible differences in settlement form. In the north there appeared to be far fewer towns, with more houses. It was recognized then that the pattern may be a function of both historical processes and the fact that surface evidence for smaller towns has been obscured, especially in the north, as a result of more recent development and land use (Mackie and Wilson 1994:29-30). On closer examination of the data, these distinctions have dissolved. Significantly, the evidence shows a surprisingly high degree of conformity not only in settlement form but also in the process of amalgamation. Amalgamation of small, independent single-lineage towns brought both allies and former enemies together as a means of accessing new sources of wealth with the advent of the maritime fur trade on the one hand, while cushioning the effects of a falling population on the other. Amalgamation offered the means of ensuring economic and social survival, while the act of amalgamation itself created a new social and economic order. It was a staged process where some pre-contact settlements, such as *SGang gwaay*, formed the nucleus of the later multilineage village, while others, such as *T'anuu*, owed their existence to the process of amalgamation.

All the considered evidence points to a pre-contact settlement pattern where the various corporate village groups residing within small, nucleated year-round settlements exploited a suite of similar resources, and many of these on a year-round rather than a seasonal basis. Most Haida of Gwaii Haanas resided on the outer exposed coasts, successfully meeting the dual needs of resource accessibility and protection. The pattern accounts for and reconciles much of the ambiguity in the ethnographic and historical literature concerning Haida social organization and political structure. The literature, in fact, is really a chronicle of the historical emergence, with all the accompanying social tensions, of a chiefdom order of political organization, including ascribed ranking, regional integration, a degree of permanence in the power of elites, and population concentrations. What may be truly ironic here is that the historical social and demographic forces that first promoted the unification of these lineages within the framework of the multilineage village would become so severe as to push these communities to the brink of extinction, if not extinction itself.

The Kunghit's story stands as an extreme though hardly unique example of the way indigenous communities of the region, and small-scale societies generally, strove to adjust to new social and economic circumstances. The shift in Kunghit settlement form with the onset of European contact was not a single dramatic event or a process divorced from the Haida themselves, but rather a complex social interaction, as autonomous corporate kin groups began to amalgamate. Faced as they were with falling populations and new economic opportunities, large multilineage settlements were a historical inevitability. For senior ranking chiefs, these amalgamated settlements, distributed as they were on the outside coast, provided an opportunity for greater political power at the expense of those seeking the material advantages and safety afforded by joining larger village units. The historical multilineage settlements of *SGang gwaay* and *T'anuu* stand as a testament to this realignment and enhancement of political authority, a trend that can be both traced and measured from the Gwaii Haanas settlement data.

Acknowledgments
Petro-Canada Resources and the British Columbia Heritage Trust generously funded the archaeological investigations on Gwaii Hanaas in the 1980s with the cooperation of the Skidegate Band Council. The field crew included Roberta Aiken, Alan and Morgan Brooks, Herman Collinson, Vicky Mills, Roberta Olson, Carmen Pollard, Bert Wilson, and Jordan Yeltatzie, all from Skidegate, and Doug Edgars of Masset. Sandra Zacharias directed much of the fieldwork with the assistance of Geordie Howe and Barbara Stucki. My thanks to Captain Gold of Skidegate, who provided valuable practical field assistance and guidance, and a special thanks to Alexander Mackie for his sustained help and interest in the study, and for the production of the figures. Parks Canada assisted with the dating of a number of radiocarbon samples, and the Archaeology Branch of the Government of British Columbia and the Royal British Columbia Museum provided field equipment and laboratory facilities.

16
Shoreline Settlement Patterns in Gwaii Haanas during the Early and Late Holocene

Alexander P. Mackie and Ian D. Sumpter

This chapter explores patterns of shoreline settlement during the early and late Holocene periods in Gwaii Haanas, southern Haida Gwaii. We examine the relationship between environmental variables and Aboriginal settlement during two time periods: 9500 to 9400 BP and 2000 BP to early post-contact times. While we are primarily interested in the early period settlement patterns, our method for discovering significant trends is to compare early site distributions with those for the relatively well known recent past. We test the relationships between four archaeological site types judged to be temporal representatives of simple (short-term) and complex (long-term) occupations. Differences in site locations and distributions that occur at either end of the Holocene may reflect changes in social organization, economic strategies, technology, settlement patterns, resource accessibility/management, environmental conditions, or perhaps differential preservation. This approach to analysis is made possible by the unusually large sample sizes we have from both early ($N = 111$) and late ($N = 325$) periods.

We propose that open-air middens and simple lithic scatters are broadly comparable as most are likely to have resulted from short-term activities related to resource procurement and processing. Some may have been campsites and others places where resources were processed without any camping. We suggest that both complex middens (towns) and complex lithic scatters were likely the result of longer-term habitation and the more complex activities that occur at such locations. There are major differences between early and late period sites that are likely largely attributable to preservation. Early sites are typically lag deposits of stone tools with all organic materials lost to erosion as they were inundated by rising sea levels. In addition, the early sites are likely to represent less than 100 years of use and thus had highly restricted opportunity to accumulate deposits, especially compared with the late period sites that are on landforms available to site formation for twenty times longer.

Paleoenvironmental work has indicated that 9500 to 9400 BP sea levels were 1 to 3 metres lower than modern-day levels in southern Haida Gwaii (Chapter 2). A basic operating assumption of this chapter is that modern configurations of most shorelines and beaches are analogous to those existing when the intertidal lithic sites were laid down. We propose that the intertidal and adjacent marine configuration and associated habitat and distributions of resources would be highly comparable because few shorelines show any signs of erosion or extensive deposition. We expect that in these areas most species available will have been much the same in the two time periods and will have existed in similar absolute or relative densities. Environmental differences between the early and late periods likely had more influence on type and distributions of terrestrial and anadromous resources than on marine resources.

These assumptions are supported to some extent by recent investigations on Ellen Island in southern Gwaii Haanas (Chapter 11). At this 9,400-year-old habitation site (1325T), the marine faunal assemblage "is similar in character to that of [nearby] recent (2000 year BP) archaeological assemblages" (Fedje et al. 2001:118). It is often noted that shellfish recovered from a site reflect the local environment (cf. Erlandson 1994; McLay 1999). Shellfish at Kilgii Gwaay occur in proportions similar to what would be expected from local modern shorelines. There is about 80 percent mussel and 12 percent clam and other bivalves in the assemblage; 80 percent of shorelines within 1 kilometre of the site could support mussels and other rock dwellers, while 20 percent was suitable for sediment dwellers like clams. Acheson's data (1998) from eight Kunghit Haida sites with large faunal samples lead to a similar conclusion. At these sites, the percent of rock dwellers that were excavated have a fairly strong correlation ($r^2 = 0.75$) with the proportion of shorelines within 1 kilometre that are suitable habitat for such species. Likewise, the percent of sediment dwellers correlates ($r^2 = 0.76$) with the proportion of nearby clam habitats.

Background

This study is based on archaeological inventory data collected over the past twenty-five years by archaeologists and Haida heritage specialists. To date, over 600 sites have been documented along 1,690 kilometres of shoreline. Almost 60 percent of the sites were recorded during six field seasons of systematic survey that commenced in 1984 and continued annually from 1991 through 1995. Information gathered from field survey programs dating between 1972 and 1999 are also presented.

Past Inventories

Archaeological inventory projects in Gwaii Haanas began with preliminary and non-intensive surveys of the east and west coasts of Moresby Island in the early to mid-1970s (Ellis 1974; Hoover 1973; Hobler and Seymour 1975; Hobler 1976, 1978). During 1984, Acheson and Zacharias (1985) conducted a systematic survey of the modern shoreline of Kunghit Island and adjacent areas, supplemented with test excavations in 1985 and 1986 (Acheson 1991, 1998). The establishment of Gwaii Haanas in the late 1980s initiated a multi-year inventory program beginning with a series of surveys of the modern shoreline of all Gwaii Haanas areas north of the Kunghit study area from 1991 through 1994 (Fedje 1993; Fedje et al. 2002; Zacharias and Wanagun 1993; Eldridge et al. 1993; Mackie and Wilson 1994, 1995). This was fol-lowed by inventories of selected inland raised beach landforms and inter-tidal zones on the east coast (Christensen 1997; Chapter 12). While some surveys were made of lakeshores and into the upland areas, no inland sites were found that are not associated with past or present shorelines, so we are able to look only at site distributions along the marine edge.

Site Survey Methods
The Gwaii Haanas shoreline surveys consisted of detailed inspection of all coastal margins with archaeological potential that could be accessed. In 1984, survey of the Kunghit area was usually confined to 30 horizontal metres from the beach (Acheson and Zacharias 1985). Subsequent coastal surveys were concentrated in a 100-metre-wide margin, or up to elevations of about 15 metres above high tide, whichever came first. Prior to 1993, single visits were usually made to particular locations, which were recorded and mapped in detail. Beginning in 1993, crews adopted a multiple-visit survey technique that increased site yields. Table 16.1 shows that as survey methods improved over time, inventories achieved higher site densities along walked shorelines, with fewer sites located during subsequent visits. Also, as knowledge of sea level history improved, more intertidal lithic scatters were located.

Archaeological Site Inventory Results
A total of 604 site locations were identified on survey programs in Gwaii Haanas between 1972 and 1999 (Table 16.1). These sites are diverse in con-tent, featuring evidence of pre-contact and/or post-contact cultural activ-ity. Some locations have evidence of only a single type of activity; others appear to have greater complexity, with evidence of multiple activities at the same location for substantial periods of time.

Early and Late Period Sites
To investigate early and late Holocene period settlement patterns in Gwaii Haanas, the distribution of four site types and their relationships to spe-cific environmental data were compared. For this study, our four site types include: (1) early period simple (intertidal lithic scatters); (2) early period

Table 16.1

Major survey program results in Gwaii Haanas

Survey area	Primary investigator	Years of main survey	Coast length (km)	% Coast walked	Intertidal lithic scatters	New site records	Sites/km walked coast
S. Coast & Kunghit Island	Acheson,	1984	496	55	1	78	0.53
	Hobler	1974-75			3	17	
	Others	Other			15	49	
SE Coast	Zacharias	1991	235	76	11	55	0.69
	Christensen	1995			1	6	
	Hobler	1974-75			4	12	
	Others	Other			9	50	
Central E. Coast	Eldridge	1992	365	60	10	52	0.66
	Christensen	1995			4	8	
	Hobler	1974-75			2	34	
	Others	Other			24	51	
NE Coast	Mackie	1993	279	58	24	97	0.85
	Christensen	1995			2	12	
	Hobler	1974-75			1	14	
	Others	Other			0	14	
W. Coast	Mackie	1994	315	16	0	45	1.11
	Hobler	1974-75			0	3	
	Others	Other			0	7	
All Gwaii Haanas			1,690	53	111	604	0.68

complex (intertidal lithic concentrations); (3) late period simple (open-air middens); and (4) late period complex (Haida towns). Types 1 and 3 represent remnants of short-term, temporary habitation or use, while types 2 and 4 are from longer-term residential use. These site types can be assigned to two Haida Gwaii archaeological culture types based on sea level, elevation, and geographical indicators. The early period intertidal lithic sites are from the Kinggi culture type (Fedje and Christensen 1999) and date to between approximately 9500 and 9400 BP. The late period sites fall within the latter part of the Graham Tradition (Fladmark 1990; Chapter 14), ranging from approximately 2000 to 200 BP.

The archaeological data used for this analysis include information recorded to the end of 1999. We have limited our analysis to 436 sites (111 early, 325 late components) at 418 site locations, including 18 that have both an early and a late site component. A random sample of 400 non-site locations was selected to assist in the analysis and is used to provide expected values representative of all Gwaii Haanas shorelines for comparison with all variables.

Because early period sites tend to be found in protected locations and are unlikely to survive in more exposed locations, it is possible that differences are attributable to differential preservation, and so we also test relationships just within the Hecate North Inner Coastal Region (HNI) (Figure 16.1), one of five coastal regions defined by Harper et al. (1994) for Gwaii Haanas. This region has almost entirely protected and semi-protected shores, with a very small proportion (4 percent) of semi-exposed shores. As we have the greatest confidence in survey results from this area, their use also controls for inter-observer variability.

Early Period Sites

Early period sites ($N = 111$) are those lithic scatters that are most certain to be in situ, albeit heavily eroded during marine transgression and regression. For greater certainty, we have removed from our sample any intertidal lithic sites associated with nearby raised beach sites that may have eroded and redeposited lithics in the intertidal zone.

Complex Intertidal Lithic Scatters

Complex intertidal lithic scatters ($N = 18$) are defined as those locations with seventeen or more surface lithics that display clustering in their distributions and usually include formed tools. We chose seventeen lithics as a natural break in the distribution of numbers of flakes and tools present at all the intertidal lithic scatters, which also coincides well with the presence of clustering within the lithics. Some are associated with broken rock that appears to be from fires. Having evidence for multiple activities and higher-intensity use, we suggest that these complex sites result from longer-term residence.

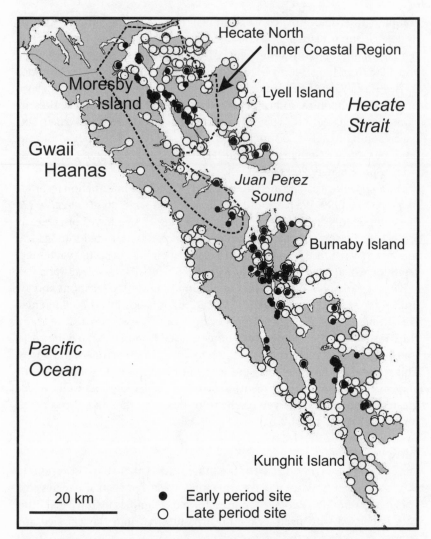

Figure 16.1   Distribution of early and late period sites, Gwaii Haanas.

Simple Intertidal Lithic Scatters

Simple intertidal lithic scatters ($N = 93$) contain fewer than seventeen surface lithics and have no clear evidence of clustering or spatial structure. These likely represent short-term, less intensive site use.

In trying to understand how much may be missing from these sites and thus how comparable they could be to their modern equivalents, we look to the Kilgii Gwaay 9450 BP shell midden on Ellen Island in the southern part of Gwaii Haanas (Fedje et al. 2001; Chapter 11). This site is similar to many more recent shell middens, although it has chipped stone and pre-served wood artifacts. We note that it is not uncommon for shell middens on the BC North Coast to have only one artifact (perishable or stone) per cubic metre of deposit. Thus, a lithic scatter with only ten flakes could in fact be all that is left of 10 or more cubic metres of midden, perhaps spread thinly over a large area.

Late Period Sites

Late Period sites ($N = 325$) are defined as open-air middens (shell and shell-free) and subdivided into simple (open-air middens) and complex (towns) categories. Because relative sea level is falling, we know that low-elevation benches at the ocean margin are less than 2,000 years old and thus sites on them can be assigned to the latter part of the Graham Tradition (Fladmark 1990).

Complex Towns

Towns[1] ($N = 72$) are defined here as sites with physical or documentary evidence for at least one house. Forty-four of the towns in the study area have surviving evidence of house features. The number of houses observed at these towns ranges from one to twenty-six. Twenty-eight towns do not have surviving surface house features but do have middens and a reference to use as towns in early ethnographic or historic sources. Excluded are a number of ethnographic towns with no associated archaeological evidence, and forts (including those with houses) that occur on higher landforms that might have been used at any time during the last 9,000 years.

Simple Open-Air Middens

The open-air midden sample includes 253 sites that do not qualify as towns. We analyze only open-air shell and non-shell middens that can be confi-dently dated as no older than about 2000 BP. Of the 253 middens exam-ined, 226 contain shell-rich deposits that also include some fire-cracked rock, charcoal, bone, artifacts, and/or other discarded debris. The 27 non-shell middens in our sample have deposits that contain no shell or chipped stone (the latter are raised beach sites) but usually have fire-cracked rock with charcoal, and sometimes calcined bone or other kinds of artifacts.

These late simple sites range from 1 to 10,000 square metres in area. In some cases, numerous pockets or larger areas of midden can be found widely scattered and may comprise a large, complex site or a few discrete activity areas. Fifty-one of the 253 open-air midden sites are larger than 1,000 square metres in area. Large open-air shell matrix sites lacking houses are excluded from our town sample, contrary to common practice by Northwest coast archaeologists (Acheson 1998; Haggarty and Inglis 1985; Mackie 1986; Maschner 1997; Mason and Haggarty 1999).

Table 16.2

Significant differences (chi-square results) between early and late sites and random non-sites ("expected"), Gwaii Haanas and Hecate North Inner Coastal Region (HNI)

	Late	Early	Early simple	Early complex	Late simple	Late complex	Early vs. late	Early simple vs. late simple	Early complex vs. late complex
			vs. expected						
All Gwaii Haanas									
Island size	Yes	Yes	Yes	–	Yes	–	No	No	–
HNI island size	–	–	–	–	–	–	–	–	–
Aspect 8	Yes	Yes	Yes	–	Yes	–	Yes	Yes	–
HNI aspect 8	–	–	–	–	–	–	–	–	–
Aspect 4	Yes	No	No	–	Yes	No	Yes	Yes	–
HNI aspect 4	Yes	No	No	–	Yes	No	Yes	Yes	–
Shoreline intricacy	Yes	Yes	Yes	–	Yes	No	Yes	Yes	–
HNI shoreline intricacy	Yes	Yes	Yes	–	Yes	–	–	–	–
Shoreline productivity	Yes	Yes	Yes	–	Yes	Yes	–	–	–
HNI shoreline productivity	–	–	–	–	–	–	–	–	–
Habitat	Yes	Yes	Yes	–	Yes	No	Yes	Yes	–
HNI habitat	–	–	–	–	–	–	–	–	–
Distance to seals	Yes	Yes	Yes	–	Yes	–	No	No	–
HNI distance to seals	No	No	No	–	No	–	–	–	–
Distance to seabirds	Yes	Yes	Yes	–	Yes	Yes	Yes	Yes	–
HNI distance to seabirds	–	–	–	–	–	–	–	–	–
Distance to salmon	Yes	Yes	Yes	–	Yes	–	Yes	Yes	–
HNI distance to salmon	Yes	–	–	–	Yes	–	No	No	–
Distance to stream	Yes	No	No	No	Yes	No	No	No	–
HNI distance to stream	No	No	No	–	Yes	–	No	No	–

Notes: Yes = Significant difference ($p < 0.05$) between $Type_1$ and $Type_2$ for each variable.
No = No significant difference.
– = Too few cases for chi-square analysis.

Variables and Results

We looked at biophysical variables of shorelines at and near site locations, including island size; aspect; intricacy; productivity; habitat; distance to concentrations of seals, seabirds, sea lions, and salmon; and distance to mapped streams. Island size and distance to sea lions and streams were inconclusive or showed no significant differences or trends between early and late sites, while productivity criteria were too similar to the habitat variable for meaningful interpretation. We focus on the remaining variables for this analysis, including also the degree to which early and late period sites occur at the same locations.

The following analysis includes results of chi-square (x^2) tests of significance where there are enough cases (Table 16.2), and general discussion of similarities and differences between the sites.[2] We use a significance level of 95 percent to accept or reject hypotheses. If chi-square analysis shows a significant difference between two site types or a site type and the expected value (derived from random non-sites), the table reads "yes" (reject the null hypothesis of no difference); otherwise it reads "no" (accept the null hypothesis). Too few cases for reliable chi-square analysis are indicated with a dash (–). Table 16.2 includes data for each variable from all of Gwaii Haanas and from the protected Hecate North Inner Coastal Region (HNI).

Site Co-occurrence

If intertidal and adjacent marine environments were similar during the early and late periods, and if similar choices of site location were being made during the two time periods, then we can expect a significant incidence of early sites occurring on the beaches in front of late sites. This is not the case. Of the 436 site locations, only 18 (4 percent) share an early and late period component (Figures 16.2 and 16.3). Only 2 of the 90 complex site types in our sample co-occur. This trend is apparent for all site types.

We also looked at the distance that separates early and late sites (Figures 16.4 and 16.5). The results are partly related to the larger sample of late sites, but they do clearly indicate that there is much less variety in site location during the early period than during the late period, and that many late period sites occur in areas where early sites are few and far between. Conversely, the locations where early sites are most frequently found are in areas where late sites are common. The average distance that separates towns from the nearest early site is consistently greater than for open-air middens, reflecting the tendency for towns to be in more exposed and marginal locations.

Of the 111 sites in the HNI, only 5 (5 percent) have both early and late sites at one location. This is about the same proportion of co-occurrence as found in all of Gwaii Haanas and suggests that differential preservation is not a significant factor in this overall pattern.

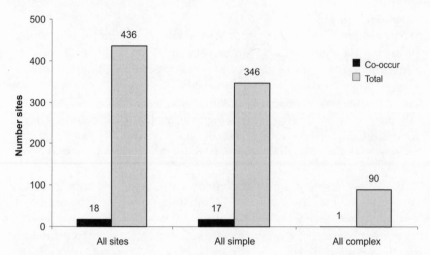

Figure 16.2   Co-occurrence of early and late sites at the same location, Gwaii Haanas.

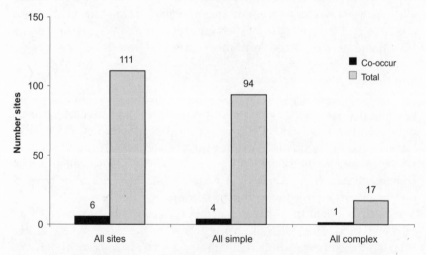

Figure 16.3   Co-occurrence of early and late sites at the same location, Hecate North Inner Coastal Region.

Next we examined the four regions where early period sites were found. The inner regions are protected and should have a higher proportion of early sites surviving if they are differentially preserved. Outer region sample sizes are smaller, but even so the average distance that separates an early site from the nearest late site is lower in the two outer regions than it is in the inner regions. The differences may be less pronounced if early period sites have been buried in protected estuaries during the early Holocene, as has been observed at Arrow Creek (Fedje et al. 1996). We are more confident

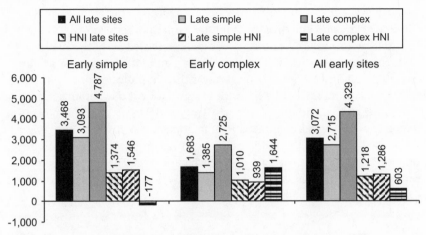

Figure 16.4 Average distance from late sites to the nearest early site: difference from expected distance (m), Gwaii Haanas.

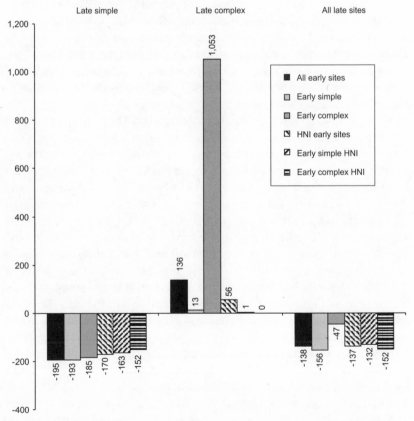

Figure 16.5 Average distance from early sites and the nearest late site: difference from expected distance (m), Gwaii Haanas.

that surveys of the northern Hecate regions returned a higher proportion of surviving early and late sites than did the work in other regions. It is likely that the two southern regions are underrepresented in both small shell middens and early sites. In any case, if early and late sites are on average closer to each other in more exposed areas than in protected ones, differential preservation may not be a contributing factor to co-occurrence results.

We now seek explanations as to why early and late sites do not co-occur, which could include a combination of factors such as environment, population growth, seasonal round, social organization, littoral zone food production, technology, or accessibility. We have a variety of digitally mapped biophysical variables with which to analyze some of these possible explanations.

Aspect

Cardinal direction or aspect has been found to correlate with site location in other areas on the Northwest Coast. In Tebenkof Bay in southeastern Alaska, Maschner (1997) found that "site present locations" have a significant orientation to the south, although they divided their sample into north and south only. In Clayoquot Sound on Vancouver Island, Mason and Haggarty (1999:160), using eight directions, report that villages and shell middens tend to be facing south and west, and that "northern exposures appear to be highly undesirable." These aspect trends are presumed to relate to exposure to solar heat.

Many analysts do not appear to consider whether the predominant cardinal directions are related to prevailing directions of shoreline in their study areas. Our study area is generally oriented northwest to southeast, and the northwestern edge of Gwaii Haanas is a boundary drawn across Moresby Island; the result is a skewed distribution of shorelines. If shorelines were evenly distributed on the compass rose, we would expect approximately 12.5 percent to occur facing each of eight directions, such as is observed for late simple sites (Figure 16.6). We used the random non-sites to establish physiographic trends (our expected values) and found that nearly half of the Gwaii Haanas shorelines face southwest and northeast (Figure 16.7). All other directions are less than expected, with north-facing shores occurring only 7 percent and northwest-facing shores 5 percent of the time. Thus, the nearly equal distribution of late simple sites is in fact significantly different from the expected.

There are significant differences in distribution of aspect between early and late sites. In the HNI especially, early sites generally exhibit a distribution similar to expected while late sites tend not to, especially towns. Northeast-facing shores are most common in the HNI (Figure 16.6) but all site types, with the exception of early complex sites, are much less likely than expected

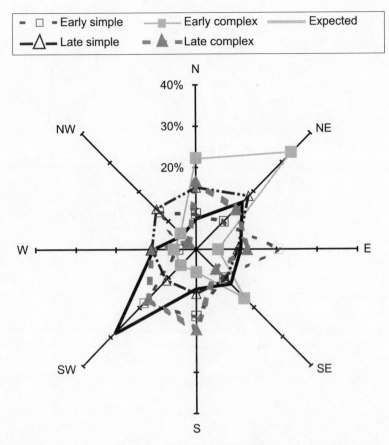

Figure 16.6 Relative frequency of sites by cardinal direction, Hecate North Inner Coastal Region.

to occur in these locations. Again, with the exception of early complex sites, all site types occur more than expected at southwest-facing shorelines. There are no complex lithic sites on southwest-, west-, or northwest-facing HNI shores. Early simple sites are the least likely to face northeast and late simple sites have a strong tendency to occur on the various north-trending shores in the HNI. A much larger proportion of towns than expected face north, especially in the HNI. For Gwaii Haanas as a whole, there appears to be an unexpected pattern of aspect for early complex lithic sites, with far more occurring on north- and northeast-facing shorelines and far fewer on southwest- and west-facing shores (Figure 16.7), but this is in fact an artifact of the large proportion of such sites in the Hecate North Inner Coastal Region, where they closely match the expected pattern (Figure 16.6).

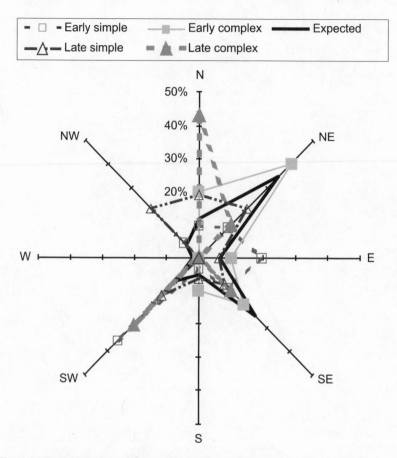

Figure 16.7   Relative frequency of sites by cardinal direction, Gwaii Haanas.

We also look at aspect with four cardinal directions in order to overcome sample size limitations in the HNI and find statistically significant differences for all of Gwaii Haanas and for the HNI. Generally, late sites are more likely than expected at north-facing shores, while early period sites are more commonly east facing. Early complex sites are also much more common than expected at north-facing locations.

Shoreline Intricacy

A combination of shoreline form and length called shoreline intricacy (Figures 16.8 and 16.9) was developed as a proxy for local productivity and biodiversity. Our premise was that with more shore near a site, there would be larger amounts of readily accessible intertidal and subtidal zone and thus

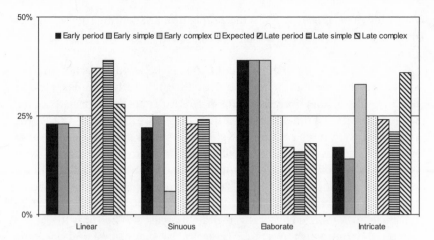

Figure 16.8 Relative proportions of shoreline intricacy at early and late period sites, Gwaii Haanas.

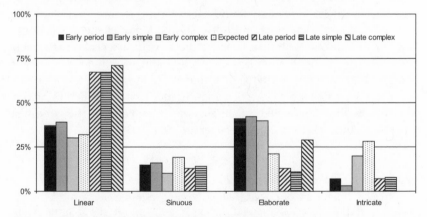

Figure 16.9 Relative proportions of shoreline intricacy at early and late period sites, Hecate North Inner Coastal Region.

greater potential for food production. Also, the more intricate a shoreline is, the greater the variations in microenvironment (exposure, beach substrate, slope) would be, with a greater likelihood of more biodiversity. Thus, we hypothesized that if local productivity and biodiversity were important to site location, then different choices made in the early and late periods should be reflected in shoreline intricacy near sites.

To test this relationship, the lengths of shoreline types within a 1-kilometre radius of each site and the 400 random non-sites were measured. The random data were used to establish four categories of expected shoreline intricacy based on the quartiles of their distribution comprising 100 random non-sites each: linear (< 3,579 metres of shoreline within 1-kilometre radius), sinuous (< 4,811 metres), elaborate (< 6,461 metres), and intricate (≥ 6,461 metres).

Figures 16.8 and 16.9 show the differences between expected and observed locations of sites in the two periods. While early complex sites are few in number, they have a strong difference from the expected values, while towns do not differ significantly. During the early period, sites in the study area were most common at elaborate shores and least common at intricate locations. Late period site locations differ from the expected, with most late simple sites having a strong tendency to be located along linear shorelines and not elaborate ones. Some differences might be explained by a lack of early period sites recorded on the west coast of Gwaii Haanas, a linear region dominated by locally intricate shorelines. When only the largely protected Hecate North Inner Coastal Region is examined we find (for those types with enough cases) that there are also significant differences from the expected pattern. Compared with the whole study area, late and early period sites in the HNI are rarely found behind intricate shores and late sites are much more common behind linear shores. Many of the linear shorelines in this area are sediment beaches and may be associated with a few resources that occur in abundance, such as clams or salmon. This might indicate that the early period sites favoured biodiversity in site locations and could have had more generalized subsistence strategies when using this area, whereas the late period inhabitants may have come to the same area to procure fewer resources, but in larger amounts.

Habitat

A habitat or community type variable for each shore unit was created in a biophysical inventory of Gwaii Haanas coastal resources by combining exposure and shore type variables (Harper et al. 1994:58-60). Ten habitats were identified, including five bedrock types that grade from very exposed to protected locations; four sand and sand-and-gravel types that occur at a variety of exposures; and channels defined by a strong tidal effect rather than exposure.

For this study we took eight of Harper and colleagues' ten habitat types and reduced them to three types (Table 16.3): exposed rock/boulder beaches (ERB) (Harper and colleagues' Type 1, 2, and 3); protected bedrock beaches (PBB) (Types 4 and 6); and protected sand/gravel/mud beaches (PGB) (Types 5, 7, and 8). The remaining two types are too rare for use with chi-square analysis.

Early and late period sites are not in front of the same kinds of habitat (Figure 16.10). The main difference is that most (86 percent) early sites are found at PGB shorelines even though these are only 24 percent of all shorelines in Gwaii Haanas. Late period sites are much more likely (30 percent)

Table 16.3

Observed habitat types and archaeological site distributions in Gwaii Haanas

Habitat type[a]	Descriptor	Length (km)	Early simple	Early complex	Late simple	Late complex
0	Sand and sand and gravel, very exposed to semi-exposed	30	1	0	10	7
1	Bedrock/boulder, very exposed	338	0	0	5	8
2	Bedrock/boulder, exposed	210	1	0	26	11
3	Bedrock/boulder, semi-exposed	280	1	0	37	15
4	Bedrock, semi-protected	230	8	1	31	9
5	Sand and gravel, semi-protected	327	26	4	51	4
6	Bedrock, protected	27	1	0	7	5
7	Sand and gravel, protected	111	23	10	53	4
8	Estuary sand/mud, semi-protected and protected	100	30	3	33	8
9	Channel – heavily influenced by tidal currents	3	2	0	1	1
Total		1,656	93	18	253	72

a As defined in Harper et al. 1994.

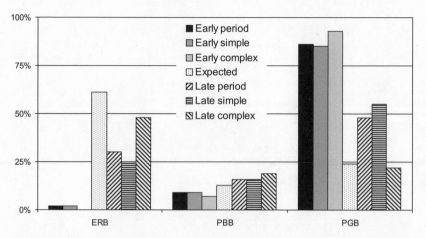

Figure 16.10   Habitat categories for shorelines at early and late period sites, Gwaii Haanas.

than early sites (2 percent) to be located at ERB locations, which represent 61 percent of all shorelines. While the kind of habitat in front of a site appears to be an important factor for early and simple site locations, it does not appear to be so for towns. This may be in part an artifact of differential preservation – protected gravel beaches are the kinds of places where early period sites are most likely to survive.

We were unable to test this variable using just the Hecate North Inner Coastal Region because it has almost no ERB shorelines, and sites do not occur in sufficient frequencies for chi-square testing. Thus, where there are sufficient exposed rock beaches for a meaningful test, we find that early and late sites do occur in these locations, but early sites are rare and late ones are marginally less than expected. It is likely that some more exposed early sites were lost during fluctuations in sea level.

Distance to Known Marine Resource Concentrations

We investigated the straight-line distance to four major resource concentrations for which we have digital locations (sea lion [$N = 9$], harbour seal [$N = 33$], seabird nesting colonies [$N = 185$], and salmon streams [$N = 78$]). All of these resources are present in the faunal collections at Kilgii Gwaay (Fedje et al. 2001), with seals and ground-nesting birds being common. All species are present at the late period sites tested by Acheson (1998), with salmon also being abundant. Sea lion places are too uncommon to permit meaningful analysis. Distance values for the three remaining resource concentrations are broken into three categories to facilitate chi-square analysis.

Harbour Seals   The three distance categories – close (< 1 kilometre), near (1 to 5 kilometres), and far (> 5 kilometres) – are used for the thirty-three

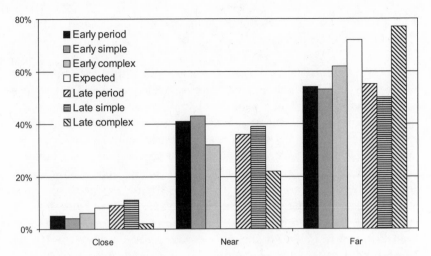

Figure 16.11 Distance of site types to nearest seal rookery and/or haulout, Gwaii Haanas.

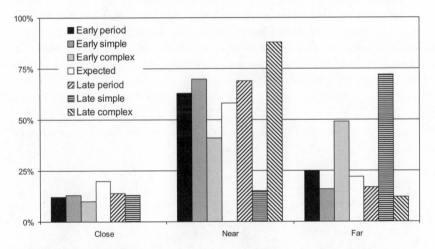

Figure 16.12 Distance of site types to nearest seal rookery and/or haulout, Hecate North Inner Coastal Region.

harbour seal locations. Early and late sites are not significantly different from each other in distance from seal concentrations (Figure 16.11) but do differ from the expected pattern. Seal places tend to be found in the northern Hecate portions of Gwaii Haanas so we tested to see whether the larger trends may be a result of regional variations or differential preservation of early sites; there were no significant differences in distance from the expected or from each other (Figure 16.12). We conclude that these seal locations are not a significant factor in the settlement patterns of either period in the HNI. It is possible that there was an influence that is now obscured by a relocation of seal rookeries and haulouts after hunting stopped and habitation in Gwaii Haanas ceased.

Seabird Nesting Areas   Seabird nesting areas are widely distributed in all parts of the study area. We used the same three-part distance classification – close (< 1 kilometre), near (1 to 5 kilometres), and far (> 5 kilometres) – to the known nesting areas, and found some significant results with regard to site locations in the two periods. High relative frequencies of all four site types from both periods are located over 5 kilometres from seabird concentrations.

Early sites and late sites have significantly different distributions with respect to distance from seabird nesting areas (Figure 16.13). All site types show a statistically different distribution from expected. Towns almost never occur more than 5 kilometres away. Early and late sites occur much more than expected near (1 to 5 kilometres) seabird nesting sites. The Hecate North Inner Coastal Region sites and non-sites almost never occur in the close category, so chi-square analysis is not possible on any of these site types. In Figure 16.14 the expected values are proportionately more likely to be far from nesting areas than in Gwaii Haanas as a whole, and yet the early and late period sites are more likely than expected to be near and less likely to be far. However, modern distributions of bird nesting areas may be substantially different from those in the early Holocene patterns due to the introduction of predators and the depopulation of the Haida 200 years ago.

Salmon   Salmon are coded for distance from sites to the lower reaches of the nearest salmon run river. Salmon escapements cited here are the average

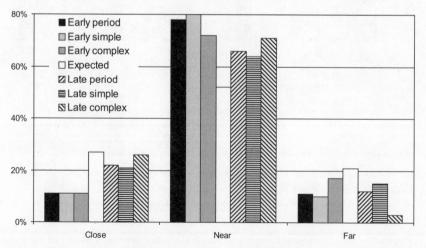

Figure 16.13   Distance of site types to nearest seabird nesting areas, Gwaii Haanas.

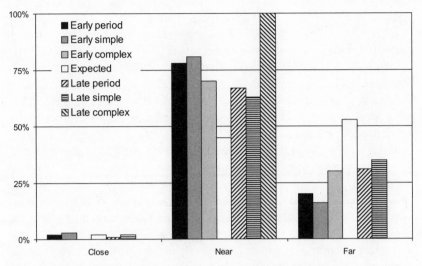

Figure 16.14 Distance of site types to nearest seabird nesting areas, Hecate North Inner Coastal Region.

combined runs of sockeye, coho, pink, and chum salmon. The twentieth-century salmon data are uneven: some runs have decades of measurement, others are hindered by intermittent observations. Three categories of distance to salmon were used in this study: close (< 500 metres), near (500 metres to 1 kilometre), and far (> 1 kilometre).

If salmon had a significant influence on settlement patterns, site distributions would differ statistically from the expected with respect to distance from salmon. Our analysis shows that there are significant differences in

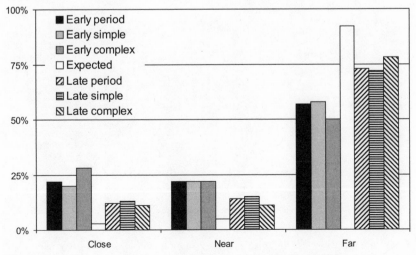

Figure 16.15 Distance of site types to nearest salmon run, Gwaii Haanas.

distance (Figure 16.15) – in all cases sites are closer to salmon than expected, but this trend is strongest for early sites, with 22 percent close (versus 3 percent expected) and 22 percent near (versus 5 percent expected). Early complex sites are even more likely than expected (28 percent) to be within 500 metres of a salmon stream. Late sites are much less often found at these distances (12 percent close and 14 percent near) than the early sites. Towns are least likely to be near salmon, with less than one-quarter being within 1 kilometre of a salmon stream.

In the Hecate North Inner Coastal Region, the overall distributions look very similar to those for Gwaii Haanas as a whole (Figure 16.16). It would seem that proximity to a salmon stream is an important consideration in both the early and late periods, but considerably more so in the early period. It is interesting that in the early period, complex sites are the class of site likely to occur most often within 1 kilometre of salmon, while in the late period, complex sites are the least likely in this zone. The association of early sites with salmon may be even stronger, as any early sites situated on early Holocene estuaries (close) will probably have been buried by Holocene alluvium.

In Gwaii Haanas early sites are closer to larger runs than are late sites. Perhaps the better streams of today were the most productive in the early period, and those that have small runs now had not established runs then. As salmon streams are usually associated with estuaries abundant in a vari-

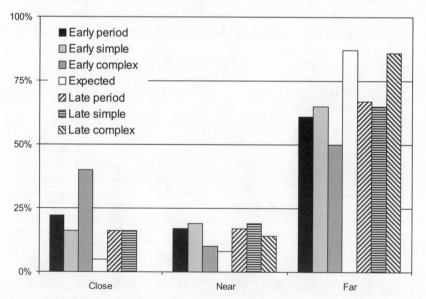

Figure 16.16 Distance of site types to nearest salmon run, Hecate North Inner Coastal Region.

ety of plant and animal resources, the sites may have been placed there to use several resources.

Distance to Nearest Mapped Stream

In order to test whether nearness to stream-related resources influences site associations with fish streams, three categories were created for the distance that sites and non-sites are from the nearest mapped streams (1:20,000 BCGS TRIM map base). There are hundreds of small potable water sources that are not mapped in this rain forest environment, so the results of this variable are not applicable to questions regarding drinking water availability. The three categories (close, near, and far) are created by dividing the 400 random non-sites into three even-sized groups (< 185 metres, 185 to 539 metres, and ≥ 540 metres).

There is no significant difference in distance to streams between the early and late period sites or early and late simple sites (Figure 16.17). In the Hecate North Inner Coastal Region, the expected distances to streams are in very different proportions, with few non-sites occurring far from streams (Figure 16.18). Even so, similar relationships occur in all Gwaii Haanas, with no significant difference between early and late sites and expected distributions. Because mapped streams does not seem to have been a factor in choosing site locations, we conclude that the associations we see with salmon streams are more likely because they have fish than because of other resource values commonly associated with streams. However, the characteristics of good salmon streams (low gradient, abundant sand and gravel) make it possible that they are also indicative of larger estuaries and good clam beds, as well as trail heads for access to upland resources.

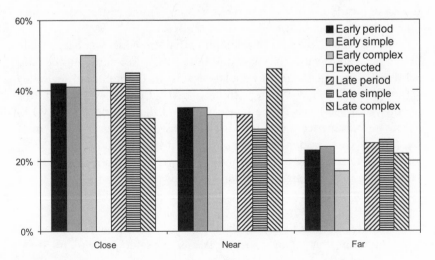

Figure 16.17 Distance of site types to nearest mapped stream, Gwaii Haanas.

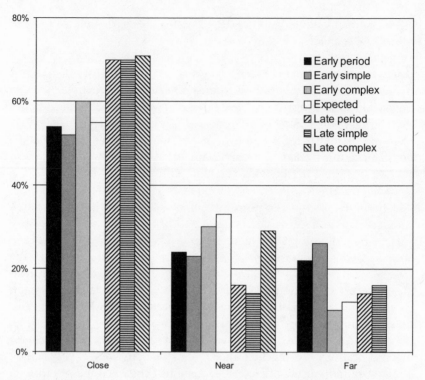

Figure 16.18   Distance of site types to nearest mapped stream, Hecate North Inner Coastal Region.

Discussion

In this chapter we have asked why early and late period sites rarely occur at the same location. In this section, we examine some of the assumptions underlying our approach, and consider our results.

Central to this chapter is the assumption that shorelines will have similar biodiversity and relative biomass during both the early and late periods. Substantive arguments might be made against this assumption, including (1) the possibility that sediment shores remained underdeveloped during rapidly rising sea levels (Fedje et al. 2001) and that during the early Holocene warmer surface waters may have increased toxic algal blooms, making filter feeders seasonally dangerous or fatal to eat (Mudie et al. 2002); and (2) there are likely to be substantially fewer anadromous fish such as salmon due to drowning of spawning grounds by rapidly rising sea levels and to unsuitable early period riparian environments (Erlandson 1994; Fladmark 1975; Lichatowich 1999).

The Kilgii Gwaay and Kunghit shellfish assemblages provide support for our contention that modern shore types are a useful analogue for those during the Kinggi Complex era because both assemblages exhibit shellfish in proportions very similar to those in nearby habitats. Evidence for the availability of Gwaii Haanas early period salmon is discussed below. Recent red-tide studies are of very high resolution and show that there were much larger blooms of harmful algae in the early period on both coasts of North America. On the BC coast there were very high frequencies of algal blooms until just before 9500 BP, although the toxicity of the taxa causing these blooms is uncertain. There followed a series of intermittent larger blooms of algae associated with paralytic shellfish poisoning beginning at just after 9400 BP until 9100 BP, after which heavy toxic blooms were frequent for nearly 2,000 years (Mudie et al. 2002:172). It is possible the Kilgii Gwaay assemblage, dating to 9450 BP, is from a time when shellfish toxins were at consistently safer levels, or that shellfish at the site are representative of general early period usage. The latter scenario implies that toxicity was understood well enough to permit managed access to the resource.

Our analysis is probably influenced by interdependence of some variables, including those used in this analysis and others not digitally mapped. Other variables are likely to covary with shoreline intricacy and probably indicate nearby productivity, such as bird and seal concentrations, both taxa that are at the top of the food chain. Certain types of habitat are also more likely to be intricate or linear than others. Town distributions do not differ significantly from the expected for aspect, shoreline intricacy, and habitat. It could be that these variables (or another unknown one) are interdependent. Certainly aspect is related to exposure and habitat is a composite variable consisting in part of exposure.

Settlement choices related to aspect may include variables other than exposure to sun, such as prevailing winds. At Cape St. James, at the southern tip of the study area, stronger summer winds tend to be from the west and northwest and winter winds from the southeast (Harper et al. 1994). It might be expected that site locations would tend to be away from west, northwest, and southeast shores, at least on a seasonal basis. In Gwaii Haanas, such exposures are among the least common, so sites are infrequent on these shores (Figure 16.7). Compared with the expected, early sites are less likely and late sites are more likely to be found on west-facing shores, but there are very few such shores in the inner protected areas where early sites are common. Simple sites from both periods are more common than expected facing northwest, and early complex sites are more likely than expected to face southeast, although most of them face north and northeast. Towns are more likely than expected to face north and south, and less likely to face southwest and southeast. Perhaps this indicates that exposure to summer storms was not considered when choosing town sites, but winter storms were planned for.

In the HNI, a place where people could shelter from winter wind and waves, all site types occur less often than expected on southeast-facing shores and early simple sites tend strongly towards southwest- and east-facing shores (Figure 16.6). Here simple late period sites are four times more likely than expected to occur at northwest-facing locations; perhaps many were chosen for protection from winter storms, or these sites are less likely to survive on beaches exposed to such weather.

There are significant differences in intricacy of shorelines at different site types. This variable was developed as a measure of differences in productivity such as biomass and biodiversity in the immediate vicinity of sites. Late period sites are much more likely to be present at linear places while early period sites are most likely at elaborate places. It is interesting that the late period sites, presumably from a time of much higher population density, would not tend towards the most productive locations. This may reflect the large number of simple sites that are expected to have specialized functions and consequent placement close to particular resources, often on more linear shorelines. Towns, which have a wide range of subsistence activities, have a strong tendency to the more productive intricate shorelines.

On a regional scale, Quentin Mackie has looked at the importance of shoreline involution for predicting early site locations (Mackie 2001). He summarizes a part of Wobst's modelling theory: "The demographic costs of linearity can only be overcome by high population density or high mobility" (Fedje et al. 2004). These demographic costs include the reproductive viability of a society, with higher costs (lower viability) proposed for peripheral groups. Mackie proposes that highly involuted shorelines may be the places that the first coastal migrants occupied until they had adjusted to the local maritime setting and established large enough populations to sustain expansion into more linear settings. He suggests that colonizing groups could also return to involuted areas during a demographic crisis. The latter part of the model fits the Kunghit Haida pattern, where, following contact and the decimation of populations by introduced diseases, towns on the west coast amalgamated with those on more involuted shores to the south, north, and east, and eventually were concentrated along Hecate Strait (Chapter 15).

The involution theory could also help explain the distribution of precontact sites in Gwaii Haanas, particularly the lack of early period sites on the linear west coast. Following Mackie (2001:15), we have created an involution index for each of Harper and colleagues' five biophysical regions (1994) in Gwaii Haanas. The HNI contains 332 kilometres of shoreline but only 43 kilometres of straight-line shoreline would be needed to cross the length of the region, hence the involution index is 332:43 or 7.72:1. We use this index to compare the relationship between involution and the density

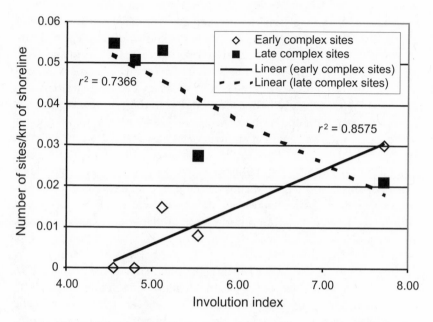

Figure 16.19 Relationship between involution of shorelines in five biophysical regions and density of complex sites from the early and late periods, Gwaii Haanas.

of early and late complex sites per kilometre of shoreline for each region. Complex sites are an indicator of population size, since by definition they are the principal residential sites for both time periods. We find that (1) the more involuted a region's shoreline, the higher the density of early complex sites in the region, and (2) the more linear the shoreline, the higher the density of late complex sites (Figure 16.19). Thus, the west coast region may not have been occupied during the Kinggi period at least in part because human populations were too low to overcome the social costs associated with inhabiting a linear shoreline.

Differential preservation may be a factor in these results, but if intertidal lithic sites were present in any numbers on the west coast, we should have found some on the suitable beaches that were all inspected more than once at low tide by the same experienced crew that surveyed the HNI. Also, any preservation effect could be offset if early sites are underestimated due to burial in aggrading deltas in the Hecate regions. It is very likely that parts of the west coast were used in the early period, even if they were accessed only on an occasional basis overland from the Hecate Strait inlets. There are numerous short trails across Moresby Island, and day-trips were made on foot by groups of Haida in the mid-1800s to get resources, such as a drift whale, even though by that time they had moved away from most west coast towns (Newcombe n.d.b). There are a few undated raised beach sites recorded on the west coast, and from what is known of their content and elevation, any could date from the early period to about 5,000 years ago. Also, there are proportionately few areas where one would expect survival of lithics on the west coast, so the lack of sites may be a sample size issue.

Archaeological evidence from excavated sites in the culture area has been used to suggest that salmon runs were not well established until salmon (or other fish) started to appear in abundance in post-5000 BP sites (Fladmark 1975). There is evidence, however, that salmon are sufficiently flexible and adaptable to environmental change and to new opportunities to have been spawning in Gwaii Haanas streams in the early Holocene, including successful introductions and spread in streams around the Great Lakes and New Zealand, rapid colonization of recently deglaciated streams in Alaska, and survival of runs following metres of subsidence and uplift caused by the 1964 Alaska earthquake (Baxter 1971; Kwain 1987; Milner and Bailey 1989; Quinn et al. 2001; Roys 1971; Taylor 1997; Thorsteinson et al. 1971). There is also recent evidence for a glacial refugium for salmon in Haida Gwaii (Smith et al. 2001). Thus, we conclude that sea level change, even of the magnitude seen in our study area, does not contraindicate persistent runs of salmon throughout the marine transgression, although it is likely that runs would have been smaller.

There is evidence of the presence of early Holocene salmon runs in Gwaii Haanas (Chapter 6). Our analyses of site distributions suggest a strong correlation with salmon streams during the early Holocene. Excavations at Kilgii Gwaay and Richardson Island confirm that salmon were present in the waters around Gwaii Haanas during the early Holocene and imply that salmon were spawning in some of the same streams that have modern salmon runs. Salmon bones have been recovered from paleomarine sediments in the beds of modern salmon streams and date back to 5300 BP (D. Fedje, personal communication).

Gwaii Haanas salmon runs are limited even now; the total combined escapement of approximately 190,000 salmon is smaller than many single runs in other parts of the coast. Even so, Acheson's tests (1998) of many late period sites found significant numbers of salmon and yet are well removed from large-sized salmon streams. On average the eight Acheson sites with salmon and sizable faunal assemblages are 1.4 kilometres from the nearest salmon run and the recorded escapements of these runs average about eighty fish annually. It is most likely that the salmon in these sites are marine-caught, and could have been feeding in the area on the way to spawning grounds hundreds of kilometres to the south.

The Kilgii Gwaay site has a number of identified specimens (NISP) of only 2 salmon out of more than 3,000 identifiable fish bones. Preliminary analy-

Table 16.4

Distance from Richardson Island and Kilgii Gwaay to the five nearest salmon streams

Creek name	Mean run size	No. of species	Water distance (km)	Exposed travel (km)	Protected travel (km)
Distance from Richardson Island site					
Longfellow Creek	26	3	4.73	0	4.73
Echo Harbour Creek	11,000	4	5.23	0	5.23
Salmon River	27,735	4	5.29	0	5.29
Anna Inlet Creek	2,447	4	6.66	0	6.66
Crescent Inlet Creek	14,247	4	10.91	0	10.91
Distance from Kilgii Gwaay Site					
Rose Harbour Creek	27	1	1.09	0	1.09
Raspberry Cove Creek	497	2	2.29	1.94	0.35
Fanny Creek	49	2	6.40	2.92	3.48
Sedmond Creek	8,552	2	8.31	2.92	5.39
Moody Creek	419	2	10.61	6.05	4.56

sis of calcined bone from Kinggi period components at the Richardson Island raised beach site shows more salmon, with a NISP of 26 salmon from a single hearth, the second most common (33 percent) identified species in that context (Wigen 2003b; Q. Mackie, personal communication). While sample size is an issue at this time, one simple answer to the difference between Kilgii Gwaay and Richardson Island salmon bone assemblages is relative access to spawning salmon. Salmon abundance near the two sites is markedly different (Table 16.4). Travel to all of the salmon runs near Richardson Island is across protected waters, while accessing all but the nearest run from Kilgii Gwaay involves travelling across exposed waters. Variety in species and thus seasons of access is also greater in the streams close to Richardson. The difference between the assemblages could be seasonal, but it is also quite possible that salmon were obtained from streams during the Kinggi period, and that marine fishing technology did not include trolling methods suitable for salmon. These assemblages indicate that some salmon runs were established in the early Holocene, even during the marine transgression, and suggest that the distance-to-salmon variable is useful for early period sites.

Early complex sites are near salmon streams, but the beaches immediately in front of the sites are mostly protected sand and gravel beaches, not estuarine sand and mud. Estuaries frequently have wide intertidal zones, especially along the Hecate shores that have 8-metre tides. These shores are often unsuitable for camping because of their wet ground and difficult boat access across very wide and muddy intertidal zones. Early residential sites, while placed close to salmon estuaries, were at locations better suited for longer-term residence, including well-drained land and narrower intertidal zones with little mud.

In the absence of mapped bivalve distributions, we see that estuaries (17 percent of all Gwaii Haanas, 18 percent HNI shorelines) that are generally good clam habitat are associated with 30 percent (20 percent in HNI) of early period sites, and only 13 percent (16 percent in HNI) of late period sites (Table 16.3). We suggest that some of the early sites were probably placed so as to make use of sediment-dwelling shellfish as well as anadromous fish. During the early period, rocky shore shellfish such as mussels may have been much more productive because of the huge organic nutrient load released from drowning land. At Kilgii Gwaay, however, the faunal data indicate that shellfish were utilized at a much lower proportion than fish, birds, and mammals when compared with late period sites. It is not clear whether this difference is related to sampling or to other factors (e.g., an early focus on other resources such as bear, or environmental differences such as high levels of shellfish toxicity).

Our analysis has been necessarily confined to the mapped variables along the intertidal zone and, by inference, adjacent marine edge. We do not have mapped terrestrial variables for the biology of the adjacent foreshore or the more remote upland areas. It is possible that some of the differences we see in site distributions are related to terrestrial changes. A warmer, drier climate and much more open terrestrial environment (Chapter 3) may have favoured a different adaptation in the early period. The early Holocene terrestrial habitat was probably much better suited to bears (Heaton 2002). They may have been much more abundant during the Kinggi period and were probably a more important part of the diet than intertidal or anadromous resources, at least during some seasons. The Kilgii Gwaay site has a very high incidence of bears in its faunal assemblage compared with any of Acheson's sites or others in Haida Gwaii. Also, we have participated in small tests at four other intertidal sites, and every one of them has produced bear, although almost no other fauna. Bear were clearly a more important species in the Kinggi period economy than during the late period, and bear distributions could be a factor in the placement of early sites. Modern black bears congregate at salmon runs, and although there is isotopic evidence that the diet of early Holocene bears was primarily terrestrial (Heaton 2002; D. Fedje, personal communication), it could be that the nearness of early complex sites to salmon runs (Figures 16.15 and 16.16) is partly explained by the fish streams being attractive to bears. A potential consequence of heavy human predation might be to limit use of salmon by bears, with a consequent weaker marine signal in their bones. Estuaries also "serve as gateways to the upland" (Harper et al. 1994:105) and as trailheads for access to the west coast of Moresby Island. So, if bears did not eat salmon in the early period, sites near estuaries might still be staging areas for bear hunting.

A possible explanation for part of the relationship in the distance-to-resource-concentration variables is that some locations may have been sited to optimize access to multiple resource locations, with the effect of generally not being too close or too far from any one resource concentration. Towns do seem to follow this pattern, while early complex sites are consistently further away from bird nesting areas, for instance, than all other site types, but may be sited so that salmon, estuarine, and inland resources can all be readily accessed.

Some observed differences between early and late sites might reflect technological differences. The end of the Kinggi Complex is identified by a shift in lithic technology marked by the abrupt introduction of microblades and subsequent decline in bifacial tools. Martin Magne has suggested that this technological shift, which coincides with the beginning of sea level maximum, may correlate with the development of mature salmon runs (Chapter 12; Magne 2004:115-116). The small amount of salmon in early sites may also indicate differences in marine fishing technology between the two periods, with salmon only incidentally caught on marine gear designed to catch the kinds of fish most common in the Kilgii Gwaay assemblage. Perhaps trolling technology had not developed sufficiently for marine-caught salmon to be widely represented in the early sites. An association of early sites with salmon runs means it is possible that fish traps were used in the early period. The well-preserved wooden artifacts from Kilgii Gwaay suggest that it could be worthwhile to sample the fish traps in Gwaii Haanas to see whether any date to the early period.

There are aspects of the environment that are constant in the early and late Holocene, and it is clear that some aspects of the maritime adaptation were similar. For instance, the environment requires that people have effective watercraft, and the archaeological assemblages point to sophisticated fishing and hunting technologies during both time periods. There would have been many aspects of survival that were similar in the two time periods, but there are clear indications that the people organized such activities differently in the early and late periods. Haida towns are permanent locations owned by corporate groups that have elaborate structures capable of housing many people and storing large quantities of preserved food and possessions. They are usually in fairly exposed areas with access to both inland and offshore waters and enough space to fit a fairly large settlement, are often close to more than one beach (each with different exposures to provide access in different weathers), and are in a good defensive location. Late simple sites would have seen mobile and temporary housing (if any), but often are places used repeatedly for many generations with clearly defined ownership of, and controlled access to, the sites and adjacent resources. A gradually receding sea level might require towns to relocate or expand closer to the beach or onto a new site every few centuries, while the foci of activity at simple sites would imperceptibly shift with the beach edge. There is almost no archaeological or ethnographic evidence for inland residences, although extensive use of inland resources, particularly cedar, is well documented.

In stark contrast, the extremely rapid rate of marine transgression would have had an important influence on adaptive strategies and settlements in the early period. Coast margins used by one generation could often have been unsuitable for the same use by the next generation, and partially drowned within two generations. This would have had a profound effect on the strategies for survival; a high degree of flexibility in settlement placement and a low degree of sedentism would have been essential. Houses are likely to have been small and mobile. Repeated use of sites would have been possible for only a few decades. Large populations and long-term accumulations of wealth and possessions would be more difficult to sustain. Food is more likely to have been stored in purpose-built caches or procured as needed. There could have been a tendency to place the more complex sites behind steep foreshores or on small heights of land where they would not be overrun as quickly by rising sea levels. Ownership or other control of access to resources is likely to have been generalized across a territory, and territory boundaries would, by definition, be fluid. Consequently, a highly stratified society would have been unlikely.

Conclusion

This study investigated relationships between specific marine edge biophysical data and sites from either end of the Holocene in order to identify variables and decision-making processes that likely influenced the placement of pre-contact settlements on the coastal margins of Gwaii Haanas. In particular we have tried to shed some light on the poorly understood settlement patterns of the early period. In view of the large and diverse archaeological sample for both time periods, we have a unique opportunity to describe aspects of early period settlement patterns on the Northwest Coast.

Our study shows varying degrees of association between certain site types and specific environmental variables, and we are reasonably confident that the broad characteristics of the intertidal zone of Gwaii Haanas were similar in the early and late periods. We suggest, therefore, that an explanation of differences in site location is more likely to lie with different strategies for adaptation than with changes in the marine environments. We also conclude that salmon runs were established in some Gwaii Haanas streams during the marine transgression and thus proximity to salmon runs is worth considering in both periods. With the data currently available, it is not possible to compare terrestrial environments with these distributions, but differences in the upland area in the early Holocene could have influenced site distributions along the marine margin.

We find that early and late period sites are unlikely to occur at the same locations and that there are significant differences in their placement. These differences include aspect, habitat, intricacy (with all that this might imply for biodiversity and biomass), and proximity to seabird nesting sites and salmon spawning streams at Gwaii Haanas. Early sites are, compared with expected values, most likely behind elaborate shorelines, protected gravel beaches, on east-facing shores, near accessible marine resources as indicated by seabird nesting areas, and close to or near salmon streams. Late sites are most likely behind linear shorelines (except towns that tend towards intricate places), protected gravel beaches (but are surprisingly common at exposed rock beaches), and on north-facing shores, and do not differ from expected in their distance from bird and salmon concentrations.

In the sheltered Hecate North Inner Coastal Region, early sites are, compared with expected values, almost always behind protected gravel beaches, and are most likely behind elaborate and linear shorelines, on west-facing shores, near seals and seabird concentrations, and within 500 metres of salmon runs. Late sites are usually at protected gravel beaches, on north-facing shores, near seals and seabirds and within 1 kilometre of salmon streams.

There is less variety in the kinds of site location during the early period than during the late period, but the locations of early sites tend to have greater variety of shoreline and resources and may have been optimized to access multiple resources. The early period site locations seem to favour greater biodiversity, as do towns. It may be that early peoples had more generalized subsistence strategies using moderate amounts of a large number of resources from fewer sites, whereas in the late period people would live at a more exposed place with intricate shores, and come to the protected areas for larger amounts of a few specific resources. Early site locations are found in areas where late sites are also common, except for towns. The smaller early period populations may have made it advantageous for early settlements to locate in involuted regions, with a consequent limited use of the peripheral areas in which towns are often found.

Complex early sites are relatively few in number and proportion compared with the late period, and this probably reflects the existence of smaller populations possibly operating out of residential base camps with many more stops on the seasonal round than those that prevailed in the late period. The extreme rate at which sea levels were rising must have required a flexible settlement pattern with mobile non-sedentary or semi-sedentary groups, likely limited in size. Once sea level stabilized at the end of the Kinggi period, effective group sizes were more likely to expand. By the time of contact there was a considerable degree and precision of control of access to specific resources that would tightly limit the places where people could live and the resources they used. Thus, the early period people likely had fewer social constraints on their choice of residential sites and resources.

Early peoples appear to have taken river-run salmon, leading us to infer the use of fish traps. Their marine fishing technology may not have been suitable for systematically catching salmon in the ocean, but there was an ability to catch other fish to considerable depths, probably with lines and baited hooks. Birds, such as albatross, were caught on the open ocean but some species were probably also taken from nesting sites while early people stayed at camps and residential sites most likely located between 1 and 5 kilometres distant. Seals were probably taken at or near rookeries and haulouts, with people using small sites as base camps or butchering stations and returning to residential sites generally located over 5 kilometres away. Protected gravel beaches, including estuaries, were an important focus of activity. Early complex sites are most likely found at sand and gravel beaches near estuaries. They were probably chosen because they had well-drained land with accessible beaches in front, and were sheltered from winter storms but located within easy distance for procuring resources associated with estuaries (and the inland access they provide), such as salmon, sediment-dwelling shellfish, and bears.

Despite limitations arising from some environmental variables and the small sample size of complex early period sites, we believe that the differences we have identified between early and late site distributions do shed light on the early period in a way not possible with other types of data and in the absence of such a generally robust sample of sites as we have. Other areas may provide similar opportunities if early period sites can be identified in large enough numbers.

Acknowledgments
We would like to acknowledge several individuals who have collaborated in gathering, collating, and interpreting Gwaii Haanas site information over the past years. First and foremost, our thanks go to Martin Magne and Daryl Fedje of Parks Canada for their enthusiasm and support of the various inventory programs during the 1990s, and invaluable input into many aspects of this chapter. Several Haida individuals have been active in most of the past field programs, and our warmest thanks go to Bert Wilson, Captain Gold, Jordan Yeltatzie, and Alan Brooks. *Howa'a!* Many thanks to Steven Acheson for sharing his

knowledge and notes. Chris Scott, Cynthia Lake, Trevor Orchard, and Patrick Bartier carried out post-field data preparation for this chapter. Quentin Mackie provided valuable insights and assistance. Last, but by no means least, we wish to thank Kjerstin and Andrea for their understanding and support during our long absences in the field and lab.

Notes

1 The term *town* is used in this analysis rather than village or settlement in order to be consistent with the modern preferences of the Haida people and the terminology of early twentieth-century ethnographers.
2 In the interests of simplicity and brevity, we have reduced the amount of data shown in this chapter. The authors would be pleased to forward data upon request.

Conclusion:
Synthesis of Environmental
and Archaeological Data

Daryl W. Fedje and Rolf W. Mathewes

Although much has been learned in recent years, archaeological knowledge of Haida Gwaii remains sketchy, with most research over the last decade emphasizing site survey rather than detailed investigation of known sites. However, the handful of excavations carried out during this time has significantly enhanced our understanding of human history on the archipelago (Chapters 11-15; Fedje et al. 2004b). The archaeological record now extends to at least 10,500 BP. The depth of history is constrained in no small part by the dynamic environmental history of the archipelago, especially that of sea level change, which has resulted in shorelines older than 9500 BP being drowned by rapid marine transgression.

We know that between approximately 15,000 and 12,000 BP the landscape of Haida Gwaii and surrounding continental shelf was biologically productive, with cool climatic conditions and diverse herb and dwarf shrub vegetation (Chapters 1, 3, and 4). The 13,000 to 10,000 BP marine environment was varied, with cold, low-salinity water in a much-restricted paleo-Hecate Strait and milder, full marine conditions along the west coast and Dixon Entrance shores. Significant warming occurred by about 12,500 BP, although the environs of Hecate Strait maintained a more continental climate than today as a consequence of lowered sea levels. At this time, temperate plant communities began to replace the late glacial flora. Trees become established: pine appeared by 12,500 BP, spruce by about 11,000 BP, and hemlock by about 10,000 BP. Pine and spruce parkland dominated the landscape continuously between 12,500 and 10,500 BP. Many of the herbs and dwarf shrubs of the previous tundra-like landscape became restricted to alpine sites and edge habitats, or disappeared entirely from Haida Gwaii as these forests developed. The vertebrate faunal record for the time between 14,000 and 10,000 BP includes black bear, brown bear, caribou, deer, dog, river otter, mouse, and shrew (Chapter 6). By 11,500 BP shellfish were abundant in western Hecate Strait, and a number of intertidal species, including those used by prehistoric people, were recovered during offshore investigations of drowned early postglacial landscapes (Chapters 2 and 10).

The end of the Younger Dryas cold period and increased ocean circulation associated with rising sea levels resulted in a more temperate maritime environment by 10,000 BP (Chapter 3). The return to temperate maritime conditions at 10,000 and to a climate even warmer than today by 9600 BP resulted in development of closed coniferous forests to elevations considerably higher than at present. The earliest securely dated archaeological evidence for maritime adaptation dates to 9500 BP (Chapter 11). Cultural assemblages between 9500 and 9000 BP have been recovered from a number of intertidal stone tool sites, a few of which have been test excavated, and also from the lowest levels at the Richardson Island site (Chapters 11, 12, and 16). Our knowledge of human adaptations at this time is fragmentary because of the limited range of archaeological evidence recovered at these sites, but recent and ongoing work at the 9300 to 9000 BP levels at Richardson Island and the 9450 BP component at Kilgii Gwaay in southernmost Haida Gwaii are enhancing interpretation for this time. While much of the direct evidence is limited to stone tools, the Kilgii Gwaay work is providing a rich faunal and paleobotanical record. Additionally, indirect evidence for other aspects of technology can be gained from site locations. Preliminary interpretations from the archaeological and environmental evidence at these sites suggest that people were using a broad range of maritime environments, including marine, intertidal, and terrestrial resources. These data suggest that a fully functioning marine environment was established by the early Holocene. Faunal remains recovered from this period include bear, harbour seal, sea otter, river otter, sea lion, and at least twenty-four taxa of birds, fourteen fish taxa, and a variety of intertidal shellfish, including mussels, clams, and univalves (Chapters 6 and 11). Stone tool technology is characterized by bifacial technology, large stone tools (especially scraperplanes and chopping tools), and a variety of simple flake tools.

Around 9000 BP sea levels stabilized in Haida Gwaii. Microblade technology was added to the stone tool technology at this time, but no obvious shifts in adaptation are seen from site location and the very limited faunal record from this time (Chapter 12). The introduction of microblade technology presupposes significant shifts in adaptation, possibly environmentally driven, but data are too few to isolate the character of these changes. Over the following millennium, bifacial technology waned in importance, disappearing completely by about 8000 BP, although the remainder of the stone tool assemblage shows little change. Faunal remains are limited to the period prior to 8000 BP and after about 6000 BP. For the early period, only Kilgii Gwaay at 9400 BP exhibits a rich faunal assemblage. The 9300 to

8000 BP raised beach assemblages are limited to a few calcined bones of marine fish, birds, and unidentified mammals.

There is evidence for climatic deterioration in Haida Gwaii commencing about 7000 BP, and by 6000 BP the environment was significantly cooler and wetter. By about 5500 BP, shell middens became a significant part of the archaeological record (Chapter 13). It is not clear to what extent the appearance of this site type in the archaeological record is a function of preservation or of shifts in human adaptation to the landscape. From about 6000 to 5000 BP, stone tool technology appears to have changed little, which argues for the former. At this time we see substantial evidence of organic tools, preserved in the alkaline shell midden soils. The faunal record is much more substantial than in preceding millennia, with a number of mammal, bird, and fish species added to the assemblage documented for earliest Holocene time. It is unclear whether differences other than an abundance of intertidal shellfish reflect sampling and geographic location or adaptational change.

At about 5000 BP, lithic technology, as seen in northern Haida Gwaii, shifted from that characteristic of the Northwest Coast Microblade Tradition to a more general technology of multidirectional and bipolar core reduction, with the latter producing small flakes that were possibly functionally equivalent to Microblade Tradition bladelets (Chapters 13 and 14). Over the next few millennia, a broad range of lithic and organic tools were added to the basic chipped stone technology. Ground stone tools appeared about 4000 BP, but were secondary to bone-working technology throughout the Graham Tradition.

By 3000 BP cedar forests were well established in Haida Gwaii. At this time climate was cool and wet, with conditions similar to those of today. Around 2000 BP a number of new elements were added to the material culture and adaptational repertoire of the people of Haida Gwaii (Chapters 14 and 15). Many of the same stone tools were present but in significantly lower frequencies. Added to the tool assemblages that have been found are a large variety of organic artifacts, many of which are associated with woodworking and more advanced fishing technology. There was a correspondingly significant increase in use of anadromous fish and a decrease in use of terrestrial fauna. These changes were pan-coastal and reflected a more intensive adaptation to a now more mature and productive coastal environment similar to that of historical times. This development may have been enabled in part by the maturing of intertidal environments and anadromous fish habitat, along with the expansion of red cedar forests into the northern Northwest Coast between 5000 and 2000 BP. Together these elements facilitated increased access to a variety of resources, residential stability, and possibly population pressure on resources.

Overall, the archaeological record demonstrates significant technological change and changes in adaptation, at least in resource procurement and settlement patterns. While some of this may have been tied to environmental change, the lag time between adaptive shifts and technological change, seen again and again through the millennia, suggests that cultural change was most likely additive – that is, new technologies and other aspects of prehistoric lifeways were introduced by diffusion, trade, or the introduction of new members to the communities, but not by population replacement. The stability and time depth of Haida culture as inferred from oral history (Chapters 7 and 8) and from linguistic and genetic studies (Greenberg 1986, 1996; Wallace et al. 1999) are consistent with the conservative nature of the archaeological record.

References

Abbott, D.N., and S.D. Keen. 1993. Report on Excavations around Totem Pole Bases at Anthony Island. Royal British Columbia Museum Heritage Record, Victoria.

Acheson, S.R. 1982. Archaeological Investigations at SgA'ngwa-i Inaga'-i. Report on file, British Columbia Archaeology Branch, Victoria.

–. 1985. *Ninstints* Village: A Case of Mistaken Identity. *BC Studies* 67:47-56.

–. 1987. Kunghit Haida Culture History Project Archaeological Investigations for 1986. Unpublished report on file, British Columbia Archaeology Branch, Victoria.

–. 1991. In the Wake of the Ya'áats' Xaatgáay [Iron People]: A Study of Changing Settlement Strategies among the Kunghit Haida. PhD dissertation, Department of Ethnology and Prehistory, University of Oxford, Oxford.

–. 1995. The Clonard Bay Point: Evidence of Lanceolate Bifaces in the Queen Charlotte Islands. *Canadian Journal of Archaeology* 19:141-148.

–. 1998. *In the Wake of the Ya'áats' Xaatgáay [Iron People]: A Study of Changing Settlement Strategies among the Kunghit Haida*. British Archaeological Reports, International Series, No. 711, Oxford.

–. 2003. The Thin Edge: Evidence for Precontact Use and Working of Metal on the Northwest Coast. In *Emerging from the Mist*, edited by R.G. Matson, G. Coupland, and Q. Mackie, pp. 213-229. UBC Press, Vancouver.

Acheson, S.R., and R.J. Wigen. 1989. Did the Haida Whale Prehistorically? Paper presented at the Circum-Pacific Prehistory Conference, Seattle, August.

Acheson, S.R., and S.K. Zacharias. 1985. Kunghit Haida Culture History Project. Results of Phase I: 1984 Archaeological Site Inventory. Report on file, British Columbia Archaeology Branch, Victoria.

Acheson, S.R., S.K. Zacharias, and R.J. Wigen. 1986. Kunghit Haida Culture History Project Archaeological Investigations 1985. Permit Report 1985-9. Report on file, British Columbia Archaeology Branch, Victoria.

Ackerman, R.E. 1988. Early Subsistence Patterns in Southeast Alaska. In *Proceedings of the Nineteenth Annual Conference of the Archaeological Association of the University of Calgary*, edited by Brenda V. Kennedy and Genevieve M. LeMoine, pp. 124-133. University of Calgary Press, Calgary.

–. 1992. Earliest Stone Industries on the North Pacific Coast of North America. *Arctic Anthropology* 20:18-27.

–. 1996a. Cave I, Lime Hills. In *American Beginnings: The Prehistory and Palaeoecology of Beringia*, edited by F. Hadleigh-West, pp. 470-477. University of Chicago Press, Chicago.

–. 1996b. Early Maritime Culture Complexes of the Northern Northwest Coast. In *Early Human Occupation in British Columbia*, edited by R.L. Carlson and L. Dalla Bona, pp. 123-132. UBC Press, Vancouver.

–. 1996c. Ground Hog Bay, Site 2. In *American Beginnings: The Prehistory and Palaeoecology of Beringia*, edited by F. Hadleigh-West, pp. 424-429. University of Chicago Press, Chicago.

–. 1996d. Ilnuk Site. In *American Beginnings: The Prehistory and Palaeoecology of Beringia,* edited by F. Hadleigh-West, pp. 464-469. University of Chicago Press, Chicago.

Ackerman, R.E., T.D. Hamilton, and R. Stuckenrath. 1979. Early Culture Complexes on the Northern Northwest Coast. *Canadian Journal of Archaeology* 3:195-208.

Ackerman, R.E., K.C. Reid, J.D. Gallison, and M.E. Roe. 1985. Archaeology of Heceta Island: A Survey of 16 Timber Harvest Units in the Tongass National Forest, Southeastern Alaska. Project Report No. 3, Center for Northwest Anthropology, Washington State University, Pullman.

Allen, G.B., K.J. Brown, and R.J. Hebda. 1999. Surface Pollen Spectra from South Vancouver Island, British Columbia, Canada. *Canadian Journal of Botany* 77:786-789.

Alley, N.F., and R. Thomson. 1978. *Aspects of Environmental Geology, Parts of Graham Island, Queen Charlotte Islands.* British Columbia Ministry of Environment, Resource Analysis Branch, Bulletin No. 2, Victoria.

Ames, K.M., and H.D. Maschner. 1999. *Peoples of the Northwest Coast: Their Archaeology and Prehistory.* Thames and Hudson, London.

Amos, C.L., J.V. Barrie, and J.T. Judge. 1995. Storm-Enhanced Sand Transport in a Macrotidal Setting, Queen Charlotte Islands, British Columbia, Canada. *Special Publication of the International Association of Sedimentology* 24:53-68.

Anderson, E. 1994. Evolution, Prehistoric Distribution and Systematics of *Martes.* In *Martens, Sables, and Fishers: Biology and Conservation,* edited by S.W. Buskirk, A.S. Harestad, and M.G. Raphael, pp. 13-25. Cornell University Press, Ithaca, NY.

Andrefsky, W. Jr. 1998. *Lithics: Macroscopic Approaches to Analysis.* Cambridge University Press, Cambridge.

Archer, D.J. 1998. Early Holocene Landscapes on the North Coast of British Columbia. Paper presented at the 31st annual meeting of the Canadian Archaeological Association, Victoria.

Arnold, T.G. 2002. Radiocarbon Dates from the Ice-Free Corridor. *Radiocarbon* 44: 437-454.

Atmospheric Environment Service. 1993. Canadian Climate Normals, 1961-1990 British Columbia/Normales Climatiques au Canada, 1961-1990 Colombie-Britannique. Environment Canada, Ottawa.

Avise, J.C. 1994. *Molecular Markers, Natural History, and Evolution.* Chapman and Hall, New York.

Banfield, A.W. 1961. *A Revision of the Reindeer and Caribou, Genus* Rangifer. National Museums of Canada, Bulletin No. 177, Biological Series 66:1-106, Ottawa.

–. 1974. *The Mammals of Canada.* University of Toronto Press, Toronto.

Banner, A., W. MacKenzie, S. Haeussler, S. Thomson, J. Pojar, and R. Trowbridge. 1993. *A Field Guide to the Site Identification and Interpretation for the Prince Rupert Forest Region.* Research Program, British Columbia Ministry of Forests, Victoria.

Barbeau, M. 1953. *Haida Myths Illustrated in Argillite Carvings.* National Museums of Canada, Bulletin No. 127, Anthropological Series 32, Ottawa.

Barrie, J.V. 1991. Contemporary and Relict Titaniferous Sand Facies on the Western Canadian Continental Shelf. *Continental Shelf Research* 11:67-79.

Barrie, J.V., and B.D. Bornhold. 1989. Surficial Geology of Hecate Strait, British Columbia Continental Shelf. *Canadian Journal of Earth Sciences* 26:1241-1254.

Barrie, J.V., and K.W. Conway. 1996a. Evolution of a Nearshore and Coastal Macrotidal Sand Transport System, Queen Charlotte Islands, Canada. In *Geology of Siliciclastic Shelf Seas,* edited by M. DeBatist and J. Jacobs, pp. 233-248. Geological Society Special Publication No. 117, London.

–. 1996b. Sedimentary Processes and Surficial Geology of the Pacific Margin of the Queen Charlotte Islands, British Columbia. In *Current Research 1996-E,* pp. 1-6. Geological Survey of Canada, Ottawa.

–. 1999. Late Quaternary Glaciation and Postglacial Stratigraphy of the Northern Pacific Margin of Canada. *Quaternary Research* 51:113-123.

Barrie, J.V., B.D. Bornhold, K.W. Conway, and J.L. Luternauer. 1991. Surficial Geology of the Northwestern Canadian Continental Shelf. *Continental Shelf Research* 11:701-715.

Barrie, J.V., K.W. Conway, R.W. Mathewes, H.W. Josenhans, and M.J. Johns. 1993. Submerged Late Quaternary Terrestrial Deposits and Paleoenvironments of Northern Hecate Strait, British Columbia Continental Shelf, Canada. *Quaternary International* 20:123-129.

Bartlein, P.J., K.H. Anderson, P.M. Anderson, M.E. Edwards, C.J. Mock, R. Thompson, R.S. Webb, T. Webb III, and C. Whitlock. 1998. Paleoclimate Simulations for North America over the Past 21,000 Years: Features of the Simulated Climate and Comparisons with Paleoenvironmental Data. *Quaternary Science Reviews* 17:549-585.

Bartlett, J. N.d. Remarks on Board the Ship Massachusett's [*sic*] Capt. Joab Prince from Boston, towards Canton. Typescript of manuscript, Special Collections Division, University of British Columbia Library, Vancouver.

Baxter, R.E. 1971. Earthquake Effects on Clams in the Prince of William Sound. In *The Great Alaska Earthquake of 1964: Biology*, National Research Council Publication No. 1604, pp. 238-245. National Academy of Sciences, Washington, DC.

Bell, M.A., and S.A. Foster. 1994. Introduction to the Evolutionary Biology of the Threespine Stickleback. In *Evolution of the Threespine Stickleback*, edited by M.A. Bell and S.A. Foster, pp. 2-27. Oxford University Press, Oxford.

Benninghoff, W.S. 1962. Calculation of Pollen and Spores Density in Sediments by Addition of Exotic Pollen in Known Quantities. *Pollen et Spores* 4:332-333.

Berger, A. 1978. Long-Term Variations of Daily Insolation and Quarternary Climatic Changes. *Journal of Atmospheric Science* 35:2362-2367.

Bernick, K. 1984. Haida Trees: Remains of Canoe Manufacture in the Forests of Southern Masset Inlet. Report of a Detailed Analysis of a Select Sample of Aboriginal Forest Utilization Features in the Area of Masset Inlet, Queen Charlotte Islands. Permit 1984-5. Report on file, British Columbia Archaeology Branch, Victoria.

Bever, M.R. 2001. An Overview of Alaskan Late Pleistocene Archaeology: Historical Themes and Current Perspectives. *Journal of World Prehistory* 15(2):125-191.

Bird, A.L. 1997. Earthquakes in the Queen Charlotte Islands Region: 1982-1996. MSc thesis, Department of Geography, University of Victoria.

Bishop, C. 1967. *The Journal and Letters of Captain Charles Bishop on the North-west Coast of America, in the Pacific and in New South Wales 1794-1799*, edited by Michael Roe (Hakluyt Society, 2nd series, No. 131). Cambridge University Press, Cambridge.

Blackman, M.B. 1979. Northern Haida Land and Resource Utilization: A Preliminary Overview. In *Tales from the Queen Charlotte Islands, Senior Citizens of the Queen Charlotte Islands, Masset*, edited by G.G. Scudder and N. Gessler, pp. 43-55. D.W. Friesen and Sons, Cloverdale, BC.

–. 1981. *Window on the Past: The Photographic Ethnohistory of the Northern and Kaigani Haida*. National Museum of Man, Mercury Series, Ethnology Paper 74. National Museums of Canada, Ottawa.

–. 1990. Haida: Traditional Culture. In *Handbook of North American Indians*. Vol. 7: *Northwest Coast*, edited by W. Suttles, pp. 240-260. Smithsonian Institution, Washington, DC.

Blaise, B., J.J. Clague, and R.W. Mathewes. 1990. Time of Maximum Late Wisconsin Glaciation, West Coast of Canada. *Quaternary Research* 34:282-295.

Boas, F. 1889. First General Report on the Indians of British Columbia. *Fifth Report of the Committee Appointed for the Purpose of Investigating and Publishing Reports on the Physical Characters, Languages, and Industrial and Social Condition of the North-Western Tribes of the Dominion of Canada*, pp. 5-97. British Association for the Advancement of Science, London.

–. 1895. *Indianische Sagen von der Nord-Pacifischen Küste Amerikas – A Translation of Franz Boas' 1895 Edition*. Edited and annotated by Randy Bouchard and Dorothy Kennedy, 2002. Talonbooks, Vancouver.

–. 1898. The Social Organisation of the Haida. *Twelfth and Final Report on the North-Western Tribes of Canada*, pp. 21-27. British Association for the Advancement of Science, London.

Boelscher, M. 1989. *The Curtain Within: Haida Social and Mythical Discourse*. UBC Press, Vancouver.

Boit, J. 1981. *Log of the Union 1794-1796*, edited by Edmund Hays. Massachusetts Historical Society/Oregon Historical Society, Portland, OR.

Bonnichsen, R., and K.L. Turnmire. 1999. An Introduction to the Peopling of the Americas. In *Ice Age Peoples of North America: Environments, Origins, and Adaptations*, edited by R. Bonnichsen and K. Turnmire, pp. 1-27. Oregon State University Press, Corvallis.

Borden, C.E. 1969. Dicussion: Current Archaeological Research on the Northwest Coast. *Northwest Anthropological Research Notes* 3(2):255-263.

Bostwick, T.K. 1984. A Re-examination of the 1949 Queen Charlotte Earthquake. MSc thesis, Department of Geology, University of British Columbia, Vancouver.

Boyd, R.T. 1990. Demographic History, 1774-1874. In *Handbook of North American Indians*. Vol. 7: *Northwest Coast*, edited by W. Suttles, pp. 135-148. Smithsonian Institution, Washington, DC.

–. 1999. *The Coming of the Spirit of Pestilence*. UBC Press, Vancouver.

Breffitt, J. 1993. The Skoglund's Landing Complex: A Re-examination of the Transitional Complex of Artifacts from Skoglund's Landing, Queen Charlotte Islands, British Columbia. MA thesis, Department of Archaeology, Simon Fraser University, Burnaby, BC.

Brooks, A., and H.S. Swarth. 1925. A Distributional List of the Birds of British Columbia. Pacific Coast Avifauna No. 17. Cooper Ornithological Club, Berkeley, CA.

Brown, R. 1869. On the Physical Geography of the Queen Charlotte Islands. *Proceedings of the Royal Geographical Society Journal* 13(5):381-392.

Brown, W.M. 1985. The Mitochondrial Genome of Animals. In *Molecular Evolutionary Genetics*, edited by R.J. MacIntyre, pp. 95-130. Plenum Press, New York.

Bryan, K. 1941. Geologic Antiquity of Man in America. *Science* 93:505-514.

Buckland-Nicks, J., and T.E. Reimchen. 1995. A Novel Association between an Endemic Stickleback and a Parasitic Dinoflagellate. 3: Details of the Life Cycle. *Arch. Protistenkd.* 145:165-175.

Buckland-Nicks, J., T.E. Reimchen, and D.J. Garbary. 1997. *Haidadinium gasterosteophilum* gen. et. sp. nov. (Phytodiniales, Dinophyceae), a Freshwater Ectoparasite on Stickleback (*Gasterosteus aculeatus*) from the Queen Charlotte Islands, Canada. *Canadian Journal of Botany* 75:1936-1940.

Byun, S.A. 1998. Quaternary Biogeography of Western North America: Insights from mtDNA Phylogeography of Endemic Vertebrates from Haida Gwaii. PhD dissertation, University of Victoria.

Byun, S.A., B. Koop, and T.E. Reimchen. 1997. North American Black Bear mtDNA Phylogeography: Implications for Morphology and the Haida Gwaii Refugium Controversy. *Evolution* 51:1647-1653.

–. 1999. Coastal Refugia and Postglacial Recolonization Routes: Reply to Dembowski, Stone and Cook. *Evolution* 53:2013-2015.

–. 2002. Evolution of Dawson Caribou. *Canadian Journal of Zoology* 80:956-960.

Calder, J.A., and R.L. Taylor. 1968. Flora of the Queen Charlotte Islands. Part 1, Systematics of Vascular Plants. Research Branch, Canada Department of Agriculture Monograph No. 4, Pt. 1, 659 pp., Ottawa.

Canada. N.d. Federal Census Returns, 1881. Microfilm copy. British Columbia Archives and Records Service, Victoria.

Cannon, A. 1991. *The Economic Prehistory of Namu*. Department of Archaeology, Simon Fraser University, Burnaby.

–. 2000. Settlement and Sea-Levels on the Central Coast of British Columbia: Evidence from Shell Midden Cores. *American Antiquity* 65:67-77.

Cannon, A., H. Schwarcz, and M. Knyf. 1999. Marine-Based Subsistence Trends and the Stable Isotope Analysis of Dog Bones from Namu, British Columbia. *Journal of Archaeological Science* 26:4.

Carey, J.S., T.F. Moslow, and J.V. Barrie. 1995. Origin and Distribution of Holocene Temperate Carbonates, Hecate Strait, Western Canada Continental Shelf. *Journal of Sedimentary Research* A65:185-194.

Carlson, C.C. 1979. The Early Component at Bear Cove. *Canadian Journal of Archaeology* 3:177-194.

Carlson, R.L. 1990. Cultural Antecedents. In *Handbook of North American Indians*. Vol 7: *Northwest Coast*, edited by W. Suttles, pp. 60-69. Smithsonian Institution, Washington, DC.

Carlson, R.L. 1972. Excavations at Kwatna. In *Salvage '71: Reports on Salvage Archaeology Undertaken in British Columbia in 1971,* edited by R. Carlson, pp. 41-58. Department of Archaeology, Publication 1, Simon Fraser University, Burnaby.

–. 1976. The 1974 Excavations at McNaughton Island. In *Current Research Reports,* edited by R.L. Carlson, pp. 99-114. Department of Archaeology, Publication 3, Simon Fraser University, Burnaby.

–. 1994. Trade and Exchange in Prehistoric British Columbia. In *Prehistoric Exchange Systems in North America,* edited by T. Baugh and J. Ericson, pp. 307-361. Plenum Press, New York.

–. 1996. Early Namu. In *Early Human Occupation in British Columbia,* edited by R.L. Carlson and L. Dalla Bona, pp. 3-10, 83-102. UBC Press, Vancouver.

–. 2004. The Pre-microblade Horizon on the Northwest Coast and the Nenana Complex. Paper presented at the 2004 Alaska Anthropological Association Meetings, Whitehorse, April.

Chittenden, N. 1884. *Official Report of the Exploration of the Queen Charlotte Islands.* Printed by the Authority of the Government, Victoria.

Christensen, T. 1995. Archaeological Impact Assessment of Unsurveyed Crown Land, District Lot 16, Queen Charlotte District. Permit No. 1995-220A. Unpublished report on file, British Columbia Archaeology Branch, Victoria.

–. 1996. Report on the 1995 Sgan Gwaii Pole Conservation Program, Anthony Island, Haida Gwai. Unpublished report on file, Parks Canada Archaeology Services, Victoria.

–. 1997. The Gwaii Haanas Archaeological Project: Raised Beach Survey 1995 Field Report. Report on file, Cultural Resource Services (Western Canada Service Centre), Parks Canada, Victoria.

–. 1998. The Gravel Culture: A Geoarchaeological Analysis of the Lyell Bay South Raised Beach Site, Gwaii Haanas, Haida Gwaii. Manuscript on file, Parks Canada, Victoria.

–. 2000. *Massett Reserve #2 Hiellen Village/Tow Hill Clam Cannery Archaeological Impact Assessment* (Non-permit). On file, Economic Development and Heritage Resources, Old Masset Village Council, Masset, BC.

Christensen, T., and J. Stafford. 2000. *Appendix XVII: C.F.S. Masset: An Archaeological Inventory.* On file, Department of National Defence, CFB Esquimalt, Esquimalt, BC.

Christensen, T., J. Stafford, and J. Lindbergh. 1999. Qay'llnagaay Heritage Center Development, Skidegate Indian Reserve No. 1 Archaeological Impact Assessment. Report on file, Millennia Research, Victoria.

Clague, J.J. 1977. Quadra Sand: A Study of the Late Pleistocene Geology and Geomorphic History of Coastal Southwest British Columbia. Geological Survey of Canada Paper 77-17:24, Ottawa.

–. 1981. Late Quaternary Geology and Geochronology of British Columbia. Part 2: Summary and Discussion of Radiocarbon-Dated Quaternary History. Geological Survey of Canada Paper 80-35:41, Ottawa.

–. 1983. Glacio-Isostatic Effects of the Cordilleran Ice Sheet, British Columbia, Canada. In *Shorelines and Isostasy,* edited by D. Smith and A. Dawson, pp. 321-343. Academic Press, London.

–. 1984. *Quaternary Geology and Geomorphology, Smithers–Terrace–Prince Rupert Area, British Columbia.* Geological Survey of Canada Memoir No. 413, Ottawa.

–. 1989. Quaternary Geology of the Queen Charlotte Islands. In *The Outer Shores,* edited by G.G.E. Scudder and N. Gessler, pp. 65-74. Queen Charlotte Islands Museum Press, Skidegate.

Clague, J.J., and B.D. Bornhold. 1980. Morphology and Littoral Processes of the Pacific Coast of Canada. In *The Coastline of Canada,* edited by S.B. McCann, pp. 339-380. Geological Survey of Canada Paper 80-10, Ottawa.

Clague, J.J., J.R. Harper, R.J. Hebda, and D.E. Howes. 1982a. Late Quaternary Sea Levels and Crustal Movements, Coastal British Columbia. *Canadian Journal of Earth Sciences* 19:597-618.

Clague, J.J., R.W. Mathewes, and B.G. Warner. 1982b. Late Quaternary Geology of Eastern Graham Island, Queen Charlotte Islands, British Columbia. *Canadian Journal of Earth Sciences* 19:1786-1795.

Clague, J.J., R.W. Mathewes, and T.A. Ager. 2004. Environments of Northwest North America Before the Last Glacial Maximum. In *Entering America: Northeast Asia and Beringia Before the Last Glacial Maximum,* edited by D.B. Madsen, pp. 63-96. University of Utah Press, Salt Lake City.

Clark, T. 2000. Prehistoric Cultural Change on Southern Vancouver Island: The Applicability of Current Explanation of the Marpole Transition. MA thesis, Department of Anthropology, University of Victoria.

Clarke, T. 1998. Molecular Re-evaluation of the *Nebria gregaria* Infragroup and the Implications for the Existence of an Ice Age Refugium on the Queen Charlotte Islands. MSc thesis, Department of Biology, University of Victoria.

Clarke, T.E., T.E. Reimchen, D. Kavanaugh, and D.B. Levin. 2001. Rapid Evolution in *Nebria* (Coleoptera: Carabidae) and the Paleogeography of the Queen Charlotte Islands. *Evolution* 55: 1408-1418.

COHMAP. 1988. Climatic Changes of the Last 18,000 Years: Observation and Model Simulations. *Science* 241:1043-1052.

Cole, D., and D. Darling. 1990. History of the Early Period. In *Handbook of North American Indians.* Vol. 7: *Northwest Coast,* edited by W. Suttles, pp. 119-134. Smithsonian Institution. Washington, DC.

Collison, W.H. 1915. *In the Wake of the War Canoe.* Seeley, Service, London.

Colnett, J. N.d. A Voyage to the N.W. Side of America 1786-1788. Unpublished journal, Public Record Office, London.

Compton, B.D. 1993. The North Wakashan "Wild Carrots": Clarification of Some Ethnobotanical Ambiguity in a Pacific Northwest Apiaceae. *Economic Botany* 47:297-303.

Cook, J.P. 1996. Healy Lake. In *American Beginnings: The Prehistory and Palaeoecology of Beringia,* edited by F. Hadleigh-West, pp. 323-328. University of Chicago Press, Chicago.

Cooper, J. N.d. Letter to Colonial Secretary, 10 October 1860. Colonial Correspondence File 347/26a. British Columbia Archives and Records Service, Victoria.

Coupland, G. 1988. *Prehistoric Cultural Change at Kitselas Canyon.* Canadian Museum of Civilization, Mercury Series 138. National Museums of Canada, Ottawa.

–. 1998. Maritime Adaptation and Evolution of the Developed Northwest Coast Pattern on the Central Northwest Coast. *Arctic Anthropology* 35(1):36-56.

Cowan, I. McT. 1989. Birds and Mammals on the Queen Charlotte Islands. In *The Outer Shores,* edited by G.G.E. Scudder and N. Gessler, pp. 175-186. Queen Charlotte Islands Museum Press, Skidegate.

Cowan, I. McT., and C.J. Guiget. 1978. *The Mammals of British Columbia.* Handbook No. 11. British Columbia Provincial Museum, Victoria.

Crawford, W.R., M.J. Woodward, G.G. Foreman, and R.E. Thomson. 1995. Oceanographic Features of Hecate Strait and Queen Charlotte Sound in Summer. *Atmosphere-Ocean* 33:639-681.

Crockford, S.J. 1994. Faunal Analysis Report for 922TA1. Unpublished report on file, Parks Canada, Victoria.

Croes, D.L. 1995. *The Hoko River Archaeological Site Complexes.* Washington State University Press, Pullman.

Cronin, M.A., S.C. Armstrup, G.W. Garner, and E.R. Vyse. 1991. Interspecific and Intraspecific Mitochondrial DNA Variation in North American Bears (*Ursus*). *Canadian Journal of Zoology* 69:2985-2992.

Cross, D. N.d. *Journal of a Voyage Round the World in the Brig* Rob Roy *in the Years 1821, 1822, 1823, 1824.* Nantucket Historical Society, Nantucket, MA.

Cruikshank, J. 1990. *Life Lived Like a Story.* UBC Press, Vancouver.

Curtis, E.S. 1916. The Nootka. The Haida. *The North American Indian: Being a Series of Volumes Picturing and Describing the Indians of the United States, the Dominion of Canada, and Alaska,* edited by E.S. Curtis, vol. 11. E.S. Curtis, Seattle; The University Press, Cambridge, MA.

Cwynar, L.C. 1990. A Late Quaternary Vegetation History from Lily Lake, Chilkat Peninsula, Southeast Alaska. *Canadian Journal of Botany* 68:1106-1112.

Cwynar, L.C., E. Burden, and J.C. McAndrews. 1979. An Inexpensive Method for Concentrating Pollen and Spores from Fine-Grained Sediments. *Canadian Journal of Earth Sciences* 16:1115-1120.

Cybulski, J.S. 1973. *Haida Burial Practices: Three Archaeological Examples*. National Museum of Man, Mercury Series, Archaeological Survey of Canada Paper 9. National Museums of Canada, Ottawa.

–. 2001. Human Biological Relationships for the Northern Northwest Coast. In *Perspectives on Northern Northwest Coast Prehistory*, edited by J. Cybulski, pp. 107-144. Canadian Museum of Civilization, Mercury Series, Archaeological Survey of Canada Paper 160. National Museums of Canada, Ottawa.

Dady, P., and T. Christensen. 2000. Archaeological Inventories at Select Department of National Defence Properties, C.F.B Esquimalt – Vol. 2: Heals Rifle Range (Saanich), Nanaimo Rifle Range, C.F.M.E.T.R. Nanoose Bay, C.F.S. Masset. Report on file, British Columbia Archaeology Branch, Victoria.

Dalzell, K.E. 1968. *The Queen Charlotte Islands 1774-1966*. Bill Ellis, Queen Charlotte City.

Davis, S.D. 1989. *The Hidden Falls Site, Baranof Island, Alaska*. Alaska Anthropological Association Series, No. 5. Anchorage.

–. 1996. Hidden Falls. In *American Beginnings: The Prehistory and Palaeoecology of Beringia*, edited by F. Hadleigh-West, pp. 413-423. University of Chicago Press, Chicago.

Dawson, G.M. 1880. Report on the Queen Charlotte Islands, 1878. *Geological Survey of Canada Report of Progress for 1878-79*, vol. 4. Ottawa.

–. 1993. *To the Charlottes: George Dawson's 1878 Survey of the Queen Charlotte Islands*, edited by Douglas Cole and Bradley Lockner. UBC Press, Vancouver.

de Laguna, F. 1934. *The Archaeology of Cook Inlet, Alaska*. University of Pennsylvania Museum Press, Philadelphia.

–. 1952. Some Dynamic Forces in Tlingit Society. *Southwestern Journal of Anthropology* 8:1-12.

–. 1956. Chugash Prehistory: The Archaeology of Prince William Sound, Alaska. *University of Washington Publications in Anthropology*, No. 13, Seattle.

–. 1960. *The Story of a Tlingit Community (Angoon): A Problem in the Relationship between Archaeological, Ethnological, and Historical Methods*. Bureau of American Ethnology, Bulletin No. 172. Smithsonian Institution, Washington, DC.

–. 1972. Under Mount Saint Elias: The History and the Culture of the Yakutat Tlingit. 3 pts. *Smithsonian Contributions to Anthropology*, vol. 7. Smithsonian Institution, Washington, DC.

de Laguna, F., F.A. Riddell, D.F. McGeein, K.S. Lane, J.A. Freed, and C. Osborne. 1964. *Archaeology of the Yakutat Bay Area, Alaska*. Bureau of American Ethnology, Bulletin No. 192. Smithsonian Institution, Washington DC.

Deagle, B.E., T.E. Reimchen, D. Levin. 1996. Origins of Endemic Stickleback from the Queen Charlotte Islands: Mitochondrial and Morphological Evidence. *Canadian Journal of Zoology* 74:1045-1056.

Deans, J. 1888. A Strange Way of Preserving Peace amongst Neighbors. *American Antiquarian and Oriental Journal* 10:42-43.

–. 1895. The Hidery Story of Creation. *American Antiquarian* 17:61-67.

–. 1899. Tales from the Totems of the Hidery. *Archives of the International Folk-Lore Association*, vol. 2. Chicago.

Demboski, J.R., K.D. Stone, and J.A. Cook. 1999. Further Perspectives on the Haida Gwaii Glacial Refugium. *Evolution* 53:2008-2012.

Derev'anko, A. (editor). 1998. *The Paleolithic of Siberia: New Discoveries and Interpretations*. University of Illinois Press, Chicago.

Dillehay, T.D. 2000. *The Settlement of the Americas: A New Prehistory*. Basic Books, New York.

Dixon, E.J. 1993. Quest for the Origins of the First American. University of New Mexico Press, Albuquerque.

–. 1999. *Bones, Boats and Bison: Archaeology and the First Colonization of Western North America*. University of New Mexico Press, Albuquerque.

–. 2001. Human Colonization of the Americas: Timing, Technology and Process. *Quaternary Science Reviews* 20:277-300.

–. 2002. How and When Did People First Come to North America? *Athena Review* 3:23-27.

Dixon, E.J., T.H. Heaton, T.E. Fifield, T.D. Hamilton, D.E. Putnam, and F. Grady. 1997. Late Quaternary Regional Geoarchaeology of Southeast Alaska Karst: A Progress Report. *Geoarchaeology* 12:689-712.

Dixon, G. 1789. *A Voyage Round the World; but More Particularly to the North-West Coast of America: Performed in 1785, 1786, 1787, and 1788, in the* King George *and* Queen Charlotte. Geo. Goulding, London.

Douglas, G.W., G.B. Straley, and D. Meidinger (editors). 1989. The Vascular Plants of British Columbia. *British Columbia Ministry of Forests, Special Report Series 1-4*, Victoria.

Douglas, J. N.d. Private Papers, Second Series 1853. A/B/40/D75.4 British Columbia Archives and Records Service, Victoria.

Drucker, P. 1939. Rank, Wealth, and Kinship in Northwest Coast Society. *American Anthropologist* n.s. 41:55-64.

–. 1943. *Archaeological Survey on the Northern Northwest Coast*. Bureau of American Ethnology, Bulletin No. 133. Smithsonian Institution, Washington, DC.

–. 1955. *Indians of the Northwest Coast*. American Museum of Natural History (1963 ed.). The Natural History Press, New York.

–. 1965. *Cultures of the North Pacific Coast*. Chandler Publishing, Scranton, PA.

Duff, W. 1964. *The Impact of the White Man: The Indian History of British Columbia*. Anthropology in British Columbia, Memoir 5. Provincial Museum of British Columbia, Victoria.

–. N.d. Field Notebooks for 1953, 1954, and 1957 Trips to the Queen Charlotte Islands. Anthropological Collections Section, Royal British Columbia Museum, Victoria.

Duff, W., and M. Kew. 1958. Anthony Island: A Home of the Haidas. In *British Columbia Provincial Museum of Natural History and Anthropology Report for 1957*, pp. 37-64. Victoria.

Dumond, D.E. 1969. Toward a Prehistory of the Na-Dene, with a General Comment on Population Movements among Nomadic Hunters. *American Anthropologist* 71:857-863.

–. 1998. The Archaeology of Migration: Following the Fainter Footprints. *Arctic Anthropology* 35:59-76.

Dunn, J. 1844. *History of the Oregon Territory and British North-American Fur Trade; with an Account of the Habits and Customs of the Principal Native Tribes on the Northern Continent*. Edwards and Hughes, London.

Durlach, T.M. 1928. The Relationship Systems of the Tlingit, Haida and Tsimshian. *Publications of the American Ethnological Society* 11. New York.

Earle, T. 1989. The Evolution of Chiefdoms. *Current Anthropology* 30:1:84-88.

Easterbrook, D.J. 1992. Advance and Retreat of Cordilleran Ice Sheets, Washington. *USA Geographie Physique et Quaternaire* 46:51-68.

Easton, N.A. 1992. Mal de Mer above Terra Incognita, or, "What Ails the Coastal Migration Theory?" *Arctic Anthropology* 29:28-42.

Ebbits, J. N.d. *Log of the Ship* Pearl *1804-1808*. Massachusetts Historical Society, Boston.

Eger, J.L. 1990. Patterns of Geographic Variation in the Skull of Nearctic Ermine (*Mustela erminea*). *Canadian Journal of Zoology* 68:1241-1249.

Eldridge, M., A.P. Mackie, and B. Wilson. 1993. Archaeological Inventory of Gwaii Haanas National Park Reserve, 1992. Report on file, Cultural Resource Services (Western Canada Service Centre), Parks Canada, Victoria.

Elliot, G.E. 1957. *Empire and Enterprise in the North Pacific, 1785-1825: A Survey and an Interpretation Emphasizing the Role and Character of Russian Enterprise*. PhD dissertation, University of Toronto.

Ellis, D. 1974. The Diary of a Queen Charlotte Island Kayaker. *The Charlottes, A Journal of the Queen Charlotte Islands* 3:50-53.

Engstrom, D.R., B.C.S. Hansen, and H.E. Wright. 1990. A Possible Younger Dryas Record in Southeastern Alaska. *Science* 250:1383-1385.

Enrico, J. N.d. Haida Place Names. Manuscript on file, Queen Charlotte Islands Museum, Skidegate.

–. 1995. *Skidegate Haida Myths and Histories*. Collected by J.R. Swanton. Queen Charlotte Islands Museum Press, Skidegate.

Erlandson, J.M. 1994. *Early Hunter-Gatherers of the California Coast*. Plenum Press, New York.

Erlandson, J.M., and M.L. Moss. 1996. The Pleistocene-Holocene Transition along the Pacific Coast of North America. In *Humans at the End of the Ice-Age,* edited by L.G. Straus, B.V. Eriksen, J.M. Erlandson, and D.R. Yesner, pp. 277-302. Plenum Press, New York.
–. 2001. Shellfish Feeders, Carrion Eaters and the Archaeology of Aquatic Adaptations. *American Antiquity* 66(3):413-432.
Erlandson, J.M., T.C. Rick, R.L. Bellanoweth, and D.J. Kennett. 1999. Marine Subsistence at a 9300-Year-Old Shell Midden on Santa Rosa Island, California. *Journal of Field Archaeology* 26:255-265.
Eschmeyer, W.N., and E.S. Herald. 1983. *A Field Guide to Pacific Coast Fishes: North America.* Houghton Mifflin, Boston.
Fægri, K.J., and J. Iversen. 1989. *Textbook of Pollen Analysis,* 4th ed. Wiley, London.
Fairbanks, R.G. 1989. A 17,000-Year Glacio-Eustatic Sea Level Record: Influence of Glacial Melting Rates on Younger Dryas Event and Deep-Ocean Circulation. *Nature* 352:637-642.
Faught, M.K. 2003. Geophysical Remote Sensing and Underwater Cultural Resource Management of Submerged Prehistoric Sites in Apalachee Bay: A Deep Water Example, Site Predictive Models, and Site Discoveries. In *Proceedings: Twenty-Second Annual Gulf of Mexico Information Transfer Meetings, 2002,* edited by M. McKay. US Geological Survey, Minerals Management Service, New Orleans.
Fedje, D.W. 1991. Pollen Analysis, South Skung-Wai Meadow. Unpublished paper, Department of Archaeology, University of Calgary.
–. 1993. Sea-Levels and Prehistory in Gwaii Haanas. MA thesis, Department of Archaeology, University of Calgary.
–. 1995. Early Human Presence in Banff National Park, Alberta. In *Early Human History of British Columbia,* edited by R.L. Carlson and L. Dalla Bona, pp. 35-44. UBC Press, Vancouver.
–. 2002. The Early Post-Glacial History of the Northern Northwest Coast: A View from Haida Gwaii and Hecate Strait. *Athena Review* 3:28-30.
–. 2003. Earliest Holocene Maritime Occupation on Haida Gwaii (Queen Charlotte Islands). Paper presented at the 3rd annual conference of the International Geological Correlation Program – Project 464 (IGCP464), Wollongong, Australia.
–. 2005. Karst Caves and Drowned Landscapes: Windows on Environmental Change and Archaeological Visibility at the Pleistocene-Holocene Transition. Paper presented at the 2005 Canadian Archaeological Association meetings, Nanaimo, May.
Fedje, D.W., and T. Christensen. 1999. Modeling Paleoshorelines and Locating Early Holocene Coastal Sites in Haida Gwaii. *American Antiquity* 64(4):635-652.
Fedje, D.W., and H. Josenhans. 2000. Drowned Forests and Archaeology on the Continental Shelf of British Columbia, Canada. *Geology* 28:99-102.
Fedje, D.W., and J.R. Southon. N.d. Parks Canada Radiocarbon Database, Victoria.
Fedje, D.W., and I.D. Sumpter. 2004. 2003 Season Gwaii Haanas Archaeology and Paleoecology Report. Manuscript on file, Cultural Resources Services (Western Canada Service Centre), Parks Canada, Victoria.
Fedje, D.W., Captain Gold, and Guujaw. 1995. Graham Island Site Reconnaissance, 1995. Report submitted to British Columbia Archaeology Branch, Victoria.
Fedje, D.W., J.B. McSporran, and A.R. Mason. 1996. Early Holocene Archaeology and Paleoecology at the Arrow Creek Sites in Gwaii Haanas. *Arctic Anthropology* 33:116-142.
Fedje, D.W., R.J. Wigen, Q. Mackie, C.R. Lake, and I.D. Sumpter. 2001. Preliminary Results from Investigations at Kilgii Gwaay: An Early Holocene Archaeological Site on Ellen Island, Haida Gwaii, British Columbia. *Canadian Journal of Archaeology* 25:98-120.
Fedje, D.W., I.D. Sumpter, A.P. Mackie, and J. Morton. 2002. Gwaii Haanas Archaeological Resource Description and Analysis. Manuscript on file, Cultural Resource Services (Western Canada Service Centre), Parks Canada, Victoria.
Fedje, D.W., Q. Mackie, E.J. Dixon, and T.H. Heaton. 2004a. Late Wisconsin Environments and Archaeological Visibility on the Northern Northwest Coast. In *Entering America: Northeast Asia and Beringia before the Last Glacial Maximum,* edited by David B. Madsen, pp. 97-138. University of Utah Press, Salt Lake City.
Fedje, D.W., R.J. Wigen, D. McLaren, and Q. Mackie. 2004b. Archaeology and environments of karst landscapes in southern Haida Gwaii (Queen Charlotte Islands), West Coast,

Canada. Paper presented at the 2004 Northwest Anthropological Conference, Eugene, OR, March.

Fedduccia, A. 1996. *The Origin and Evolution of Birds.* Yale University Press, New Haven, CT.

Fisher, R. 1977. *Contact and Conflict: Indian-European Relations in British Columbia, 1774-1890.* UBC Press, Vancouver.

Fladmark, K.R. 1969. Preliminary Report on the Archaeology of the Queen Charlotte Islands – 1969 Field Season. Manuscript on file, British Columbia Archaeology Branch, Victoria.

–. 1970. A Preliminary Report on the Archaeology of the Queen Charlotte Islands. In *Archaeology in BC, New Discoveries,* edited by Roy Carlson, pp. 18-45. *BC Studies* Special Issue No. 6-7.

–. 1971a. New Radiocarbon Dates May Push Back History in the Queen Charlotte Islands. *The Midden* 3(5):11-15.

–. 1971b. Early Microblade Industries on the Queen Charlotte Islands, British Columbia. Manuscript on file, British Columbia Archaeology Branch, Victoria.

–. 1973. The Richardson Ranch Site: A 19th Century Haida House. In *Historical Archaeology in Northwest North America,* edited by R. Geddy and K. Fladmark, pp. 53-107. University of Calgary, Archaeological Association, Calgary.

–. 1975. *A Paleoecological Model for Northwest Coast Prehistory.* National Museum of Man, Mercury Series, Archaeological Survey of Canada Paper 43. National Museums of Canada, Ottawa.

–. 1979a. Routes: Alternate Migration Corridors for Early Man in North America. *American Antiquity* 44:55-69.

–. 1979b. The Early Prehistory of the Queen Charlotte Islands. *Archaeology* 32(2):38-45.

–. 1982. An Introduction to the Prehistory of British Columbia. *Canadian Journal of Archaeology* 6:95-156.

–. 1983. Times and Places: Environmental Correlates of Mid-to-Late Wisconsinan Human Population Expansion in North America. In *Early Man in the New World,* edited by R. Shutler, pp. 13-41. Sage Publications, Beverly Hills, CA.

–. 1986. Lawn Point and Kasta: Early Microblade Sites on the Queen Charlotte Islands, British Columbia. *Canadian Journal of Archaeology* 10:39-58.

–. 1989. The Native Culture History of the Queen Charlotte Islands. In *The Outer Shores,* edited by G.G.E. Scudder and N. Gessler, pp. 199-222. Queen Charlotte Islands Museum Press, Skidegate.

–. 1990. Possible Early Human Occupation of the Queen Charlotte Islands, British Columbia. *Canadian Journal of Archaeology* 14:183-197.

–. 2001. From Land to Sea. Late Quaternary Environments of the Northern Northwest Coast. In *Perspectives on Northern Northwest Coast Prehistory,* edited by Jerome S. Cybulski, pp. 25-48. Canadian Museum of Civilization, Mercury Series, Archaeological Survey of Canada Paper 160. National Museums of Canada, Ottawa.

Fladmark, K.R., K.M. Ames, and P.D. Sutherland. 1990. Prehistory of the Northern Coast of British Columbia. In *Handbook of North American Indians.* Vol. 7: *The Northwest Coast,* edited by W. Suttles, pp. 229-239. Smithsonian Institution, Washington, DC.

Fleurieu, C.P. 1801. *A Voyage Round the World Performed during the Years 1790, 1791 and 1792,* by Etienne Marchand. 2 vols. T.N. Longman and O. Rees, London.

Foster, J.B. 1965. The Evolution of the Mammals of the Queen Charlotte Islands, British Columbia. *Occasional Papers of the British Columbia Provincial Museum,* No. 14. British Columbia Provincial Museum, Victoria.

Fox, R. 1967. *Kinship and Marriage: An Anthropological Perspective.* Penguin, Harmondsworth, Middlesex.

Friele, P.A., and I. Hutchinson. 1993. Holocene Sea-Level Change on the Central West Coast of Vancouver Island, British Columbia. *Canadian Journal of Earth Sciences* 30:832-840.

Furgerson, S. N.d. Journal of a Voyage from Boston to the North-West Coast of America, in the Brig *Otter,* Samuel Hill Commander, March 31, 1809 to March 24, 1811. Beinecke Library, Yale University.

Gach, M.H., and T.E. Reimchen. 1989. Mitochondrial DNA Patterns among Endemic Stickleback from the Queen Charlotte Islands: A Preliminary Survey. *Canadian Journal of Zoology* 67:1324-1328.

Gale, W.A. N.d. Journal Kept on Board the Ship *Albatross* 1809-1812. Bancroft Library, University of California, Berkeley.

Gessler, N. N.d. Dating the Early Component at Kiusta, Queen Charlotte Islands. Paper presented at the 21st annual Canadian Archaeological Association Meetings, Whistler, BC, May.

—. 1974. Archaeology in the Queen Charlottes: A Preliminary Report. *The Midden* 4(2):2-7.

—. 1975. Archaeology at K'Yuust'aa (Kiusta), Interim Report [1975]. Haida Museum, Masset. Report on file, British Columbia Archaeology Branch, Victoria.

—. 1988. Initial Radiocarbon Dates Kiusta, Queen Charlotte Islands, British Columbia, Canada. On file, Anthropological Collections Section, Royal British Columbia Museum, Victoria.

Gessler, N., and L. Watney. 1976. Archaeological reconnaisance from Rennel Sound to Tian Head, Queen Charlotte Islands, British Columbia. Report on file, British Columbia Archaeology Branch, Victoria.

Giannico, G.R., and D.W. Nagorsen. 1989. Geographic and Sexual Variation in the Skull of Pacific Coast Marten (*Martes americana*). *Canadian Journal of Zoology* 67:1386-1393.

Gibson, J.R. 1992. *Otter Skins, Boston Ships and China Goods: The Maritime Fur Trade of the Northwest Coast, 1785-1841.* McGill-Queen's University Press, Montreal and Kingston.

Gilbert, G.R., and J.V. Barrie. 1985. Provenance and Sedimentary Processes of Ice-Scoured Surficial Sediments, Labrador Shelf. *Canadian Journal of Earth Sciences* 22:1066-1079.

Gingerich, P.D. 1993. Rates of Evolution in Plio-Pleistocene Mammals: Six Case Studies. In *Morphological Change in Quaternary Mammals of North America*, edited by R.A. Martin and A.D. Barnosky, pp. 84-106. Cambridge University Press, New York.

Goebel, T. 1999. Pleistocene Human Colonization of Siberia and Peopling of the Americas: An Ecological Approach. *Evolution Anthropology* 8:208-227.

Goebel, T., and S.B. Slobodin. 1999. The Colonization of Western Beringia: Technology, Ecology, and Adaptations. In *Ice Age People of North America: Environments, Origins, and Adaptations*, edited by R. Bonnichsen and K.L. Turnmire, pp. 104-155. Oregon State University Press, Corvallis.

Goebel, T., W.R. Powers, N.H. Bigelow, and A.S. Higgs. 1996. Walker Road. In *American Beginnings: The Prehistory and Palaeoecology of Beringia*, edited by F. Hadleigh-West, pp. 356-362. University of Chicago Press, Chicago.

Goebel, T., M.R. Waters, I. Buvit, M.V. Konstantinov, and A.V. Konstantinov. 2000. Studenoe-2 and the Origins of Microblade Technologies in the Transbaikal, Siberia. *Antiquity* 74:567-575.

Gottfried, M., H. Pauli, and G. Grabherr. 1998. Prediction of Vegetation Patterns at the Limits of Plant Life: A New View of the Alpine-Nival Ecotone. *Arctic and Alpine Research* 30:207-221.

Green, J.S. 1915. *Journal of a Tour on the Northwest Coast of America in the Year 1829*. Frederick Heartman, New York.

Greenberg, J.H. 1986. *Language in the Americas*. Stanford University Press, Stanford, CA.

—. 1996. Beringia and New World Origins II: The Linguistic Evidence. In *American Beginnings: The Prehistory and Palaeoecology of Beringia*, edited by F. Hadleigh-West, pp. 525-536. University of Chicago Press, Chicago.

Greenberg, J.H, C.G. Turner II, and S. Zegura 1986. The Settlement of the Americas: A Comparison of the Linguistic, Dental and Genetic Evidence. *Current Anthropology* 25: 477-497.

Grimm, E. 1991. TILIAGRAPH 2.0.b.5 (computer software). Illinois State Museum, Research and Collections Center, Springfield, IL.

—. 1993. TILIA v2.0 (computer software). Illinois State Museum, Research and Collections Center, Springfield, IL.

Grinnell, J., and J.S. Dixon. 1926. Two New Races of the Pine Marten from the Pacific Coast of North America. *University of California Publications in Zoology* 21:411-417.

Haggarty, J.C., and R.I. Inglis. 1985. Historical Resources Site Survey and Assessment Pacific Rim National Park. National Historic Parks and Sites Branch, Parks Service, Environment Canada, Ottawa.

Hagmeier, E.M. 1955. The Genus *Martes* (Mustelidae) in North America: Its Distribution, Variation, Classification, Phylogeny, and Relationship to Old World Forms. PhD dissertation, Department of Zoology, University of British Columbia.

–. 1961. Variation and Relationships in North American Marten. *Canadian Field-Naturalist* 75:122-137.

Hall, E.R. 1981. *The Mammals of North America*, vol. 2. 2nd ed. John Wiley and Sons, New York.

Ham, L.C. 1988. An Archaeological Impact Assessment of the Cohoe Creek Site (FjUb 10), Port Clements, Queen Charlotte Islands, British Columbia. Report on file, British Columbia Archaeology Branch, Victoria.

–. 1990. The Cohoe Creek Site: A Late Moresby Tradition Shell Midden. *Canadian Journal of Archaeology* 14:199-221.

Hamann, A., Y.A. El-Kassaby, M.P. Koshy, and G. Namkoong. 1998. Multivariate Analysis of Allozymic and Quantitative Trait Variation in *Alnus rubra*: Geographic Patterns and Evolutionary Implications. *Canadian Journal of Forest Research* 28:1557-1565.

Hamel, P.J. 1989. A Bird Population Study of the Delkatla Wildlife Sanctuary, Masset, Queen Charlotte Islands. In *The Outer Shores*, edited by G.G.E. Scudder and N. Gessler, pp. 187-194. Queen Charlotte Islands Museum Press, Skidegate.

Hamilton, T.D., and T. Goebel. 1999. Late Pleistocene Peopling of Alaska. In *Ice Age People of North America: Environments, Origins, and Adaptations*, edited by R. Bonnichsen and K.L. Turnmire, pp. 156-199. Oregon State University Press, Corvallis.

Hansen, B.C., and D.R. Engstrom. 1996. Vegetation History of Pleasant Island, Southeastern Alaska, since 13,000 Yr BP. *Quaternary Research* 46:161-175.

Hare, S.R., and R.C. Francis. 1995. Climate Change and Salmon Production in the Northeast Pacific Ocean. In *Climate Change and Northern Fish Populations*, edited by R.J. Beamish, pp. 357-372. Canadian Special Publication on Fishery and Aquatic Sciences No. 121.

Harington, C.R. 1975. Pleistocene Musk Oxen (*Symbos*) from Alberta and British Columbia. *Canadian Journal of Earth Sciences* 12:903-919.

Harington, C.R., and F.V. Clulow. 1973. Pleistocene Mammals from Gold Run Creek, Yukon Territory. *Canadian Journal of Earth Sciences* 10:697-759.

Harper, J.R. 1980a. Coastal Processes on Graham Island, Queen Charlotte Islands, British Columbia. In *Current Research 80-1A*, pp. 13-18. Geological Survey of Canada, Ottawa.

–. 1980b. Seasonal Changes in Beach Morphology along the BC Coast. In *Proceedings of the Canadian Coastal Conference, 1980*, pp. 136-150. National Research Council, Ottawa.

Harper, J.R., W.T. Austin, M. Morris, P.D. Reimer, and R. Reitmeier. 1994. A Biophysical Inventory of the Coastal Resources in Gwaii Haanas. Report prepared by Coastal and Ocean Resources Inc., on file, Parks Canada, Victoria.

Harris H. 1997. Remembering 10,000 Years of History: The Origins and Migrations of the Gitksan. In *At a Crossroads: Archaeology and First Peoples in Canada*, edited by G.P. Nicholas and T.D. Andrews, pp. 190-196. Simon Fraser University Press, Burnaby, BC.

Haskins, R. N.d. 3d Vol[e] of a Journal Kept by R. Haskins on the Ship *Atahualpa* Bound on a Voyage from Boston 'round the World, 1800 to 1803. Journal, Columbia River Maritime Museum, Astoria, OR.

Haswell, R. N.d. A Voyage on Discoveries in the Ship *Columbia Rediviia* by Robert Haswell with Remarks on Board the Sloop *Adventure*. Photocopy of manuscript, Special Collections Division, University of British Columbia Library, Vancouver.

Havinga, A.J. 1984. A 20-Year Experimental Investigation into the Differential Corrosion Susceptibility of Pollen and Spores in Various Soil Types. *Pollen et Spores* 26:541-558.

Heaton, T.H. 1995a. Interpretation of d13 Values from Vertebrate Remains of the Alexander Archipelago, SE Alaska. *Current Research in the Pleistocene* 12:95-97.

–. 1995b. Middle Wisconsin Bear and Rodent Remains Discovered on Prince of Wales Island, Alaska. *Current Research in the Pleistocene* 12:93-95.

–. 2002. Ice Age Paleontology of Southeast Alaska, <http://www.usd.edu/esci/alaska/index.html>, accessed February 2003.

Heaton, T.H., and F. Grady. 2003. The Late Wisconsin Vertebrate History of Prince of Wales Island, Southeast Alaska. In *Vertebrate Paleontology of Late Cenozoic Cave Deposits in North America*, edited by B.W. Schubert, J.I. Mead, and R.W. Graham, pp. 17-53. Indiana University Press, Bloomington.

Heaton, T.H., S.L. Talbot, and G.F. Shields. 1996. An Ice Age Refugium for Large Mammals in the Alexander Archipelago, Southeastern Alaska. *Quaternary Research* 46:186-192.

Hebda, R.J. 1977. The Paleoecology of a Raised Bog and Associated Deltaic Sediments of the Fraser River Delta. PhD dissertation, Department of Botany, University of British Columbia.

–. 1983. Late-Glacial and Postglacial Vegetation History at Bear Cove Bog, Northeast Vancouver Island, British Columbia. *Canadian Journal of Botany* 61:3172-3192.

–. 1985. Pollen Morphology of *Ligusticum* (Apiaceae) in Canada. *Canadian Journal of Botany* 63:1880-1887.

–. 1987. Long Term Succession in Coastal Forests of British Columbia. *BC Vegetation Working Group Newsletter* 2(1):6.

–. 1995. British Columbia Vegetation and Climate History with a Focus on 6 KA BP. *Geographie physique et Quaternaire* 49:55-79.

–. 1997. Late Quaternary Paleoecology of Brooks Peninsula. In *Brooks Peninsula: An Ice Age Refugium on Vancouver Island*, edited by R.J. Hebda and J.C. Haggarty, pp 9.1-9.48. Occasional Paper No. 5. British Columbia Parks, Ministry of Environment, Lands and Parks, Victoria.

Hebda, R.J., and G.B. Allen. 1993. Modern Pollen Spectra from West Central British Columbia. *Canadian Journal of Botany* 71:1486-1495.

Hebda, R.J., and S.G. Frederick. 1990. History of Marine Resources of the North-East Pacific since the Last Glaciation. *Transactions of the Royal Society of Canada Series* 1, 1:319-341.

Hebda, R.J., and J.C. Haggarty (editors). 1997. *Brooks Peninsula: An Ice Age Refugium on Vancouver Island*. Occasional Paper No. 5. British Columbia Parks, Ministry of Environment, Lands and Parks. Victoria.

Hebda, R.J., and R.W. Mathewes. 1984. Holocene History of Cedar and Native Indian Cultures of the North American Pacific Coast. *Science* 225:711-713.

–. 1986. Radiocarbon Dates from Anthony Island, Queen Charlotte Islands, and Their Geological and Archaeological Significance. *Canadian Journal of Earth Sciences* 23(12):2071-2076.

Hebda, R.J., and C. Whitlock. 1997. Environmental History. In *The Rain Forests of Home: Profile of a North American Bioregion*, edited by P.K. Schoonmaker, B. von Hagen, and E.C. Wolf, pp. 227-254. Island Press, Covelo, CA.

Henderson, R.W. 1985. *These Hundred Years: The United Church of Canada in the Queen Charlotte Islands 1884-1984*. Official Board of the Queen Charlotte United Church, Queen Charlotte Islands.

Hetherington, R., and R.G. Reid. 2003. Malacological Insights into the Marine Ecology and Changing Climate of the Late Pleistocene: Early Holocene Queen Charlotte Islands Archipelago, Western Canada, and Implications for Early Peoples. *Canadian Journal of Zoology* 81:626-661.

Hetherington, R., J.V. Barrie, R.G. Reid, R. MacLeod, and D.J. Smith. 2004. Paleogeography, Glacially Induced Crustal Displacement, and Late Quaternary Coastlines on the Continental Shelf of British Columbia, Canada. *Quaternary Science Reviews* 23:295-318.

Heusser, C.J. 1955. Pollen Profiles from the Queen Charlotte Islands, British Columbia. *Canadian Journal of Botany* 33:429-449.

–. 1960. Late-Pleistocene Environments of North Pacific North America. *American Geographical Society Special Publication* No. 35, New York.

–. 1985. Quaternary Pollen Records from the Pacific Northwest Coast: Aleutians to the Oregon-California Boundary. In *Pollen Records of Late-Quaternary North American Sediments*, edited by V.M. Bryant Jr. and R.G. Holloway, pp. 141-165. American Association of Stratigraphic Palynologists, Dallas.

–. 1989. North Pacific Coastal Refugia: The Queen Charlotte Islands in Perspective. In *The Outer Shores*, edited by G.G.E. Scudder and N. Gessler, pp. 91-106. Queen Charlotte Islands Museum Press, Skidegate.

–. 1990. Late Quaternary Vegetation of the Aleutian Islands, Southwestern Alaska. *Canadian Journal of Botany* 68:1320-1326.

–. 1995. Late-Quaternary Vegetation Response to Climatic-Glacial Forcing in North Pacific America. *Physical Geography* 16:118-149.

Heusser, C.J., L.E. Heusser, and D.M. Peteet. 1985. Late-Quaternary Climatic Change on the American North Pacific Coast. *Nature* 315:485-487.

Hicock, S.R., and E.A. Fuller. 1995. Lobal Interactions, Rheologic Superposition, and Implications for a Pleistocene Ice Stream on the Continental Shelf of British Columbia. *Geomorphology* 14:167-184.

Hobler, P.M. 1976. Archaeological Sites on Moresby Island, Queen Charlotte Islands. Report on file, British Columbia Archaeology Branch, Victoria.

–. 1978a. The Relationship of Archaeological Sites to Sea Levels on Moresby Island, Queen Charlotte Islands. *Canadian Journal of Archaeology* 2:1-14.

–. 1978b. A Cache of Aboriginal Fishing Gear from the Queen Charlotte Islands. *BC Studies* 37:37-47.

Hobler, P.M., and B. Seymour. 1975. Archaeological Site Inventory, Southern Queen Charlotte Islands, 1974 Field Work. Report on file, British Columbia Archaeology Branch, Victoria.

Hodgetts, L., and F. Rahemtulla. 2001. Land and Sea: Use of Terrestrial Mammal Bones in Coastal Hunter-Gatherer Communities. *Antiquity* 75:56-62.

Hoffecker, J.F., W.R. Powers, and T. Goebel. 1993. The Colonization of Beringia and the Peopling of the New World. *Science* 259:46-53.

Hoffecker, J.F., W.R. Powers, and N.H. Bigelow. 1996. Dry Creek. In *American Beginnings: The Prehistory and Palaeoecology of Beringia*, edited by F. Hadleigh-West, pp. 343-352. University of Chicago Press, Chicago.

Holder, K., R. Montgomerie, and V.L. Friesen. 1999. A Test of the Glacial Refugium Hypothesis Using Patterns of Mitochondrial and Nuclear DNA Sequence Variation in Rock Ptarmigan (*Lagopus mutus*). *Evolution* 53:1936-1950.

Holland, S.S. 1964. *Landforms of British Columbia: A Physiographic Outline*. British Columbia Department of Mines and Petroleum Resources, Bulletin 48:138, Victoria.

Holmes, C.E. 1996. Broken Mammoth. In *American Beginnings: The Prehistory and Paleoecology of Beringia*, edited by F. West, pp. 312-318. University of Chicago Press, Chicago.

Hoover, A. 1973. Site Records and Brief Observations. Report on file, British Columbia Archaeology Branch, Victoria.

Hopkins, G.F. 1885. Letter from the Rev. Geo. F. Hopkins, dated Skidegate, Q.C. Is., Oct. 2nd, 1885. *The Missionary Outlook* 5(10):174-175.

Hoskins, J. N.d. The Narrative of a Voyage to the North West Coast of America and China on Trade and Discoveries by John Hoskins Performed in the Ship *Columbia Rediviva* 1790, 1791, 1792 & 1793. Copy of manuscript, Special Collections Division, University of British Columbia Library, Vancouver.

Howay, F.W. 1925. Indian Attacks upon Maritime Fur Traders of the North-West Coast, 1785-1805. *Canadian Historical Review* 6:287-309.

–. 1930. A List of Trading Vessels in the Maritime Fur Trade, 1785-1794. *Transactions of the Royal Society of Canada*, 3rd series 24, Section 2:111-134.

–. 1931. A List of Trading Vessels in the Maritime Fur Trade, 1795-1804. *Transactions of the Royal Society of Canada*, 3rd series 25, Section 2:117-149.

–. 1932. A List of Trading Vessels in the Maritime Fur Trade, 1805-1814. *Transactions of the Royal Society of Canada*, 3rd series 26, Section 2:43-86.

–. 1933. A List of Trading Vessels in the Maritime Fur Trade, 1815-1819. *Transactions of the Royal Society of Canada*, 3rd series 27, Section 2:119-147.

–. 1934. A List of Trading Vessels in the Maritime Fur Trade, 1820-1825. *Transactions of the Royal Society of Canada*, 3rd series 28, Section 2:11-49.

–. (editor). 1941. *Voyages of the* Columbia *to the Northwest Coast, 1787-1790 and 1790-1793*. Massachusetts Historical Society, Boston.

Howes, D.E. 1983. Late Quaternary Sediments and Geomorphic History of Northern Vancouver Island, British Columbia. *Canadian Journal of Earth Sciences* 18:1-12.

Hudson's Bay Company. N.d.a. Fort Simpson Journals, 1832-1866. Hudson's Bay Company Archives, B 201/a/1-9. Archives of Manitoba, Winnipeg.

–. N.d.b. Fort Simpson Journals May 12, 1842 – June 22, 1843. A/C/20/si 2.1. British Columbia Archives and Records Service, Victoria.

–. N.d.c. Fort Simpson Journals Sept. 15, 1859 – Dec. 31, 1862. A/B/20/si. British Columbia Archives and Records Service, Victoria.

Hutchings, W.K. 1996. The Namu Obsidian Industry. In *Early Human Occupation in British Columbia*, edited by R.L. Carlson and L. Dalla Bona, pp. 167-176. UBC Press, Vancouver.

Hutchinson, I., and A.D. McMillan. 1997. Archaeological Evidence for Village Abandonment Associated with Late Holocene Earthquakes at the Northern Cascadia Subduction Zone. *Quaternary Research* 47:79-87.

Ingraham, J. 1971. *Voyage to the Northwest Coast of North America 1790-1792*, edited by Mark Kaplanoff. Imprint Society, MA.

Inskip, G.H. N.d. Journal of a Voyage from England to the Pacific Including the Northwest Coast of North America, Master of H.M.S. *Virago*, 1851-1855. Add. Mss. 805, 2 vols. British Columbia Archives and Records Service, Victoria.

Jackman, N. 1998. Archaeobotanical Analysis of Site 1127T12, Richardson Island, Gwaii Haanas. Manuscript on file, Parks Canada, Victoria.

James, T.S., J.J. Clague, K. Wang, and I. Hutchinson. 2000. Postglacial Rebound at the Northern Cascadia Subduction Zone. *Quaternary Science Reviews* 19:1527-1541.

Johnson, L.S., and E.B. Taylor. 2004. The Distribution of Divergent Mitochondrial DNA Lineages of Threespine Stickleback (*Gasterosteus aculeatus*) in the Northeastern Pacific Basin: Post-Glacial Dispersal and Lake Accessibility. *Journal of Biogeography* 31:1073-1083.

Johnson, J.R., T.W. Stafford, H.O. Ajie, and D.P. Morris. 2000. Arlington Springs Revisited. In *Proceedings of the Fifth California Islands Symposium*, pp. 541-545. US Department of the Interior, Camarillo, CA.

Jones, T.L., R.T. Fitzgerald, D.J. Kennett, C.H. Miksicek, J.L. Fagan, J. Sharp, and J.M. Erlandson. 2002. The Cross Creek Site (CA-SLO-1797) and Its Implications for New World Colonization. *American Antiquity* 67:213-230.

Jongman, R.H., C.J.F. ter Braak, and O.F.R. van Tongeren. 1987. *Data Analysis in Community and Landscape Ecology.* Pudoc., Wageningen, The Netherlands.

Jordan, R.H. 1992. A Maritime Paleoarctic Assemblage from Kodiak Island, Alaska. Anthropological Papers of the University of Alaska 24. Fairbanks.

Josenhans, H.W., J.V. Barrie, K.W. Conway, T. Patterson, R. Mathewes, and G.J. Woodsworth. 1993. Surficial Geology of the Queen Charlotte Basin: Evidence of Submerged Proglacial Lakes at 170m on the Continental Shelf of Western Canada. In *Current Research 93-1A*, pp. 119-127. Geological Survey of Canada, Ottawa.

Josenhans, H.W., D.W. Fedje, K.W. Conway, and J.V. Barrie. 1995. Post Glacial Sea Levels on the Western Canadian Continental Shelf: Evidence for Rapid Change, Extensive Subaerial Exposure, and Early Human Habitation. *Marine Geology* 125:73-94.

Josenhans, H.W., D.W. Fedje, R. Pienitz, and J.R. Southon. 1997. Early Humans and Rapidly Changing Holocene Sea Levels in the Queen Charlotte Islands, Hecate Strait, British Columbia, Canada. *Science* 277:71-74.

Kavanaugh, D.H. 1989. The Ground-Beetle (Coleoptera: Carabidae) Fauna of the Queen Charlotte Islands: Its Composition, Affinities and Origins. In *The Outer Shores*, edited by G.G.E. Scudder and N. Gessler, pp. 131-146. Queen Charlotte Islands Museum Press, Skidegate.

–. 1992. Carabid Beetles (Insecta: Coleoptera: Carabidae) of the Queen Charlotte Islands, British Columbia. *Memoirs of the California Academy of Sciences* (16):113.

Keen, S.D. 1990. Shellfish Faunal Analyses from Sixteen Archaeological Sites in the Southern Queen Charlotte Islands. Unpublished report to the British Columbia Heritage Trust, 1990, Victoria.

Klinka, K., V.J. Krajina, A. Ceska, and A.M. Scagel. 1989. *Indicator Plants of Coastal British Columbia.* UBC Press, Vancouver.

Koppel, T. 2003. *Lost World: Rewriting Prehistory – How New Science Is Tracing America's Ice Age Mariners.* Atria Books, New York.

Kurtén, B., and E. Anderson. 1980. *Pleistocene Mammals of North America*. Columbia University Press, New York.

Kwain, W. 1987. Biology of Pink Salmon in the North American Great Lakes. American Fisheries Society Symposium 1:57-65.

Lacourse, T. 2004. Late Quaternary Vegetation Dynamics of the Queen Charlotte Islands, Northern Vancouver Island, and the Continental Shelf of British Columbia, Canada. PhD dissertation, Department of Biological Sciences, Simon Fraser University.

Lacourse, T., R.W. Mathewes, and D.W. Fedje. 2003. Paleoecology of Late-Glacial Terrestrial Deposits with in-situ Conifers from the Submerged Continental Shelf of Western Canada. *Quaternary Research* 60:180-188.

Lévi-Strauss, C. 1963. *Structural Anthropology*. Basic Books, New York.

Lian, O.B., R.W. Mathewes, and S.R. Hicock. 2001. Paleoenvironmental reconstruction of the Port Moody Interstade, a nonglacial interval in southwestern British Columbia at about 18000 ¹⁴C BP. *Canadian Journal of Earth Sciences* 38:943-952.

Lichatowich, J. 1999. *Salmon without Rivers: A History of the Pacific Salmon Crisis*. Island Press, Washington, DC.

Lister, A.M. 1993. Mammoths in Miniature. *Nature* 362:288-289.

Lowe, J.J., B. Ammann, H.H. Birks, S. Björck, G.R. Coope, L. Cwynar, J.L. De Beaulieu, R.J. Mott, D.M. Peteet, and M.J.C. Walker. 1994. Climatic Changes in Areas Adjacent to the North Atlantic during the Last Glacial-Interglacial Transition (14-9 ka BP): A Contribution to IGCP-253. *Journal of Quaternary Science* 9:185-198.

Luebbers, R.A. 1978. Excavations: Stratigraphy and Artifacts. In *Studies in Bella Bella Prehistory*, edited by James J. Hester and Sarah M. Nelson, pp. 11-66. Department of Archaeology, Simon Fraser University, Burnaby.

Luternauer, J.L., and J.W. Murray. 1983. Late Quaternary Morphologic Development and Sedimentation, Central British Columbia Continental Shelf. In *Current Research 83-21*, p. 38. Geological Survey of Canada, Ottawa.

Luternauer, J.L., J.J. Clague, K.W. Conway, J.V. Barrie, B. Blaise, and R.W. Mathewes. 1989a. Late Pleistocene Terrestrial Deposits on the Continental Shelf of Western Canada: Evidence for Rapid Sea-Level Change at the End of the Last Glaciation. *Geology* 17:357-360.

Luternauer, J.L., K.W. Conway, J.J. Clague, and B. Blaise. 1989b. Late Quaternary Geology and Geochronology of the Central Continental Shelf of Western Canada. *Marine Geology* 89:57-68.

MacArthur, R.H., and E.O. Wilson. 1967. *The Theory of Island Biogeography*. Monographs in Population Biology 1. Princeton University Press, Princeton, NJ.

MacDonald, G.F. 1969. Preliminary Culture Sequence from the Coast Tsimshian Area, British Columbia. *Northwest Anthropological Research Notes* 3(2):240-254.

–. 1973. *Haida Burial Practices: Three Archaeological Examples*. National Museum of Man, Mercury Series, Archaeological Survey of Canada Paper 9. National Museums of Canada, Ottawa.

–. 1983a. Ninstints: Haida World Heritage Site. University of British Columbia Museum of Anthropology, Museum Note No. 12. Vancouver.

–. 1983b. *Haida Monumental Art: Villages of the Queen Charlotte Islands*. UBC Press, Vancouver.

–. 1989. *Chiefs of the Sea and Sky: Haida Heritage Sites of the Queen Charlotte Islands*. UBC Press, Vancouver.

MacDonald, G.F., and R.I. Inglis. 1981. An Overview of the North Coast Prehistory Project (1966-1980). *BC Studies* 48:37-63.

Mackie, A.P. 1986. A Closer Look at Coastal Survey Results. *The Midden* 18(1):3-5.

–. 1994. Archaeological Impact Assessment Gwaii Haanas Visitor Reception and Information Centre, Queen Charlotte City, BC, Archaeological Site 1248T/FhUa-58. Unpublished report on file, Cultural Resources Services, Parks Canada, Victoria.

Mackie, A.P., and B. Wilson. 1994. Archaeological Inventory of Gwaii Haanas 1993. Manuscript on file, Cultural Resource Services (Western Canada Service Centre), Parks Canada, Victoria.

–. 1995. Archaeological Inventory of Gwaii Haanas 1994. Manuscript on file, Cultural Resource Services (Western Canada Service Centre), Parks Canada, Victoria.

Mackie, A.P., D.W. Fedje, Q. Mackie, and M.L. Florian. 2003. Early Holocene Wood Artifacts from the Kilgii Gwaay Site, Southern Haida Gwaii. Paper presented at the 10th International Wetland Archaeological Research Project Conference, April, Olympia, WA.

Mackie, Q. N.d. Preliminary Results from 2001 Investigations at Richardson Island. Report on file, Department of Anthropology, University of Victoria.

Mackie, Q. 2001. *Settlement Archaeology in a Fjordland Archipelago. Network Analysis, Social Practice and the Built Environment of Western Vancouver Island, British Columbia, Canada since 2,000 BP.* British Archaeological Reports, International Series, No. 926. Oxford.

Mackie, Q., T.C. Orchard, and C.R. Lake. 2001. The Environmental Archaeology Pilot Project in Gwaii Haanas: Report to British Columbia Heritage Trust re: BC Heritage Trust Grant 00-78. Unpublished report on file, British Columbia Heritage Trust, Victoria.

MacKinnon, A., J. Pojar, and R. Coupé (editors). 1992. *Plants of Northern British Columbia.* British Columbia Ministry of Forests and Lone Pine Publishing, Edmonton.

Magne, M.P.R. 1996. Comparative Analysis of Microblade Cores from Haida Gwaii. In *Early Human Occupation in British Columbia,* edited by R. L. Carlson and L. Dalla Bona, pp. 83-102. UBC Press, Vancouver.

–. 2000. Evidence and Implications of in-situ Development of Microblade Technology in Gwaii Haanas. Paper presented at the 33rd annual meeting of the Canadian Archaeological Association, Ottawa, May.

–. 2004. Technological Correlates of Gwaii Haanas Microblades. *Lithic Technology* 29(2): 91-118.

Magne, M.P.R., and D.W. Fedje 2004. The Spread of Microblade Technology in Northwestern North America. Paper presented at the 2004 Society for American Archaeology Meetings, Montreal, April.

Mandryk, C.A.S., H.W. Josenhans, D.W. Fedje, and R.W. Mathewes. 2001. Late Quaternary Paleoenvironments of Northwestern North America: Implications for Inland Versus Coastal Migration Routes. *Quaternary Science Reviews* 20:301-314.

Mangerud, J., S.T. Andersen, B.E. Berglund, and J.J. Donner. 1974. Quaternary Stratigraphy of Norden: A Proposal for Terminology and Classification. *Boreas* 3:109-128.

Mann, D.H., and T.D. Hamilton. 1995. Late Pleistocene and Holocene Paleoenvironments of the North Pacific Coast. *Quaternary Science Reviews* 14:449-471.

Martain, W. N.d. Log of the Ship *Hamilton* 1820-1822. Essex Institute Library, Salem, MA.

Maschner, H.D. 1997. Settlement and Subsistence in the Later Prehistory of Tebenkof Bay, Kuiu Island, Southeast Alaska. *Arctic Anthropology* 34(2):74-99.

Maschner, H.D., and K.L. Reedy-Maschner. 1998. Raid, Retreat, Defend (Repeat): The Archaeology and Ethnohistory of Warfare on the North Pacific Rim. *Journal of Anthropological Archaeology* 17:19-51.

Mason, A.R. 1995. Archaeological Inventory, Impact Assessment and Traditional Land Use Study of BCBC Property, Port Clements, BC, Permit 1995-223. Report on file, British Columbia Archaeology Branch, Victoria.

Mason, A.R., and J.C. Haggarty. 1999. Archaeological Inventory of Clayoquot Sound, Results of Phase 3 Investigations (Fall 1998). Report on file, British Columbia Archaeology Branch, Victoria.

Mason, R. 2000. Archaeology and Native North American Oral Traditions. *American Antiquity* 65(2):239-266.

Mathewes, R.W. 1985. Paleobotanical Evidence for Climatic Change in Southern British Columbia during Late-Glacial and Holocene Time. In *Climatic Change in Canada 5: Critical Periods in the Quaternary Climatic History of Northern North America,* edited by C.R. Harington, Syllogeus No. 55:397-422.

–. 1989a. *Paleobotany of the Queen Charlotte Islands.* In *The Outer Shores,* edited by G.G.E. Scudder and N. Gessler, pp. 75-90. Queen Charlotte Islands Museum Press, Skidegate.

–. 1989b. The Queen Charlottes Refugium: A Paleoecological Perspective. In *Quaternary Geology of Canada and Greenland,* edited by R.J. Fulton, pp. 486-491. Geology of Canada Publication No. 1. Geological Survey of Canada, Ottawa.

–. 1993. Evidence for Younger Dryas-Age Cooling on the North Pacific Coast of America. *Quaternary Science Reviews* 12:321-331.

–. 2000a. Paleoecology of a Lost World: Postglacial Environments and Biogeography of the Continental Shelf of Western Canada. Abstract on CD, GEOCANADA 2000, University of Calgary.

–. 2000b. Paleoecology of a Lost World: Pollen Analysis and Coastal Route for the Peopling of the Americas. Abstract, Geological Association of America, Summit 2000, Reno, NV.

Mathewes, R.W., and J.J. Clague. 1994. Detection of Large Prehistoric Earthquakes in the Pacific Northwest by Microfossil Analysis. *Science* 264:688-691.

Mathewes, R.W., J.S. Vogel, J.R. Southon, and D.E. Nelson. 1985. Accelerator Radiocarbon Date Confirms Early Deglaciation of the Queen Charlotte Islands. *Canadian Journal of Earth Sciences* 22:790-791.

Mathewes, R.W., L.E. Heusser, and R.T. Patterson. 1993. Evidence for a Younger Dryas-like Cooling Event on the British Columbia Coast. *Geology* 21:101-104.

Matson, R.G. 1976. *The Glenrose Cannery Site*. National Museum of Man, Mercury Series, Archaeological Survey of Canada Paper 52. National Museums of Canada, Ottawa.

–. 1996. The Old Cordilleran Component at the Glenrose Cannery Site. In *Early Human Occupation in British Columbia*, edited by R.L. Carlson and L. Dalla Bona, pp. 111-122. UBC Press, Vancouver.

Matson, R.G., and G. Coupland. 1995. *The Prehistory of the Northwest Coast*. Academic Press, New York.

Matson, R.G., and D.L. True. 1974. Site Relationships at Quebrada Tarapaca, Chile: A Comparison of Clustering and Scaling Techniques. *American Antiquity* 39:51-73.

McLaren, D., R.J. Wigen, Q. Mackie, and D.W. Fedje. 2005. Bear Hunting at the Pleistocene/Holocene Transition on the Northern Northwest Coast of North America. *Canadian Journal of Zoology* 22:1-32.

McLay, E.B. 1999. The Diversity of Northwest Coast Shell Middens: Late Pre-Contact Settlement-Subsistence Patterns on Valdes Island, British Columbia. MA thesis, Department of Anthropology and Sociology, University of British Columbia.

McMillan, A.D. 1999. *Since the Time of the Transformers: The Ancient Heritage of the Nuu-chah-nulth, Ditidaht, and Makah*. UBC Press, Vancouver.

McMillan, A.D., and I. Hutchinson. 2002. When the Mountain Dwarfs Danced: Aboriginal Traditions of Paleoseismic Events along the Cascadia Subduction Zone of Western North America. *Ethnohistory* 49(1):41-68.

Meares, J. 1790. *Voyages Made in the Years 1788 and 1789, from China to the North West Coast of America, to Which Are Prefixed an Introductory Narrative of a Voyage Performed in 1786, from Bengal, in the Ship* Nootka; *Observations on the Probable Existence of a North West Passage and Some Account of the Trade between the North West Coast of America and China; and the Latter Country and Great Britain*. Logographic Press, London.

Meek, T. N.d. Log of the Brig *Arab*, June 15, 1821 to January 5, 1825. Bancroft Collection, Bancroft Library, University of California, Berkeley.

Meidinger, D., and J. Pojar (editors). 1991. *Ecosystems of British Columbia*. Research Branch, British Columbia Ministry of Forests, Victoria.

Miller, F.L. 1982. Caribou. In *Wild Mammals of North America*, edited by Joseph A. Chapman and George A. Feldhamer, pp. 923-959. John Hopkins University Press, Baltimore and London.

Milner, A.M., and R.G. Bailey, 1989. Salmonid Colonization of New Streams in Glacier Bay National Park, Alaska. *Aquaculture and Fisheries Management* 20:179-192.

Mitchell, D.H. 1988. Changing Patterns of Resource Use in the Prehistory of Queen Charlotte Strait, British Columbia. In *Prehistoric Economies of the Pacific Northwest Coast*, edited by B.L. Isaac, pp. 245-290. JAI Press, Greenwich, CT.

–. 1990. Prehistory of the Coasts of Southern British Columbia and Northern Washington. In *Handbook of North American Indians*. Vol. 7: *The Northwest Coast*, edited by W. Suttles, pp. 340-358. Smithsonian Institution, Washington, DC.

Mitchell, D.H., and L. Donald. 1988. Archaeology and the Study of Northwest Coast Economies. In *Prehistoric Economies of the Pacific Northwest Coast*, edited by B.L. Isaac, pp. 293-351. JAI Press, Greenwich, CT.

Moodie, G.E. 1972. Predation, Natural Selection and Adaptation in an Unusual Stickle-back. *Heredity* 28:155-167.

Moodie, G.E., and T.E. Reimchen. 1973. Endemism and Conservation of Stickleback Populations of the Queen Charlotte Islands. *Canadian Field-Naturalist* 87:173-175.

–. 1976a. Glacial Refugia, Endemism, and Stickleback Populations of the Queen Charlotte Islands, British Columbia. *Canadian Field-Naturalist* 90:471-474.

–. 1976b. Phenetic Variation and Habitat Differences in *Gasterosteus* Populations of the Queen Charlotte Islands. *Systematic Zoology* 25:49-61.

Moodie, D.W., A.J. Catchpole, and K. Abel. 1992. Northern Athapaskan Oral Traditions and the White River Volcano. *American Society for Ethnohistory* 39(2):148-171.

Moss, M.L., and J.M. Erlandson. 1992. Forts, Refuge Rocks, and Defensive Sites: The Antiquity of Warfare along the North Pacific Coast of North America. *Arctic Anthropology* 29(2): 73-90.

Mott, R.J., D.R. Grant, R. Stea, and S. Occhietti. 1986. Late-Glacial Climatic Oscillation in Atlantic Canada Equivalent to the Allerød/Younger Dryas event. *Nature* 323: 247-250.

Mudie, P.J., A. Rochon, and E. Levac. 2002. Palynological Records of Red Tide-Producing Species in Canada: Past Trends and Implications for the Future. *Palaeogeography, Palaeoclimatology, Palaeoecology* 180:159-186.

Murdock, G.P. 1934a. The Haidas of British Columbia. In *Our Primitive Contemporaries*, G.P. Murdock, pp. 221-263. Macmillan, New York.

–. 1934b. Kinship and Social Behavior among the Haida. *American Anthropologist* 36: 355-386.

–. 1936. *Rank and Potlatch among the Haida*. Yale University Publication in Anthropology 13. Yale University, New Haven, CT.

–. 1949. *Social Structure*. Macmillan, New York.

Murphy, R.C. 1938. The Need of Insular Exploration as Illustrated by Birds. *Science* 88: 533-539.

Murray, J.S. 1981. Prehistoric Skeletons from Blue Jackets Creek (FlUa 4), Queen Charlotte Islands, British Columbia. In *Contributions to Physical Anthropology, 1978-1980*, edited by Jerome Cybulski, pp. 127-175. National Museum of Man, Mercury Series, Archaeological Survey of Canada Paper 106. National Museums of Canada, Ottawa.

Nagorsen, D.W. 1990. *The Mammals of British Columbia*. Royal British Columbia Museum and the Wildlife Branch, Victoria.

Nagorsen, D.W., and G. Keddie. 2000. Late Pleistocene Mountain Goats (*Oreamnos americanus*) from Vancouver Island: Biogeographic Implications. *Journal of Mammalogy* 81(3):666-675.

Nagorsen, D.W., G. Keddie, and R.J. Hebda. 1995. Early Holocene Black Bears, *Ursus americanus*, from Vancouver Island. *Canadian Field-Naturalist* 109(1):11-18.

Neave, F., and M.G. Hanavan. 1960. Seasonal Distribution of Some Epipelagic Fishes in the Gulf of Alaska Region. *Journal of Fisheries Research Board of Canada* 17(2):221-233.

Newcombe, C.F. N.d.a. Miscellaneous papers for years 1897, 1901 and 1903. In Newcombe Family Papers 1897-1955, Add. Mss. 1077, vol. 35. British Columbia Archives and Records Service, Victoria.

–. N.d.b. Notes of a Journey Round the Southern Islands of the Queen Charlotte Group, British Columbia in the Year 1901. American Museum of Natural History, New York.

Newcombe, C.F., and W.A. Newcombe. 1914. Sea-Lions on the Coast of British Columbia. Report of the Commissioner of Fisheries for the Year Ending December 31st, 1913 with Appendices. Sessional Papers, Second Session, Thirteenth Parliament of the Province of British Columbia, Session 1914, vol. 2, pp. R 131-136, 4 Geo. 5. Victoria.

Niblack, A.P. 1890. The Coast Indians of Southern Alaska and Northern British Columbia; Based on the Collections in the United States National Museum and on the Personal Observations of the Writer in Connection with a Survey of Alaska in the Seasons of 1885, 1886 and 1887. In *Annual Report of the United States National Museum for the Year Ending June 30, 1888*, pp. 225-386. US National Museum, Washington, DC.

Nicoll, M. 1981. Report on a Survey of Haida Forest Utilization, Masset Inlet, Queen Charlotte Islands, BC. Manuscript on file, British Columbia Archaeology Branch, Victoria.

Northcote, T.G., A.E. Peden, and T.E. Reimchen. 1989. Fishes of the Coastal Marine, Riverine and Lacustrine Waters of the Queen Charlotte Islands. In *The Outer Shores,* edited by G.G.E. Scudder and N. Gessler, pp. 147-174. Queen Charlotte Islands Museum Press, Skidegate.

Nott, J. 2003. Waves, Coastal Boulder Deposits and the Importance of the Pre-Transport Setting. *Earth and Planetary Science Letters* 210:269-276.

O'Reilly, P., T.E. Reimchen, R. Beech, and C. Strobeck. 1993. Mitochondrial DNA in *Gasterosteus* and Pleistocene Glacial Refugium on the Queen Charlotte Islands. *Evolution* 47:678-684.

Ogilvie, R.T. 1989. Disjunct Vascular Flora of Northwestern Vancouver Island in Relation to Queen Charlotte Islands' Endemism and Pacific Coast Refugia. In *The Outer Shores,* edited by G.G.E. Scudder and N. Gessler, pp. 127-130. Queen Charlotte Islands Museum Press, Skidegate.

–. 1994. Rare and Endemic Vascular Plants of Gwaii Haanas (South Moresby) Park, Queen Charlotte Islands, British Columbia. Canada–British Columbia Partnership Agreement on Forest Resource Development: FRDA II Report 214. Canadian Forest Service and British Columbia Ministry of Forests, Victoria.

–. 1997. Vascular Plants and Phytogeography of Brooks Peninsula. In *Brooks Peninsula: An Ice Age Refugium on Vancouver Island,* edited by R.J. Hebda and J.C. Haggarty, pp 5.1-5.48. Occasional Paper No. 5. British Columbia Parks, Victoria.

Ogilvie, R.T., and H.L. Roemer. 1984. The Rare Plants of the Queen Charlotte Islands. *BC Naturalist* 22:17-18.

Ohman, J.L., and T.A. Spies. 1998. Regional Gradient Analysis and Spatial Pattern of Woody Plant Communities of Oregon Forests. *Ecological Monographs* 68:151-182.

Orchard, T.J. 2003. Gwaii Haanas Environmental Project 2002: Archaeology Report on 2002 Field Activities. Unpublished report on file, Gwaii Haanas National Park Reserve and Haida Heritage Site, Queen Charlotte City.

Orti, G., M.A. Bell, T.E. Reimchen, and A. Meyer. 1994. Global Survey of Mitochondrial DNA Sequences in the Threespine Stickleback: Evidence for Recent Migrations. *Evolution* 48:608-622.

Osgood, W.H. 1901. Natural History of the Queen Charlotte Islands, British Columbia. Natural History of the Cook Inlet Region, Alaska. *North American Fauna* 21:1-87.

Patterson, R.T., J. Guilbault, R.E. Thomson, and J.L. Luternauer. 1995. Foraminiferal Evidence of Younger Dryas Age Cooling on the British Columbia Shelf. *Géographie Physique et Quaternaire* 49:409-428.

Pearson, G.A. 1999. Early Occupations and Cultural Sequence at Moose Creek: A Late Pleistocene Site in Central Alaska. *Arctic* 52:332-345.

Peirce, M.T. N.d. Log of the Brig *Griffon,* October 24, 1824 to July 21, 1827. Essex Institute Library, Salem, MA.

Pellatt, M.G., and R.W. Mathewes. 1994. Paleoecology of Post-Glacial Treeline Fluctuations on the Queen Charlotte Islands, British Columbia. *Ecoscience* 1:71-81.

–. 1997. Holocene Tree Line and Climate Change on the Queen Charlotte Islands, Canada. *Quaternary Research* 48:88-99.

Pellatt, M.G., R.W. Mathewes, and I.R. Walker. 1997. Pollen Analysis and Ordination of Lake Sediment Surface Samples from Coastal British Columbia, Canada. *Canadian Journal of Botany* 75:799-814.

Pellatt, M.G., R.W. Mathewes, and J.J. Clague. 2002. Implications of the Mike Lake Pollen Record for the Glacial and Climatic History of the Fraser Lowland, British Columbia. *Palaeogeography, Palaeoclimatology, Palaeoecology* 180:147-157.

Peteet, D.M. 1991. Postglacial Migration History of Lodgepole Pine near Yakutat, Alaska (USA). *Canadian Journal of Botany* 69:786-796.

Peteet, D.M., and D.H. Mann, 1994. Late-Glacial Vegetational, Tephra, and Climatic History on Southwestern Kodiak Island, Alaska. *Ecoscience* 1:255-267.

Peteet, D.M., J.S. Vogel, D.E. Nelson, J.R. Southon, R.J. Nickmann, L.E. Heusser. 1990. Younger Dryas climatic reversal in northeastern USA? AMS Ages for an Old Problem. *Quaternary Research* 33: 219-230.

Pielou, E.C. 1992. *After the Ice Age: The Return of Life to Glaciated North America.* University of Chicago Press, Chicago.

Pienitz, R., G. Lortie, and M. Allard. 1990. Isolation of Lacustrine Basins and Marine Regression in the Kuujjuaq Area, Northern Quebec, as Inferred from Diatom Analysis. *Geographie physique et Quaternaire* 45:155-174.

Pitul'ko, V.V., and A.K. Kasparov. 1996. Ancient Arctic Hunters: Material Culture and Survival. *Arctic Anthropology* 33:1-36.

Pojar, J., and A. MacKinnon (editors). 1994. *Plants of Coastal British Columbia.* British Columbia Ministry of Forests and Lone Pine Publishing, Vancouver.

Poole, F. 1872. *Queen Charlotte Islands: A Narrative of Discovery and Adventure in the North Pacific.* Hurst and Blackett, London; J.J. Douglas, Vancouver.

Porsild, A.E., and W.J. Cody, 1980. *Vascular Plants of Continental Northwest Territories, Canada.* National Museums of Canada, Ottawa.

Porter, L. N.d. Log book of the ship *Hamilton,* March 26, 1809 to April 27, 1812. Essex Institute Library, Salem, MA.

Powers, W.R., and J.F. Hoffecker. 1989. Late Pleistocene Settlement in the Nenana Valley, Central Alaska. *American Antiquity* 54:263-287.

Prince Rupert Interagency Management Committee. 1999. Queen Charlotte Islands – Haida Gwaii Draft Background Report: An Overview of Natural, Cultural, and Socio-Economic Features, Land Uses and Resources Management. Smithers, BC.

Quickfall, G.S. 1987. Paludification and Climate on the Queen Charlotte Islands during the Past 8000 Years. MSc thesis, Department of Biological Sciences, Simon Fraser University, Burnaby.

Quinn, T., M.T. Kinnison, and M.J. Unwin. 2001. Evolution of Chinook Salmon (*Oncorhynchus tshawytscha*) Populations in New Zealand: Pattern, Rate and Process. *Genetica* 112-13:493-513.

Ramsey, C.B. 2000. OxCal 3.5, <http://www.rlaha.ox.ac.uk/orau/index.htm>, accessed 2004.

Ramsey, C.L, P.A. Griffiths, D.W. Fedje, R.J. Wigen, and Q. Mackie. 2004. K1 Preliminary Investigation of a Late Wisconsinan Fauna from K1 Cave, Queen Charlotte Islands (Haida Gwaii), Canada. *Quaternary Research* 62:105-109.

Reimchen, T.E. 1980. Spine-Deficiency and Polymorphism in a Population of *Gasterosteus aculeatus:* An Adaptation to Predators? *Canadian Journal of Zoology* 58:1232-1244.

–. 1983. Structural Relationships between Spines and Lateral Plates in Threespine Stickleback (*Gasterosteus aculeatus*). *Evolution* 37:931-946.

–. 1984. Status of Unarmoured and Spine-Deficient Populations (Charlotte unarmoured stickleback) of Threespine Stickleback, *Gasterosteus* sp., on the Queen Charlotte Islands, British Columbia. *Canadian Field-Naturalist* 98:120-126.

–. 1988. Inefficient Predators and Prey Injuries in a Population of Giant Stickleback. *Canadian Journal of Zoology* 66:2036-2044.

–. 1989. Loss of Nuptial Color in Threespine Stickleback *Gasterosteus. Evolution* 43:450-460.

–. 1991. Trout Foraging Failures and the Evolution of Body Size in Stickleback. *Copeia* 1991:1098-1104.

–. 1992a. Injuries on Stickleback from Attacks by a Toothed Predator (*Oncorhynchus*) and Some Implications for the Evolution of Lateral Plates. *Evolution* 46:1224-1230.

–. 1992b. Naikoon Provincial Park, Queen Charlotte Islands: Biophysical Data for Freshwater Habitats. Unpublished report on file, Ministry of the Environment, Government of British Columbia, Victoria.

–. 1994a. Predators and Evolution in Threespine Stickleback. In *Evolution of the Threespine Stickleback,* edited by M.A. Bell and S.A. Foster, pp. 240-273. Oxford University Press, Oxford.

–. 1994b. Biophysical Surveys of Aquatic Habitats in Gwaii Haanas 1993: Upper Victoria Lake, Lower Victoria Lake, Escarpment Lake and 14 Selected Streams. Unpublished report on file, Parks Canada, Queen Charlotte City.

–. 1995. Predator-Induced Cyclical Changes in Lateral Plate Frequencies of *Gasterosteus. Behaviour* 132:1079-1094.

Reimchen, T.E., and J. Buckland-Nicks. 1990. A Novel Association between an Endemic Stickleback and a Parasitic Dinoflagellate: Seasonal Cycle and Host Response. *Canadian Journal of Zoology* 68:667-671.

Reimchen, T.E., and P. Nosil. 2004. Variable Predation Regimes Predict the Evolution of Sexual Dimorphism in a Population of Threespine Stickleback. *Evolution* 58:1274-1281.

Reimchen, T.E., E.S. Stinson, and J.S. Nelson. 1985. Multivariate Differentiation of Parapatric and Allopatric Populations of Threespine Stickleback in the Sangan River Watershed, Queen Charlotte Islands. *Canadian Journal of Zoology* 63:2944-2951.

Reynolds, S. 1938. *The Voyage of the* New Hazard *to the Northwest Coast, Hawaii and China, 1810-1813,* edited by F.W. Howay. Peabody Museum of Archaeology and Ethnology, Cambridge, MA; and Southworth Anthoensen Press, Portland, ME.

Rick, T.C., J.M. Erlandson, and R.L. Vellanoweth. 2001. Paleocoastal Marine Fishing on the Pacific Coast of the Americas: Perspectives from Daisy Cave, California. *American Antiquity* 66:595-613.

Riddihough, R.P. 1982. Contemporary Movements and Tectonics on Canada's West Coast: A Discussion. *Tectonophysics* 86:239-242.

–. 1988. The Northeast Pacific Ocean and Margin. In *The Ocean Basins and Margins.* Vol. 7B: *The Pacific Ocean,* edited by A.E.M. Nairn, F.W. Stehli, and S. Uyeda, pp. 85-118. Plenum, New York.

Rohr, M.M., M. Scheidhauer, and A.M. Trehu. 2000. Transpression between Two Warm Mafic Plates: The Queen Charlotte Fault Revisited. *Journal of Geophysical Research* 105:8147-8172.

Roys, R.S. 1971. Effect of Tectonic Deformation on Pink Salmon Runs in Prince William Sound. In *The Great Alaska Earthquake of 1964: Biology,* National Research Council Publication No. 1604, pp. 220-237. National Academy of Sciences, Washington, DC.

Ruhlen, M. 1998. The Origin of the Na-Dene. *Proceedings of the National Academy of Sciences* 95:13994-13996.

Sahlins, M.D. 1961. The Segementary Lineage: An Organization of Predatory Expansion. *American Anthropologist* 63(2):322-343.

Sanders, W.T., and J. Marino. 1970. *New World Prehistory.* Prentice Hall, Englewood Cliffs, NJ.

Sandweiss, D.H., H. McInnis, R.L. Burger, A. Cano, B. Ojeda, R. Paredes, M.C. Sandweiss, and M.D. Glascock. 1998. Quebrada Jaguay: Early South American Maritime Adaptations. *Science* 281:1830-1832.

Savage, H. 1971. Faunal Findings Queen Charlotte Islands Archaeological Sites. Unpublished manuscript, Royal Ontario Museum, Toronto.

Schneider, D.M. 1961. The Distinctive Features of Matrilineal Descent Groups. In *Matrilineal Kinship,* edited by D.M. Schneider and K. Gough, pp. 1-29. University of California Press, Berkeley.

Schofield, W.B. 1989. Structure and Affinities of the Bryoflora of the Queen Charlotte Islands. In *The Outer Shores,* edited by G.G.E. Scudder and N. Gessler, pp. 109-120. Queen Charlotte Islands Museum Press, Skidegate.

Scudder, G.G. 1989. The Queen Charlotte Islands: Overview and Synthesis. In *The Outer Shores,* edited by G.G.E. Scudder and N. Gessler, pp. 319-327. Queen Charlotte Islands Museum Press, Skidegate.

Scudder, G.G.E., and N. Gessler (editors). 1989. *The Outer Shores.* Queen Charlotte Islands Museum Press, Skidegate.

Severs, P.D. 1972. Preliminary Report on the Archaeological Investigation of FlUa-4, the Site of Blue Jackets Creek, Queen Charlotte Islands (Permit 1972-023). Manuscript on file, British Columbia Archaeology Branch, Victoria.

–. 1973. Resume of the 1973 Field Season at Blue Jackets Creek, Queen Charlotte Islands, BC. Manuscript on file, Archaeological Survey of Canada, Ottawa.

–. 1974a. Archaeological Investigations at Blue Jackets Creek, FlUa-4, Queen Charlotte Islands, British Columbia, 1973. *Bulletin of the Canadian Archaeological Association* 6:163-205.

–. 1974b. Preliminary Report on Archaeological Investigations at Tow Hill, GaTw 5, in Naikoon Park, Queen Charlotte Islands. ASAB Permit #22. Report on file, British Columbia Archaeology Branch, Victoria.

–. 1975. Recent Research into the Prehistory of the Queen Charlotte Islands. *The Midden* 7(2):15-17.

Shackleton, D. 1999. *Hoofed Mammals of British Columbia.* Royal British Columbia Museum Handbooks Series. UBC Press, Vancouver.

Simonsen, B.O. 1973. *Archaeological Investigations in the Hecate Strait–Milbanke Sound Area of British Columbia.* National Museum of Man, Mercury Series, Archaeological Survey of Canada Paper 13. National Museums of Canada, Ottawa.

Skinner, M. 1983. Burial Excavations at DeRv-148, GaUa-2, and DfRu-42. Permit 1983-46. Unpublished report on file, Archaeology Branch, Victoria.

Small, M.P., K.D. Stone, and J.A. Cook. 2003. American Marten (*Martes americana*) in the Pacific Northwest: Population Differentiation across a Landscape Fragmented in Time and Space. *Molecular Ecology* 12:89-103.

Smith, C.I., R.J. Nelson, C.C. Wood, and B.F. Koop. 2001. Glacial Biogeography of North American Coho Salmon (*Onchorhynchus kisutch*). *Molecular Ecology* 10:2775-2785.

Smith, H.I. 1927. A Prehistoric Earthwork in the Haida Indian Area. *American Anthropologist* 29:109-111.

–. 1929. *Kitchen-Middens of the Pacific Coast of Canada.* National Museums of Canada, Annual Report for 1927, Bulletin 56:42-46. Ottawa.

Smith, N.F. 2005. A Geochemical Approach to Understanding Stone Tool Production at the Richardson Island Archaeological Site, Haida Gwaii, British Columbia. MA thesis, Department of Anthropology, University of Victoria.

Southon, J.R., and D.W. Fedje. 2003. A Post-Glacial Record of ^{14}C Reservoir Ages for the British Columbia Coast. *Canadian Journal of Archaeology* 27:95-111.

Southon, J.R., D.E. Nelson, and J.S. Vogel. 1990. A Record of Past Ocean-Atmosphere Radiocarbon Differences from the Northeast Pacific. *Paleoceanography,* 5:197-206.

Spalding, D. 2000. *The Early History of the Woodland Caribou (*Rangifer tarandus caribou*) in British Columbia.* Wildlife Bulletin No. B-100. British Columbia Ministry of Environment, Lands and Parks, Victoria.

SPSS. 1999. *SPSS Base 10.0 Applications Guide.* SPSS, Chicago.

Stafford, J., and T. Christensen. 1999. *Queen Charlotte City Secondary School Archaeological Impact Assessment: Site FhUa-52.* On file, British Columbia Archaeology Branch, Victoria.

–. 2000. Naden Harbour Archaeological Inventory Survey. Report on file, British Columbia Archaeology Branch, Victoria.

Stearns, M.L. 1984. Succession to Chiefship in Haida Society. In *The Tsimshian and Their Neighbours of the North Pacific Coast,* edited by J. Miller and C. Eastman, pp. 190-219. University of Washington Press, Seattle.

Stockmarr, J. 1971. Tablets with Spores Used in Absolute Pollen Analysis. *Pollen et Spores* 13:615-621.

Stone, K.D., and J.A. Cook. 2000. Phylogeography of Black Bears (*Ursus americanus*) of the Pacific Northwest. *Canadian Journal of Zoology* 78:1218-1223.

–. 2002. Molecular Evolution of Holarctic Martens (Genus *Martes,* Mammalia: Carnivora: Mustelidae). *Molecular Phylogenetics and Evolution* 24:169-179.

Stuiver, M., P.J. Reimer, E. Bard, J.W. Beck, G.S. Burr, K.A. Hughen, B. Kromer, G. McCormac, J. van der Plicht, and M. Spurk. 1998. INTCAL98 Radiocarbon Age Calibration, 24,000-0 Cal BP. *Radiocarbon* 40:1041-1084.

Sturgis, W. N.d.a. *My First Voyage: Remarks on Voyage of Eliza 1798 to Feb. 19th 1799.* Photocopy of original journal, Special Collections Division, University of British Columbia Library, Vancouver.

–. N.d.b. Journal of the *Eliza,* February-May 1799, of a Voyage to the NW Coast of N.A. and China. Photocopy of original, Special Collections Division, University of British Columbia Library, Vancouver.

Sumpter, I.D. 1999. 1998 Archaeological Investigations, Site 922T, Gunlai Kin (Hotspring Island), Gwaii Haanas. Report on file, Cultural Resource Services, Parks Canada, Victoria.

Sumpter, I.D., and A. Mason. 1994. Test Excavations at Site 922T, Hotsprings Island, Gwaii Haanas/South Moresby NPR. Unpublished report on file, Parks Canada, Victoria.

Suter, J. N.d.a. Log of the Ship *Atahualpa* October 1, 1811 to December 28, 1813. Harvard College Library, Harvard University, Cambridge, MA.

–. N.d.b. Log of the *Mentor* 1817-1818. Peabody Museum, Salem, MA.

Sutherland, P.D. 2001. Revisiting an Old Concept: The North Coast Interaction Sphere. In *Perspectives on Northern Northwest Coast Prehistory*, edited by J. Cybulski, pp. 49-59. Canadian Museum of Civilization, Mercury Series, Archaeological Survey of Canada Paper 160. National Museums of Canada, Ottawa.

Sutherland-Brown, A. 1968. Geology of Queen Charlotte Islands, British Columbia. Bulletin 54. British Columbia Department of Mines and Petroleum Resources, Victoria.

Sutherland-Brown, A., and H. Nasmith. 1962. The Glaciation of the Queen Charlotte Islands. *Canadian Field-Naturalist* 76:209-219.

Sutherland-Brown, A., and C.J. Yorath. 1989. Geology and Non-Renewable Resources of the Queen Charlotte Islands. In *The Outer Shores*, edited by G. Scudder and N. Gessler, pp. 3-26. Queen Charlotte Islands Museum Press, Skidegate.

Swanton, J.R. N.d. Haida Notebooks, 1900-1901. 2 vols. National Anthropological Archives, Smithsonian Institution, Washington, DC.

–. 1905a. *Contributions to the Ethnology of the Haida*. Memoir of the American Museum of Natural History No. 5, pt. 1. New York.

–. 1905b. *Haida Texts and Myths: Skidegate Dialect*. Bureau of American Ethnology Bulletin No. 29. Government Printing Office, Washington, DC.

–. 1905c. Social Organization of the Haida. *Proceedings of the International Congress of Americanists* 13:327-334.

–. 1908. *Haida Texts – Masset Dialect*. Memoir of the American Museum of Natural History, vol. 10 of *The Jesup North Pacific Expedition*, edited by Franz Boas. Stechert, New York.

–. 1912. *Haida Songs*. Publications of the American Ethnological Society, vol. 3, pt. 1. E.J. Brill, Leyden.

Talbot, S.L., and G.F. Shields. 1996. A Phylogeny of the Bears (Ursidae) Inferred from Complete Sequences of Three Mitochondrial Genes. *Molecular Phylogenetics and Evolution* 5:567-575.

Taylor, E. 1997. Local Adaptation. In *Genetic Effects of Straying of Non-Native Hatchery Fish into Natural Populations, Proceedings of the Workshop*, edited by W.S. Grant. US Department of Commerce, NOAA Tech Memo NMFS NWFSC-30, <http://www.nwfsc.noaa.gov/publications/tm30/tm30.html>, accessed January 2005.

ter Braak, C.J. 1988. CANOCO v2.1 – A FORTRAN Program for Canonical Community Ordination by (Partial) (Detrended) (Canonical) Correspondence Analysis. Agricultural Mathematics Group Technical Report LWA-88-02. Agricultural University, Wageningen, The Netherlands.

–. 1989. CANOCO v3.0. Unpublished computer program.

–. 1990. Update notes: CANOCO v3.0. Agricultural Mathematics Group, Agricultural University, Wageningen, The Netherlands.

Thorsteinson, F.V., J.H. Helle, and D.G. Birkholz. 1971. Salmon Survival in Intertidal Zones of Prince William Sound Streams in Uplifted and Subsided Areas. In *The Great Alaska Earthquake of 1964: Biology*, National Research Council Publication No. 1604, pp. 194-219. National Academy of Sciences, Washington, DC.

Torben, C.R., and J.M. Erlandson. 2000. Early Holocene Fishing Strategies on the California Coast: Evidence from CA-SBA-2057. *Journal of Archaeological Science* 27:621-633.

Trevan, H. N.d. Journal of Surgeon Henry Trevan. MG 24, F40, pp. 274-351, 1853, National Archives of Canada, Ottawa.

Turner, N.J. 1979. *Plants in British Columbian Indian Technology*. Handbook No. 38. British Columbia Provincial Museum, Victoria.

–. 1995. *Food Plants of Coastal First Peoples*. Royal British Columbia Museum Handbooks Series. UBC Press, Vancouver.

–. 1998. *Plant Technology of First Peoples in British Columbia*. Royal British Columbia Museum Handbooks Series. UBC Press, Vancouver.

United Church of Canada. 1888. Sixty-Fourth Annual Report of the Missionary Society of the Methodist Church for 1887-88. United Church/Victoria University Archives, Toronto.

Veitch, Alasdair M., and Fred H. Harrington. 1996. Brown Bears, Black Bears, and Humans in Northern Labrador: An Historical Perspective and Outlook to the Future. *Journal of Wildlife Research* 1(3):245-250.

Walker, I.R., and M.G. Pellatt 2003. Climate Change in Coastal British Columbia – A Paleoenvironmental Perspective. *Canadian Water Resources Journal* 28:531-565.

Walker, W. N.d. Log-Book of the Brig *Lydia* on a Fur-Trading Voyage from Boston to the Northwest Coast of America 1804-1805 with the Return Voyage by Way of the Sandwich Islands and Canton Aboard the Ships *Atahualpa* and *Swift* 1805-1807. Beinecke Library, Yale University, New Haven, CT.

Wallace, D.C., M.D. Brown, and M.T. Lott. 1999. Mitochondrial DNA Variation in Human Evolution and Disease. *Gene* 238:211-230.

Ward, B.C., M.C. Wilson, D.W. Nagorsen, D.E. Nelson, J.C. Driver, and R.J. Wigen. 2003. Port Eliza Cave: North American West Coast Interstadial Environment and Implications for Human Migrations. *Quaternary Science Reviews* 22:1383-1388.

Warner, B.G. 1984. Late Quaternary Paleoecology of Eastern Graham Island, Queen Charlotte Islands, British Columbia, Canada. PhD dissertation, Department of Biological Sciences, Simon Fraser University, Burnaby.

Warner, B.G., and J.G. Chmielewski. 1987. Biometric Analysis of Modern and Late Pleistocene Cones of *Picea* from Western Canada. *New Phytologist* 107:449-457.

Warner, B.G., R.W. Mathewes, and J.C. Clague. 1982. Ice-Free Conditions on the Queen Charlotte Islands, British Columbia, at the Height of Late Wisconsin Glaciation. *Science* 218:675-677.

Watts, W.A. 1980. Regional Variation in the Response of Vegetation to Lateglacial Climatic Events in Europe. In *Studies in the Lateglacial of Northwest Europe,* edited by J.J. Lowe, J.M. Gray, and J.E. Robinson, pp. 1-21. Oxford, UK: Pergamon Press.

West, C.F. 1996. Trail Creek Caves, Seward Peninsula. In *American Beginnings: The Prehistory and Palaeoecology of Beringia,* edited by F. Hadleigh-West, pp. 482-484. University of Chicago Press, Chicago.

West, F.H. 1967. The Donnelly Ridge Site and the Definition of an Early Core and Blade Complex in Central Alaska. *American Antiquity* 32:360-382.

–. 1996. Beringia and New World Origins II: The Archaeological Evidence. In *American Beginnings: The Prehistory and Palaeoecology of Beringia,* edited by F. Hadleigh-West, pp. 537-560. University of Chicago Press, Chicago.

West, F.H., and B.S. Robinson. 2000. Systematics and the Classification of American Beringian Cultures. Paper presented at the 33rd annual meeting of the Canadian Archaeological Association, Ottawa, May.

West, F.H., B.S. Robinson, and C.F. West. 1996. Whitmore Ridge. In *American Beginnings: The Prehistory and Palaeoecology of Beringia,* edited by F. Hadleigh-West, pp. 386-393. University of Chicago Press, Chicago.

Whitlock, C., and P.J. Bartlein. 1997. Vegetation and Climate Change in Northwest America during the Past 125 kyr. *Nature* 388:57-61.

Wigen, R.J. 1990. Identification and Analysis of Vertebrate Fauna from Eighteen Archaeological Sites on the Southern Queen Charlotte Islands. Unpublished report to the British Columbia Heritage Trust, Victoria.

–. 2000. Masset DND Project, GaUa T1. Unpublished Pacific ID faunal report for Millennia Research. On file, Department of Anthropology, University of Victoria.

–. 1998. Report on Fauna from Richardson Island 1127T10. Unpublished report on file, Parks Canada, Victoria.

–. 1999a. Analysis of Bone from 922T, Hotsprings Island, Units 7 and 9. Unpublished Pacific Identifications consulting report on file, Parks Canada, Victoria.

–. 1999b. Analysis of Fauna from Second Beach Site, FhTx 19. Unpublished Pacific Identifications consulting report for Millennia Research. On file, Millennia Research, Victoria.

–. 2000. Faunal Report for GaTw 7. Unpublished Pacific Identifications consulting report for Tina Christensen and Old Masset Band Council. On file, Old Massett Village Council, Old Masset, BC.

–. 2001. Analysis of Bones from K1 Cave, 2000 and 2001. Report on file, Heritage Canada, Victoria.

–. 2003a. Analysis of Bones from K1 Cave, 2003. Report on file, Heritage Canada, Victoria.

–. 2003b. Identification of Fauna from Richardson Island, 2003. Report submitted to Quentin Mackie, University of Victoria.

–. 2003c. Analysis of Bones from Kilgii Gwaay. Manuscript report on file, Parks Canada, Victoria.

–. 2003d. 1127T13 Richardson Island Site: Hearth, Bone from Hearth Q12 F1a. Manuscript on file, Department of Anthropology, University of Victoria.

–. 2004. Gaadu Din Report. Report on file, Heritage Canada, Victoria.

Wigen, R.J., and T. Christensen. 2001. The Fauna from Cohoe Creek: An Early Shell Midden in Haida Gwaii. *Canadian Zooarchaeology* 19:16-20.

Wigen, R.J., and B. Stucki. 1988. Taphonomy and Stratigraphy in the Interpretation of Economic Patterns at Hoko River Rockshelter. In *Prehistoric Economies of the Pacific Northwest Coast,* edited by B.L. Isaac, pp. 87-146. JAI Press, Greenwich, CT.

Wigen, R.J., and I.D. Sumpter. 2003. Preliminary Fauna Analysis of an Early Holocene Site – Kilgii Gwaay, on the Queen Charlotte Islands, British Columbia, Canada. Paper presented at the Wetlands Archaeology Research Project Conference, Olympia, WA, March.

Wigen, R.J., S. Crockford, and R. Greenspan. 1990. Comparison of Taphonomic Patterns in Fish Bone from Northwest Coast (North American) Sites. Paper presented at the 6th international conference, International Council for Archaeozoology, Smithsonian Institution, Washington, DC.

Wike, J. 1951. *The Effect of the Maritime Fur Trade on Northwest Coast Indian Society.* PhD dissertation, Columbia University, New York.

–. 1957. More Puzzles on the North West Coast. *American Anthropologist* 60:1086-1101.

Williams, J.W., D.M. Post, L.C. Cwynar, A.F. Lotter, and A.J. Levesque. 2002. Rapid and Widespread Vegetation Responses to Past Climate Change in the North Atlantic Region. *Geology* 30:971-974.

Wilson, M.C., and J.A. Burns. 1999. Searching for the Earliest Canadians: Wide Corridors, Narrow Doorways, Small Windows. In *Ice Age Peoples of North America: Environments, Origins, and Adaptations,* edited by R. Bonnichsen and K.L. Turnmire, pp. 213-248. Oregon State University Press, Corvallis.

Wolf, E.R. 1982. *Europe and the People without History.* University of California Press, Los Angeles.

Wood, C.C., B.E. Riddell, D.T. Rutherford, and R.E. Withler. 1994. Biochemical Genetic Survey of Sockeye Salmon (*Oncorhynchus nerka*) in Canada. *Canadian Journal of Fisheries and Aquatic Sciences* 51:114-131.

Wootton, R.J. 1984. *A Functional Biology of Sticklebacks.* University of California Press, Berkeley and Los Angeles.

Work, J. 1945. *The Journal of John Work, January to October, 1835.* Archives of British Columbia Memoir No. 10. C.F. Banfield, Victoria.

Workman, W. 2001. Reflections on the Utility of the Coastal Migration Hypothesis in Understanding the Peopling of the New World. Paper presented at the 2001 Alaska Anthropological Association meetings. Fairbanks, March.

Wylie, A. 1985. The Reaction against Analogy. In *Advances in Archaeological Method and Theory,* edited by M.B. Schiffer, vol. 8, pp. 63-111. Academic Press, New York.

Yesner, D.R. 1996. Human Adaptation at the Pleistocene-Holocene Boundary (circa 13,000 to 8,000 BP) in Eastern Beringia. In *Humans at the End of the Ice-Age,* edited by L.G. Straus, B.V. Eriksen, J.M. Erlandson, and D.R. Yesner, pp. 255-276. Plenum Press, New York.

Young, S., and M. Eldridge. 2001 Final Report for the Archaeological Inventory Study of Begbie Peninsula, Kumdis Island, Wathus Island, and Ain River, Haida Gwaii. On file, British Columbia Archaeology Branch, Victoria.

Zacharias, S., and Wanagun. 1993. Gwaii Haanas 91 Archaeology: 1991 Archaeological Resource Inventory of South-Eastern Moresby Island within the Gwaii Haanas/South Moresby National Park Reserve. Report on file, Cultural Resource Services (Western Canada Service Centre), Parks Canada, Victoria.

Zink, R.M., and D. Dittmann. 1993. Gene Flow, Refugia, and Evolution of Geographic Variation in the Song Sparrow (*Melospiza melodia*). *Evolution* 47:717-729.

Notes on Contributors

Steven Acheson is a staff archaeologist with the government of British Columbia, as well as adjunct professor of anthropology at the University of Victoria. He received his doctorate in archaeology, which dealt with the settlement history of the Kunghit Haida, from the University of Oxford in 1991. His research focuses on Northwest Coast settlement archaeology and ethnohistory. Recent publications include contributions to edited volumes of the *Encyclopaedia of Medical Anthropology: Health and Illness in the World's Cultures* (2004) and *The Archaeology of Contact in Settler Societies* (2004).

David Archer (MA, University of Victoria) is an instructor in anthropology at the Prince Rupert Campus of Northwest Community College. His research interests include lithic analysis, landscape archaeology, and the use of oral history in archaeology. He is currently part of a team of researchers investigating the history of settlement in the Dundas Island Group, west of Prince Rupert on the north coast of BC.

J. Vaughn Barrie received his MSc and PhD (1986) from the University of Wales. In 1989 Dr. Barrie joined the Pacific Division of the Geological Survey of Canada, and since 1992 he has been head of the Marine Section. He is also an adjunct professor at the School of Earth and Ocean Sciences (SEOS) of the University of Victoria and Canadian director of the Circum-Pacific Council. His research has focused on three areas: Quaternary geology of the Canadian continental shelves, geological hazards on the continental shelf and coastal zone, and mechanisms for the formation and preservation of marine mineral deposits.

Ashley Byun received her PhD from the University of Victoria in 1998. Her research focused on the molecular genetics of Haida Gwaii endemic taxa under the supervision of Thomas Reimchen and B. Koop. This was followed by a postdoctoral position at Simon Fraser University, where she worked on molecular responses of biotic and abiotic stress in plants.

Tina Christensen (BA, MA in progress, Simon Fraser University) has undertaken archaeological research on the Northwest Coast since 1994. Her archaeological research has focused on Haida Gwaii, particularly sites associated with the early Holocene.

John Clague is Shrum Professor of Science in the Department of Earth Sciences at Simon Fraser University. He conducts research on hazardous natural processes, including earthquakes, tsunamis, landslides, and floods, as well as impacts of climate change. Dr. Clague is also involved in research on the history of Ice Age glaciation in western Canada.

Kim Conway is a physical scientist who has been working with the Geological Survey of Canada at the Pacific Geoscience Centre since 1982, after graduating from the University of Victoria in 1981. Most of his career has been spent working on the Quaternary marine geology, sedimentology, and sea level history of the western Canadian continental shelf. He has also worked extensively on unique sponge reefs that today live only on the western Canadian shelf but are found worldwide as fossilized reefs.

Daryl Fedje is a staff archaeologist with Parks Canada. He completed his MA in archaeology at the University of Calgary in 1993. His research interests include lithic analysis, paleoecology, and the peopling of the Northwest Coast. He is currently conducting research into the early postglacial to early Holocene environmental and human history of Haida Gwaii.

Heather Harris is a Cree-Métis, born in British Columbia. She is a professor of First Nations Studies at the University of Northern British Columbia. Most of her writing has been academic in nature, concerned with oral history, archaeology, paleoenvironments, indigenous critique of archaeology, shamanism, and indigenous social structure. She is also an artist and poet. Heather is currently working on a book of contemporary Coyote stories.

Richard Hebda received his PhD in botany from University of British Columbia in 1977. Since 1980 as curator at the Royal British Columbia Museum, he has studied the late Quaternary vegetation and climatic history of British Columbia, and more recently the flora of alpine areas, taxonomy and geography of grasses, and impacts of climate change. Dr. Hebda also holds adjunct appointments in biology, earth and ocean sciences, and environmental studies at the University of Victoria. He is author or co-author of more than 80 scientific publications and 150 popular articles.

Heiner Josenhans is a marine geologist with the Geological Survey of Canada. Using a variety of ships, submersibles, and remote sensing equipment, he has studied and mapped large areas of Canada's marine lands. In the past thirty years, he has described the seafloor history, sediment distribution, and seafloor stability of the Nova Scotian margin, the Gulf of St. Lawrence, the Labrador Shelf, Hudson Bay, and the Queen Charlotte Basin of British Columbia.

K'ii7iljuus (Barbara J. Wilson) has worked for Gwaii Haanas National Park Reserve and Haida Heritage Site since 1989. She graduated from the University of Victoria in 1999, and holds a diploma in cultural resource management. She is a student of *X̲aayda* history and all aspects of her nation's life. K̲'ii7iljuus is the matriarch of the *St'aaw7aas X̲aaydaagaay*. Her next challenge is to earn her master's degree in environmental sciences and communications.

Terri Lacourse received her master's degree in physical geography from the University of Ottawa in 1998 and her PhD in biology from Simon Fraser University in 2004. Her doctoral research focused on the late Quaternary vegetation history of the Queen Charlotte Islands, northern Vancouver Island, and the adjacent continental shelf. For this research, she received the American Quaternary Association's Denise Gaudreau Award for Excellence in Quaternary Studies. She is currently conducting postdoctoral research at Stockholm University.

Cynthia Lake holds a double BA in anthropology and French from the University of Victoria, and was the recipient of the 1999 Jubilee Medal in Social Sciences. She has worked on several archaeological sites in Haida Gwaii, including Kilgii Gwaay (co-authoring an article on the site) and Richardson Island. She has several years of archaeological consulting experience, primarily on southern Vancouver Island, and has also worked for Parks Canada Archaeology Services.

Alexander Mackie is a staff archaeologist with the government of British Columbia. He completed a BA at the University of Victoria in 1981. His research interests are in Northwest Coast archaeology. He is currently coordinating, with the Champagne and Aishihik First Nation, research into the Kwäd¹y Dän Ts'inchá human remains and artifacts found melting from a glacier in northwestern BC. He also has active research interests in Haida and Nuu-chah-nulth traditional territories.

Quentin Mackie is an assistant professor of anthropology at the University of Victoria, specializing in the archaeology of the Northwest Coast. His thematic interests include settlement archaeology, lithic analysis, environmental archaeology, and the first peopling of the Northwest Coast. He is currently investigating early Holocene human occupation and environments in Haida Gwaii, with a focus on the Richardson Island archaeological site.

Joanne McSporran completed her BA in archaeology at the University of Victoria in 1991 and is currently an independent archaeologist living in Victoria. She has worked on many archaeological projects in Haida Gwaii, including model development, terrestrial and marine surveys, and excavations. She is a photographer and artist with considerable experience illustrating archaeological artifacts.

Martin Magne is manager of Cultural Resource Services for Parks Canada and adjunct associate professor at the University of Calgary. He obtained his PhD from the University of British Columbia (1983), his MA from the University of Manitoba (1978), and his BSc from the University of Toronto (1976). His principal research interests are lithic technology, rock art, and Athapaskan archaeology.

Rolf Mathewes is a professor in the Department of Biological Sciences at Simon Fraser University, and associate dean of the Faculty of Science. He is also an associate member of the Archaeology Department, and has been studying the environmental and archaeological history of Haida Gwaii since 1980. He has authored or co-authored more than 100 scientific publications, dealing mainly with paleoenvironmental reconstructions. He and his collaborators have used a wide range of techniques, including pollen analysis, plant macrofossils, radio-carbon dating, fossil insects, and geological approaches to study climatic changes and biological responses in western Canada.

Nang Kiing.aay7uuans (James Young) is one of the elders teaching and learning *Xaayda kil* at the Skidegate Haida Language Program in Skidegate. He is the spokes-person for his clan. Nang Kiing.aay7uuans spoke only Haida until he was 7 years old. He learned many old stories from his father, Henry Young, and also gath-ered more stories from his sister, Elizabeth Collinson, as well as stories he re-members himself. He began working as a commercial fisherman when he was 11 and joined the Canadian Army when he was 21. Nang Kiing.aay7uuans re-turned to the Northwest Coast and again worked as a seine fisherman until retirement.

Marlow Pellatt is the Coastal Ecologist for Parks Canada's Western Canada Ser-vice Centre and an adjunct professor in the School of Resource and Environ-mental Management at Simon Fraser University. He has published scientific papers concerning the paleoecology and paleoclimatology of British Columbia, par-ticularly in coastal and Cordilleran ecosystems. Dr. Pellatt's research interests are in coastal ecosystem processes, historical ecology, paleoclimatology, and paleo-ecology. Current research projects include the examination of past salmon abun-dance, fire history, and climate change in Garry oak and Coastal Douglas-fir zones, and coastal food web dynamics. Dr. Pellatt received his PhD in biological sciences at Simon Fraser University in 1996.

Thomas Reimchen received his DPhil from the University of Liverpool, Eng-land, in 1974 and is currently adjunct professor of zoology at the University of Victoria. From 1975 to 1996, he resided on Haida Gwaii and undertook a long-term research program on the adaptive radiation of endemic taxa from the is-lands. His graduate students have further developed various aspects of this program. Over the last ten years, he has also examined ecological relationships and nutrient cycling between marine and terrestrial ecosystems, with a focus on salmon, bear, and riparian communities. Current research projects and publica-tion lists are described at <http://web.uvic.ca/~reimlab/>.

John Southon is a researcher in the Department of Earth System Science at the University of California, Irvine, and is co-director of the Keck Carbon Cycle Accelerator Mass Spectrometry (AMS) facility. His research interests include ra-diocarbon dating and the use of ^{14}C in paleoclimate and paleoceanographic stud-ies as a tracer for past variations in the carbon cycle. His interest in paleoclimate in western Canada began more than twenty years ago, when he was appointed at Simon Fraser University during the early days of the development of the AMS technique.

Jim Stafford (BA, Simon Fraser University) operates an independent archaeology firm from Pender Island, BC, with a focus on the Northwest Coast. In addition to numerous heritage management projects, he has participated in and led large-scale archaeological inventories and excavations on the coast of BC since 1992.

Jennifer Strang is a GIS and image processing specialist working at the Geological Survey of Canada. She has a degree in geology from Dalhousie University, Halifax, Nova Scotia, and a diploma in GIS from the Centre of Geographic Sciences in Lawrencetown, Nova Scotia. Her current work focuses on the use of LIDAR in Coastal Monitoring and Climate Change.

Ian Sumpter is an archaeologist with Parks Canada Cultural Resource Services. He completed a BA in archaeology at Simon Fraser University in 1980. He has active research interests in Nuu-chah-nulth, Haida, and Central Coast Salish territories.

Rebecca Wigen (MA, University of Victoria) is senior lab instructor in the Anthropology Department at the University of Victoria. She established and manages the comparative faunal collection in that department. She is also a partner in Pacific Identifications, Inc., a company that specializes in identifying bones from biological or archaeological contexts. She has twenty-five years of experience identifying bones. Recent work has included analysis of the vertebrate fauna from K1 and Gaadu Din caves in Haida Gwaii and analysis of the bird bones from the Amaknak Bridge site in the Aleutians.

Index